Shojo Beat

# OTOMEN

Story & Art by
**Aya Kanno**

Volume
**FIFTEEN**

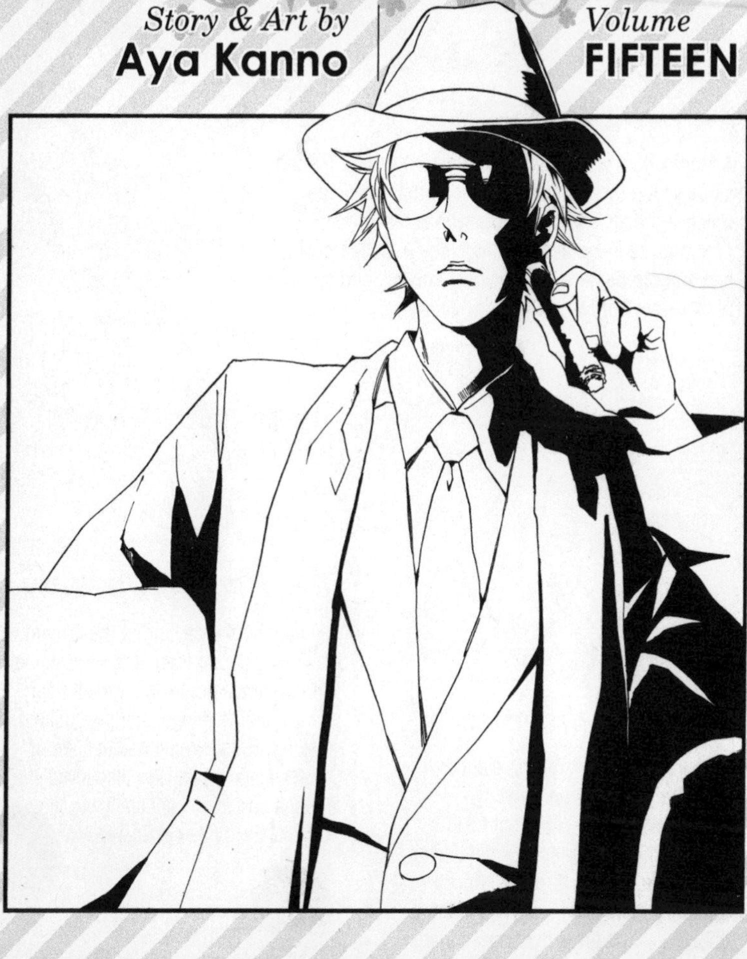

# OTOMEN Characters & Story

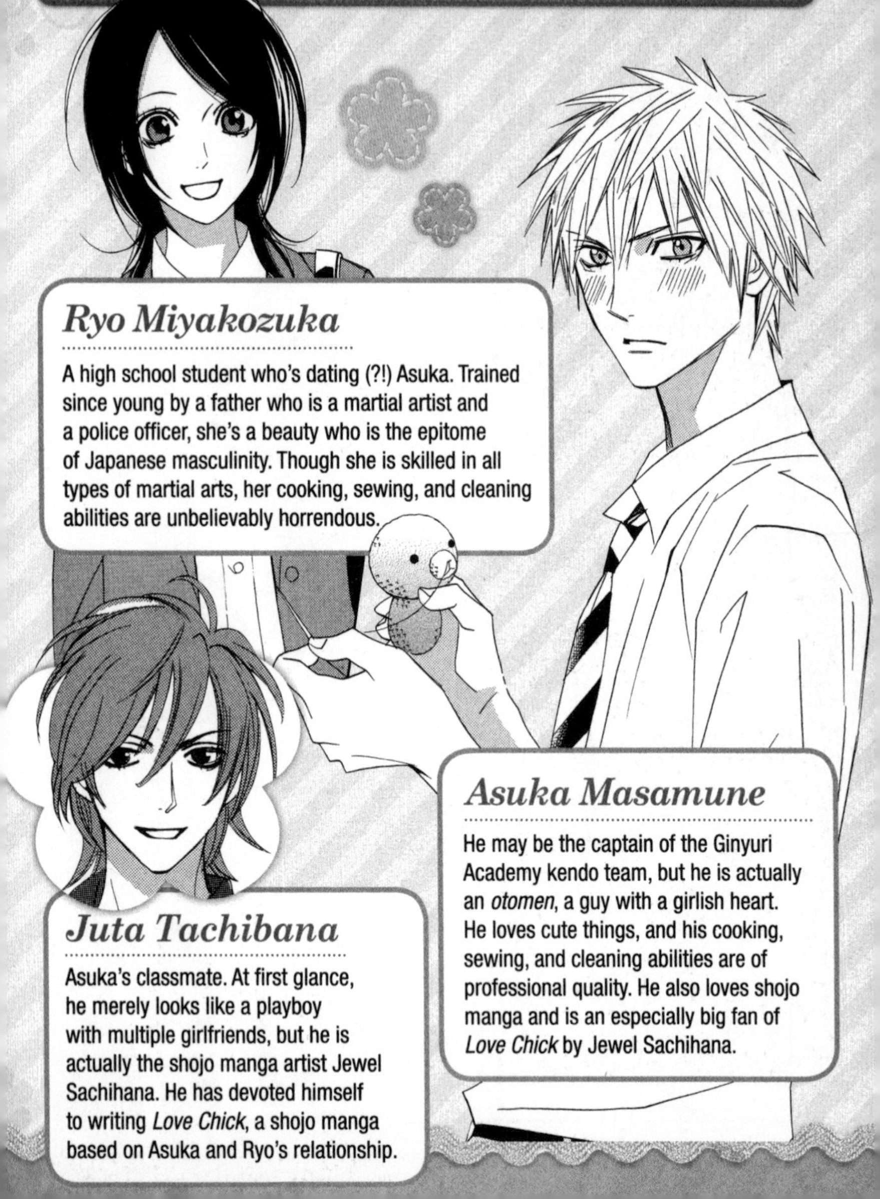

## *Ryo Miyakozuka*

A high school student who's dating (?!) Asuka. Trained since young by a father who is a martial artist and a police officer, she's a beauty who is the epitome of Japanese masculinity. Though she is skilled in all types of martial arts, her cooking, sewing, and cleaning abilities are unbelievably horrendous.

## *Asuka Masamune*

He may be the captain of the Ginyuri Academy kendo team, but he is actually an *otomen*, a guy with a girlish heart. He loves cute things, and his cooking, sewing, and cleaning abilities are of professional quality. He also loves shojo manga and is an especially big fan of *Love Chick* by Jewel Sachihana.

## *Juta Tachibana*

Asuka's classmate. At first glance, he merely looks like a playboy with multiple girlfriends, but he is actually the shojo manga artist Jewel Sachihana. He has devoted himself to writing *Love Chick*, a shojo manga based on Asuka and Ryo's relationship.

# STORY

While Asuka completes a future goals questionnaire, he imagines what his life will be like. He wants to be with Ryo and live as an otomen, but he can't tell his mother Kiyomi that. Meanwhile, Tonomine wants to become the best at kendo so that he can make his father Osamu accept his dream of becoming a makeup artist. However, his father wants him to follow in his footsteps and become a politician…

KIYOMI MASAMUNE

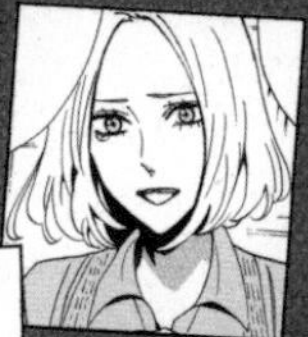

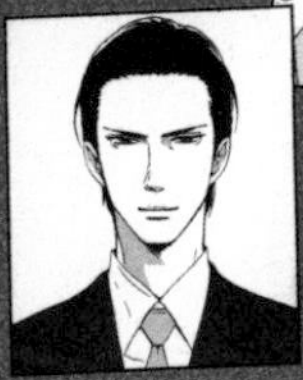

OSAMU TONOMINE

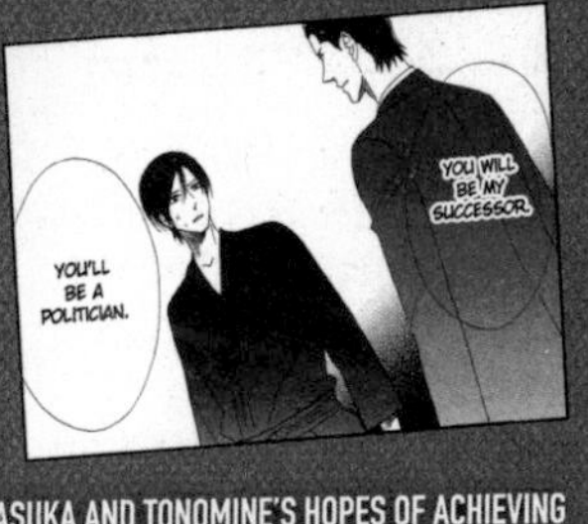
YOU WILL BE MY SUCCESSOR.
YOU'LL BE A POLITICIAN.

ASUKA AND TONOMINE'S HOPES OF ACHIEVING THEIR DREAMS ARE LOOKING GRIM…

# OTHER OTOMEN

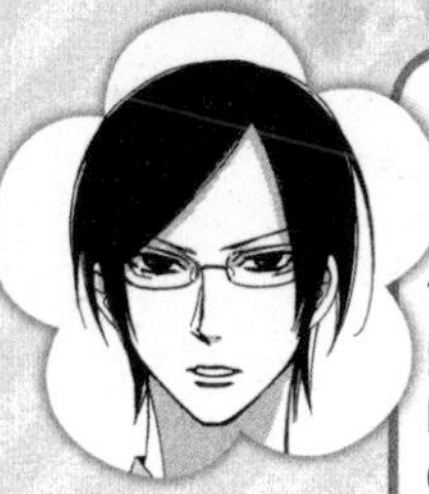

## Hajime Tonomine

The captain of the Kinbara High School kendo team, he considers Asuka his sworn rival. He is actually an *otomen* who is good with cosmetics.

## Yamato Ariake

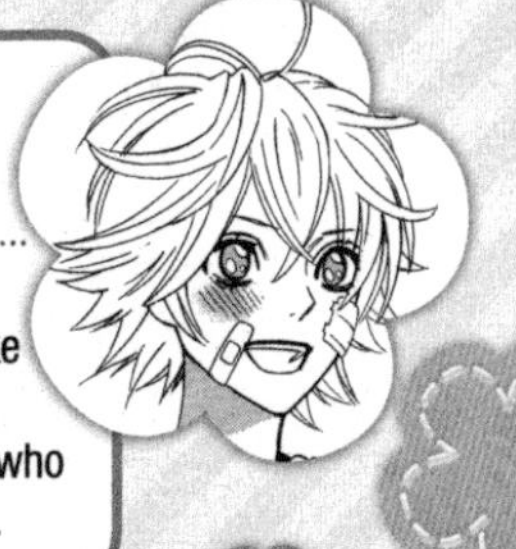

He is younger than Asuka and looks like a cute girl. He is a delusional *otomen* who admires manliness.

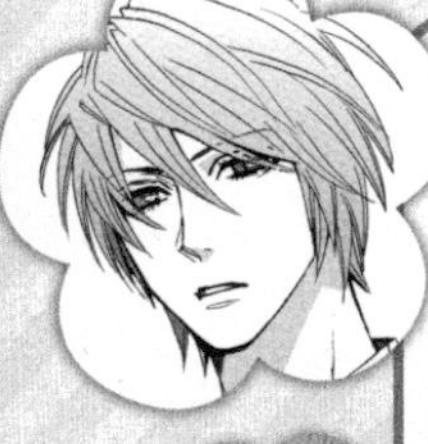

## Kitora Kurokawa

Asuka's classmate. A man who is captivated by the beauty of flowers. He is an obsessed *otomen* who wants to cover the world in flowers.

# OTOMEN

*volume 15*
## CONTENTS

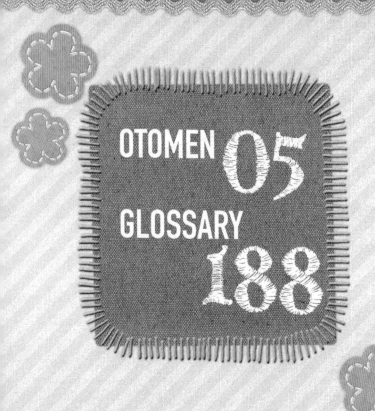

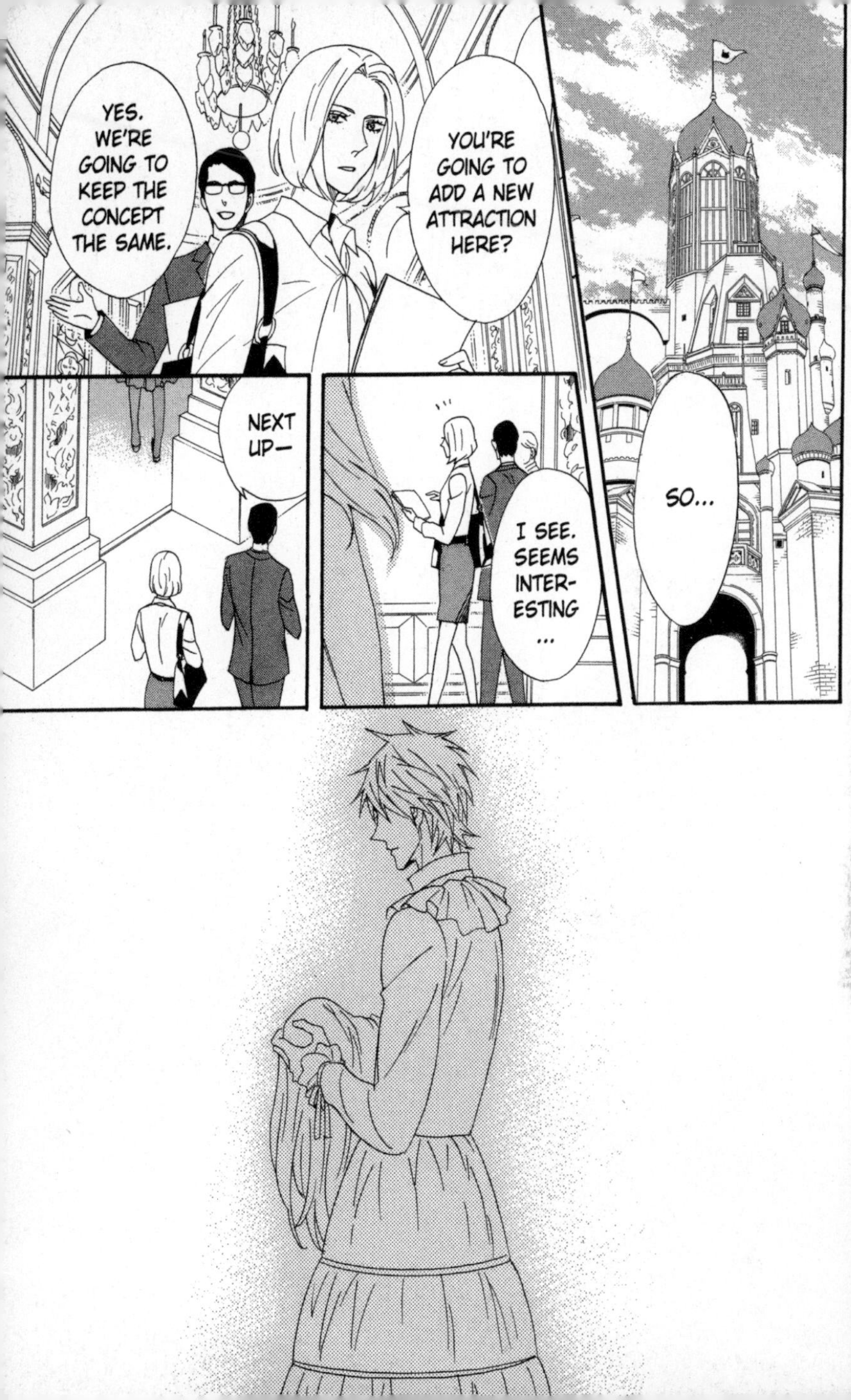
SO...
YOU'RE GOING TO ADD A NEW ATTRACTION HERE?
YES. WE'RE GOING TO KEEP THE CONCEPT THE SAME.
I SEE. SEEMS INTER-ESTING...
NEXT UP—

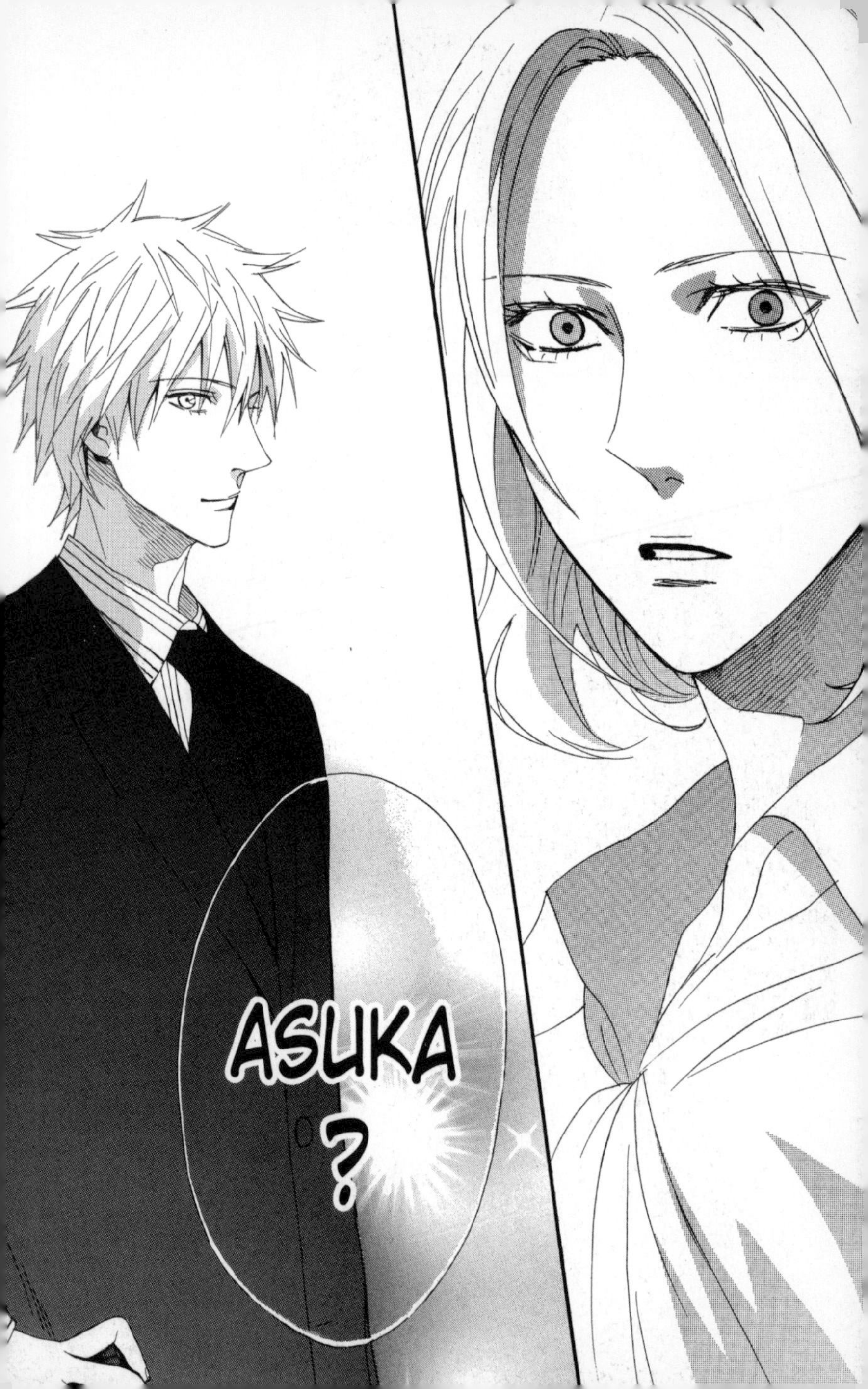
ASUKA
?

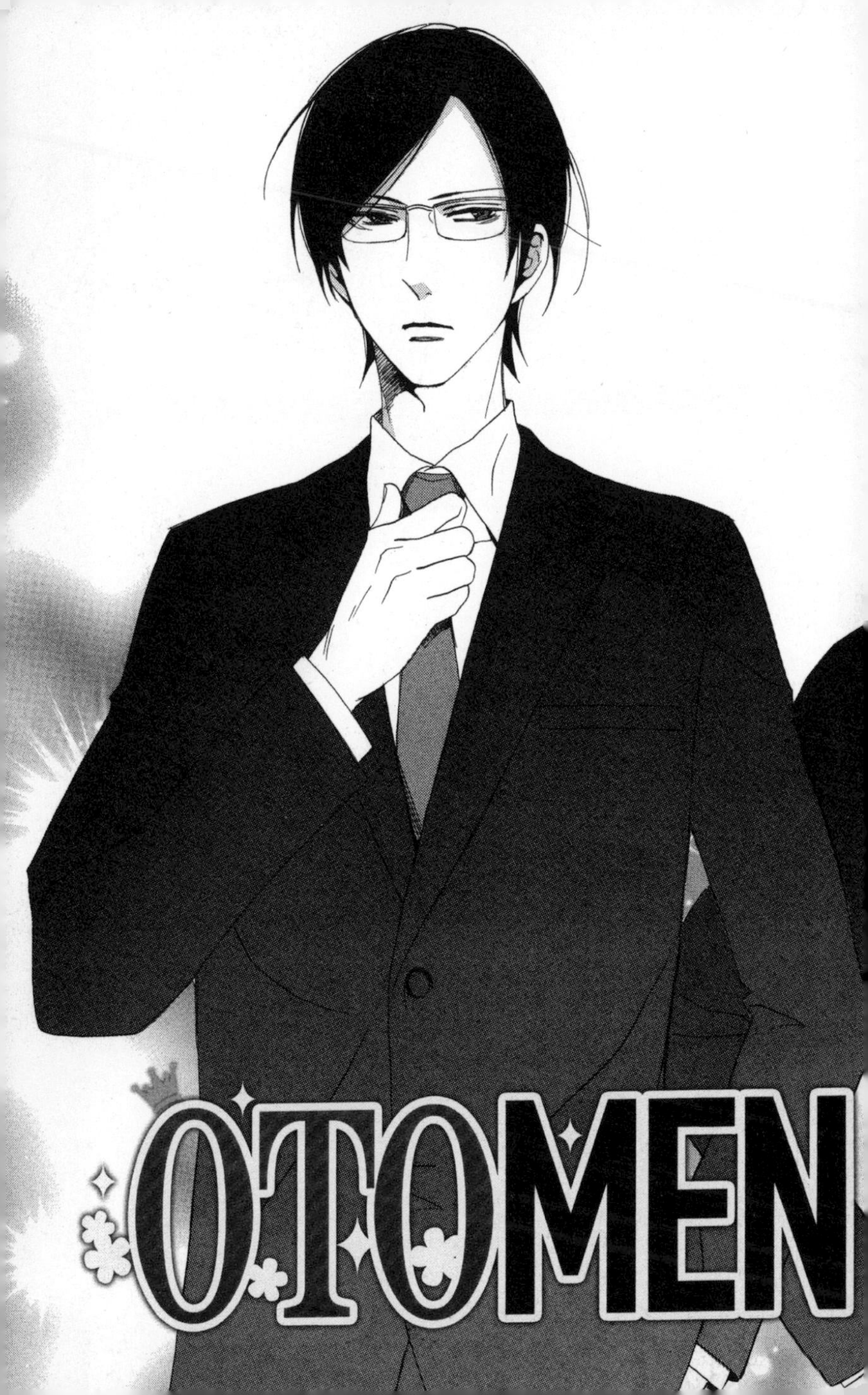
OTOMEN

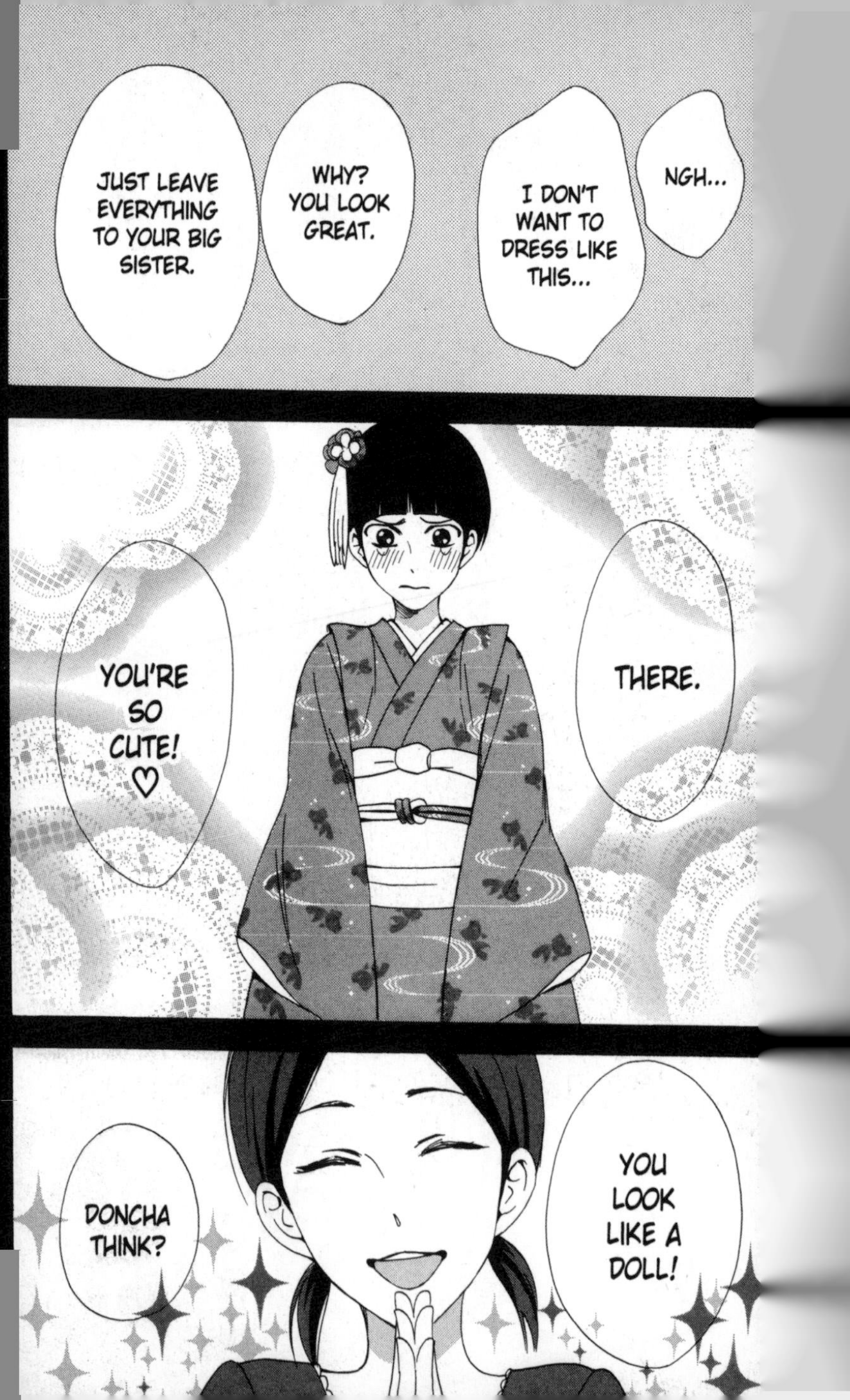
NGH...
I DON'T WANT TO DRESS LIKE THIS...
WHY? YOU LOOK GREAT.
JUST LEAVE EVERYTHING TO YOUR BIG SISTER.
THERE.
YOU'RE SO CUTE! ♡
YOU LOOK LIKE A DOLL!
DONCHA THINK?

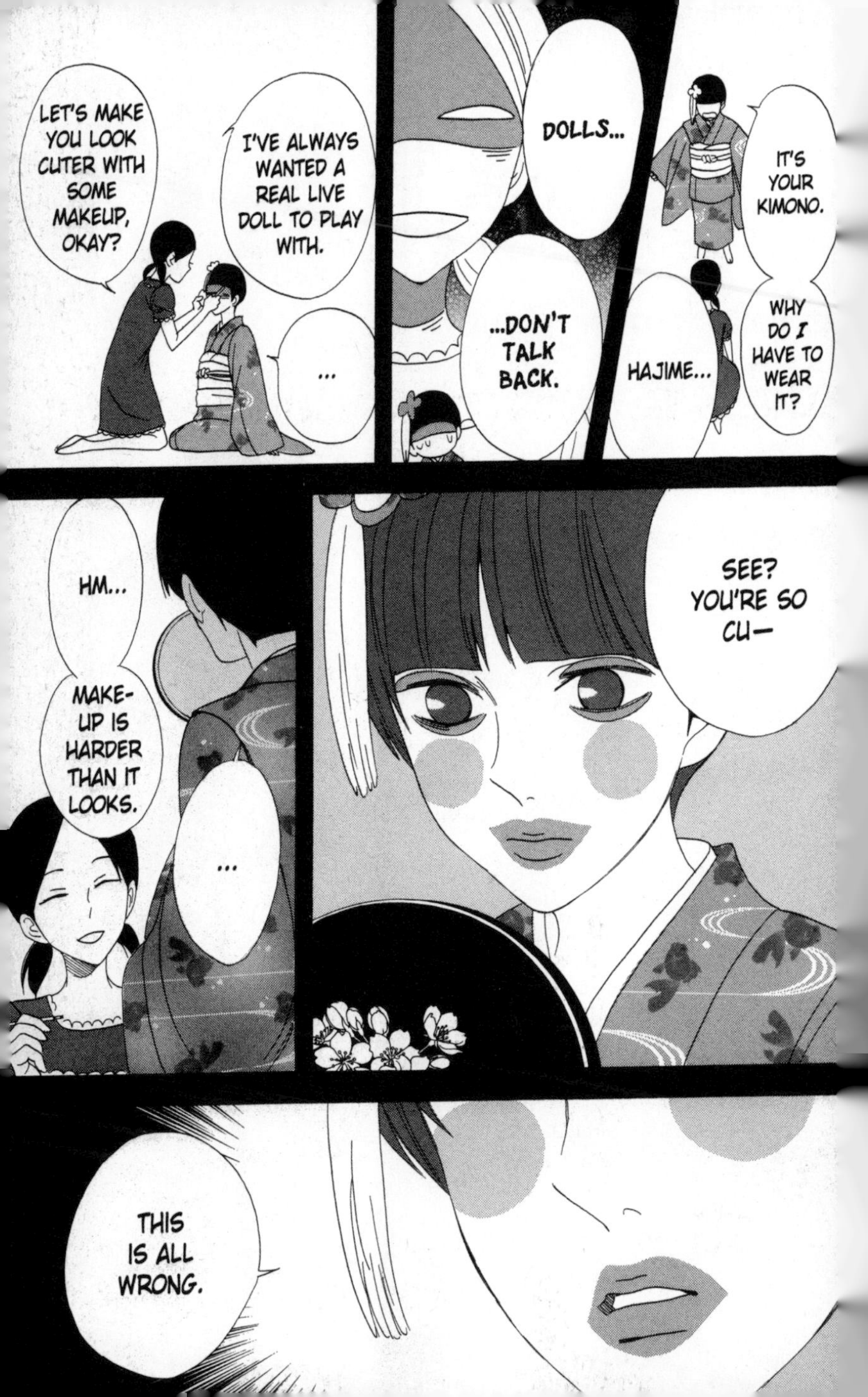
IT'S YOUR KIMONO.
WHY DO I HAVE TO WEAR IT?
HAJIME...
DOLLS...
...DON'T TALK BACK.
I'VE ALWAYS WANTED A REAL LIVE DOLL TO PLAY WITH.
LET'S MAKE YOU LOOK CUTER WITH SOME MAKEUP, OKAY?
...
SEE? YOU'RE SO CU—
HM...
MAKE-UP IS HARDER THAN IT LOOKS.
...
THIS IS ALL WRONG.

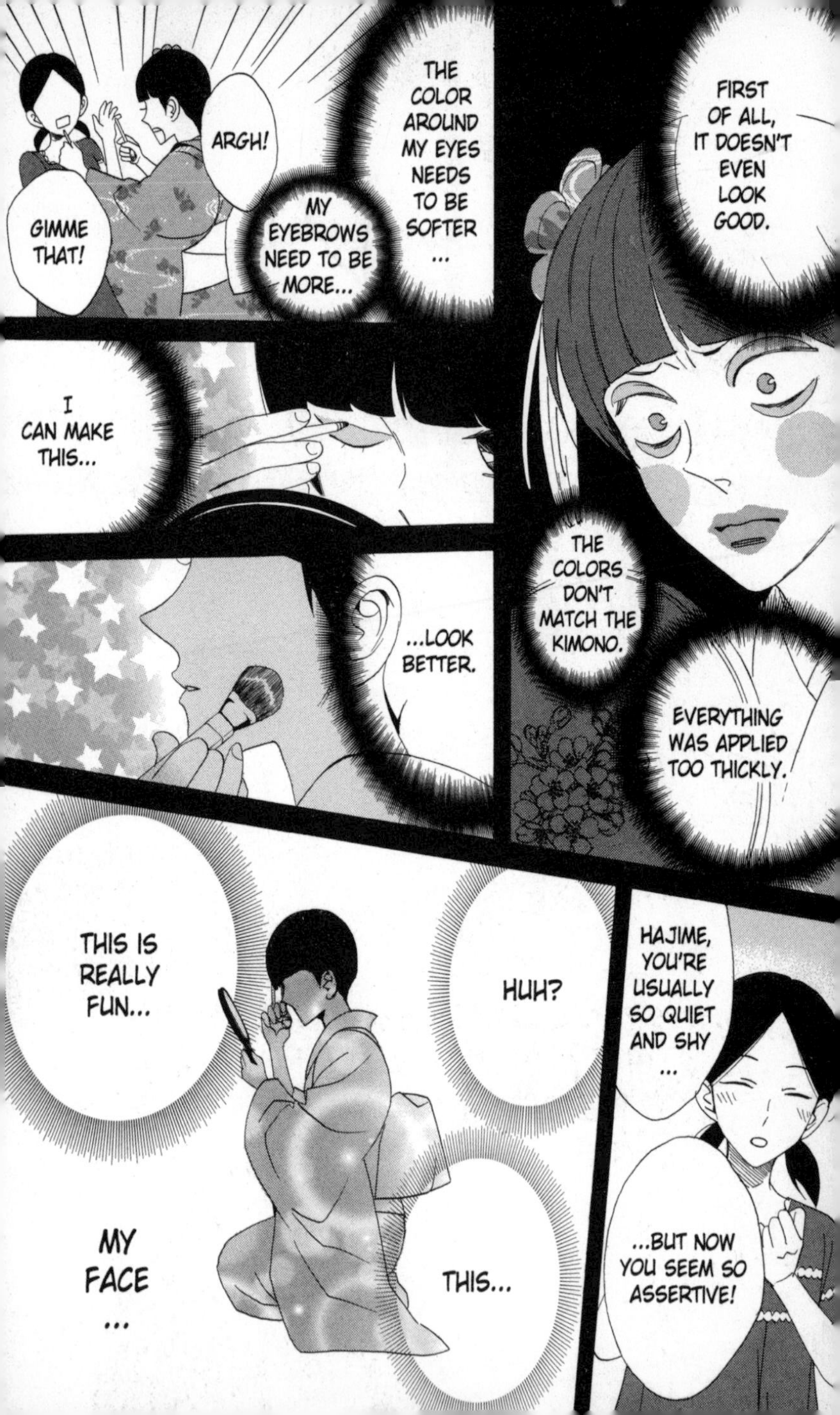
FIRST OF ALL, IT DOESN'T EVEN LOOK GOOD.
THE COLORS DON'T MATCH THE KIMONO.
EVERYTHING WAS APPLIED TOO THICKLY.
THE COLOR AROUND MY EYES NEEDS TO BE SOFTER...
MY EYEBROWS NEED TO BE MORE...
ARGH!
GIMME THAT!
I CAN MAKE THIS...
...LOOK BETTER.
HAJIME, YOU'RE USUALLY SO QUIET AND SHY...
...BUT NOW YOU SEEM SO ASSERTIVE!
HUH?
THIS IS REALLY FUN...
THIS...
MY FACE...

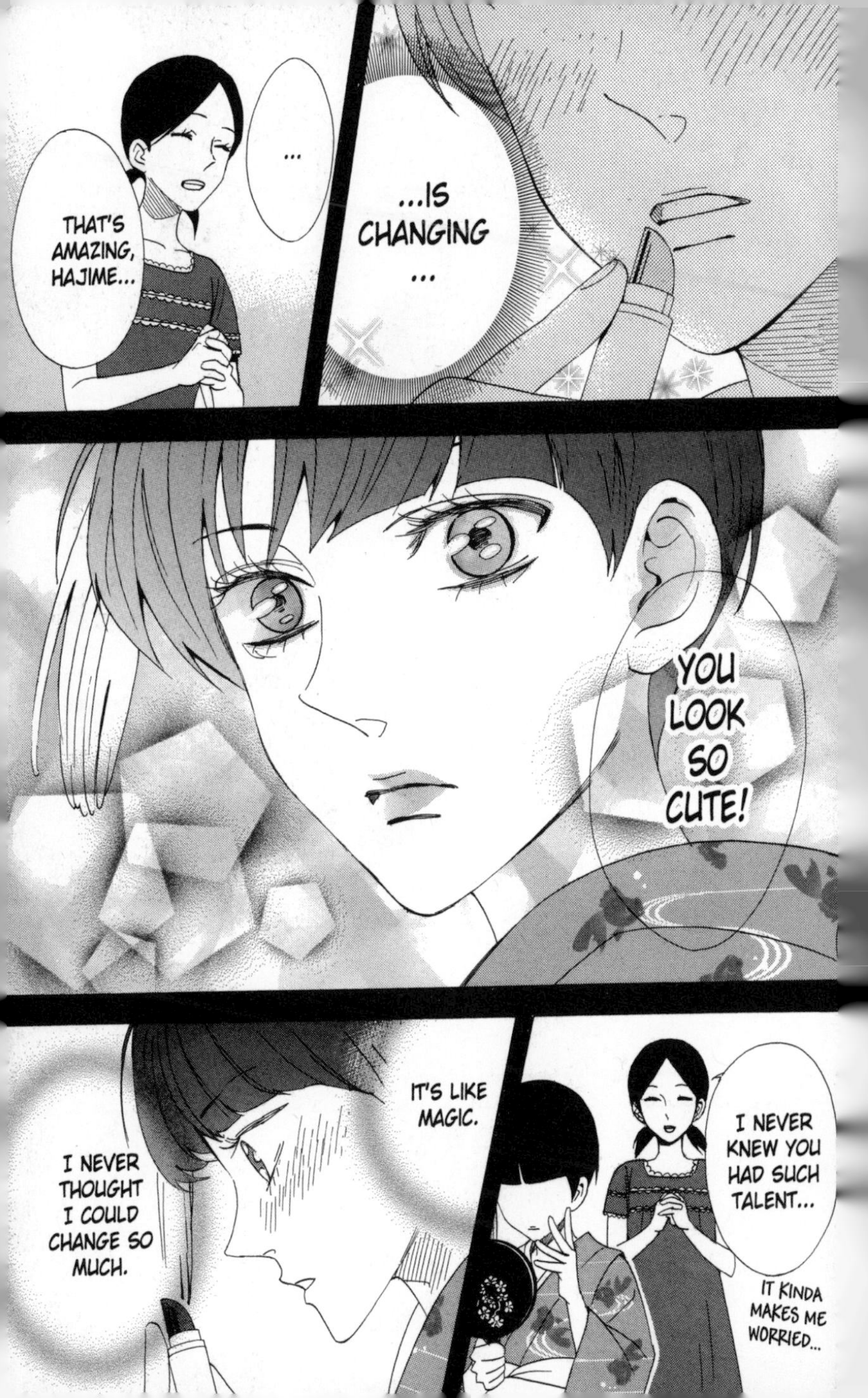
...IS CHANGING ...
...
THAT'S AMAZING, HAJIME...
YOU LOOK SO CUTE!
I NEVER KNEW YOU HAD SUCH TALENT...
IT KINDA MAKES ME WORRIED...
IT'S LIKE MAGIC.
I NEVER THOUGHT I COULD CHANGE SO MUCH.

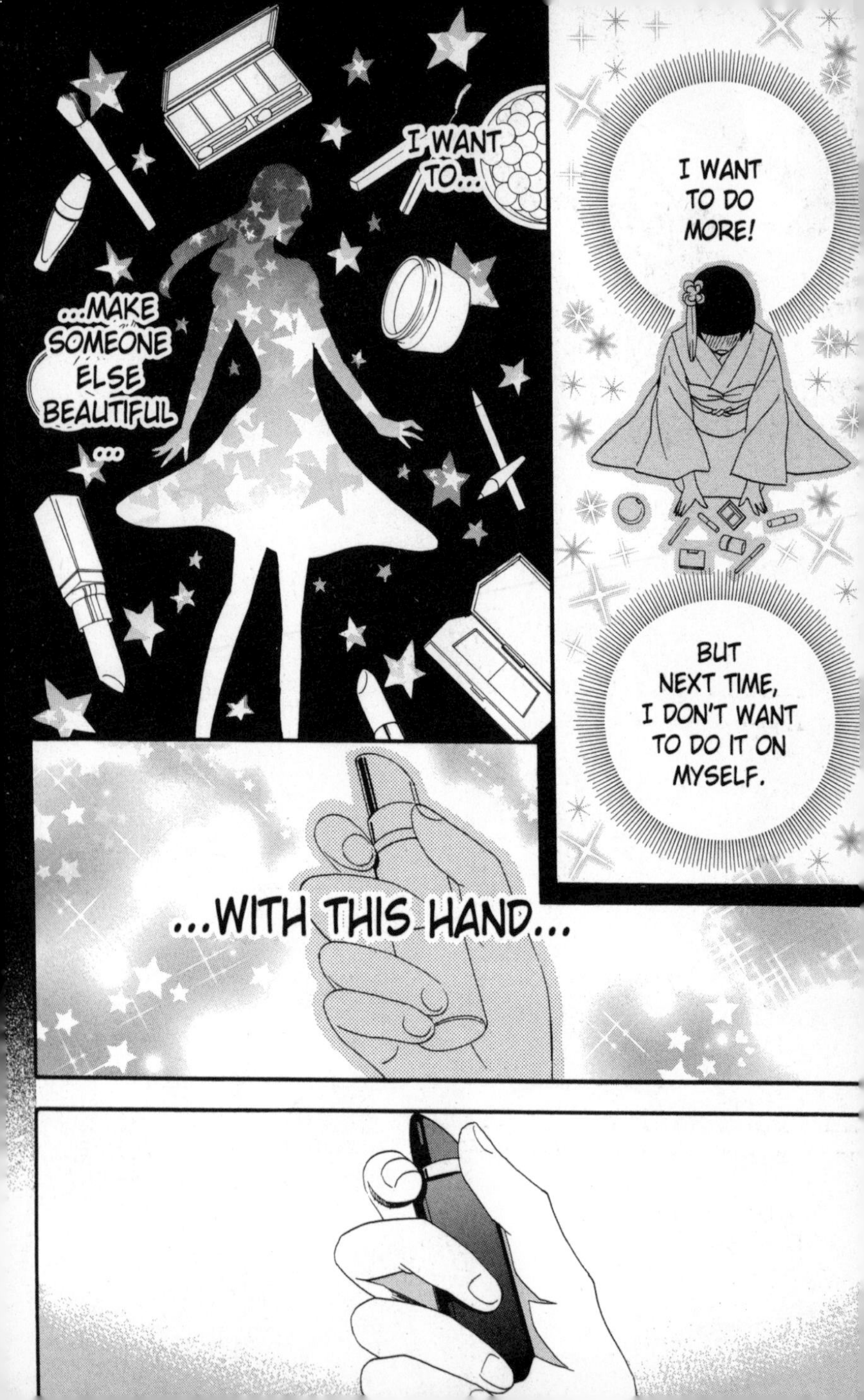
I WANT TO DO MORE!
BUT NEXT TIME, I DON'T WANT TO DO IT ON MYSELF.
I WANT TO...
...MAKE SOMEONE ELSE BEAUTIFUL...
...WITH THIS HAND...

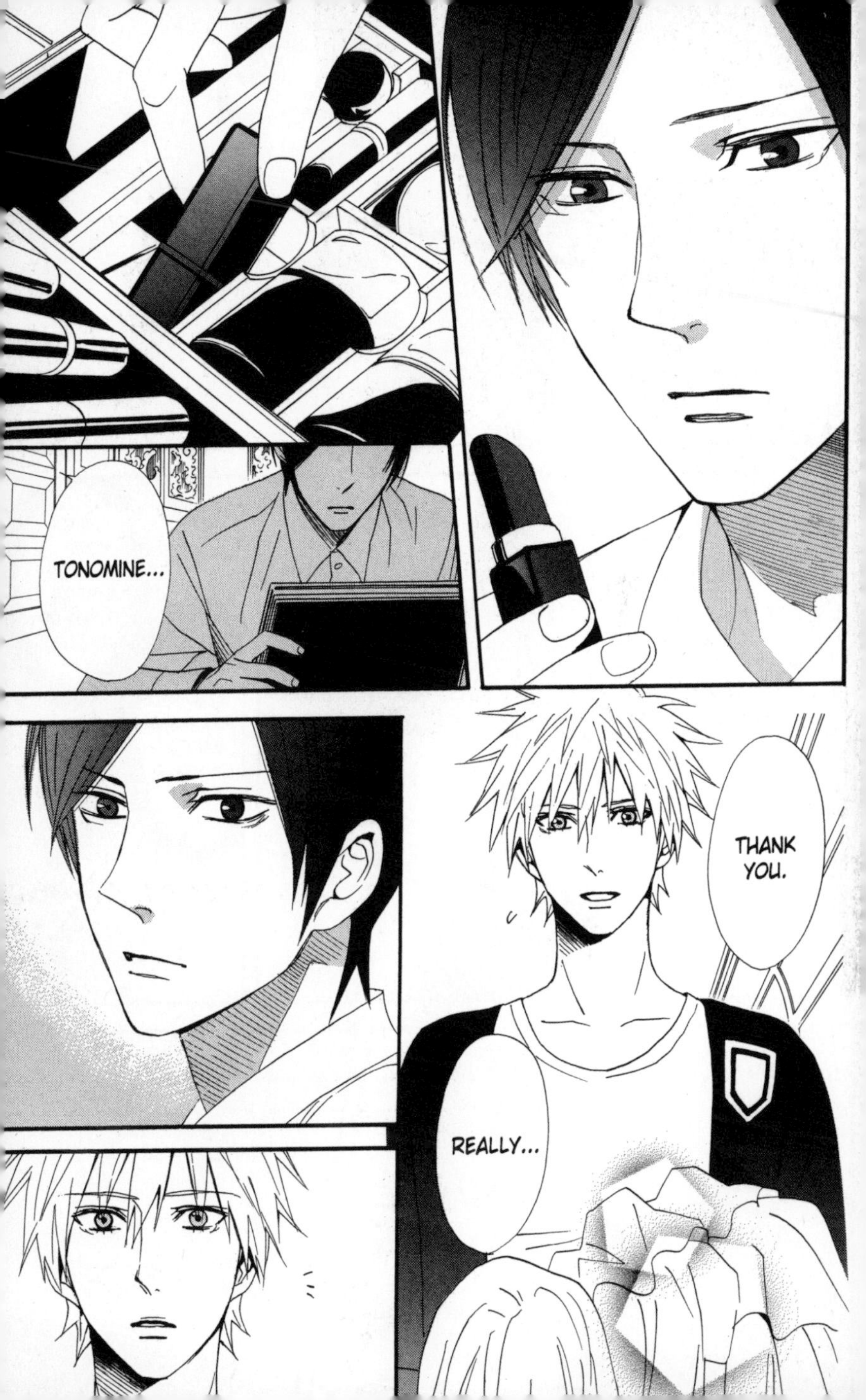
TONOMINE...
THANK YOU.
REALLY...

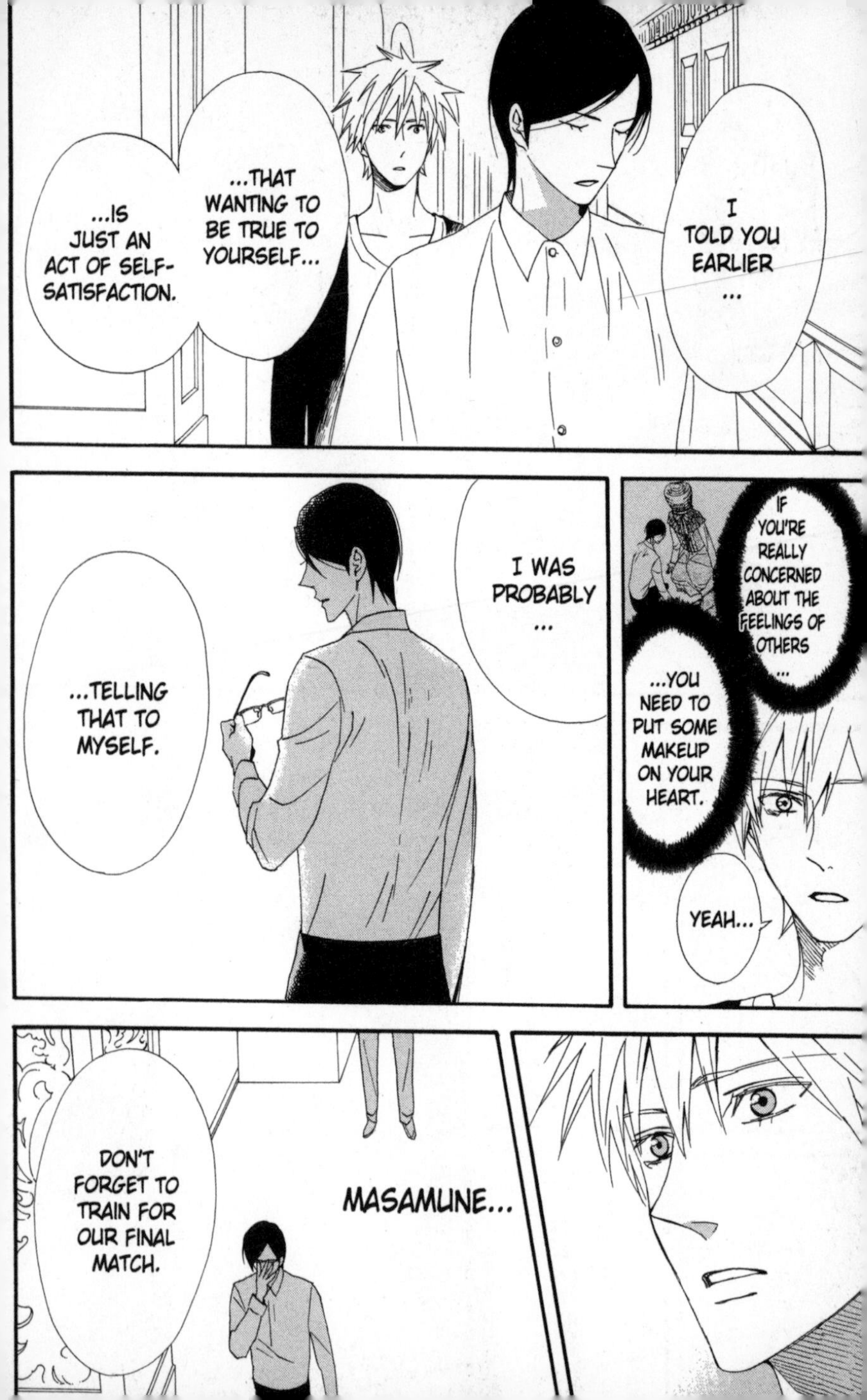
I TOLD YOU EARLIER ...
...THAT WANTING TO BE TRUE TO YOURSELF...
...IS JUST AN ACT OF SELF-SATISFACTION.
IF YOU'RE REALLY CONCERNED ABOUT THE FEELINGS OF OTHERS ...
...YOU NEED TO PUT SOME MAKEUP ON YOUR HEART.
YEAH...
I WAS PROBABLY ...
...TELLING THAT TO MYSELF.
MASAMUNE...
DON'T FORGET TO TRAIN FOR OUR FINAL MATCH.

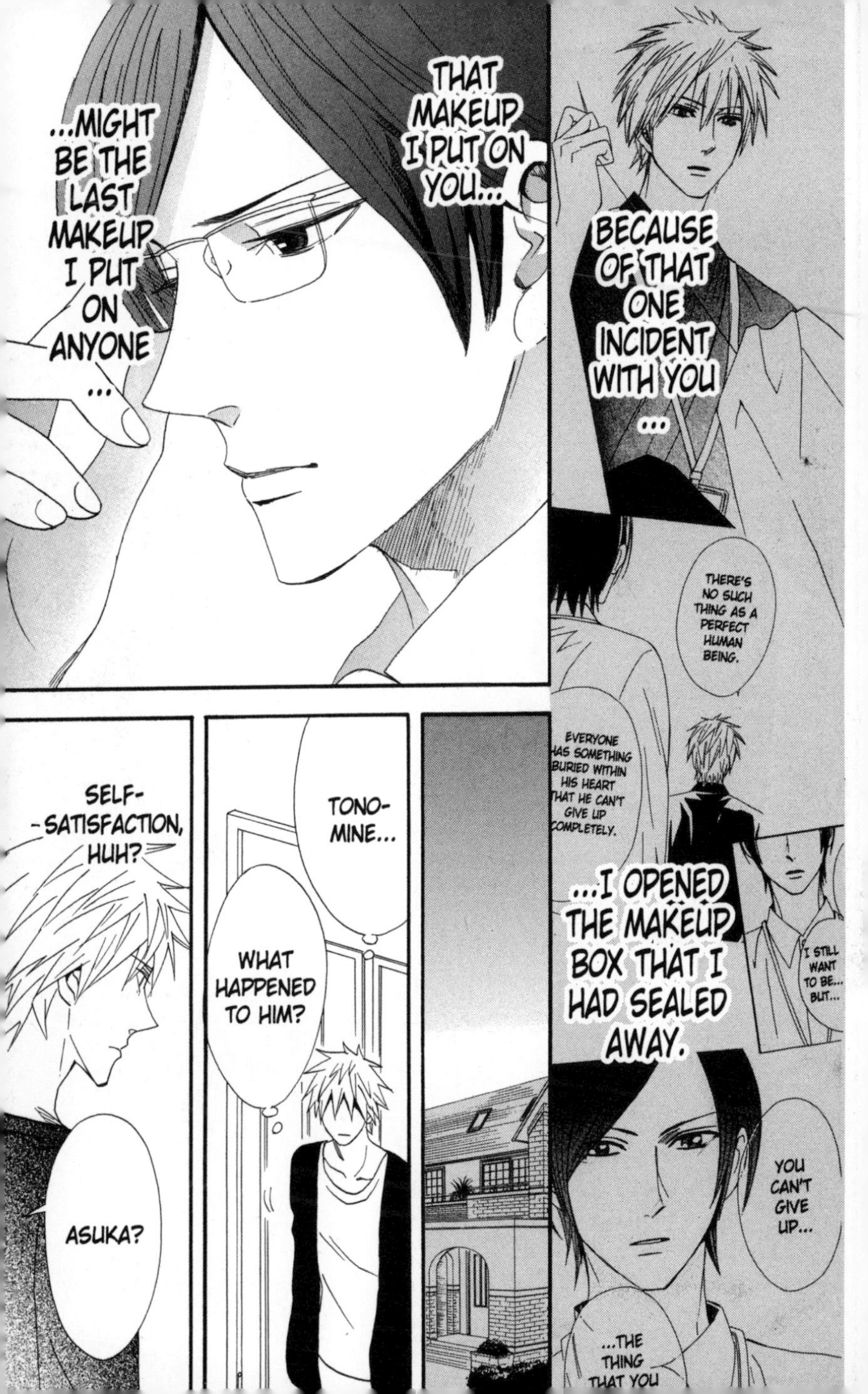
BECAUSE OF THAT ONE INCIDENT WITH YOU ...
THERE'S NO SUCH THING AS A PERFECT HUMAN BEING.
EVERYONE HAS SOMETHING BURIED WITHIN HIS HEART THAT HE CAN'T GIVE UP COMPLETELY.
...I OPENED THE MAKEUP BOX THAT I HAD SEALED AWAY.
I STILL WANT TO BE... BUT...
YOU CAN'T GIVE UP...
...THE THING THAT YOU
THAT MAKEUP I PUT ON YOU...
...MIGHT BE THE LAST MAKEUP I PUT ON ANYONE ...
TONO-MINE...
WHAT HAPPENED TO HIM?
SELF-SATISFACTION, HUH?
ASUKA?

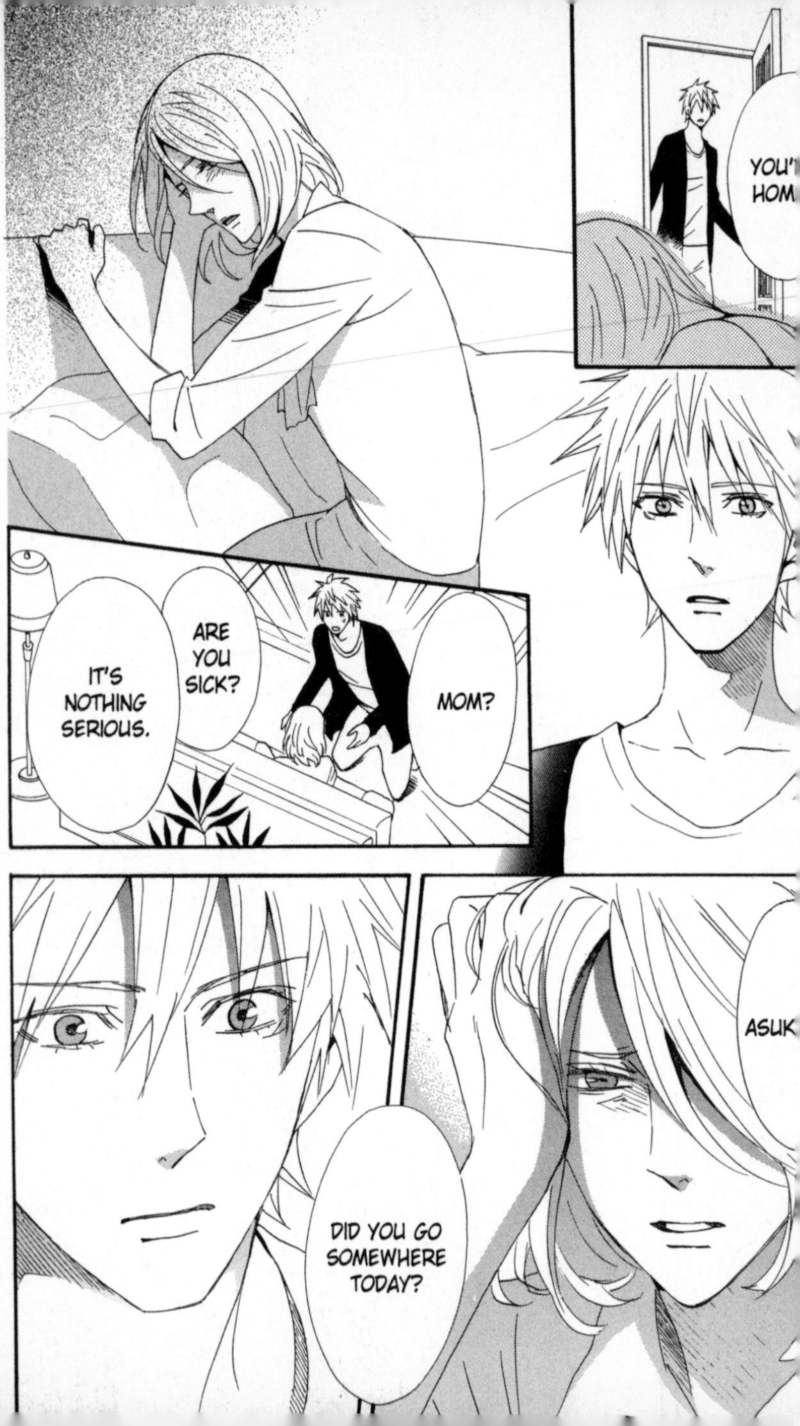

YOU' HOM
MOM?
ARE YOU SICK?
IT'S NOTHING SERIOUS.
ASUK
DID YOU GO SOMEWHERE TODAY?

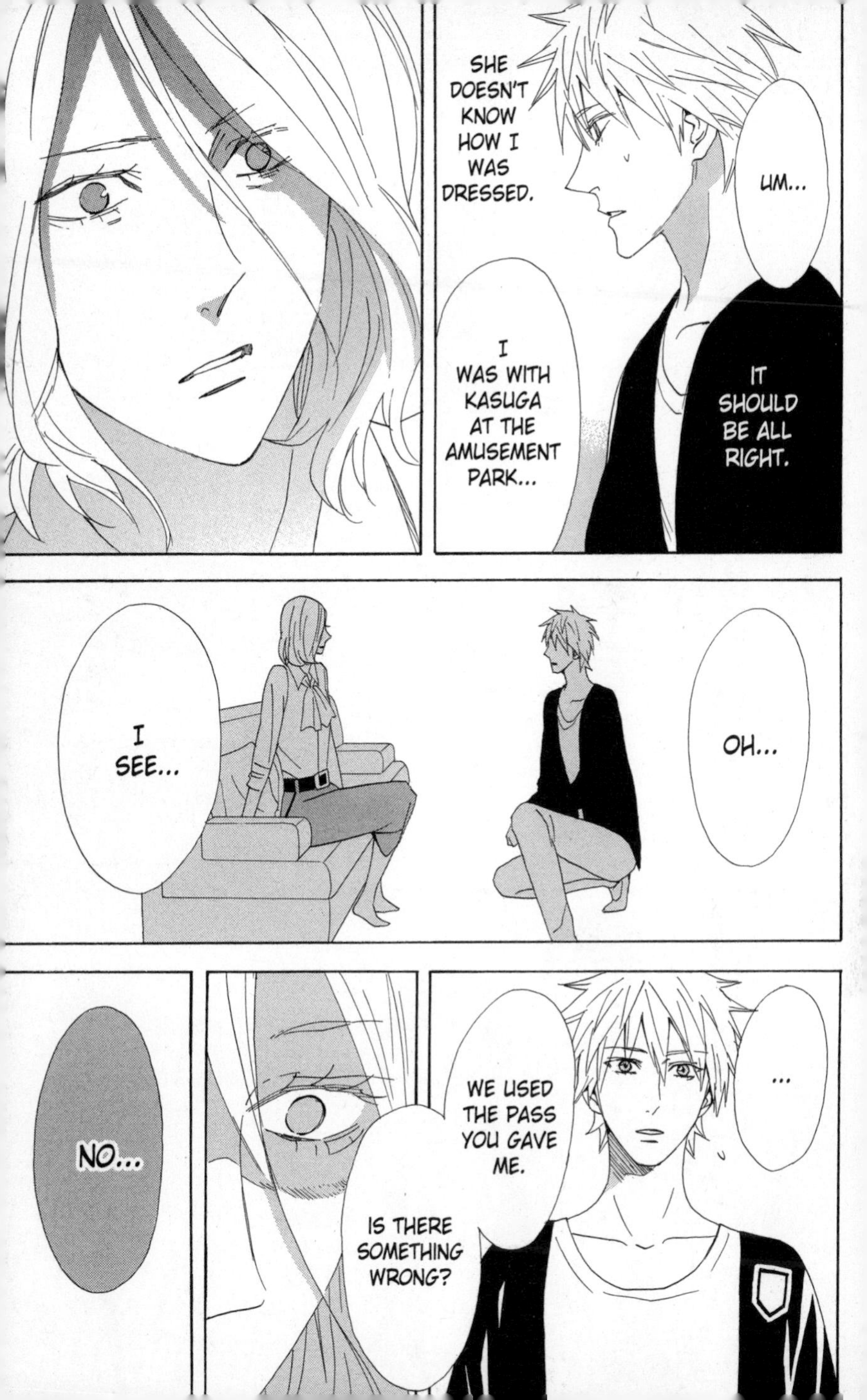
UM...
SHE DOESN'T KNOW HOW I WAS DRESSED.
IT SHOULD BE ALL RIGHT.
I WAS WITH KASUGA AT THE AMUSEMENT PARK...
OH...
I SEE...
...
WE USED THE PASS YOU GAVE ME.
IS THERE SOMETHING WRONG?
NO...

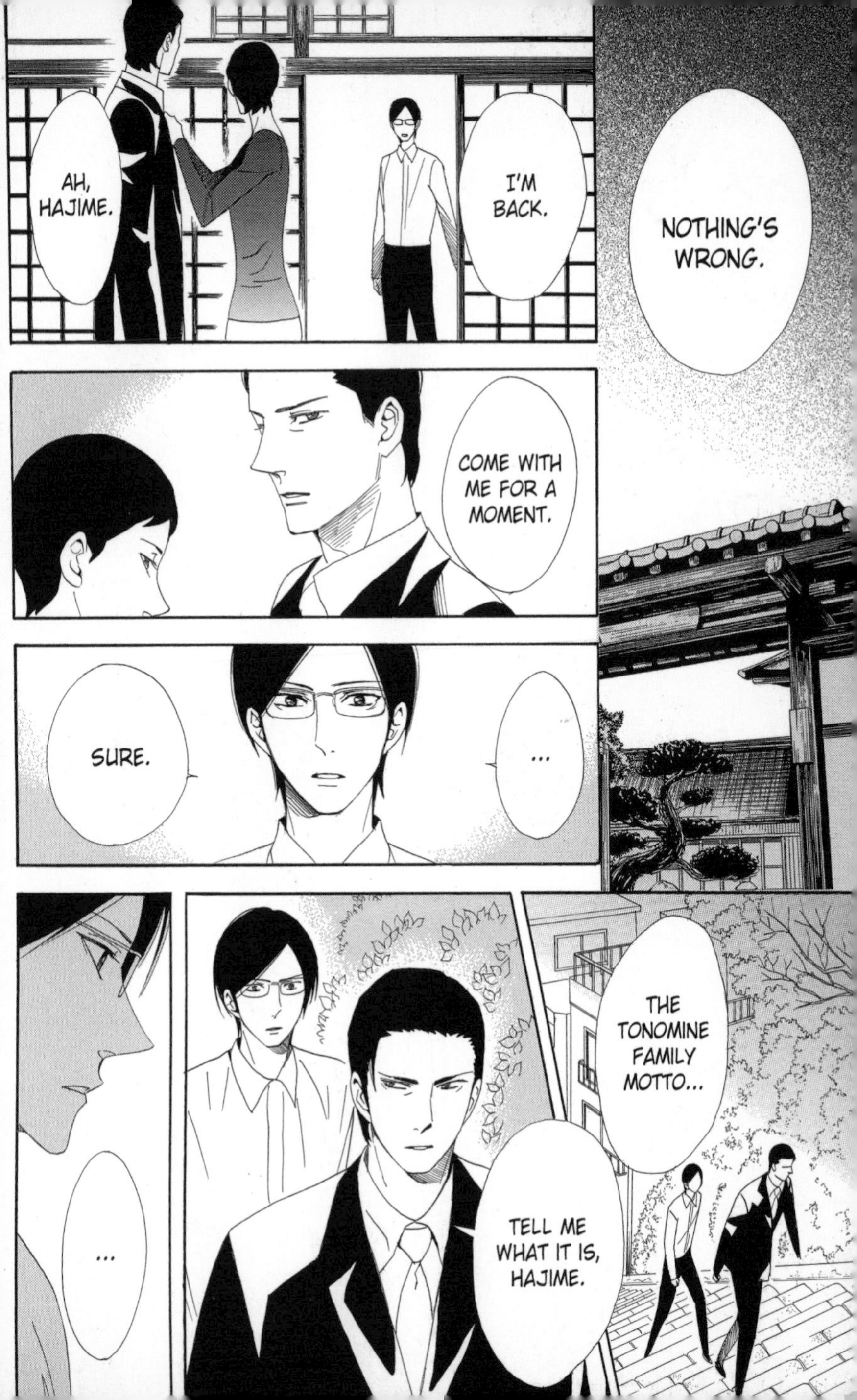
NOTHING'S WRONG.
I'M BACK.
AH, HAJIME.
COME WITH ME FOR A MOMENT.
...
SURE.
THE TONOMINE FAMILY MOTTO...
TELL ME WHAT IT IS, HAJIME.
...

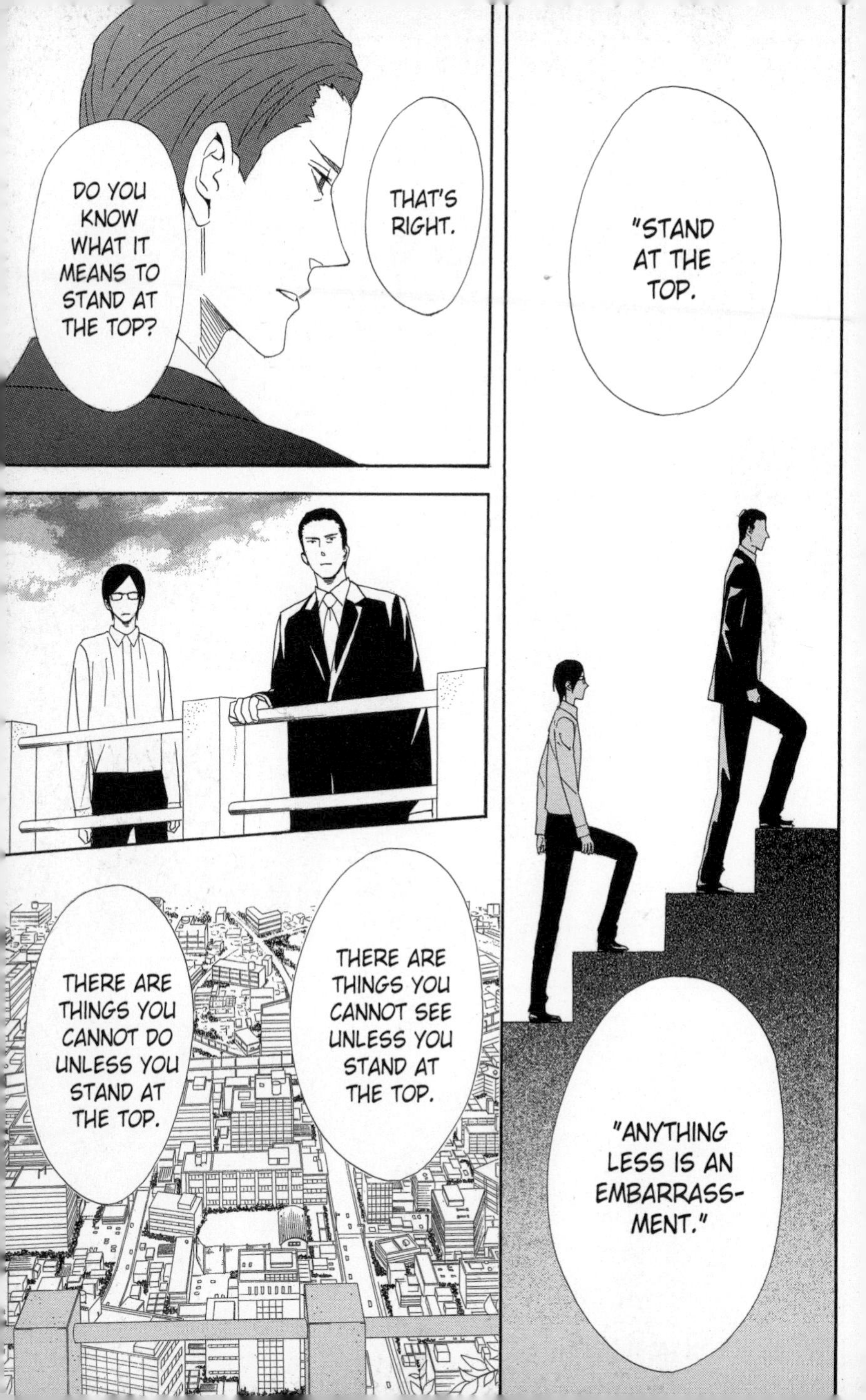
"STAND AT THE TOP.
"ANYTHING LESS IS AN EMBARRASS-MENT."
THAT'S RIGHT.
DO YOU KNOW WHAT IT MEANS TO STAND AT THE TOP?
THERE ARE THINGS YOU CANNOT SEE UNLESS YOU STAND AT THE TOP.
THERE ARE THINGS YOU CANNOT DO UNLESS YOU STAND AT THE TOP.

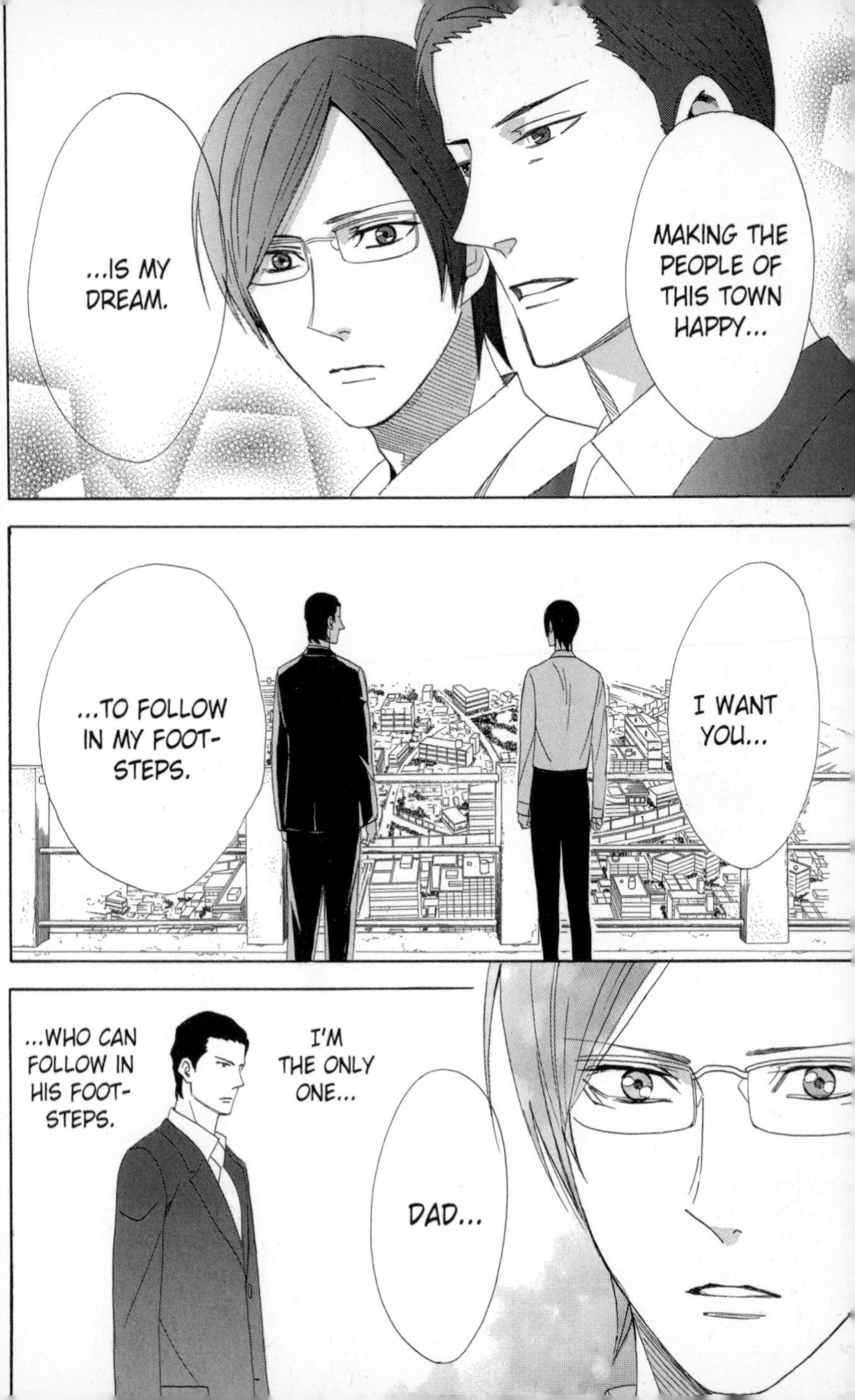
MAKING THE PEOPLE OF THIS TOWN HAPPY...
...IS MY DREAM.
I WANT YOU...
...TO FOLLOW IN MY FOOT-STEPS.
DAD...
I'M THE ONLY ONE...
...WHO CAN FOLLOW IN HIS FOOT-STEPS.

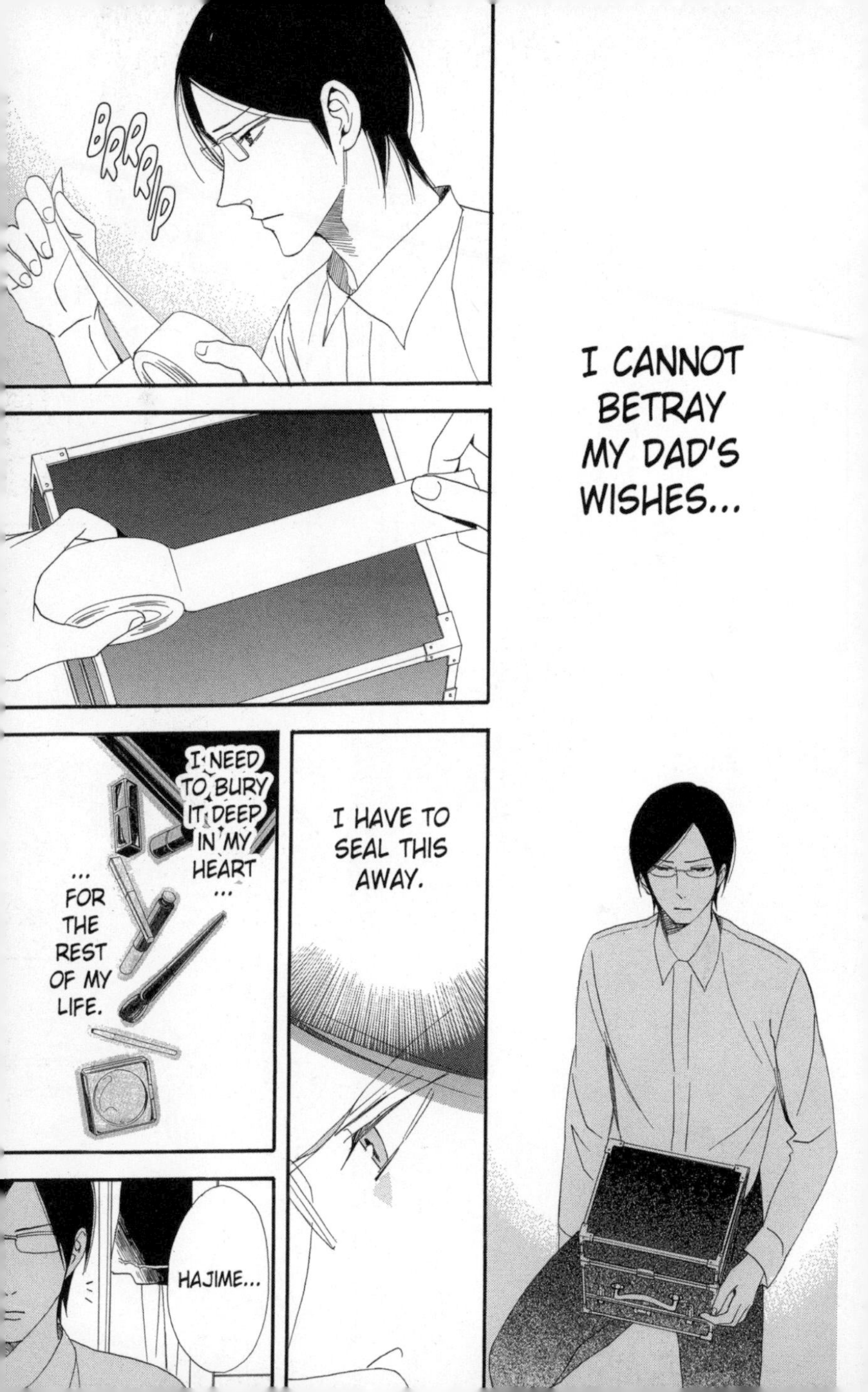
I CANNOT BETRAY MY DAD'S WISHES...
BRRRIP
I HAVE TO SEAL THIS AWAY.
I NEED TO BURY IT DEEP IN MY HEART...
...FOR THE REST OF MY LIFE.
HAJIME...

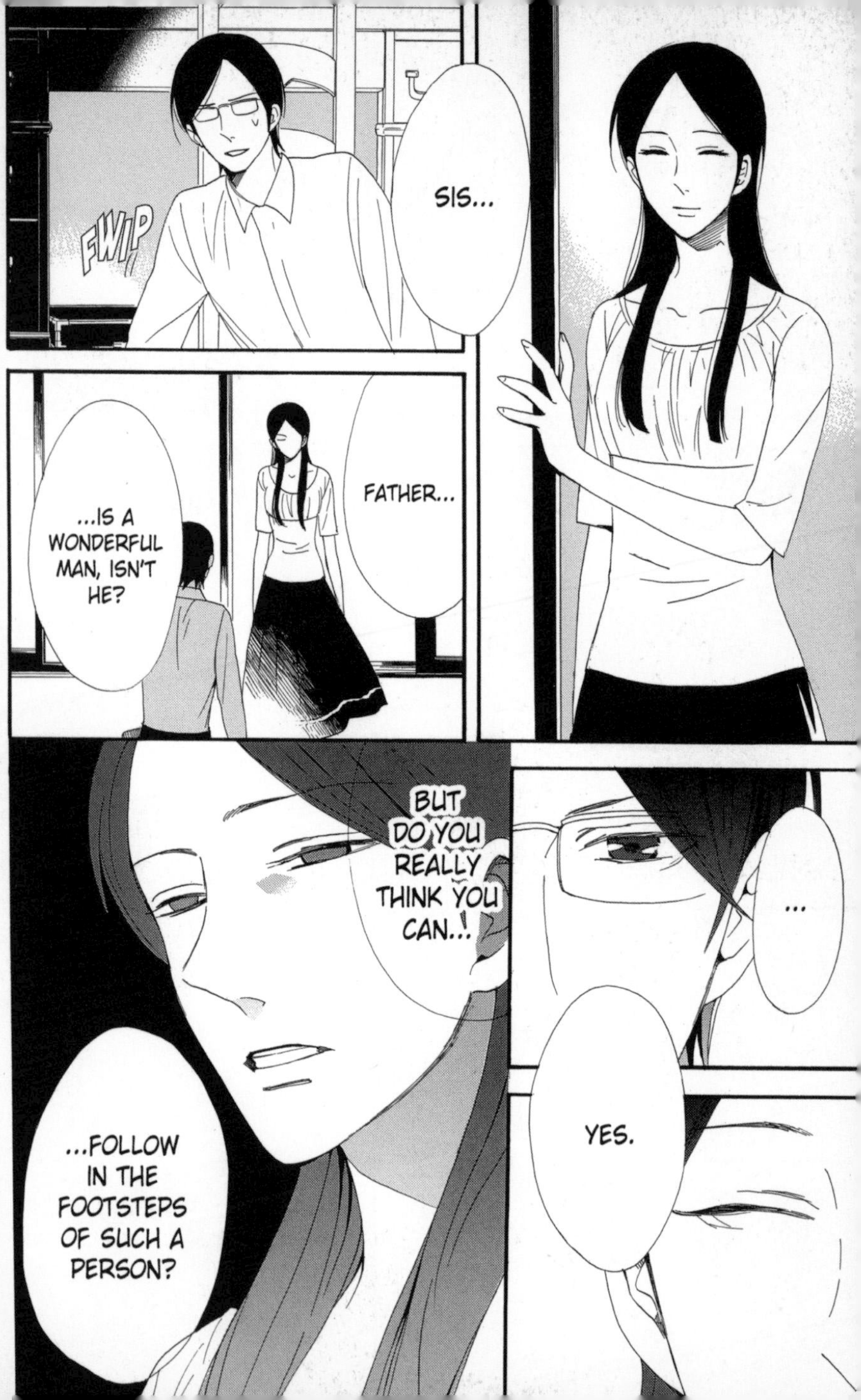
SIS...
FWIP
FATHER...
...IS A WONDERFUL MAN, ISN'T HE?
...
YES.
BUT DO YOU REALLY THINK YOU CAN..!
...FOLLOW IN THE FOOTSTEPS OF SUCH A PERSON?

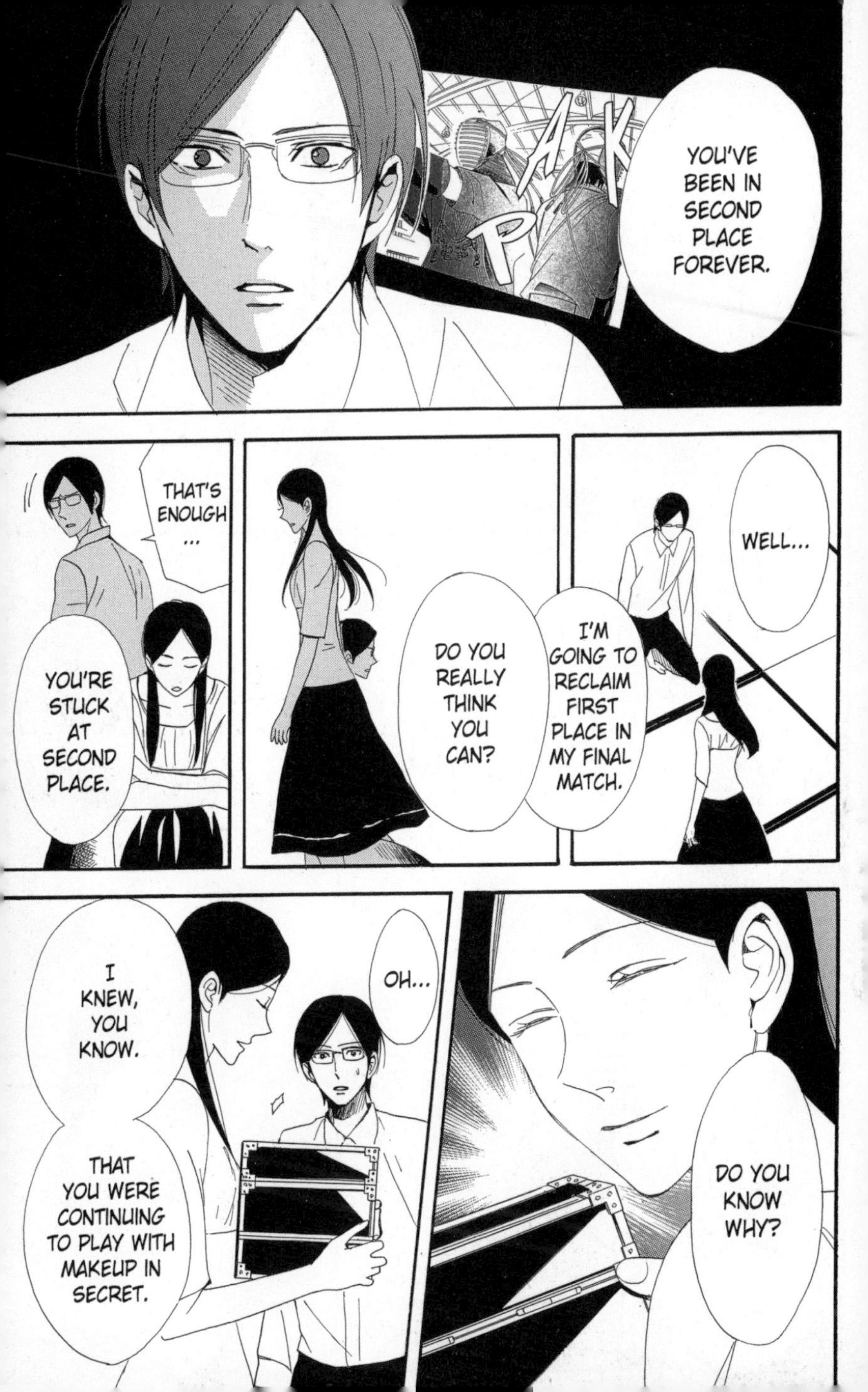
PAK
YOU'VE BEEN IN SECOND PLACE FOREVER.
WELL...
I'M GOING TO RECLAIM FIRST PLACE IN MY FINAL MATCH.
DO YOU REALLY THINK YOU CAN?
THAT'S ENOUGH...
YOU'RE STUCK AT SECOND PLACE.
DO YOU KNOW WHY?
OH...
I KNEW, YOU KNOW.
THAT YOU WERE CONTINUING TO PLAY WITH MAKEUP IN SECRET.

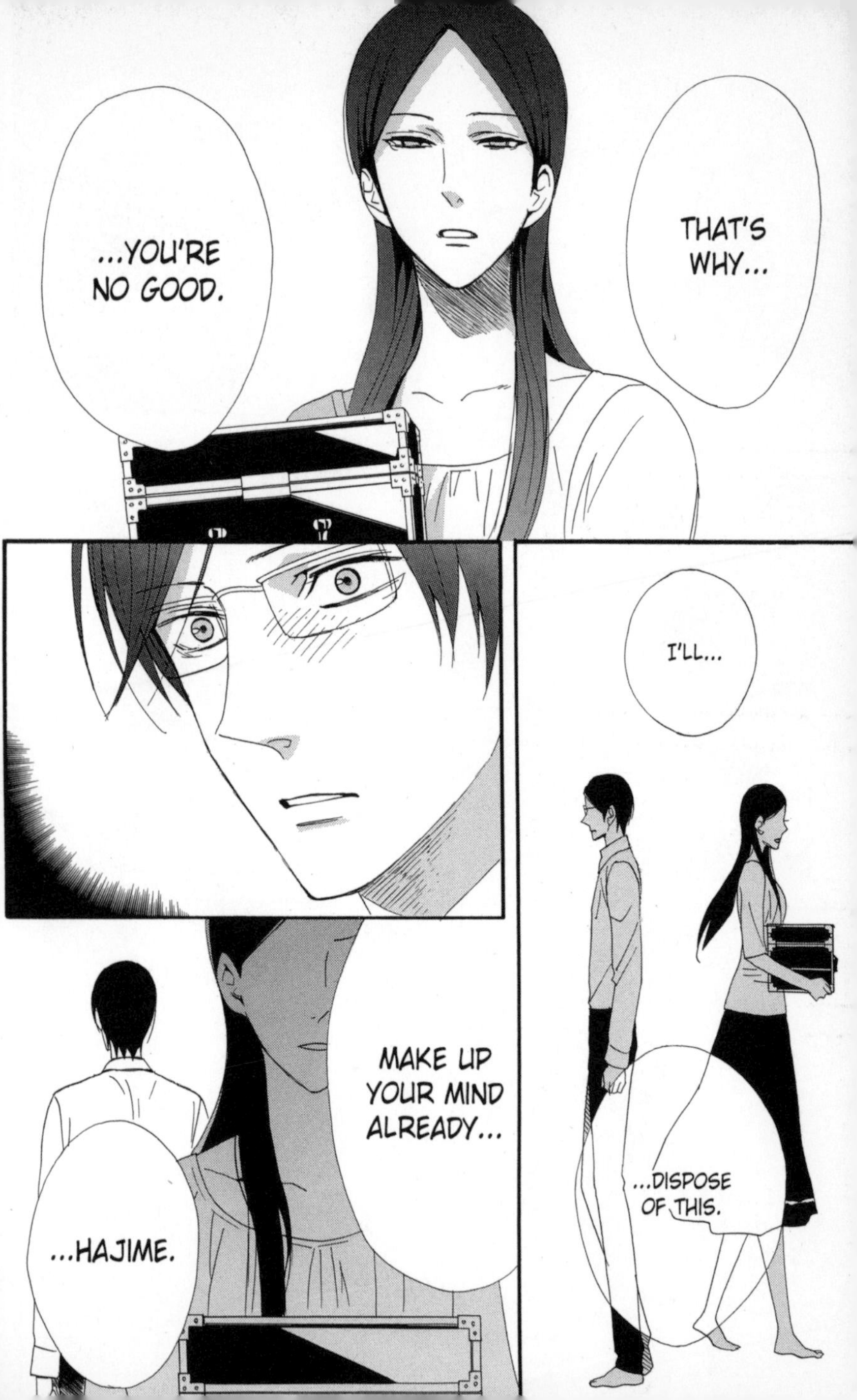
THAT'S WHY...
...YOU'RE NO GOOD.
I'LL...
...DISPOSE OF THIS.
MAKE UP YOUR MIND ALREADY...
...HAJIME.

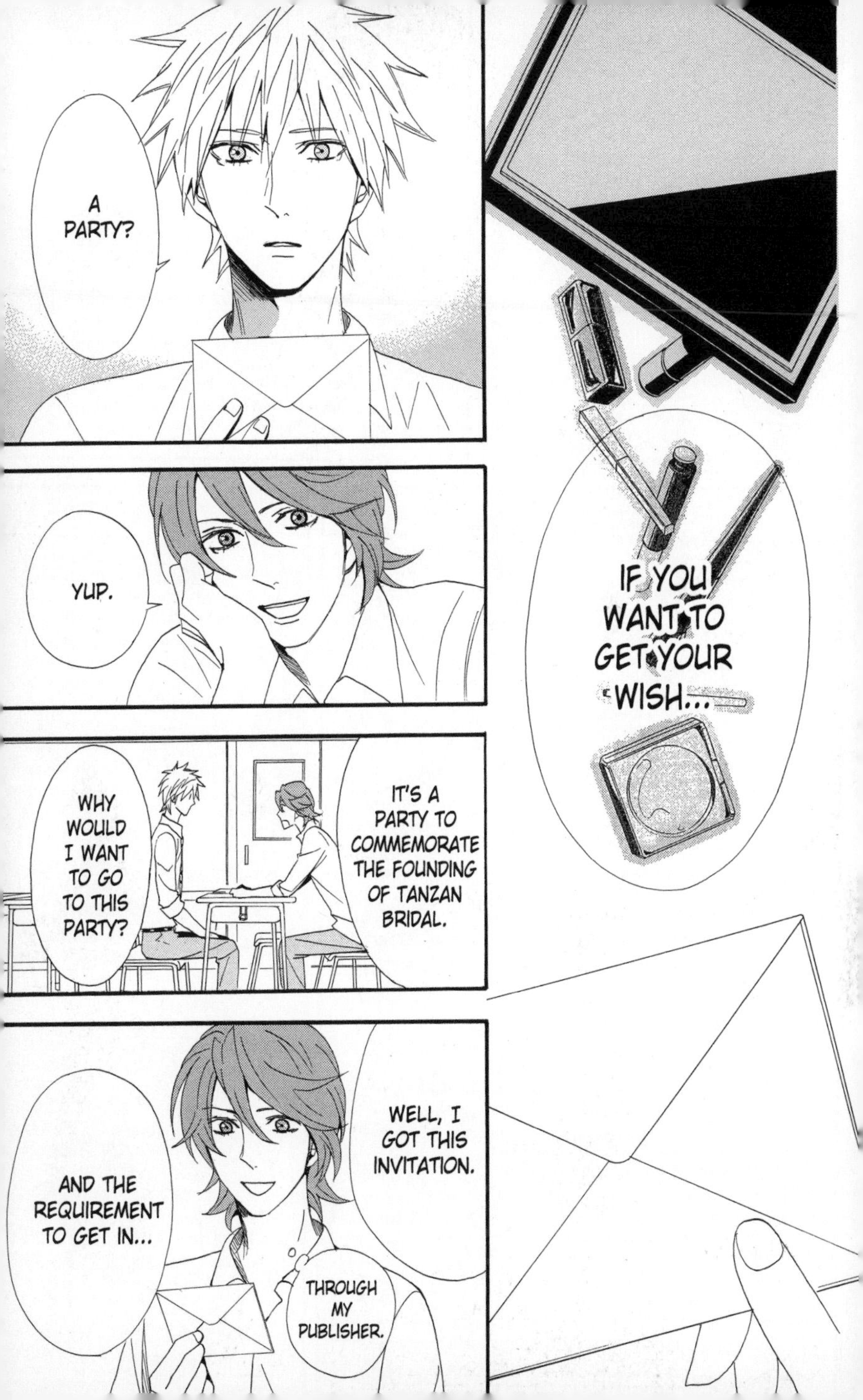
IF YOU WANT TO GET YOUR WISH...
A PARTY?
YUP.
IT'S A PARTY TO COMMEMORATE THE FOUNDING OF TANZAN BRIDAL.
WHY WOULD I WANT TO GO TO THIS PARTY?
WELL, I GOT THIS INVITATION.
THROUGH MY PUBLISHER.
AND THE REQUIREMENT TO GET IN...

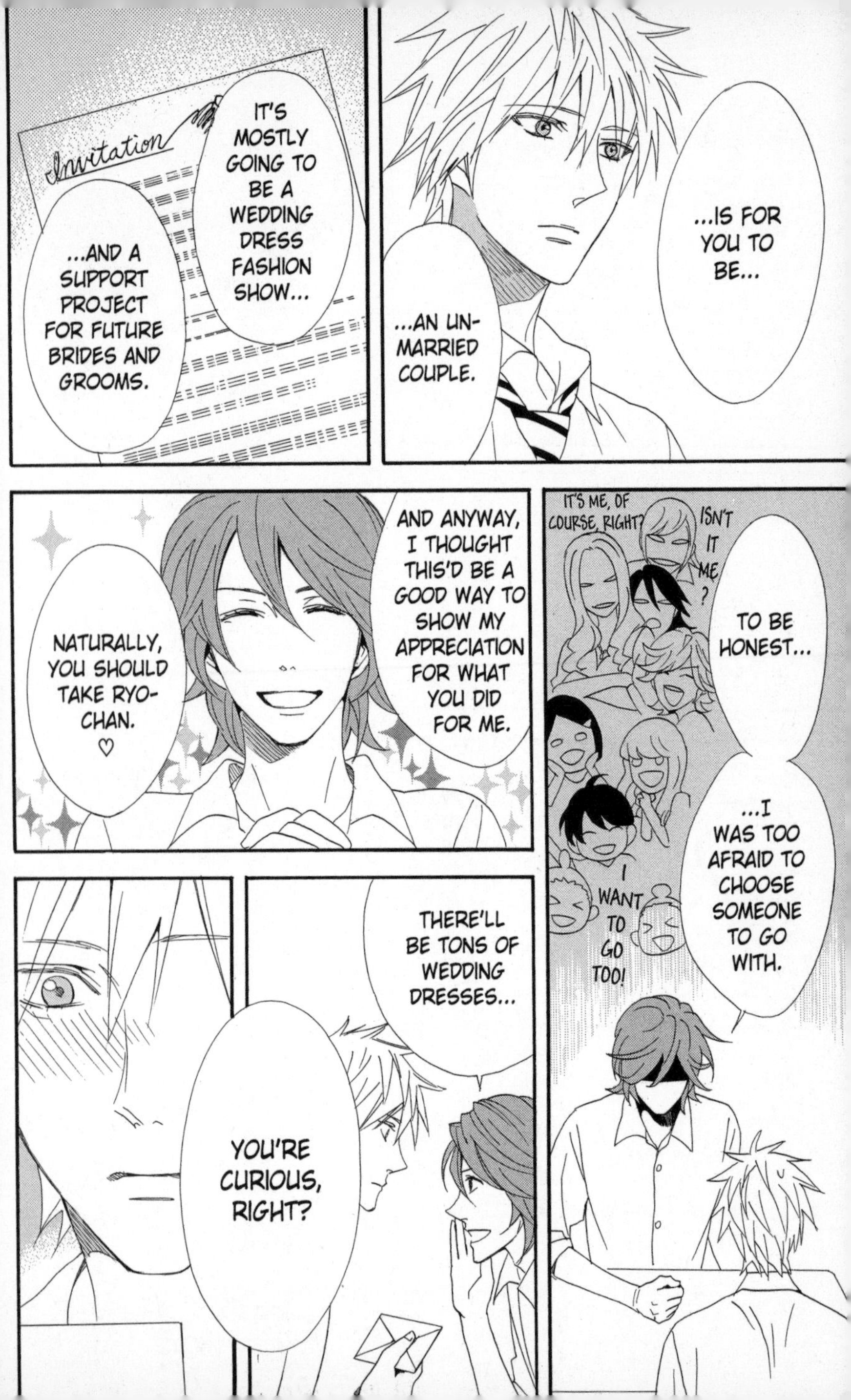
...IS FOR YOU TO BE...
...AN UN-MARRIED COUPLE.
Invitation
IT'S MOSTLY GOING TO BE A WEDDING DRESS FASHION SHOW...
...AND A SUPPORT PROJECT FOR FUTURE BRIDES AND GROOMS.
TO BE HONEST...
IT'S ME, OF COURSE, RIGHT?
ISN'T IT ME?
...I WAS TOO AFRAID TO CHOOSE SOMEONE TO GO WITH.
I WANT TO GO TOO!
AND ANYWAY, I THOUGHT THIS'D BE A GOOD WAY TO SHOW MY APPRECIATION FOR WHAT YOU DID FOR ME.
NATURALLY, YOU SHOULD TAKE RYO-CHAN. ♡
THERE'LL BE TONS OF WEDDING DRESSES...
YOU'RE CURIOUS, RIGHT?

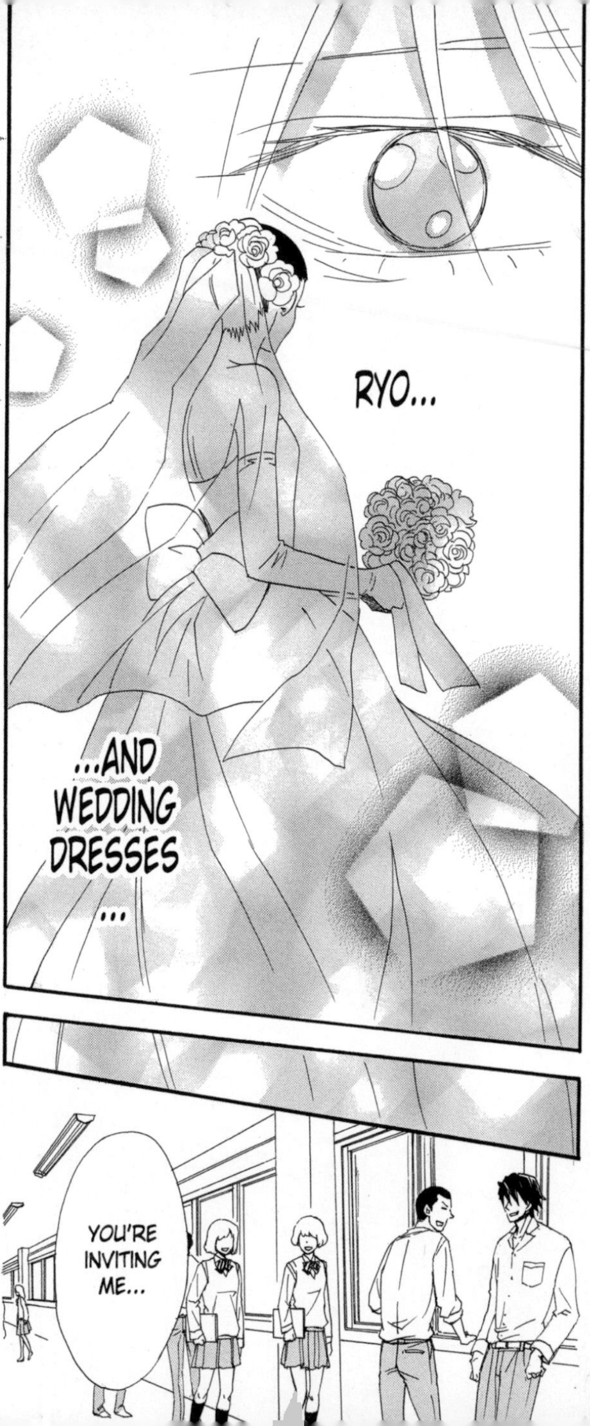
RYO...
...AND WEDDING DRESSES ...
YOU'RE INVITING ME...

Hello.
This is Kanno.

Tonomine's turn continues from the last chapter.

As the creator, I felt that he was the easiest of the characters to handle. He was quite popular with readers too.

As a side note, in regards to the characters he puts makeup on— this time, I'd first sketch them without makeup. Then I'd thicken their eye line and give them more eyelashes with pens and tones as if I was actually putting makeup on them.

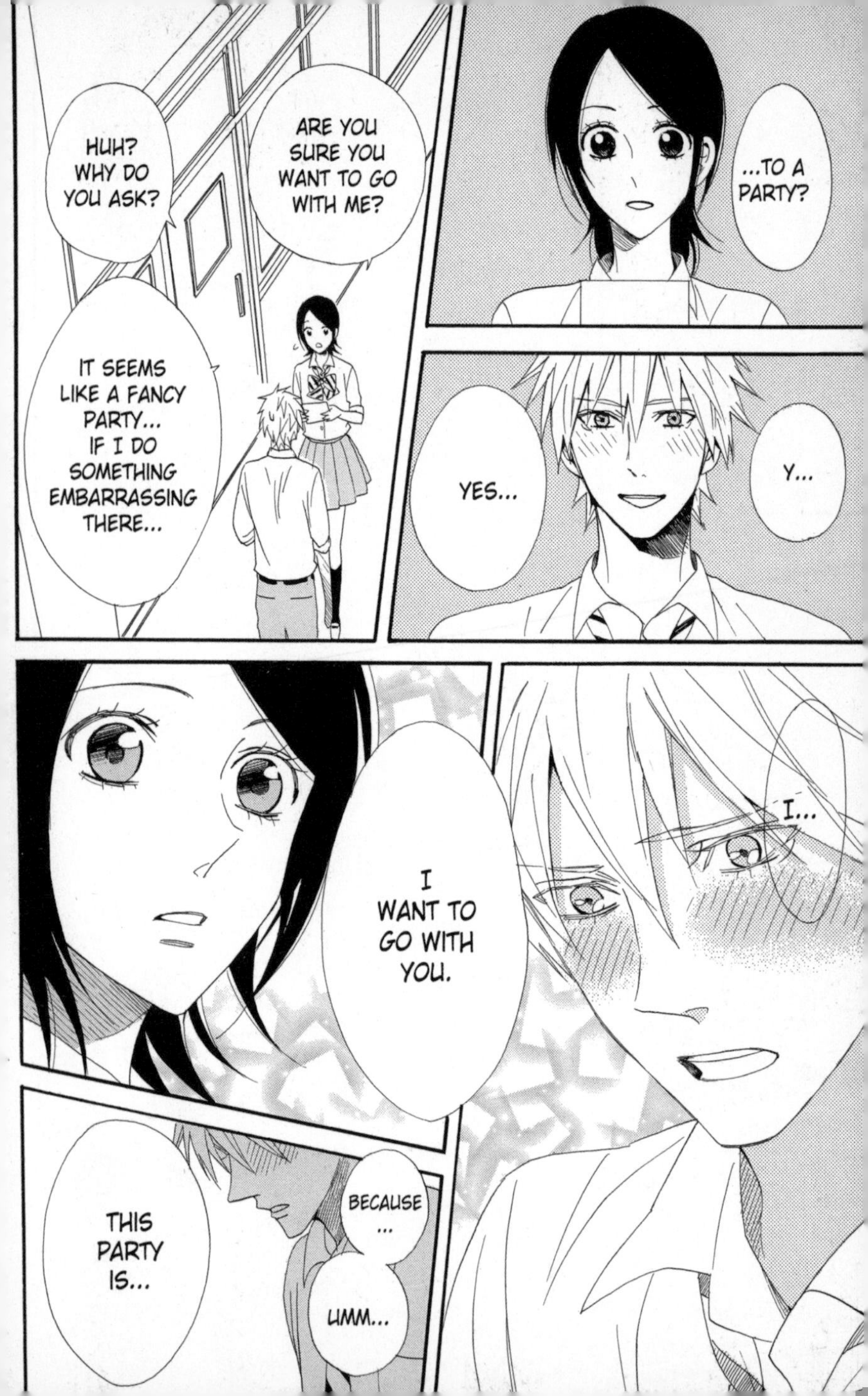
...TO A PARTY?
Y...
YES...
ARE YOU SURE YOU WANT TO GO WITH ME?
HUH? WHY DO YOU ASK?
IT SEEMS LIKE A FANCY PARTY... IF I DO SOMETHING EMBARRASSING THERE...
I...
I WANT TO GO WITH YOU.
BECAUSE...
UMM...
THIS PARTY IS...

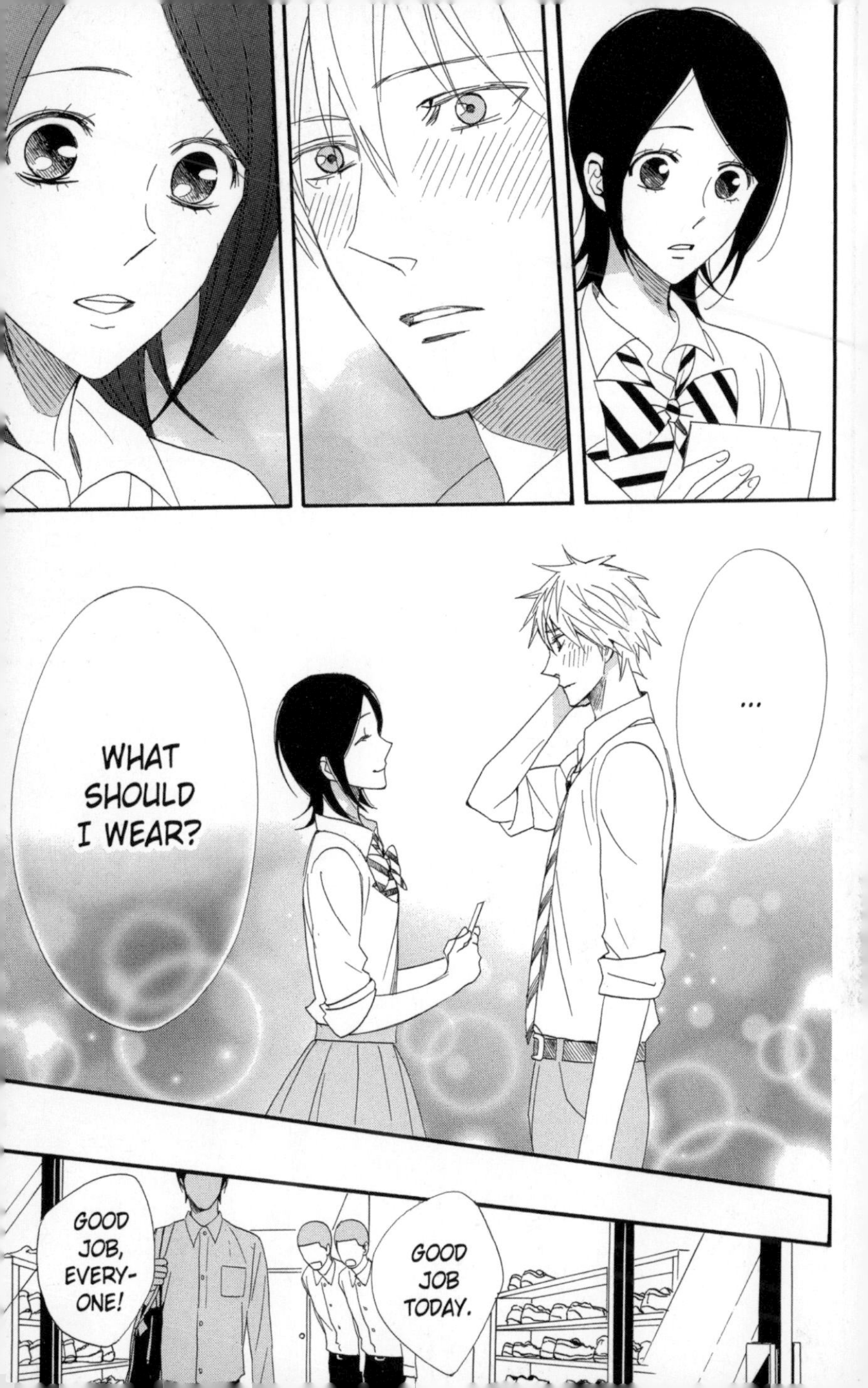
...
WHAT SHOULD I WEAR?
GOOD JOB TODAY.
GOOD JOB, EVERY-ONE!

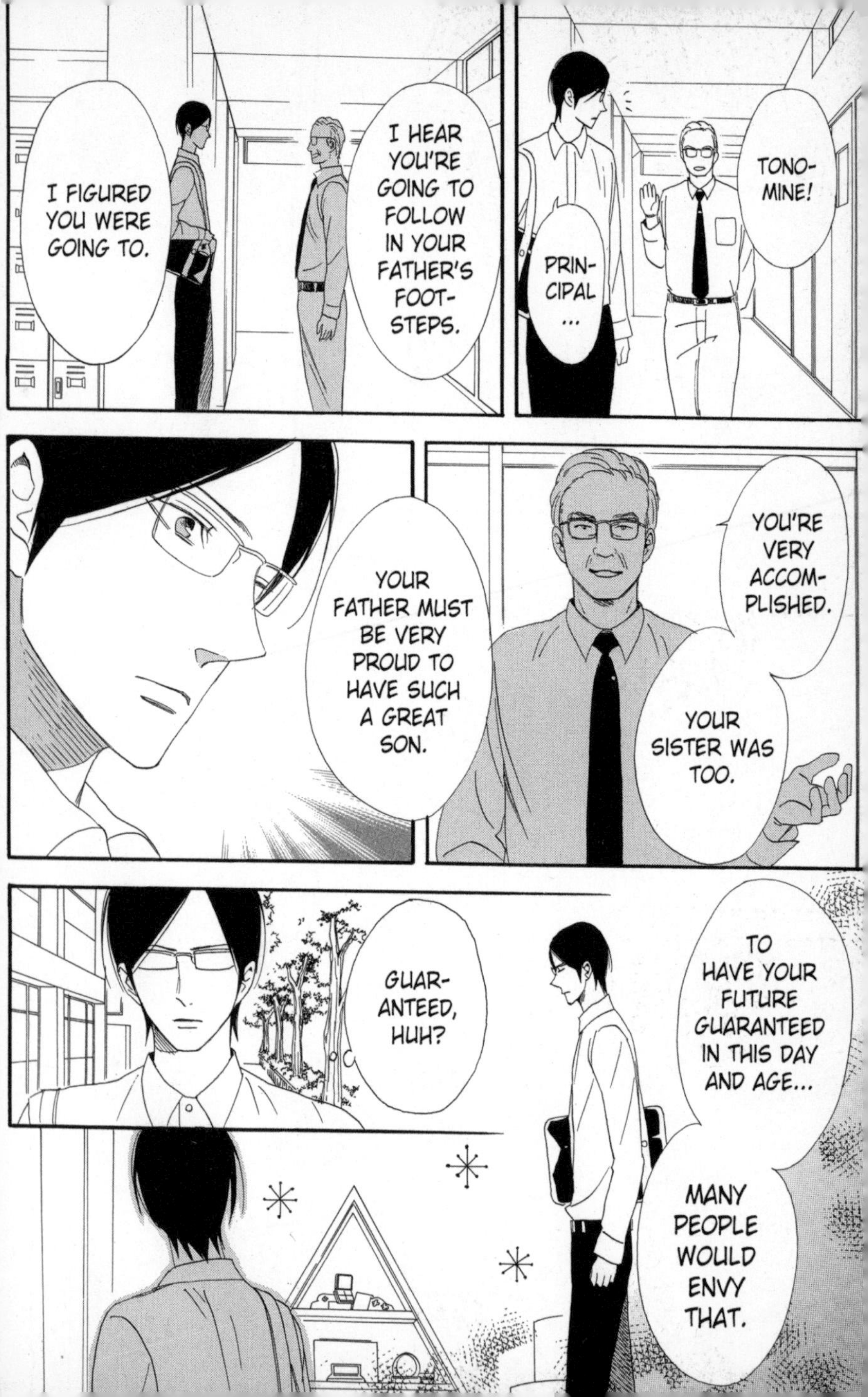
TONOMINE!
PRINCIPAL...
I HEAR YOU'RE GOING TO FOLLOW IN YOUR FATHER'S FOOTSTEPS.
I FIGURED YOU WERE GOING TO.
YOU'RE VERY ACCOMPLISHED.
YOUR SISTER WAS TOO.
YOUR FATHER MUST BE VERY PROUD TO HAVE SUCH A GREAT SON.
TO HAVE YOUR FUTURE GUARANTEED IN THIS DAY AND AGE...
MANY PEOPLE WOULD ENVY THAT.
GUARANTEED, HUH?

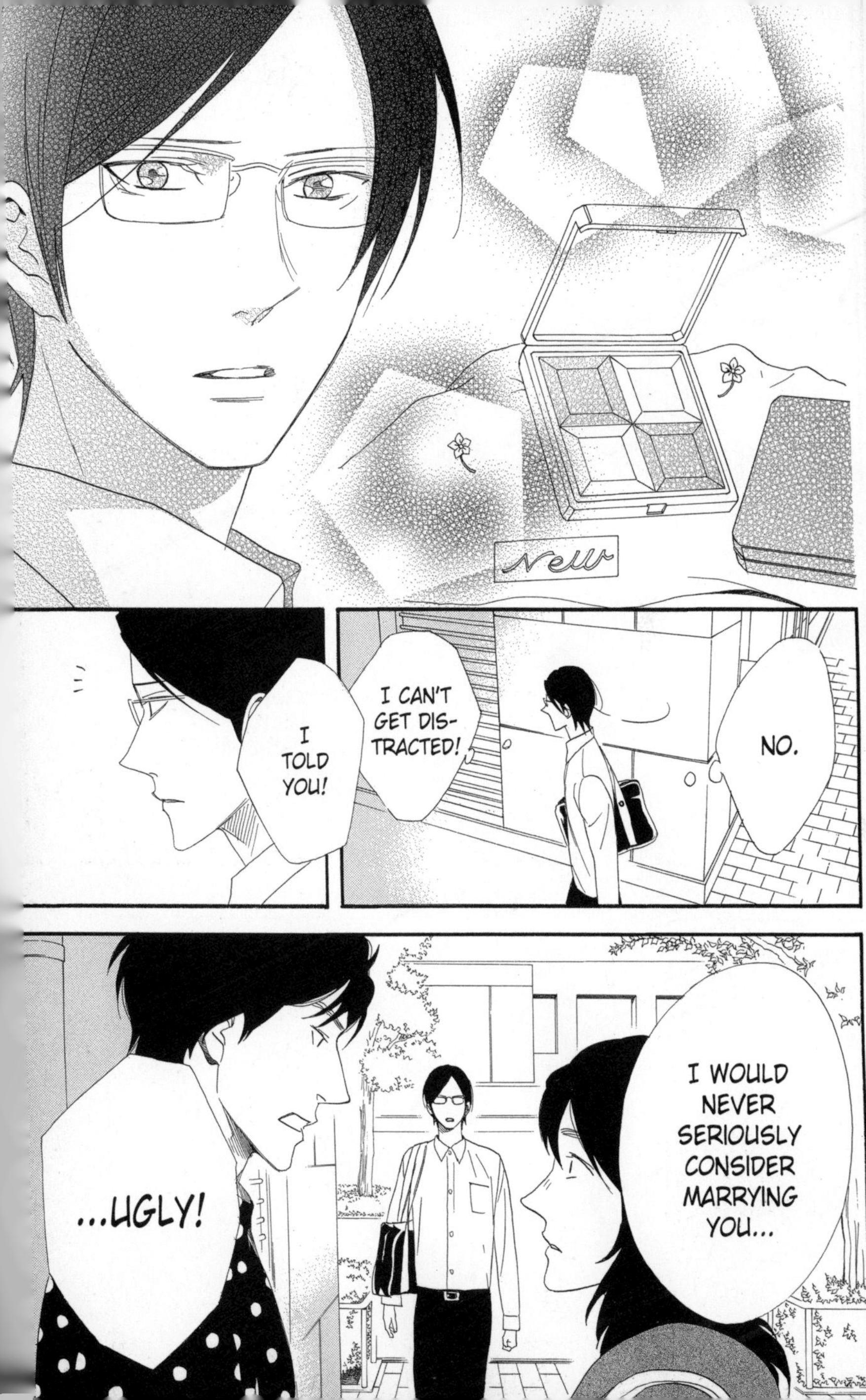
New
NO.
I CAN'T GET DIS-TRACTED!
I TOLD YOU!
I WOULD NEVER SERIOUSLY CONSIDER MARRYING YOU...
...UGLY!

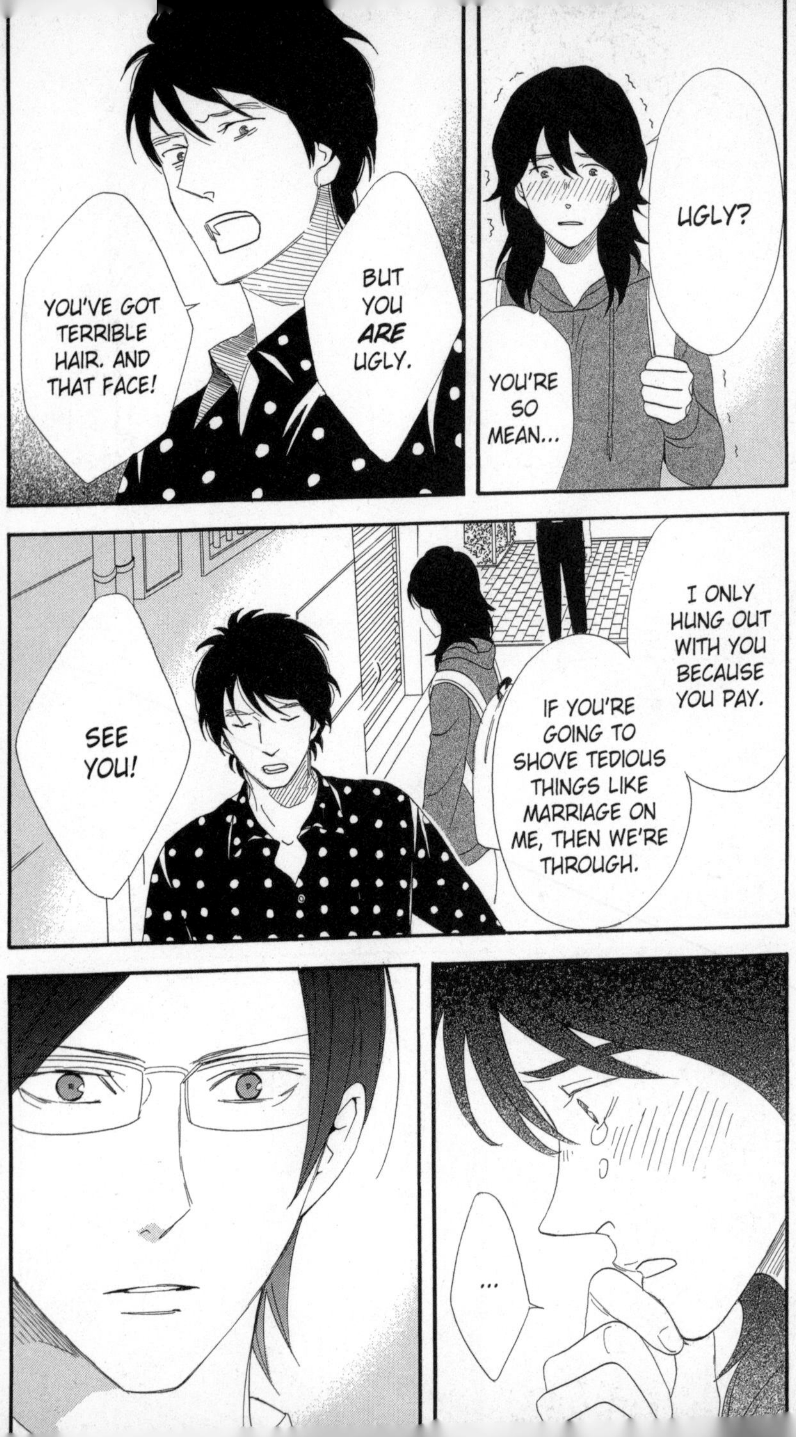
UGLY?
YOU'RE SO MEAN...
BUT YOU **ARE** UGLY.
YOU'VE GOT TERRIBLE HAIR. AND THAT FACE!
I ONLY HUNG OUT WITH YOU BECAUSE YOU PAY.
IF YOU'RE GOING TO SHOVE TEDIOUS THINGS LIKE MARRIAGE ON ME, THEN WE'RE THROUGH.
SEE YOU!
...

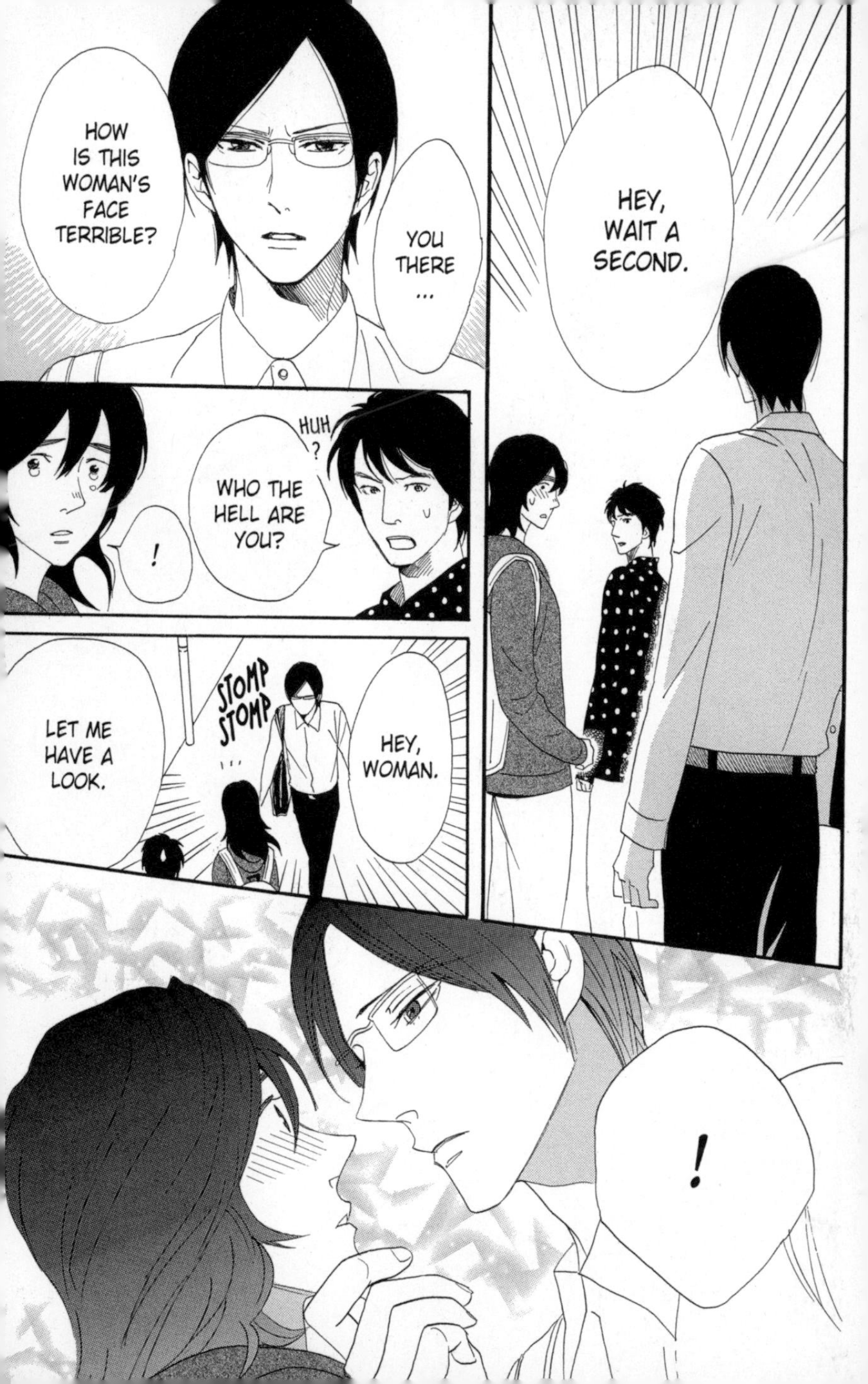
HEY, WAIT A SECOND.
YOU THERE ...
HOW IS THIS WOMAN'S FACE TERRIBLE?
HUH ?
WHO THE HELL ARE YOU?
!
HEY, WOMAN.
STOMP STOMP
...
LET ME HAVE A LOOK.
!

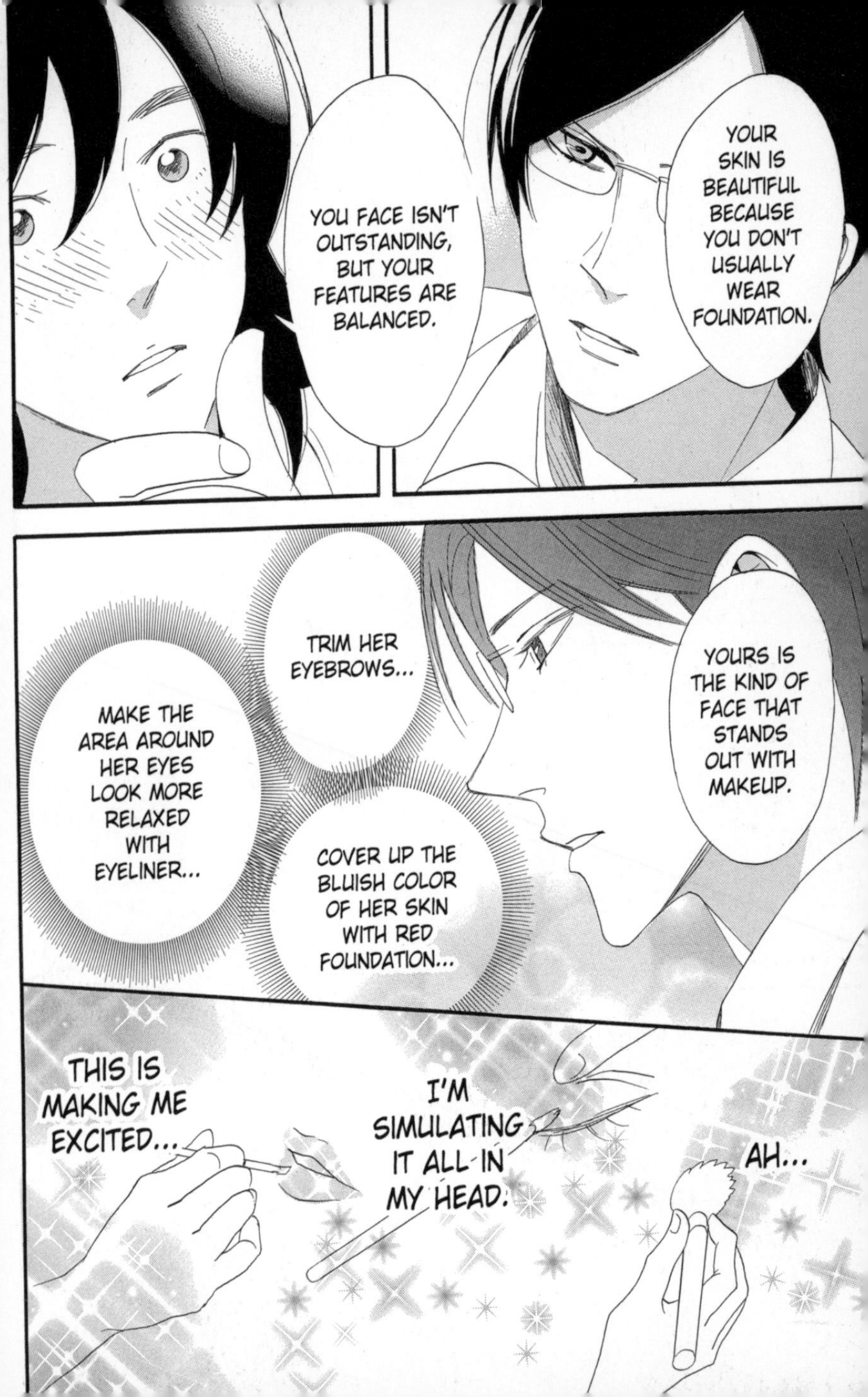
YOUR SKIN IS BEAUTIFUL BECAUSE YOU DON'T USUALLY WEAR FOUNDATION.
YOU FACE ISN'T OUTSTANDING, BUT YOUR FEATURES ARE BALANCED.
YOURS IS THE KIND OF FACE THAT STANDS OUT WITH MAKEUP.
TRIM HER EYEBROWS...
COVER UP THE BLUISH COLOR OF HER SKIN WITH RED FOUNDATION...
MAKE THE AREA AROUND HER EYES LOOK MORE RELAXED WITH EYELINER...
AH...
I'M SIMULATING IT ALL IN MY HEAD.
THIS IS MAKING ME EXCITED...

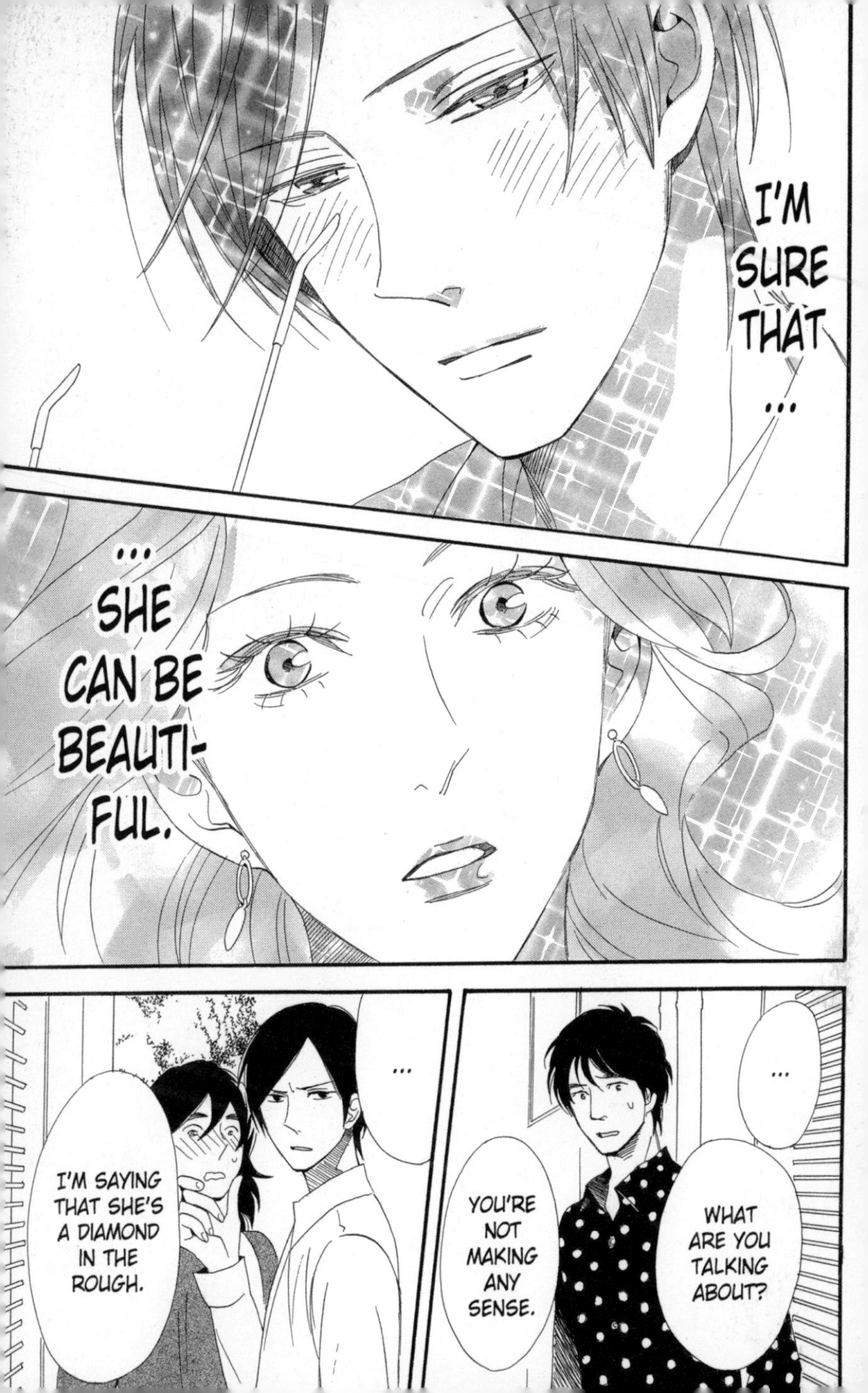
I'M SURE THAT...
...SHE CAN BE BEAUTI-FUL.
...
WHAT ARE YOU TALKING ABOUT?
YOU'RE NOT MAKING ANY SENSE.
...
I'M SAYING THAT SHE'S A DIAMOND IN THE ROUGH.

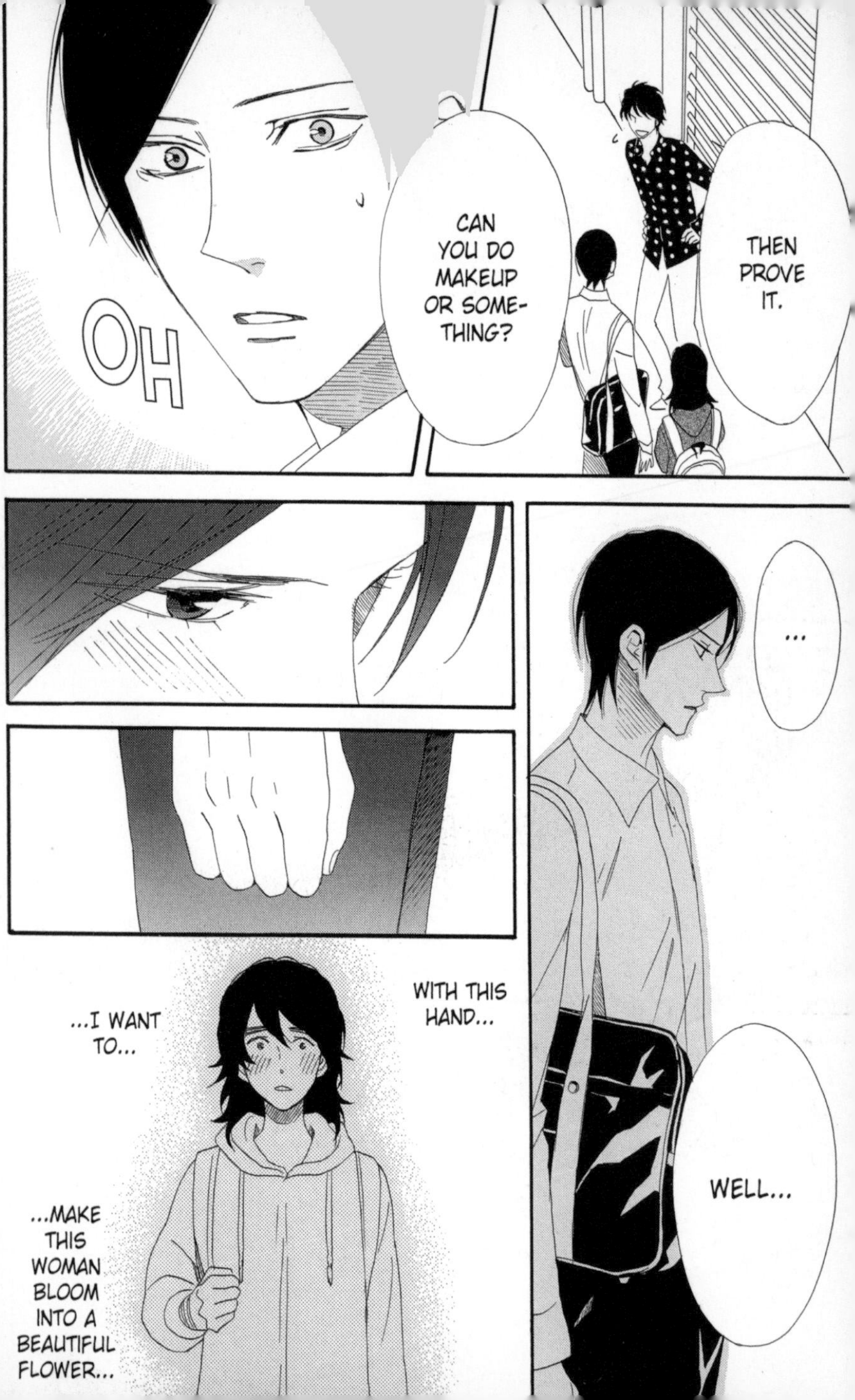
THEN PROVE IT.
CAN YOU DO MAKEUP OR SOME-THING?
OH
...
WELL...
WITH THIS HAND...
...I WANT TO...
...MAKE THIS WOMAN BLOOM INTO A BEAUTIFUL FLOWER...

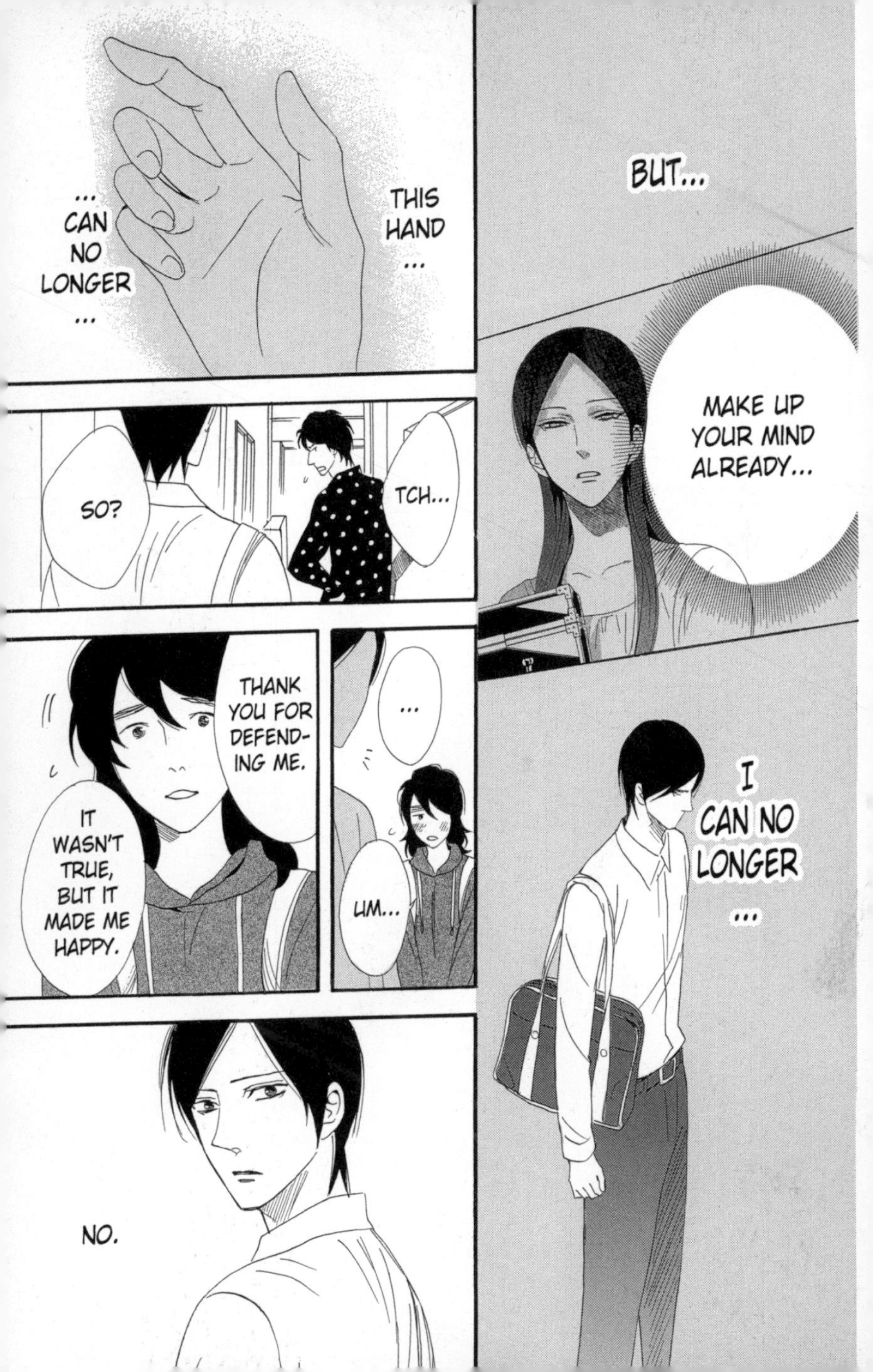
BUT...
MAKE UP YOUR MIND ALREADY...
I CAN NO LONGER ...
THIS HAND ...
... CAN NO LONGER ...
TCH...
SO?
...
UM...
THANK YOU FOR DEFENDING ME.
IT WASN'T TRUE, BUT IT MADE ME HAPPY.
NO.

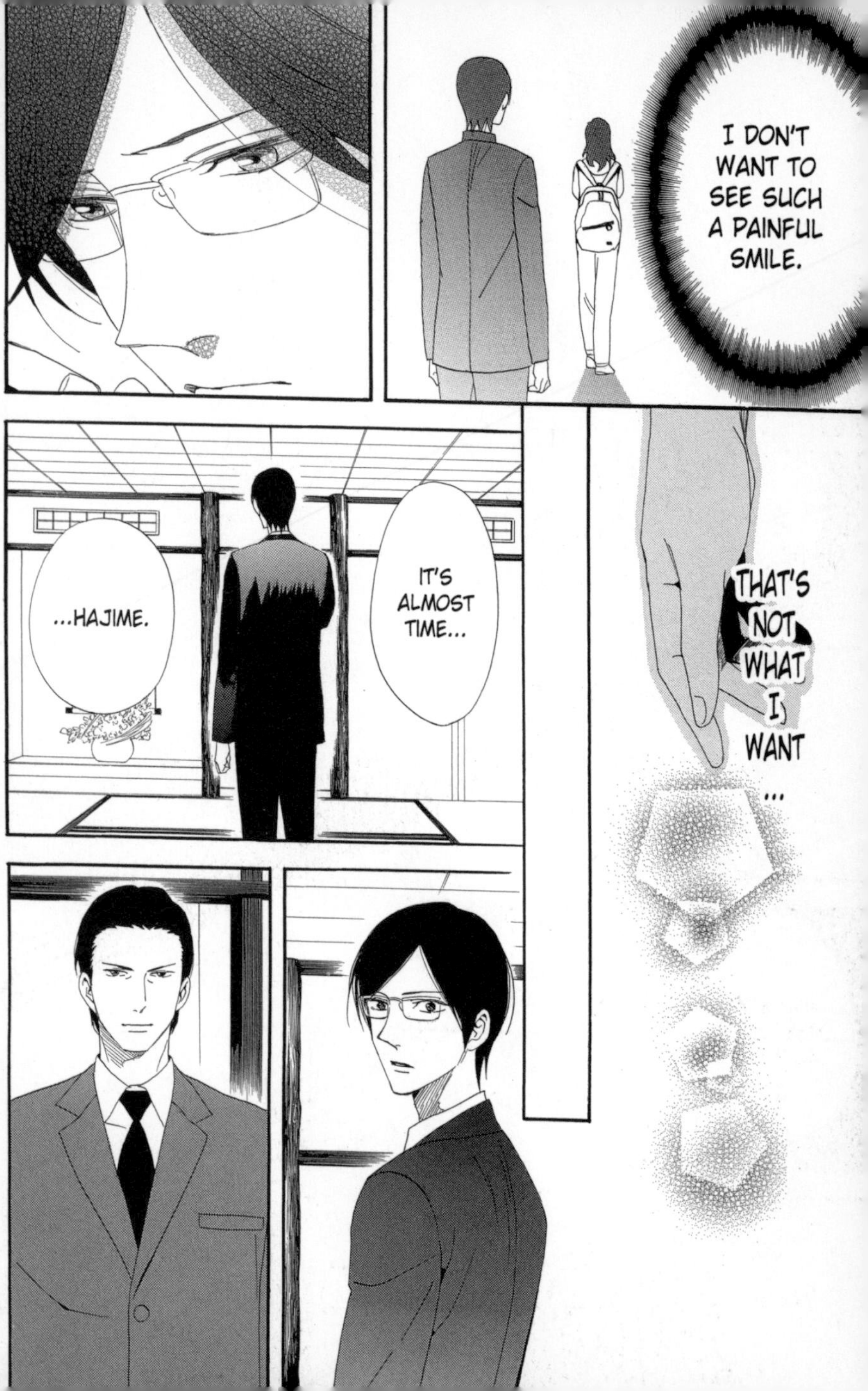
I DON'T WANT TO SEE SUCH A PAINFUL SMILE.
THAT'S NOT WHAT I WANT...
IT'S ALMOST TIME...
...HAJIME.

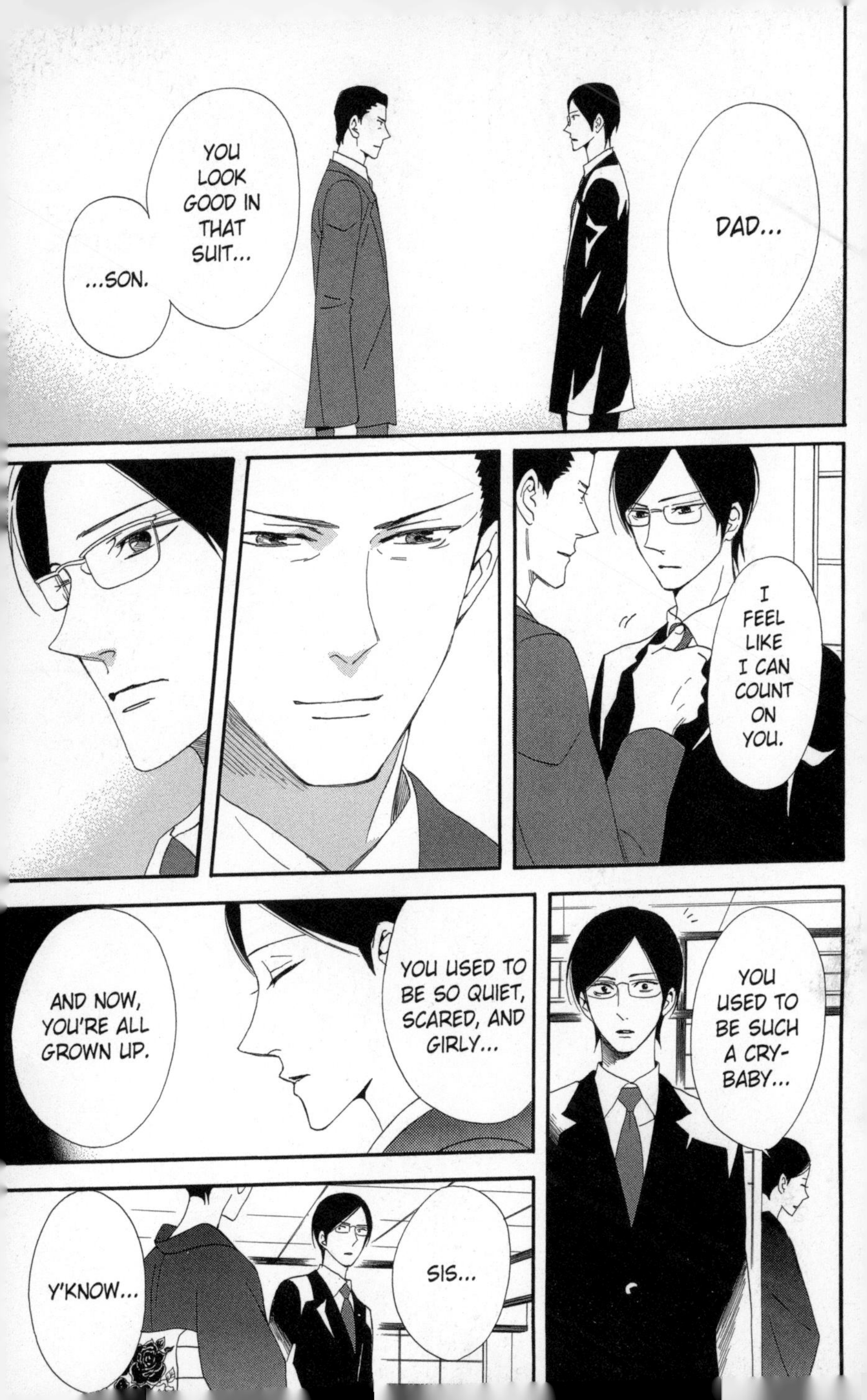
DAD...
YOU LOOK GOOD IN THAT SUIT...
...SON.
I FEEL LIKE I CAN COUNT ON YOU.
YOU USED TO BE SUCH A CRY-BABY...
YOU USED TO BE SO QUIET, SCARED, AND GIRLY...
AND NOW, YOU'RE ALL GROWN UP.
SIS...
Y'KNOW...

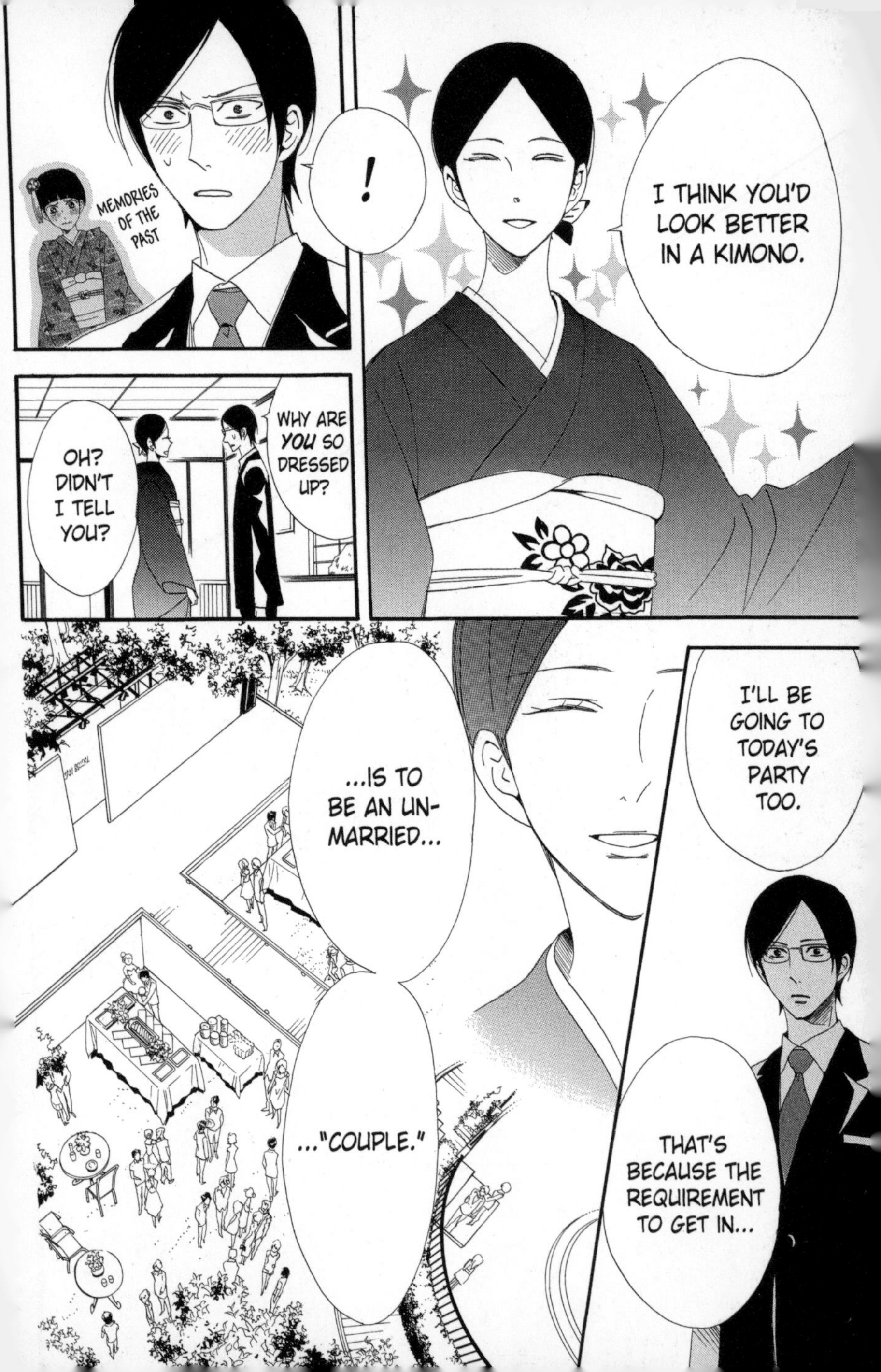
I THINK YOU'D LOOK BETTER IN A KIMONO.
!
MEMORIES OF THE PAST
WHY ARE *YOU* SO DRESSED UP?
OH? DIDN'T I TELL YOU?
I'LL BE GOING TO TODAY'S PARTY TOO.
THAT'S BECAUSE THE REQUIREMENT TO GET IN...
...IS TO BE AN UN-MARRIED...
..."COUPLE."

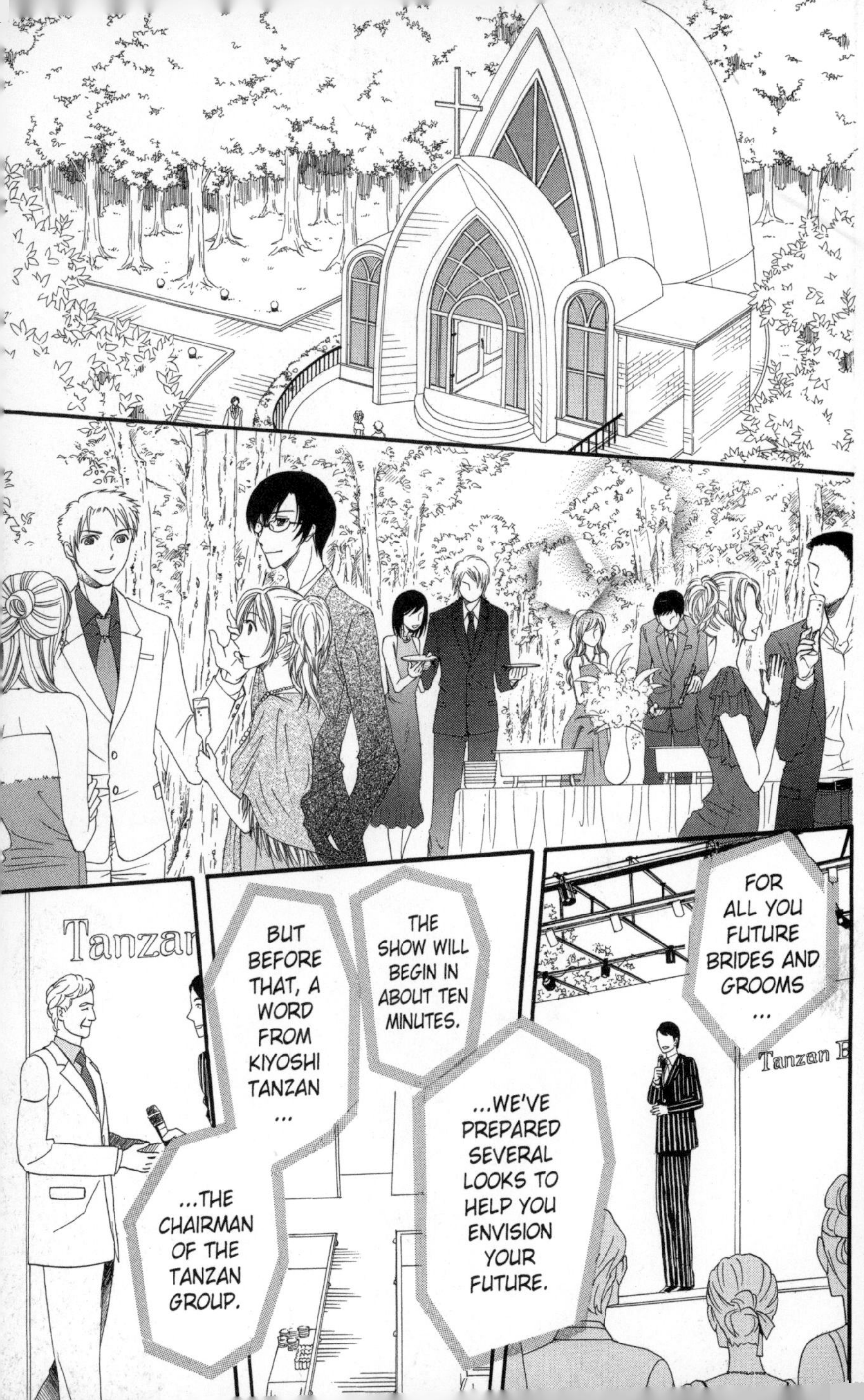
FOR ALL YOU FUTURE BRIDES AND GROOMS...
...WE'VE PREPARED SEVERAL LOOKS TO HELP YOU ENVISION YOUR FUTURE.
Tanzan
THE SHOW WILL BEGIN IN ABOUT TEN MINUTES.
BUT BEFORE THAT, A WORD FROM KIYOSHI TANZAN...
...THE CHAIRMAN OF THE TANZAN GROUP.
Tanzan

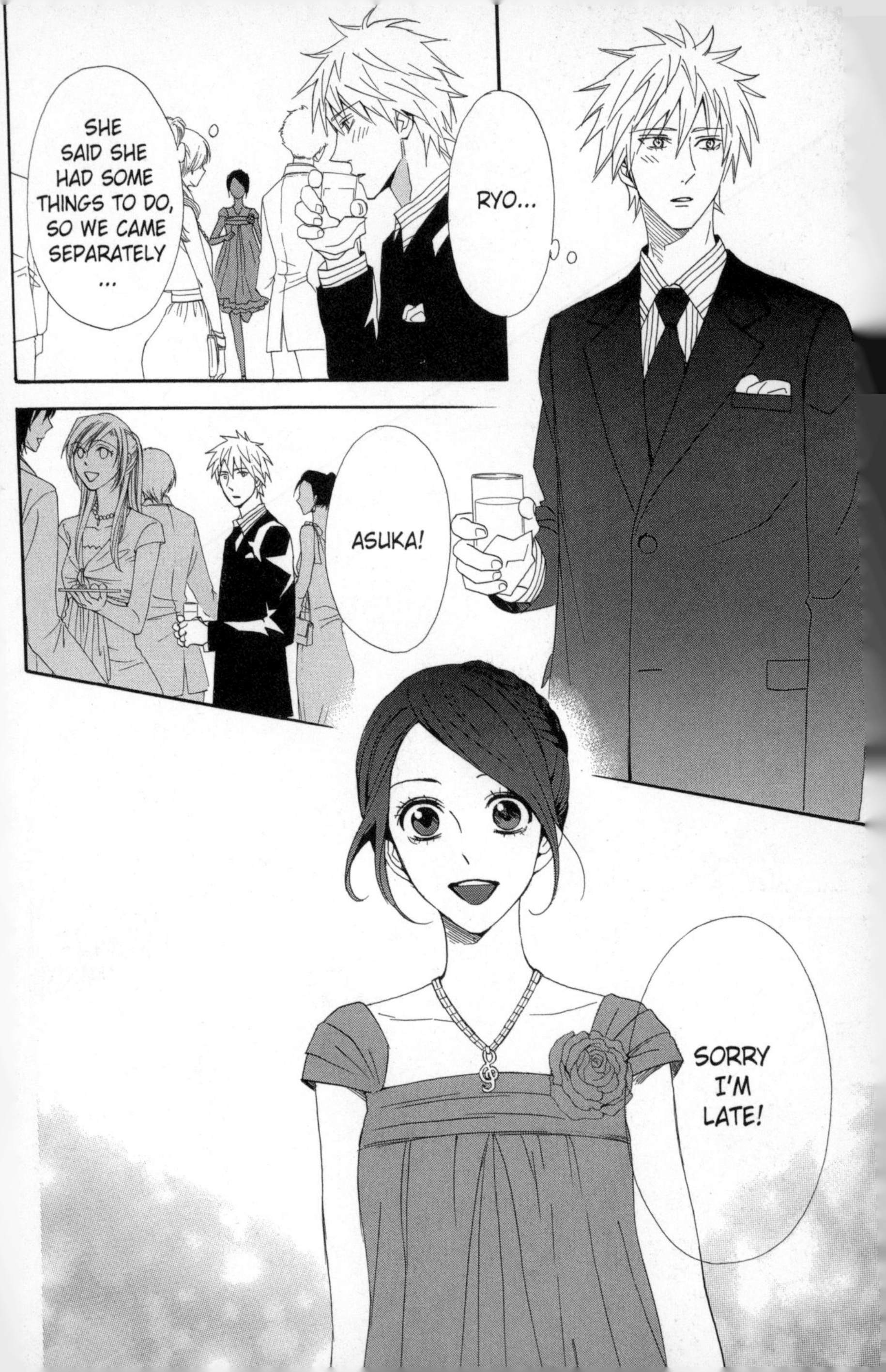
RYO...
SHE SAID SHE HAD SOME THINGS TO DO, SO WE CAME SEPARATELY ...
ASUKA!
SORRY I'M LATE!

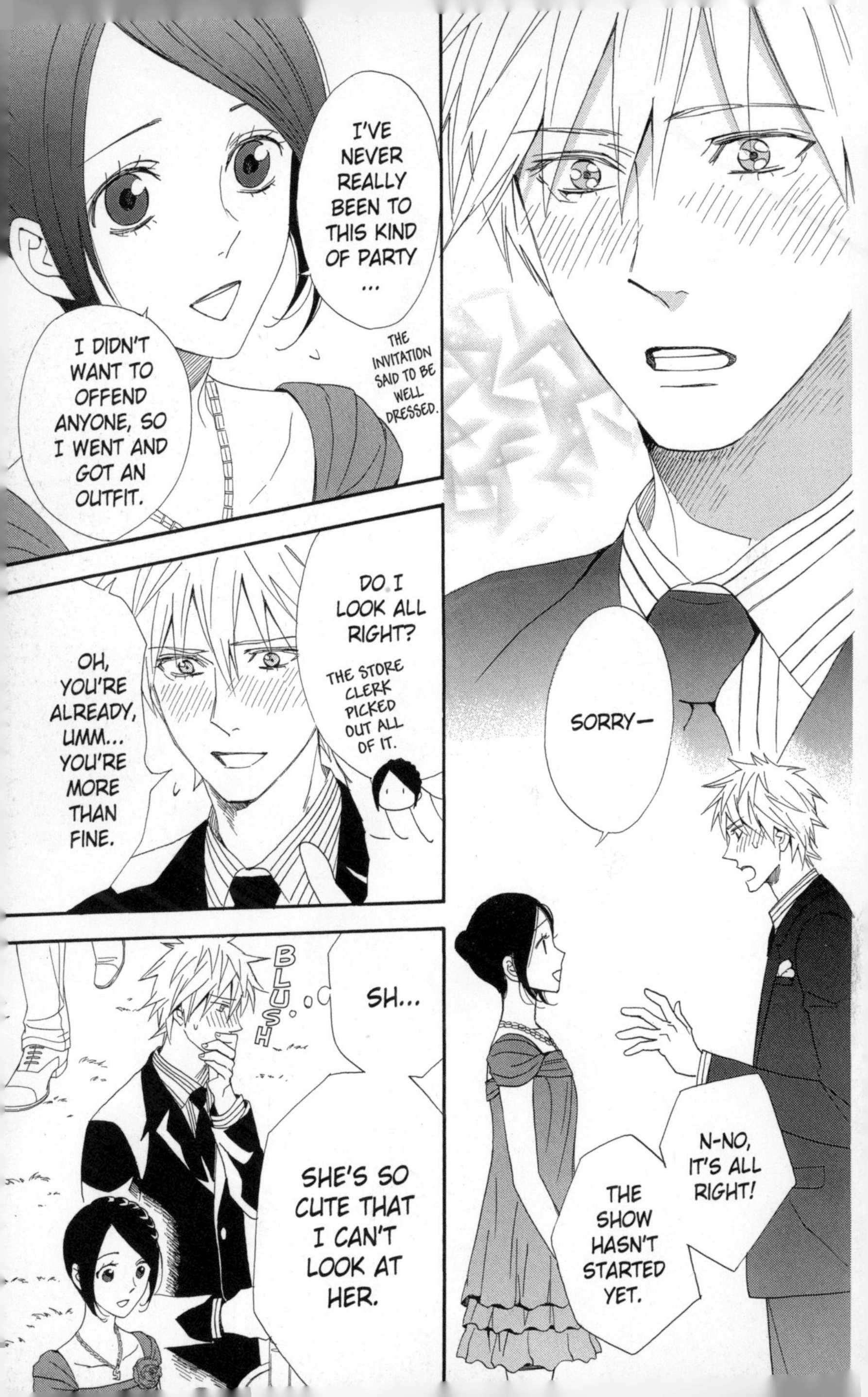
SORRY—
N-NO, IT'S ALL RIGHT!
THE SHOW HASN'T STARTED YET.
I'VE NEVER REALLY BEEN TO THIS KIND OF PARTY ...
THE INVITATION SAID TO BE WELL DRESSED.
I DIDN'T WANT TO OFFEND ANYONE, SO I WENT AND GOT AN OUTFIT.
DO I LOOK ALL RIGHT?
THE STORE CLERK PICKED OUT ALL OF IT.
OH, YOU'RE ALREADY, UMM... YOU'RE MORE THAN FINE.
SH...
BLUSH
SHE'S SO CUTE THAT I CAN'T LOOK AT HER.

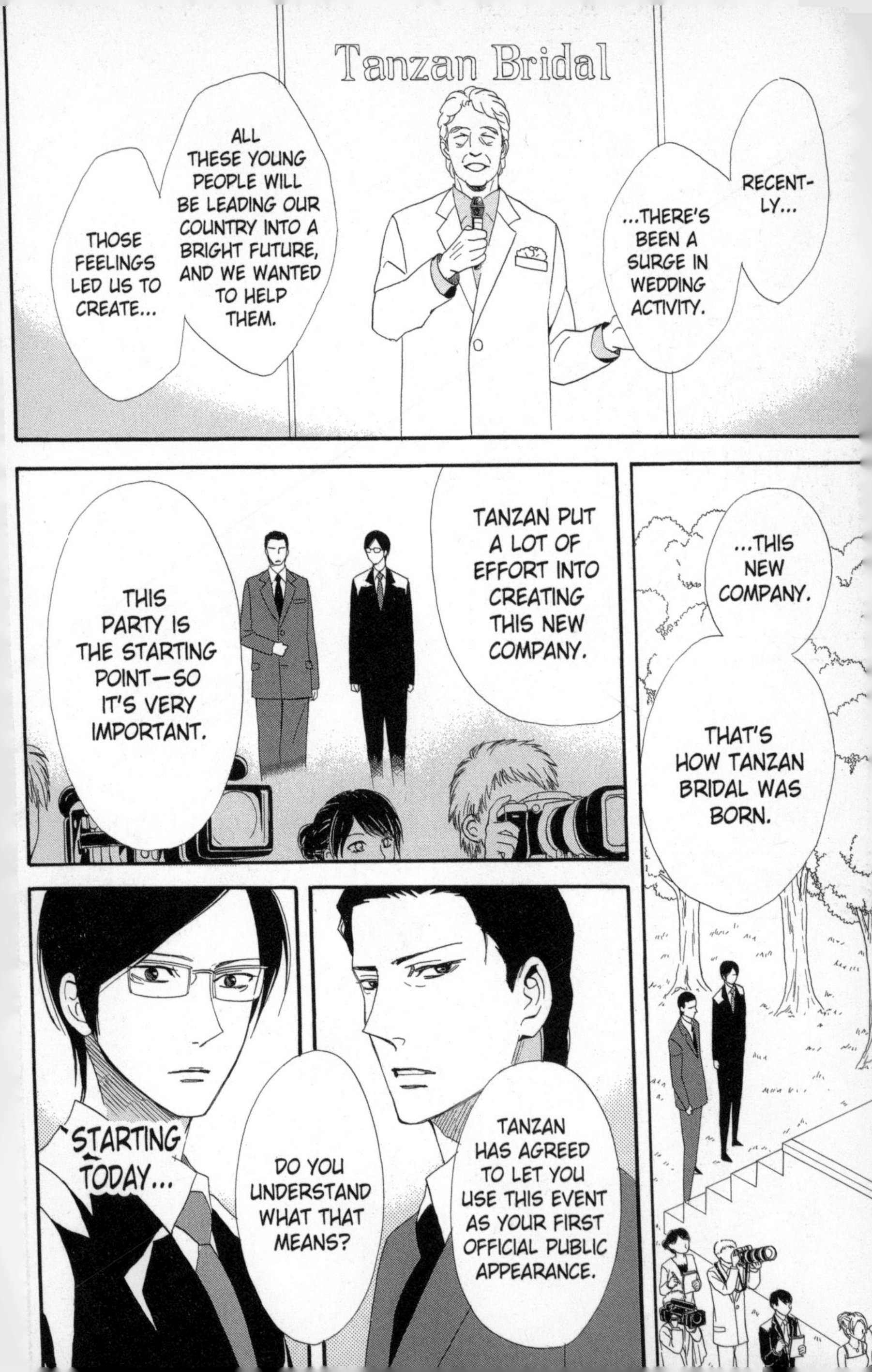
Tanzan Bridal
RECENTLY...
...THERE'S BEEN A SURGE IN WEDDING ACTIVITY.
ALL THESE YOUNG PEOPLE WILL BE LEADING OUR COUNTRY INTO A BRIGHT FUTURE, AND WE WANTED TO HELP THEM.
THOSE FEELINGS LED US TO CREATE...
...THIS NEW COMPANY.
THAT'S HOW TANZAN BRIDAL WAS BORN.
TANZAN PUT A LOT OF EFFORT INTO CREATING THIS NEW COMPANY.
THIS PARTY IS THE STARTING POINT—SO IT'S VERY IMPORTANT.
TANZAN HAS AGREED TO LET YOU USE THIS EVENT AS YOUR FIRST OFFICIAL PUBLIC APPEARANCE.
DO YOU UNDERSTAND WHAT THAT MEANS?
STARTING TODAY...

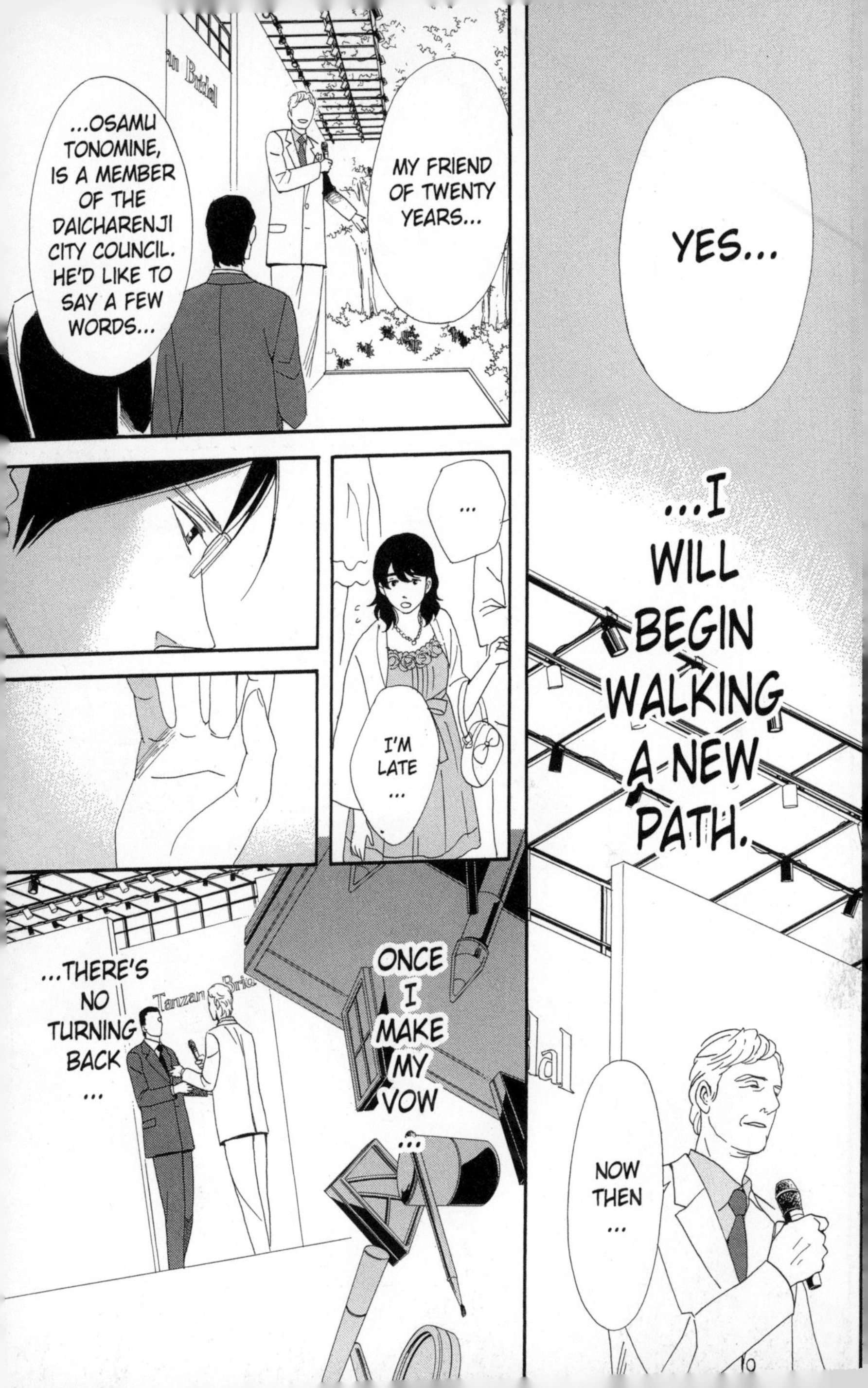
YES...
...I WILL BEGIN WALKING A NEW PATH.
NOW THEN...
MY FRIEND OF TWENTY YEARS...
...OSAMU TONOMINE, IS A MEMBER OF THE DAICHARENJI CITY COUNCIL. HE'D LIKE TO SAY A FEW WORDS...
...
I'M LATE...
ONCE I MAKE MY VOW...
...THERE'S NO TURNING BACK...

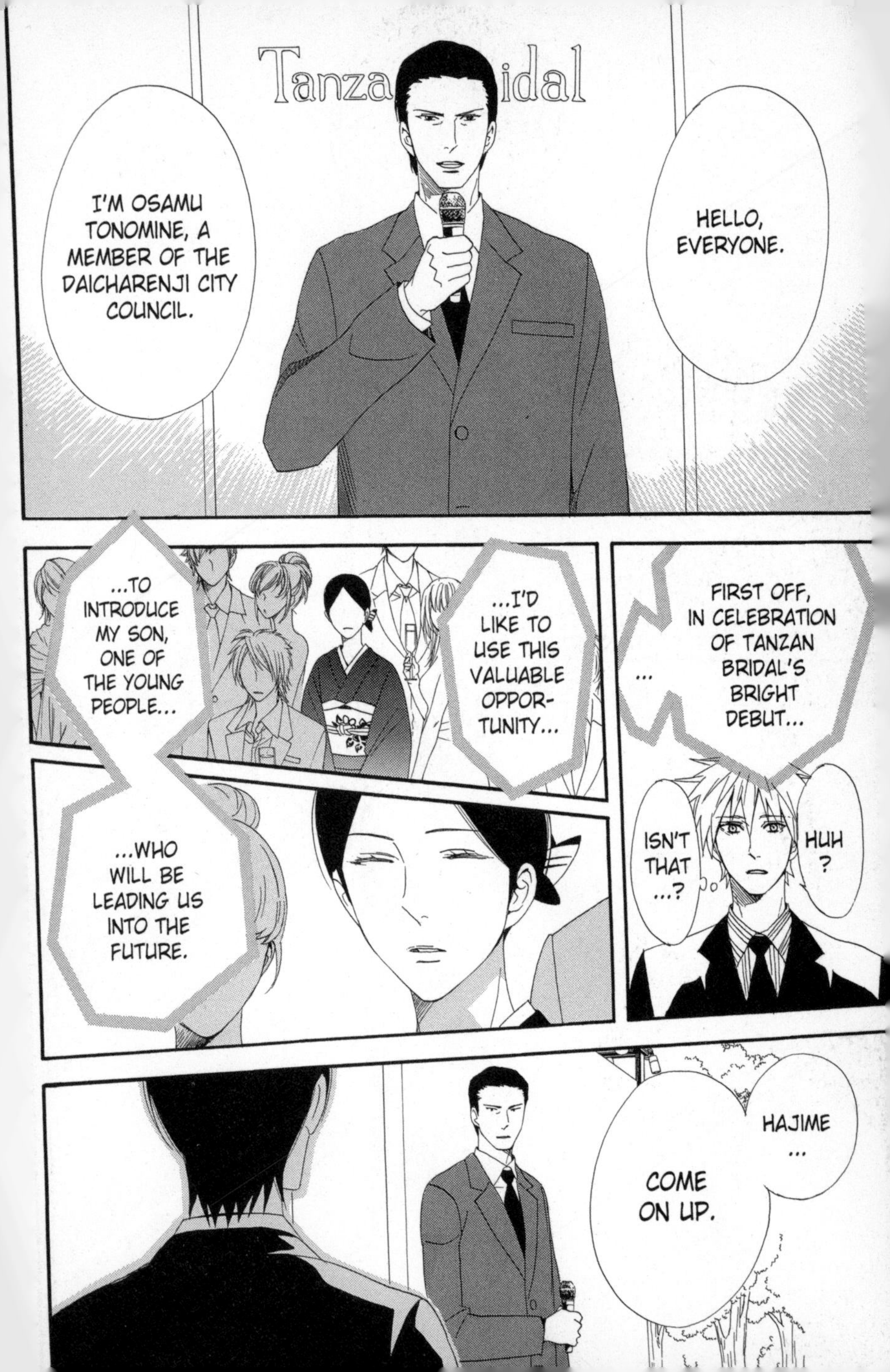
Tanza idal
HELLO, EVERYONE.
I'M OSAMU TONOMINE, A MEMBER OF THE DAICHARENJI CITY COUNCIL.
FIRST OFF, IN CELEBRATION OF TANZAN BRIDAL'S BRIGHT DEBUT...
...
HUH?
ISN'T THAT ...?
...I'D LIKE TO USE THIS VALUABLE OPPOR-TUNITY...
...TO INTRODUCE MY SON, ONE OF THE YOUNG PEOPLE...
...WHO WILL BE LEADING US INTO THE FUTURE.
HAJIME ...
COME ON UP.

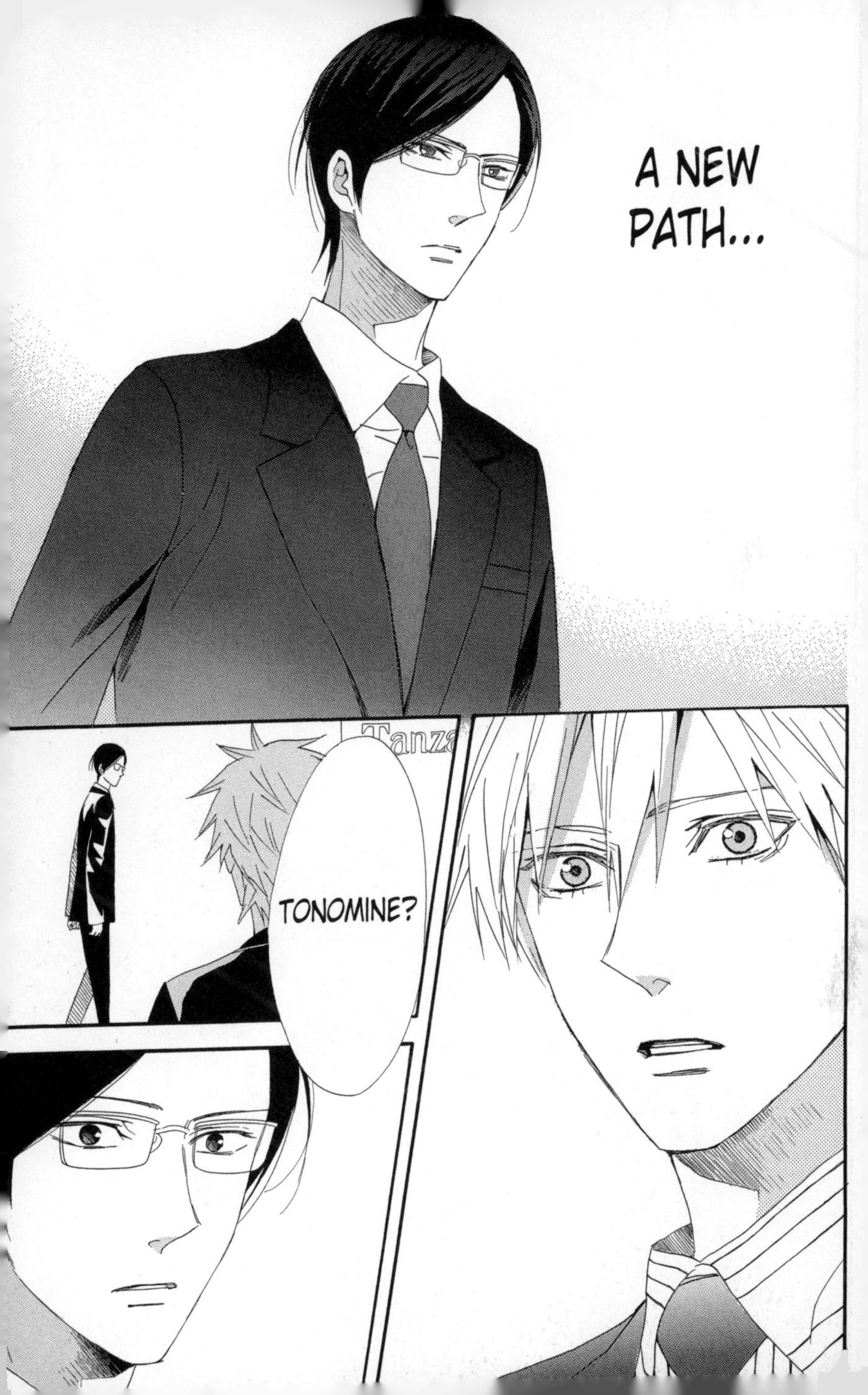
A NEW PATH...
TONOMINE?

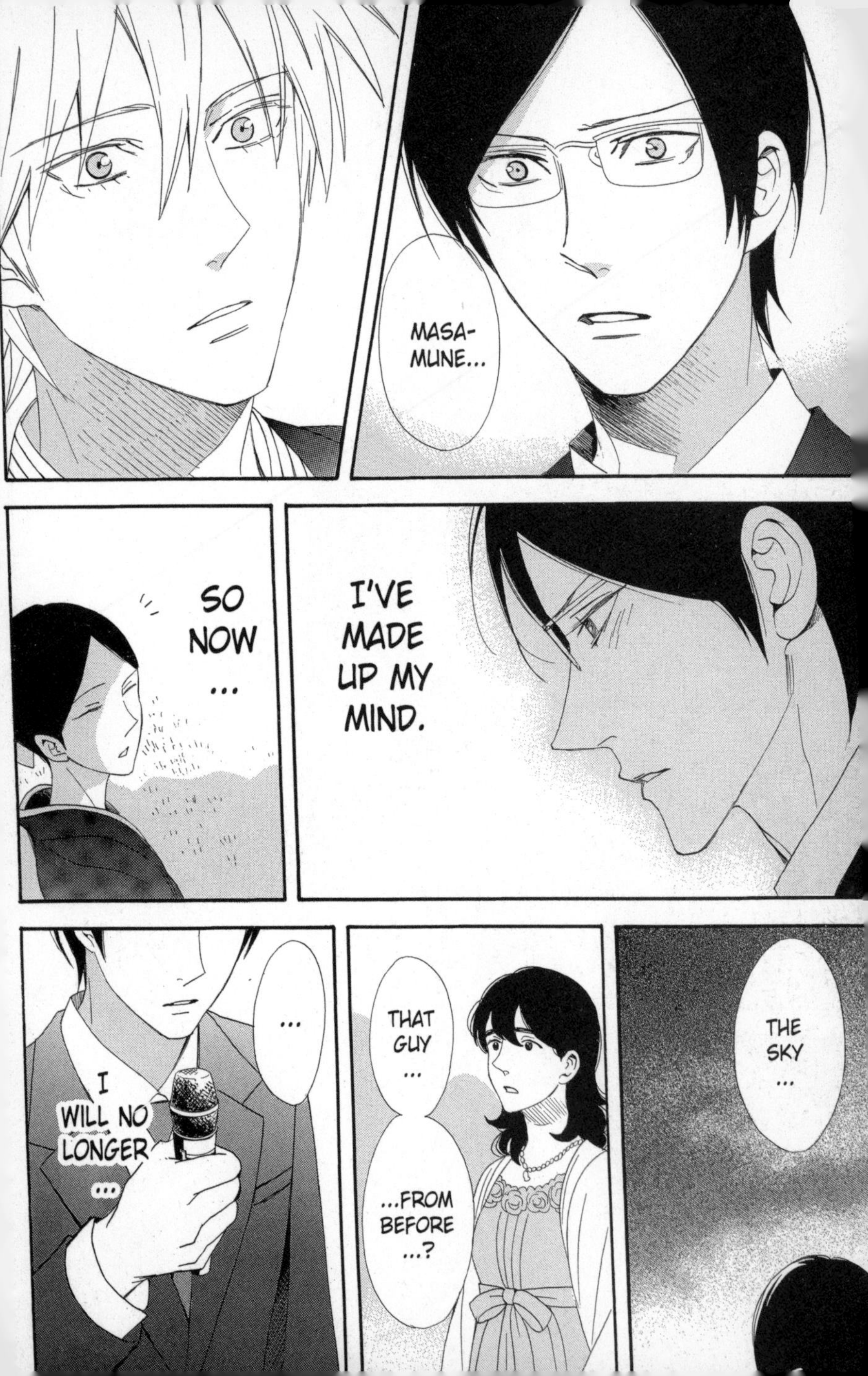
MASA-MUNE...
I'VE MADE UP MY MIND.
SO NOW ...
THE SKY ...
THAT GUY ...
...FROM BEFORE ...?
...
I WILL NO LONGER ...

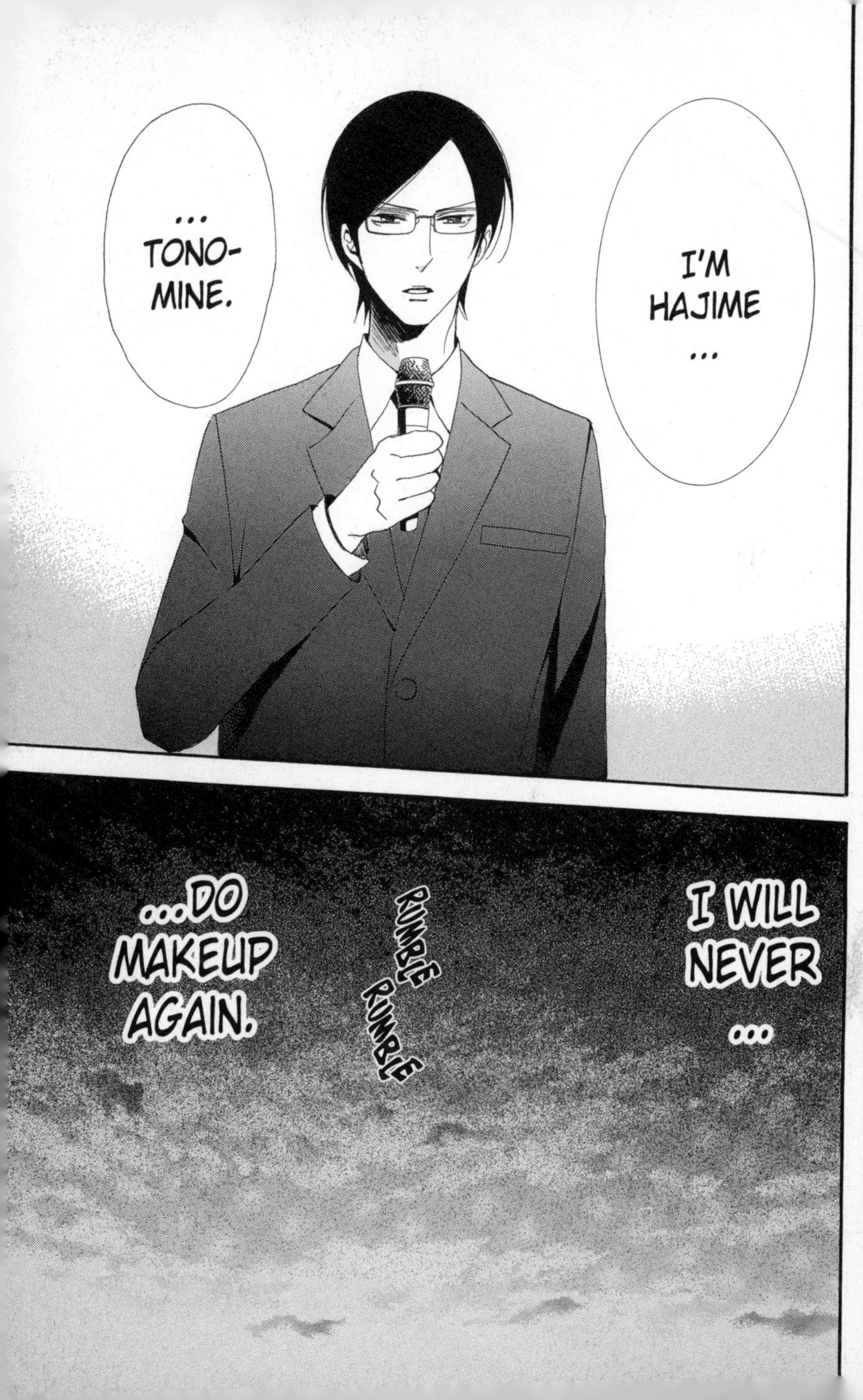
I'M HAJIME ...
... TONO-MINE.
I WILL NEVER ...
RUMBLE RUMBLE
...DO MAKEUP AGAIN.

OTOMEN

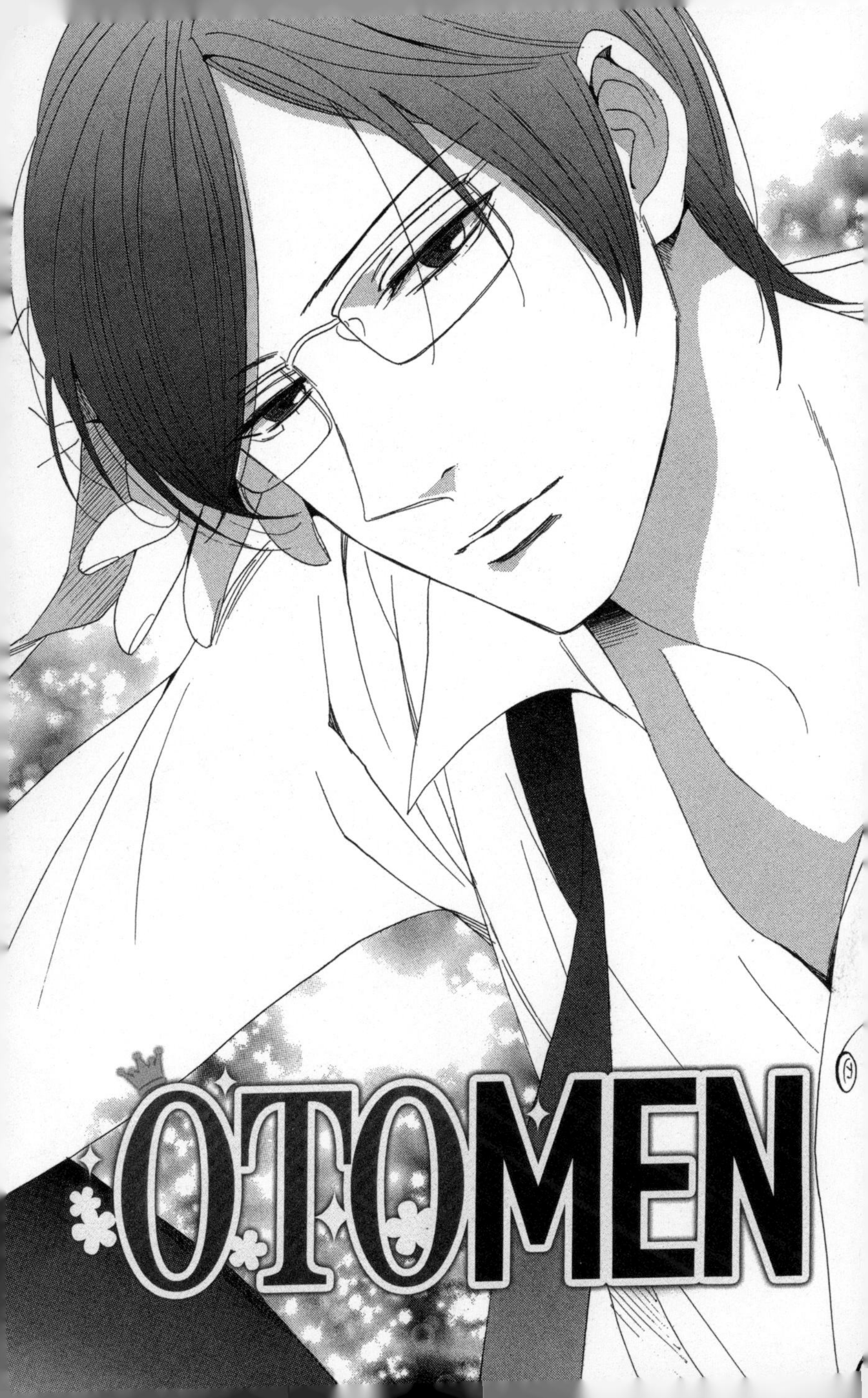
OTOMEN

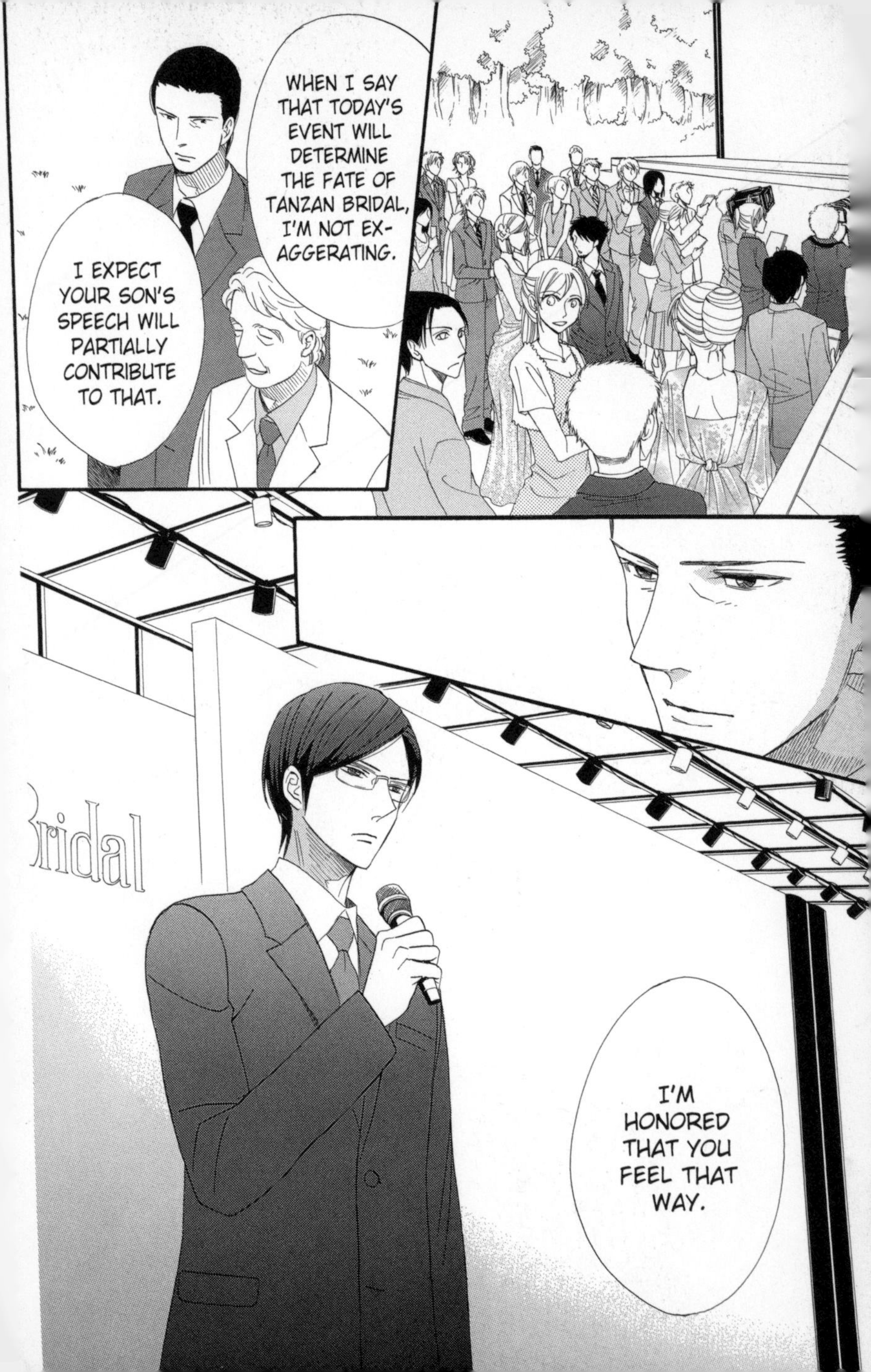
WHEN I SAY THAT TODAY'S EVENT WILL DETERMINE THE FATE OF TANZAN BRIDAL, I'M NOT EX-AGGERATING.
I EXPECT YOUR SON'S SPEECH WILL PARTIALLY CONTRIBUTE TO THAT.
I'M HONORED THAT YOU FEEL THAT WAY.

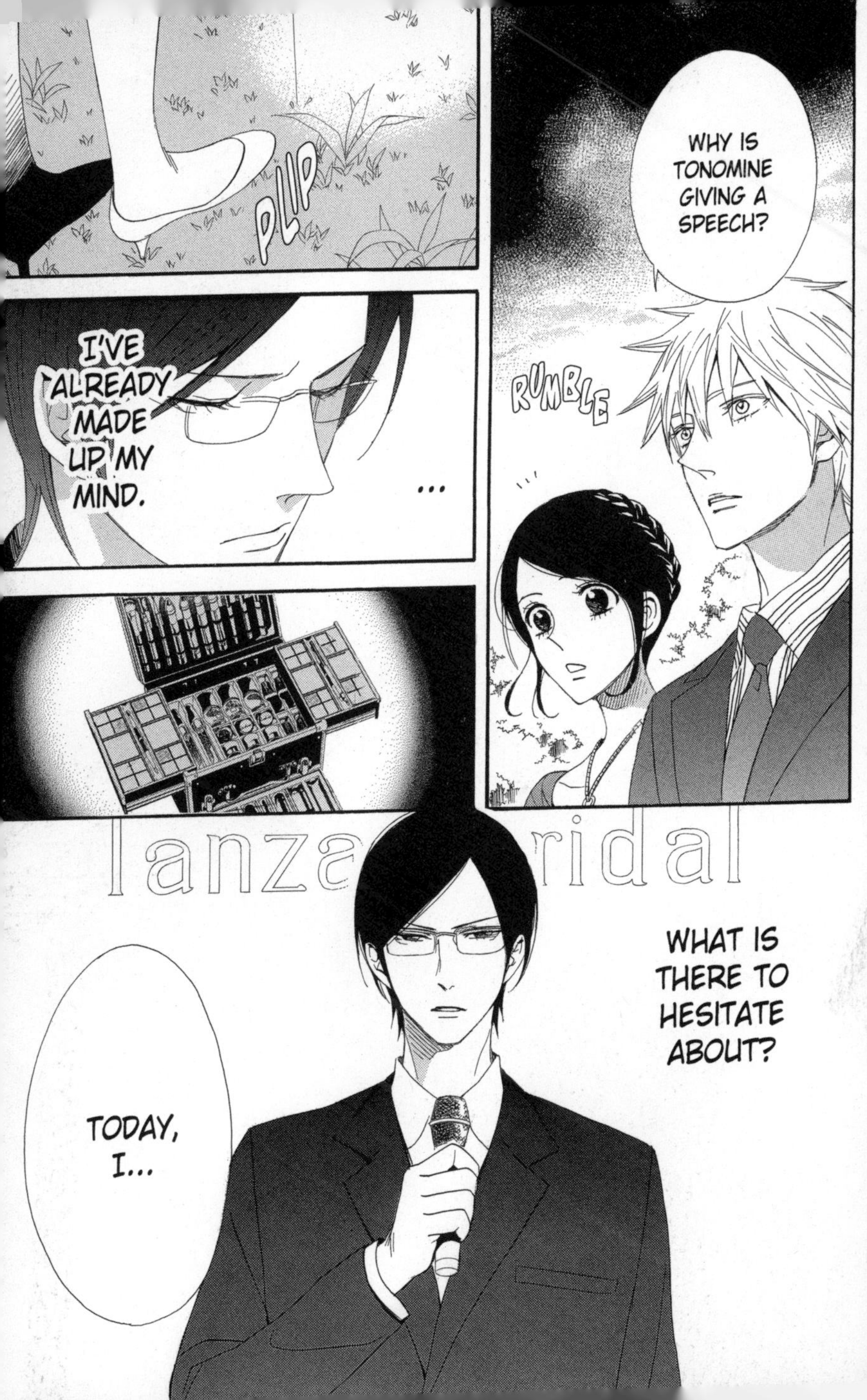
WHY IS TONOMINE GIVING A SPEECH?
RUMBLE
PLIP
I'VE ALREADY MADE UP MY MIND.
...
WHAT IS THERE TO HESITATE ABOUT?
TODAY, I...

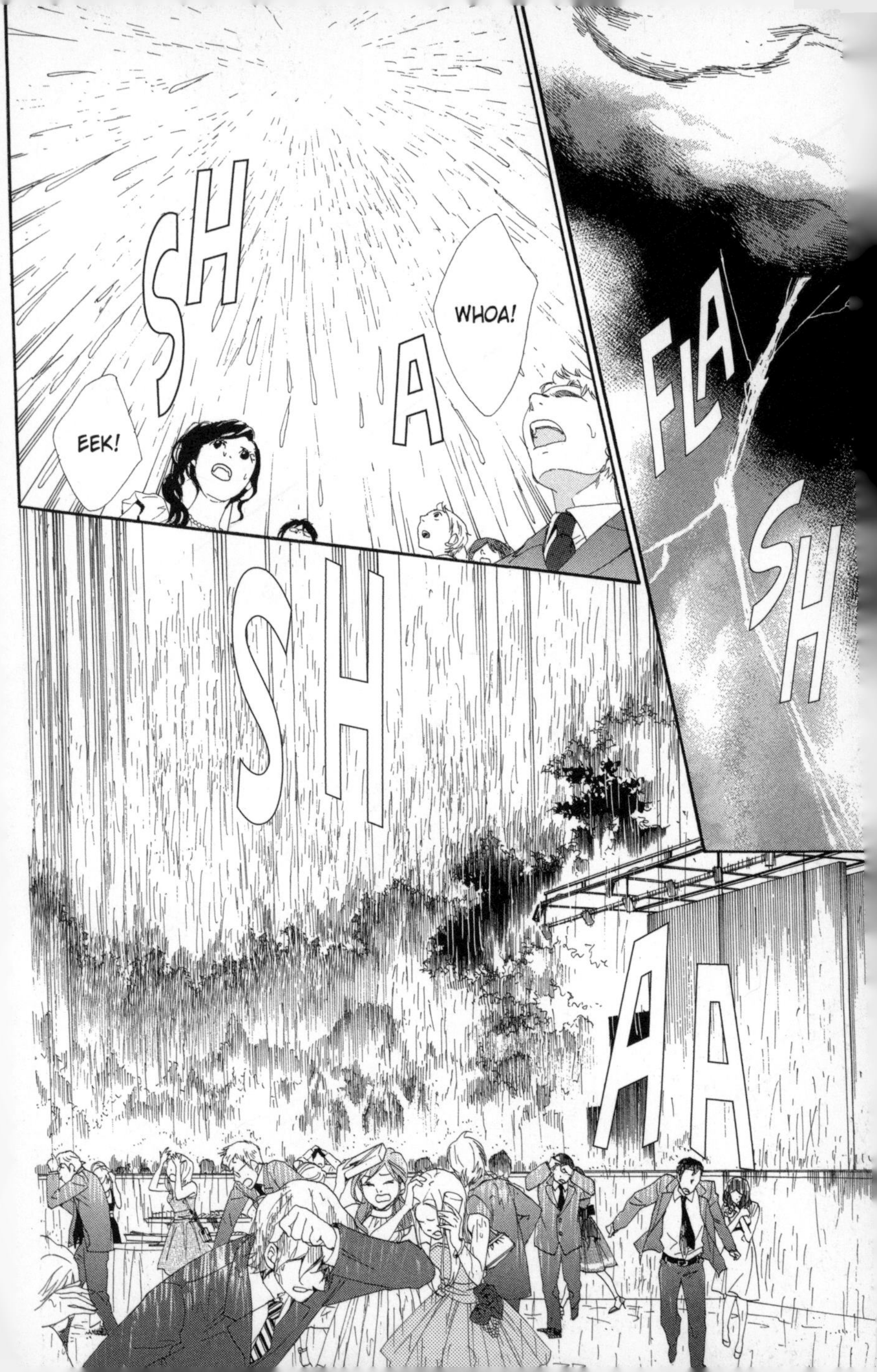
FLASH
SHA
WHOA!
EEK!
SH
AA

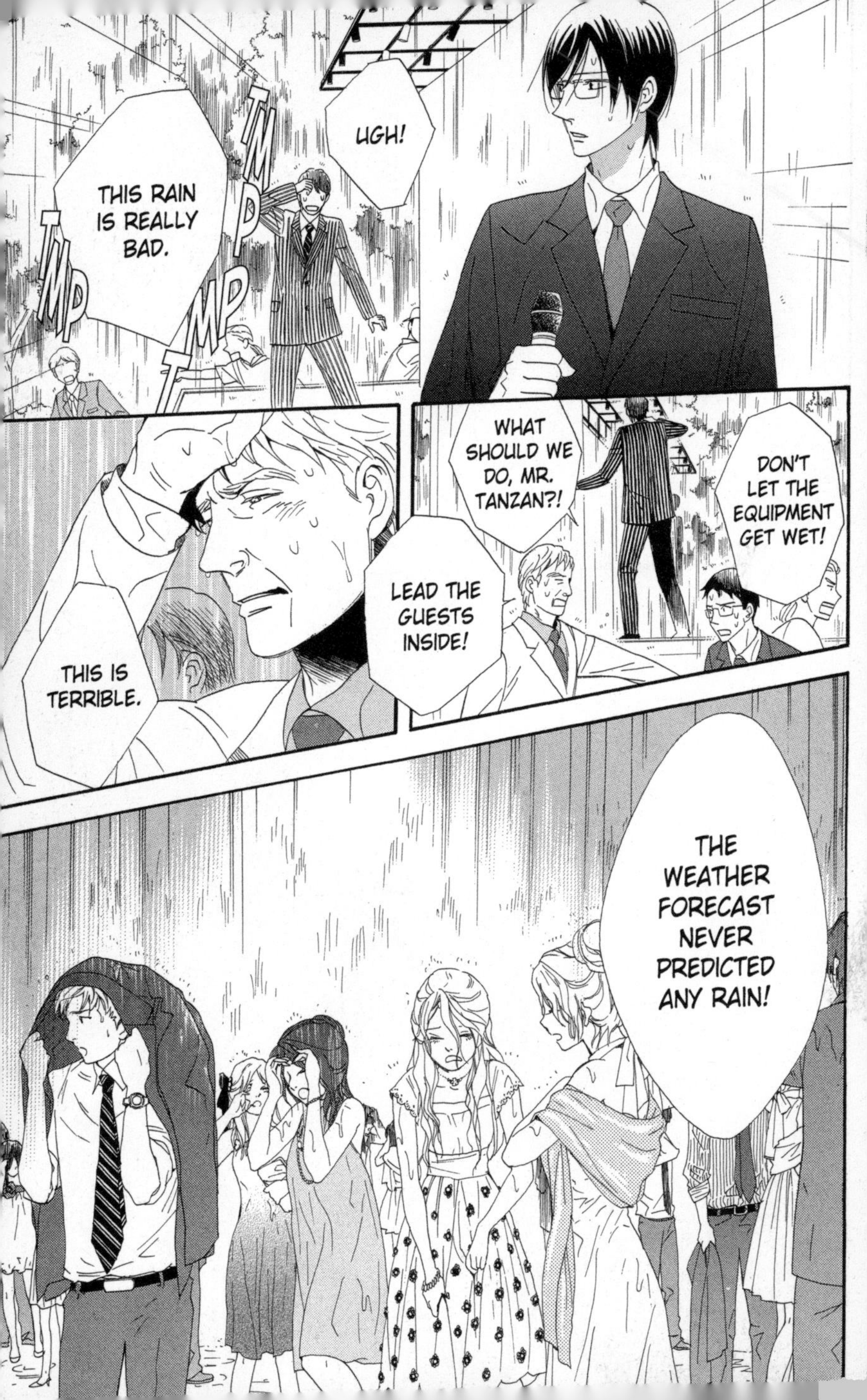
UGH!
TMP
TMP
THIS RAIN IS REALLY BAD.
TMP
DON'T LET THE EQUIPMENT GET WET!
WHAT SHOULD WE DO, MR. TANZAN?!
LEAD THE GUESTS INSIDE!
THIS IS TERRIBLE.
THE WEATHER FORECAST NEVER PREDICTED ANY RAIN!

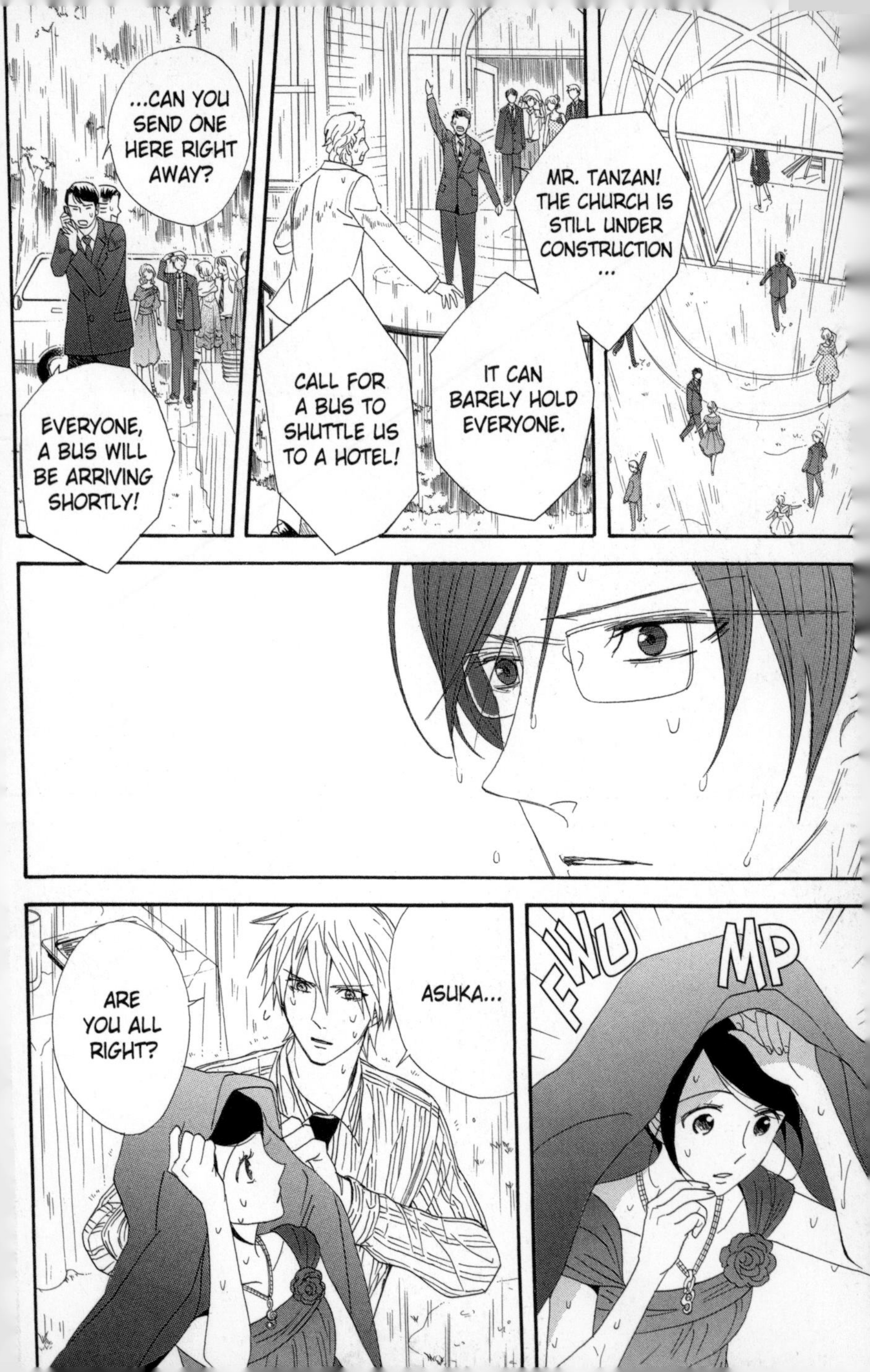
MR. TANZAN! THE CHURCH IS STILL UNDER CONSTRUCTION...
IT CAN BARELY HOLD EVERYONE.
CALL FOR A BUS TO SHUTTLE US TO A HOTEL!
...CAN YOU SEND ONE HERE RIGHT AWAY?
EVERYONE, A BUS WILL BE ARRIVING SHORTLY!
FWUMP
ASUKA...
ARE YOU ALL RIGHT?

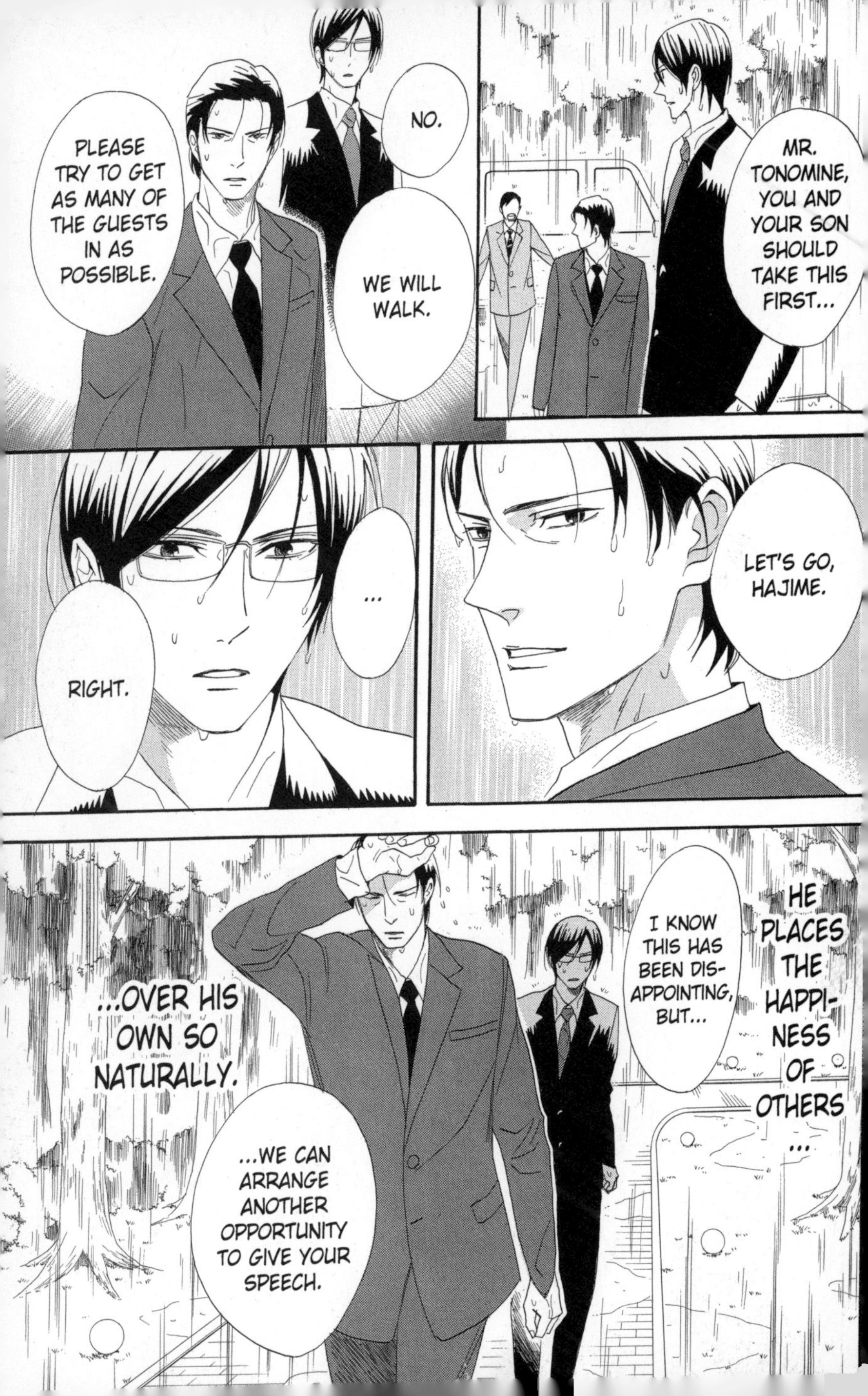
MR. TONOMINE, YOU AND YOUR SON SHOULD TAKE THIS FIRST...
NO.
WE WILL WALK.
PLEASE TRY TO GET AS MANY OF THE GUESTS IN AS POSSIBLE.
LET'S GO, HAJIME.
...
RIGHT.
HE PLACES THE HAPPINESS OF OTHERS...
I KNOW THIS HAS BEEN DISAPPOINTING, BUT...
...OVER HIS OWN SO NATURALLY.
...WE CAN ARRANGE ANOTHER OPPORTUNITY TO GIVE YOUR SPEECH.

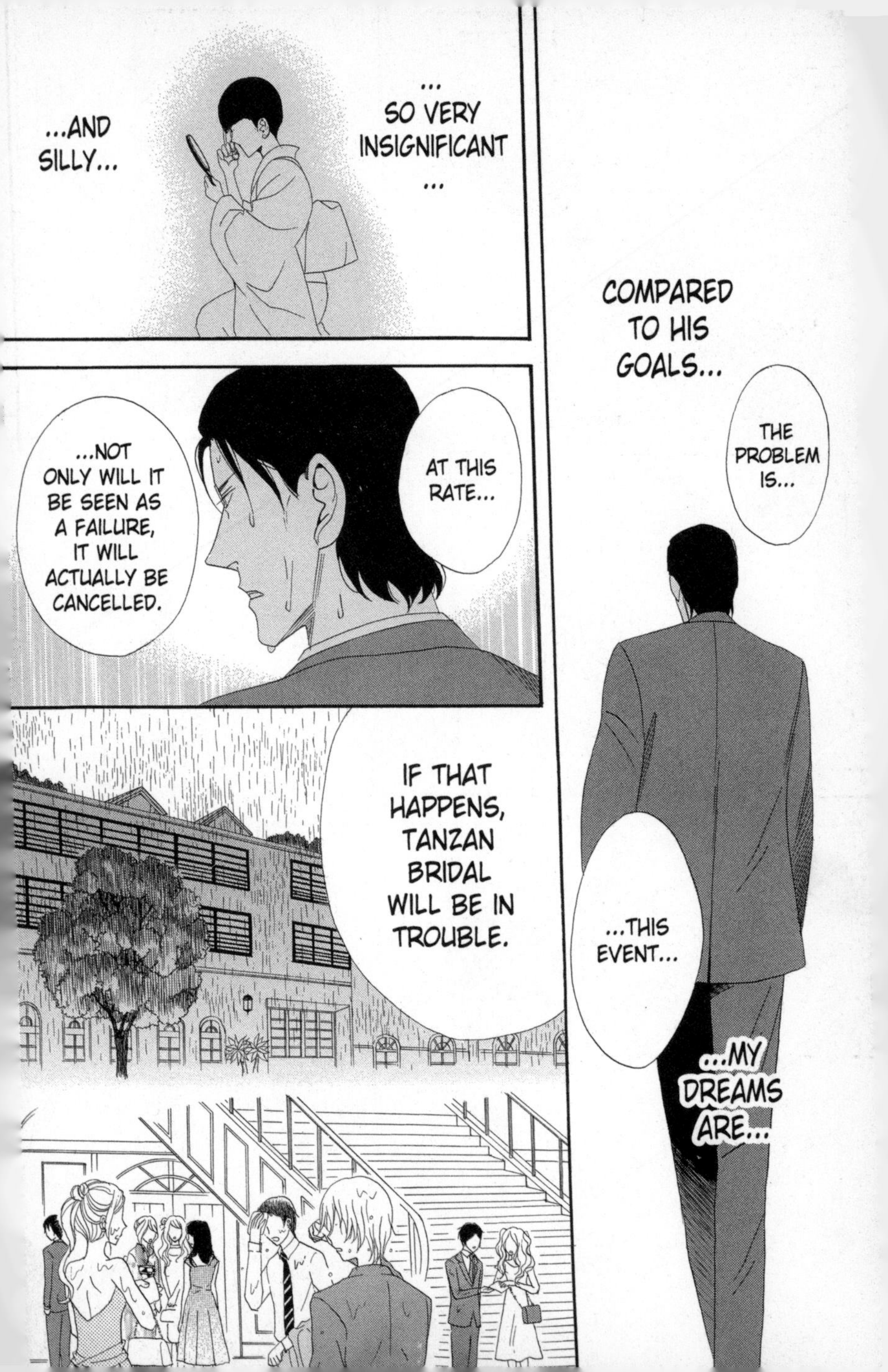
COMPARED TO HIS GOALS...
THE PROBLEM IS...
...THIS EVENT...
...MY DREAMS ARE...
... SO VERY INSIGNIFICANT ...
...AND SILLY...
AT THIS RATE...
...NOT ONLY WILL IT BE SEEN AS A FAILURE, IT WILL ACTUALLY BE CANCELLED.
IF THAT HAPPENS, TANZAN BRIDAL WILL BE IN TROUBLE.

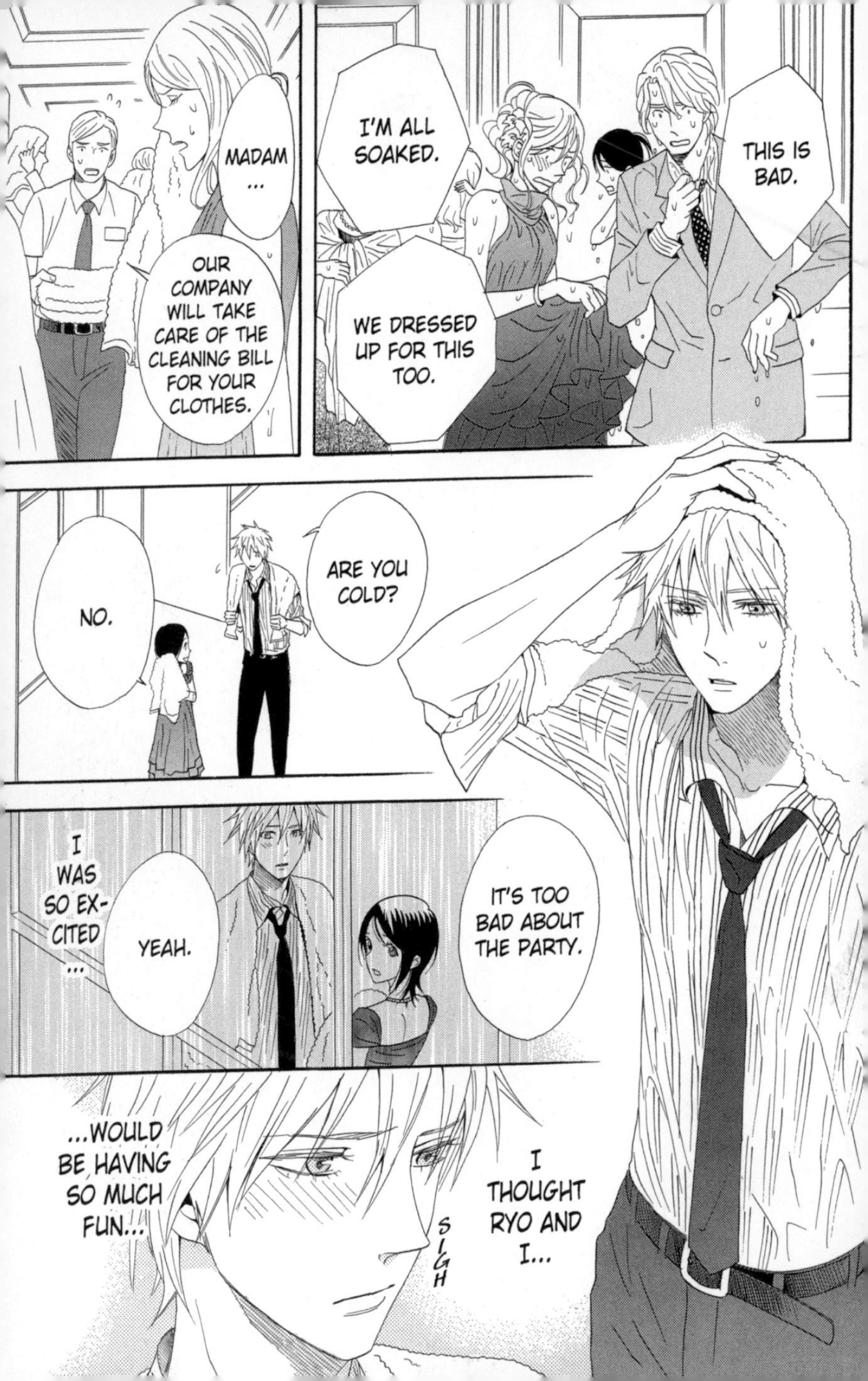
THIS IS BAD.
I'M ALL SOAKED.
WE DRESSED UP FOR THIS TOO.
MADAM ...
OUR COMPANY WILL TAKE CARE OF THE CLEANING BILL FOR YOUR CLOTHES.
ARE YOU COLD?
NO.
IT'S TOO BAD ABOUT THE PARTY.
YEAH.
I WAS SO EX-CITED ...
I THOUGHT RYO AND I...
SIGH
...WOULD BE HAVING SO MUCH FUN...

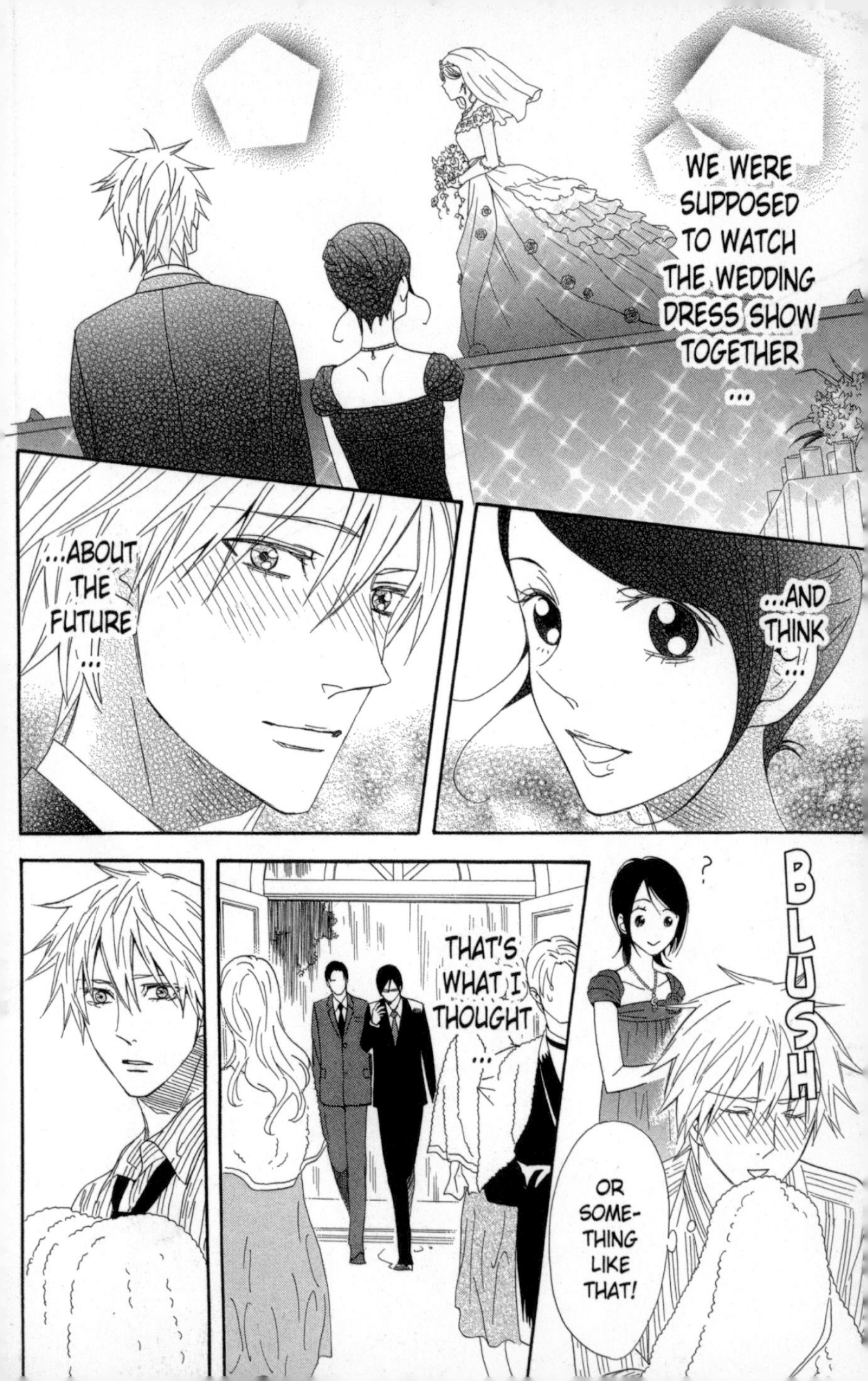
WE WERE SUPPOSED TO WATCH THE WEDDING DRESS SHOW TOGETHER ...
...AND THINK ...
...ABOUT THE FUTURE ...
BLUSH
?
OR SOME-THING LIKE THAT!
THAT'S WHAT I THOUGHT ...

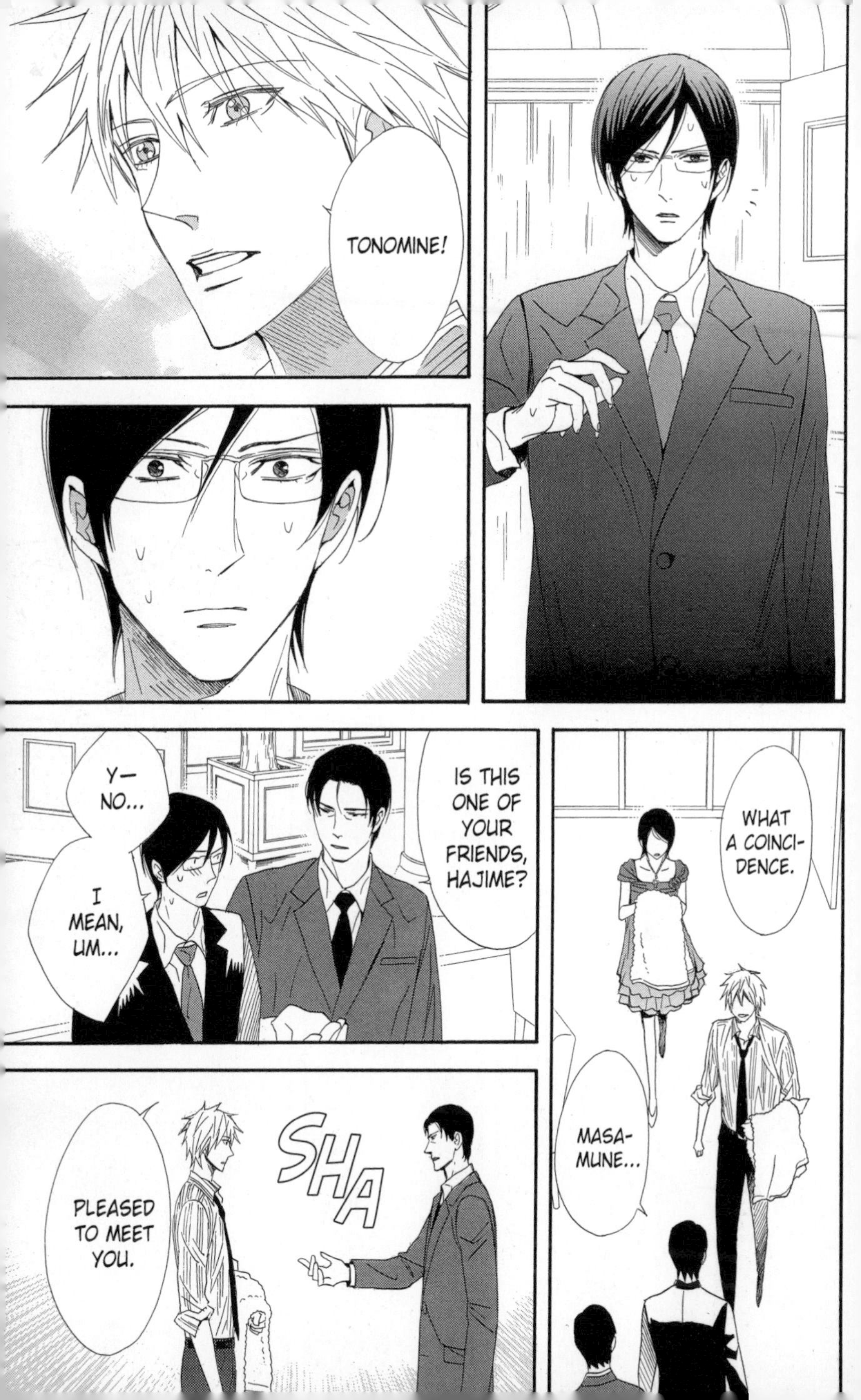
TONOMINE!
WHAT A COINCI-DENCE.
MASA-MUNE...
IS THIS ONE OF YOUR FRIENDS, HAJIME?
Y— NO...
I MEAN, UM...
SHA
PLEASED TO MEET YOU.

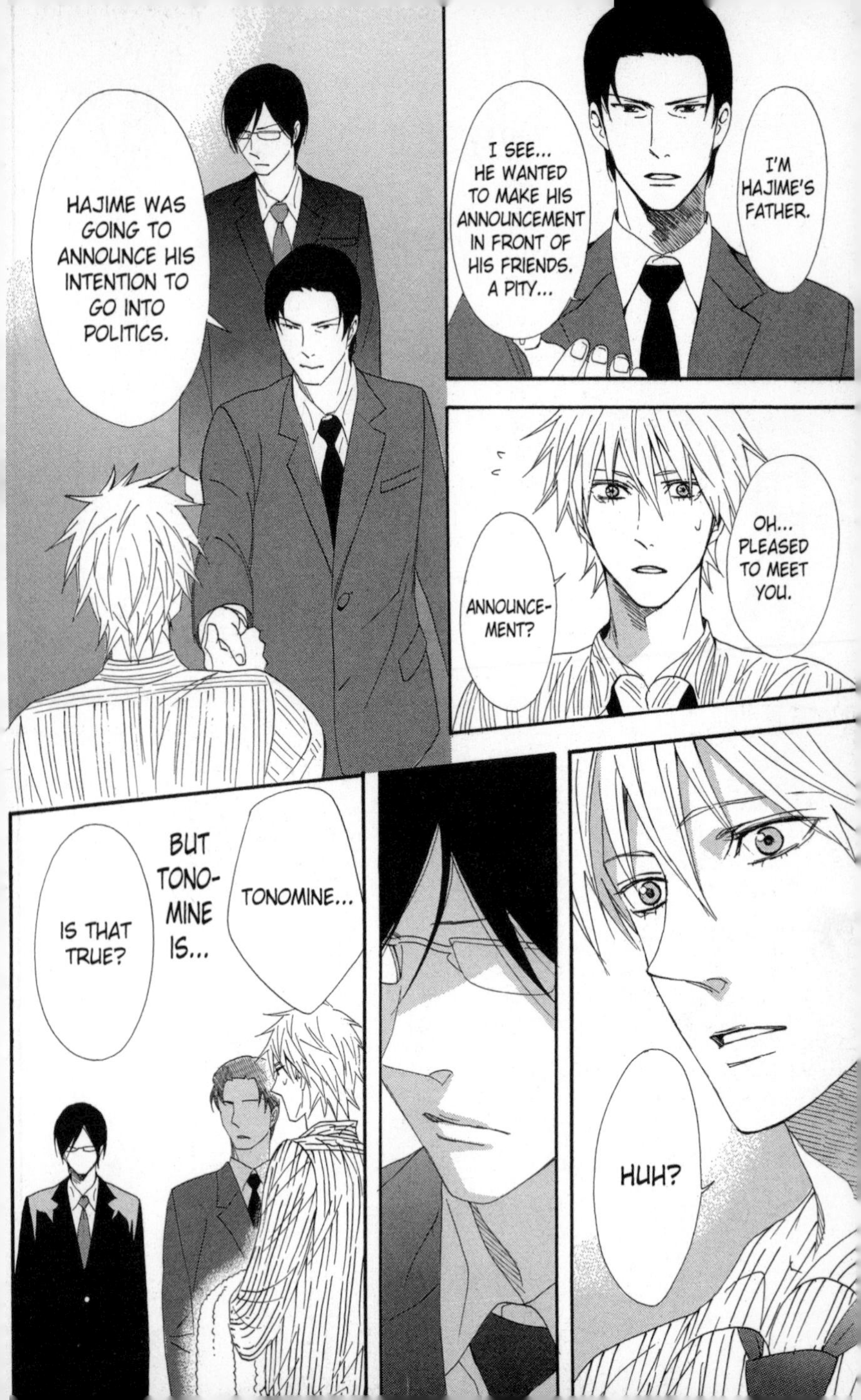
I'M HAJIME'S FATHER.
I SEE... HE WANTED TO MAKE HIS ANNOUNCEMENT IN FRONT OF HIS FRIENDS. A PITY...
OH... PLEASED TO MEET YOU.
ANNOUNCE-MENT?
HAJIME WAS GOING TO ANNOUNCE HIS INTENTION TO GO INTO POLITICS.
HUH?
TONOMINE...
BUT TONO-MINE IS...
IS THAT TRUE?

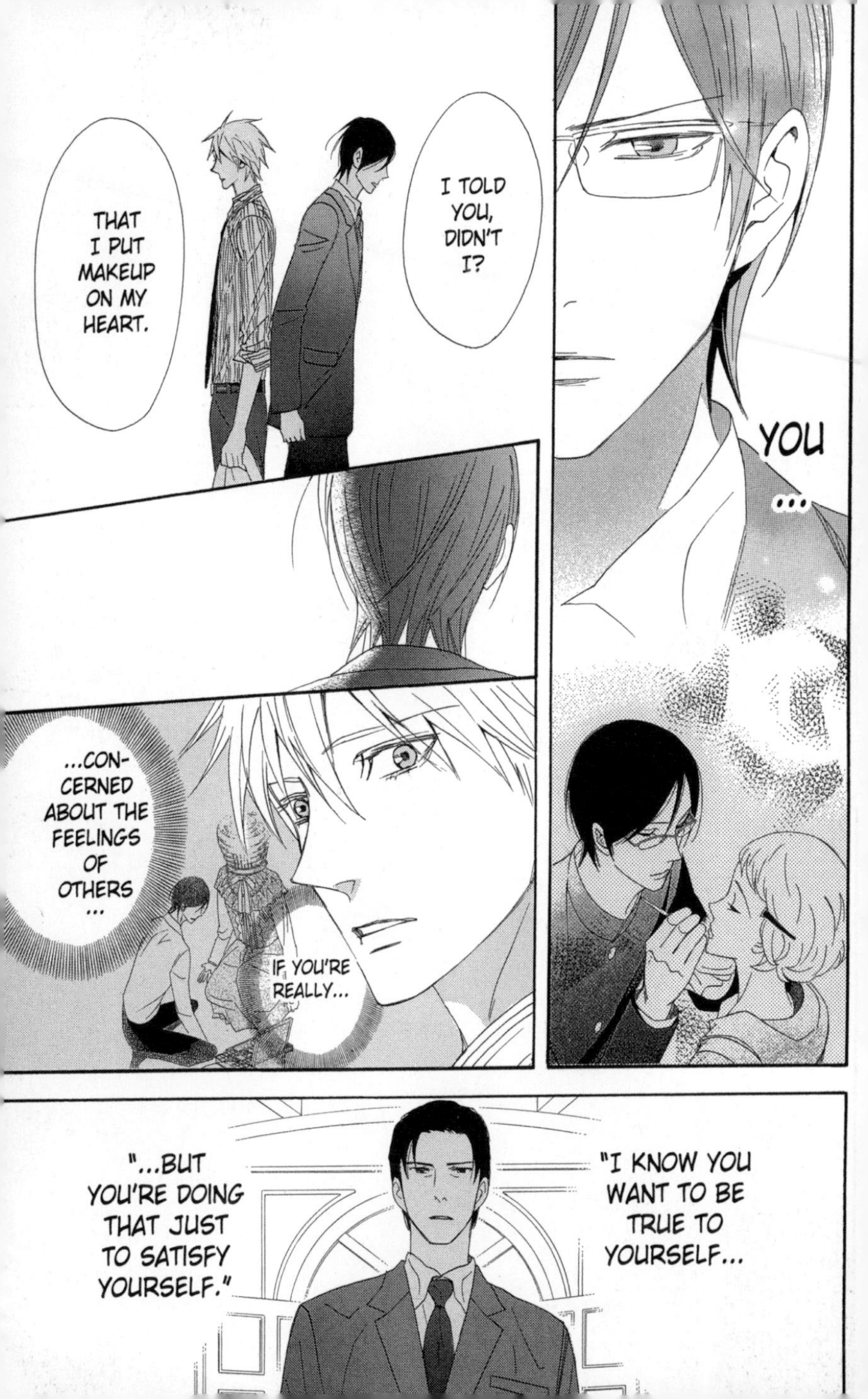
YOU
...
I TOLD YOU, DIDN'T I?
THAT I PUT MAKEUP ON MY HEART.
IF YOU'RE REALLY...
...CON-CERNED ABOUT THE FEELINGS OF OTHERS...
"I KNOW YOU WANT TO BE TRUE TO YOURSELF...
"...BUT YOU'RE DOING THAT JUST TO SATISFY YOURSELF."

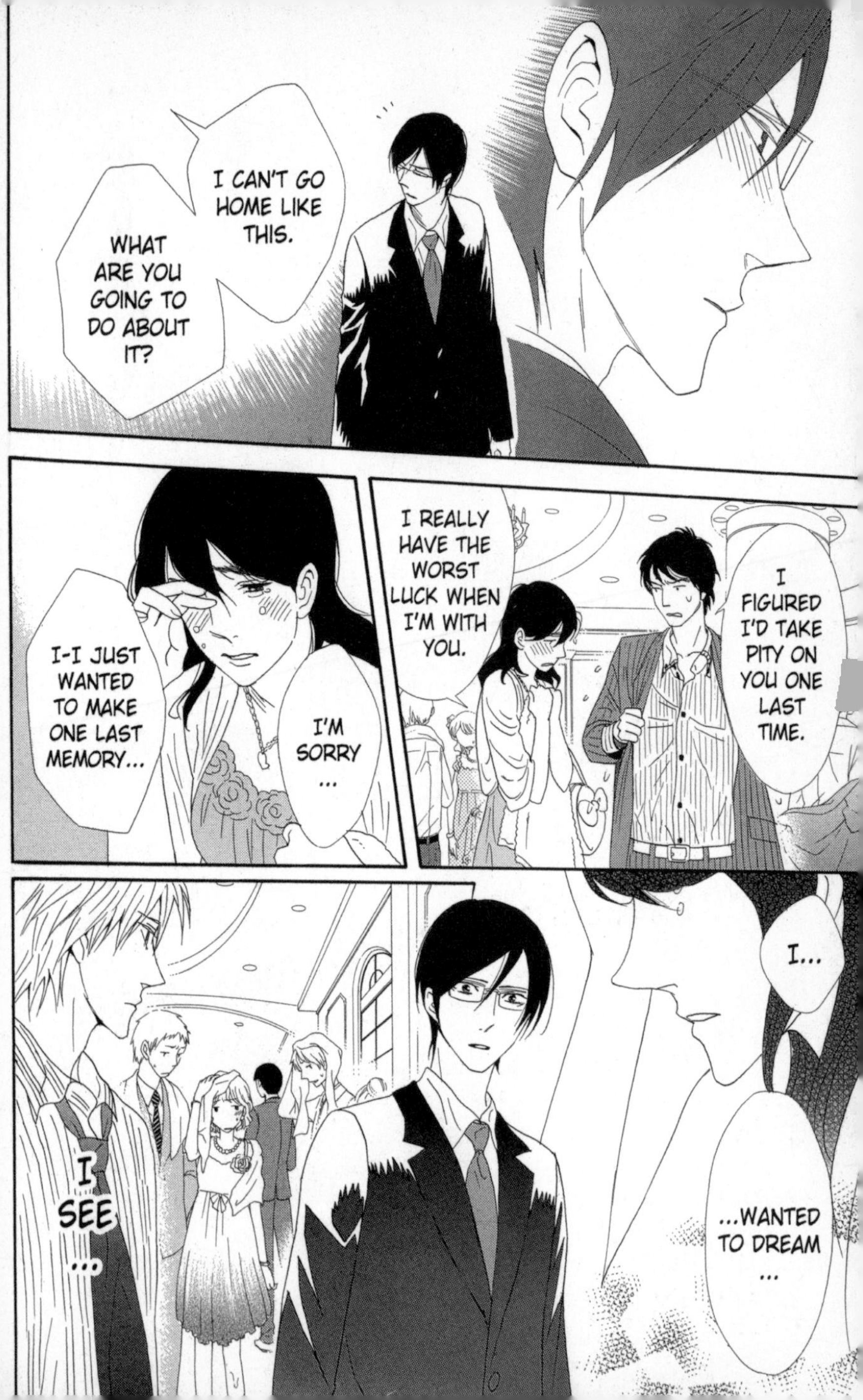
I CAN'T GO HOME LIKE THIS.
WHAT ARE YOU GOING TO DO ABOUT IT?
I FIGURED I'D TAKE PITY ON YOU ONE LAST TIME.
I REALLY HAVE THE WORST LUCK WHEN I'M WITH YOU.
I'M SORRY ...
I-I JUST WANTED TO MAKE ONE LAST MEMORY...
I...
...WANTED TO DREAM ...
I SEE ...

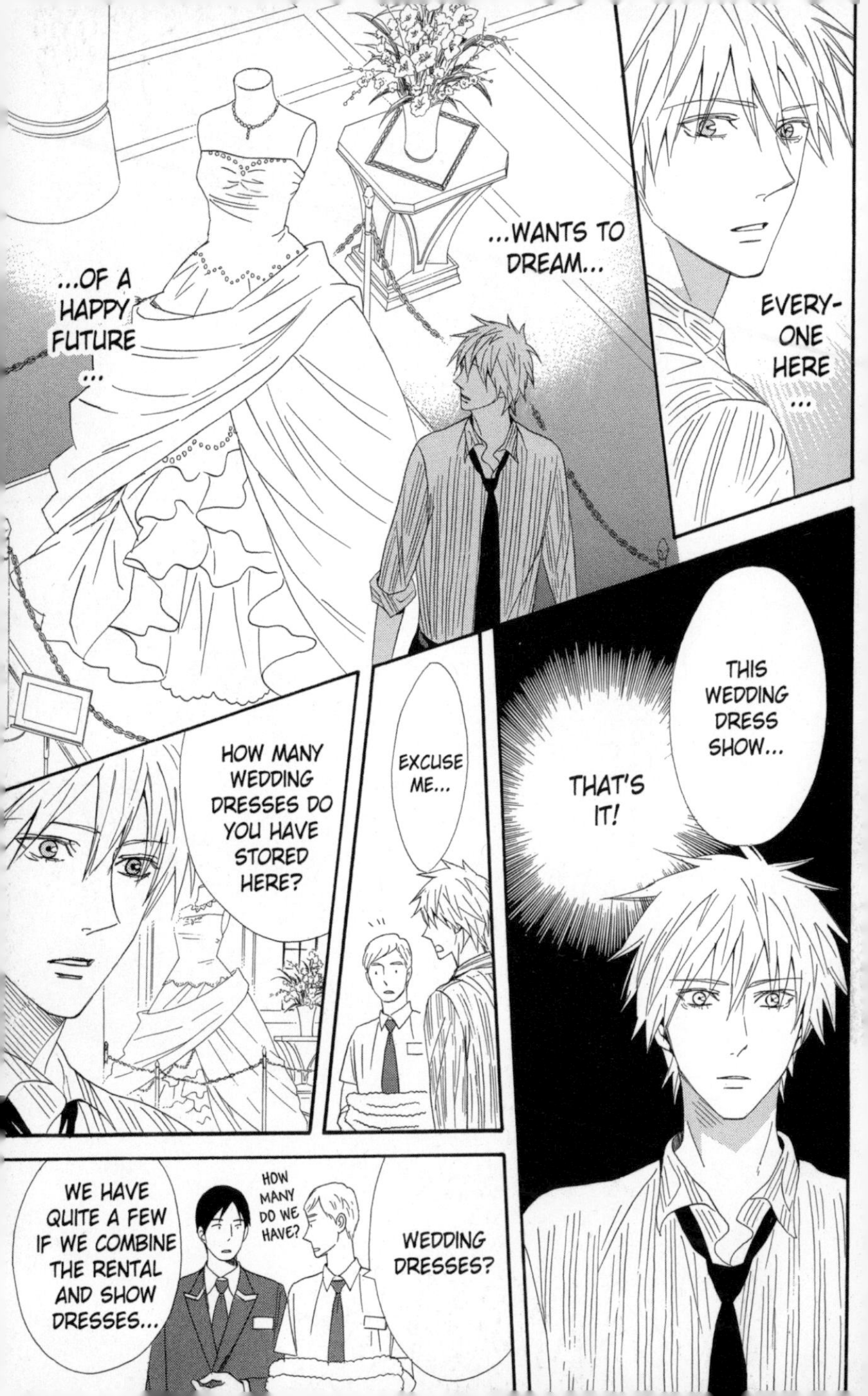
EVERY-ONE HERE ...
...WANTS TO DREAM...
...OF A HAPPY FUTURE ...
THIS WEDDING DRESS SHOW...
THAT'S IT!
EXCUSE ME...
HOW MANY WEDDING DRESSES DO YOU HAVE STORED HERE?
WEDDING DRESSES?
HOW MANY DO WE HAVE?
WE HAVE QUITE A FEW IF WE COMBINE THE RENTAL AND SHOW DRESSES...

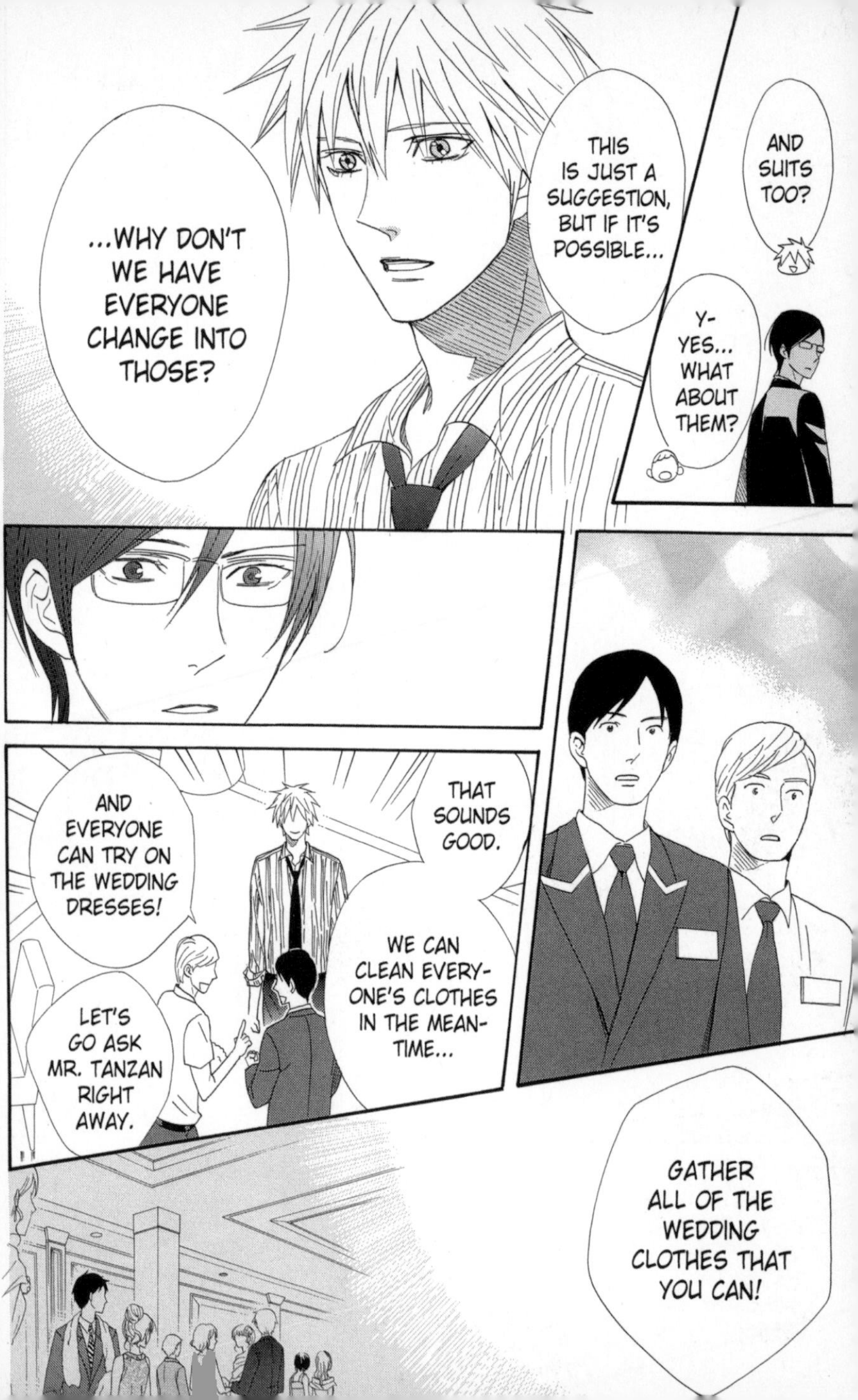
AND SUITS TOO?
Y-YES... WHAT ABOUT THEM?
THIS IS JUST A SUGGESTION, BUT IF IT'S POSSIBLE...
...WHY DON'T WE HAVE EVERYONE CHANGE INTO THOSE?
THAT SOUNDS GOOD.
WE CAN CLEAN EVERY-ONE'S CLOTHES IN THE MEAN-TIME...
AND EVERYONE CAN TRY ON THE WEDDING DRESSES!
LET'S GO ASK MR. TANZAN RIGHT AWAY.
GATHER ALL OF THE WEDDING CLOTHES THAT YOU CAN!

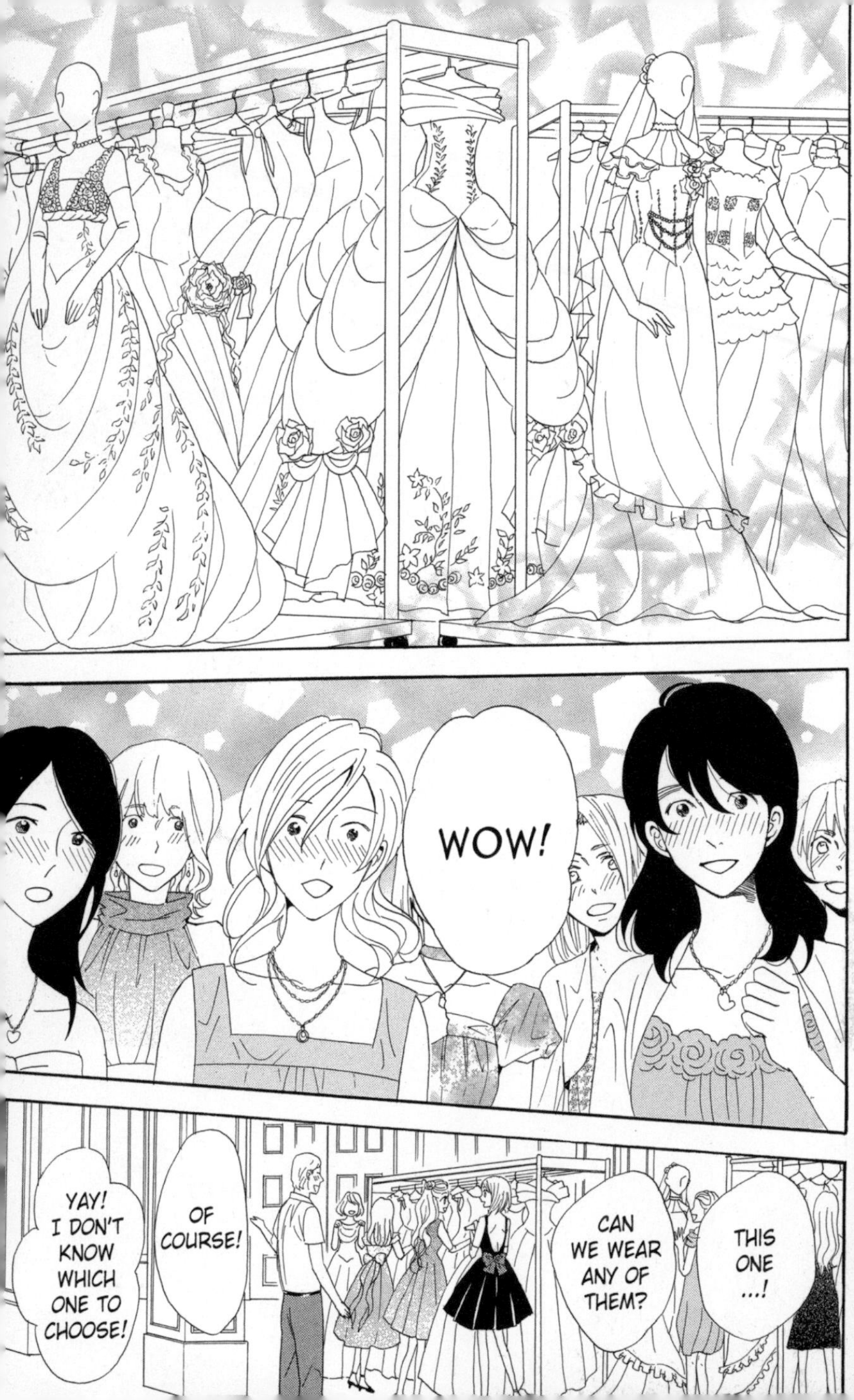
WOW!
THIS ONE ...!
CAN WE WEAR ANY OF THEM?
OF COURSE!
YAY! I DON'T KNOW WHICH ONE TO CHOOSE!

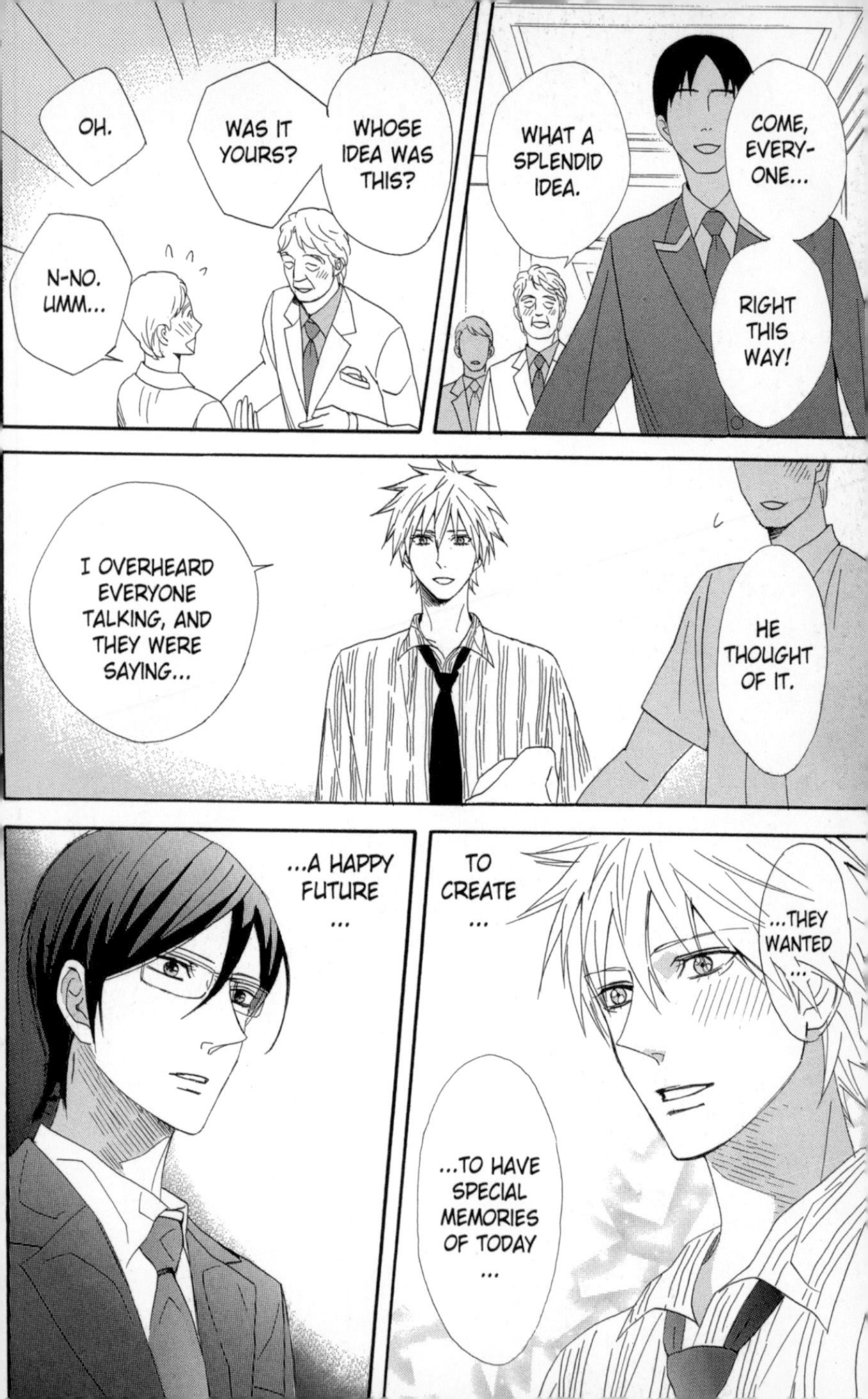
COME, EVERYONE...
RIGHT THIS WAY!
WHAT A SPLENDID IDEA.
WHOSE IDEA WAS THIS?
WAS IT YOURS?
OH.
N-NO. UMM...
HE THOUGHT OF IT.
I OVERHEARD EVERYONE TALKING, AND THEY WERE SAYING...
...THEY WANTED...
...TO HAVE SPECIAL MEMORIES OF TODAY...
TO CREATE...
...A HAPPY FUTURE...

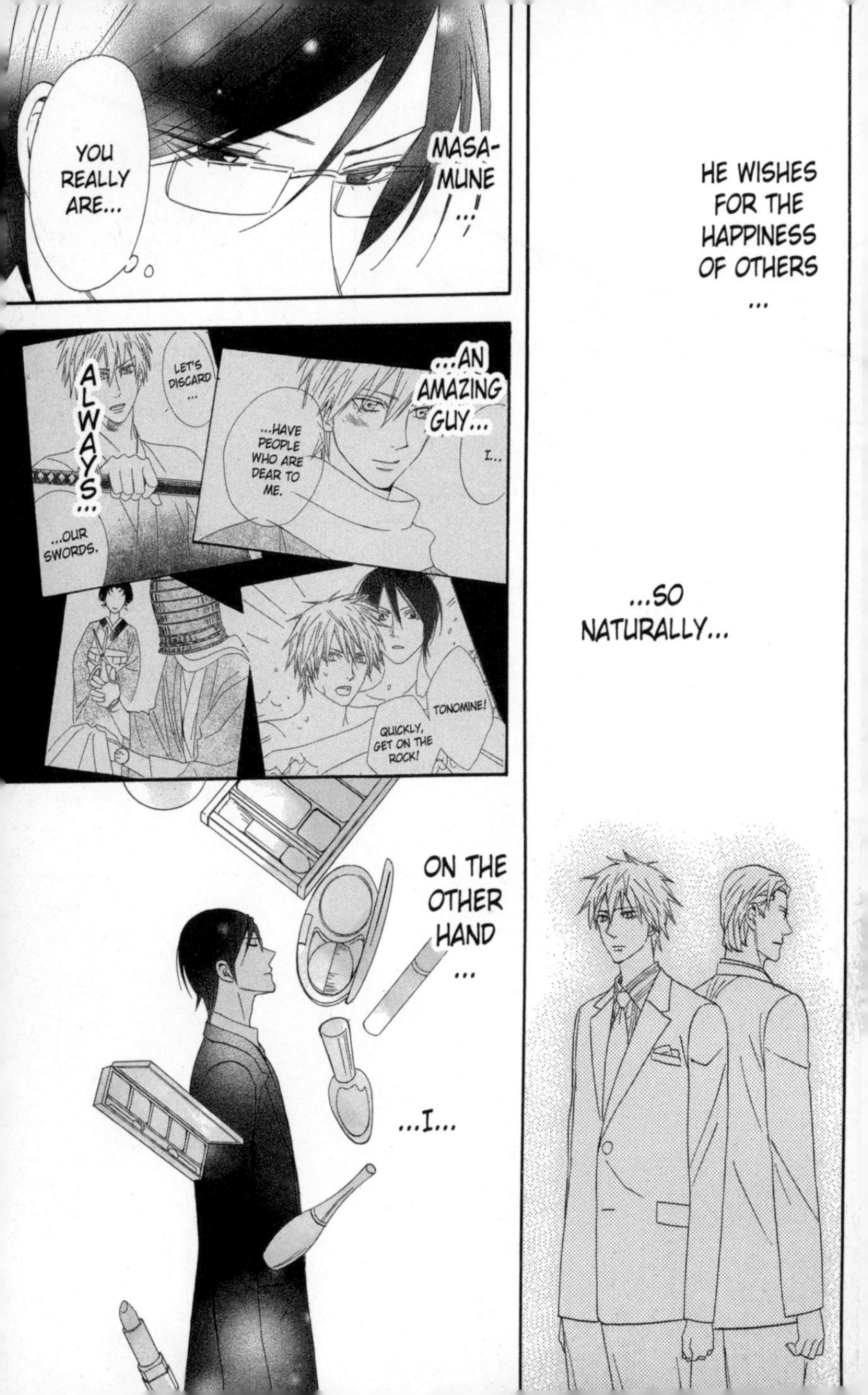
HE WISHES FOR THE HAPPINESS OF OTHERS ...
...SO NATURALLY...
MASA-MUNE ...
YOU REALLY ARE...
...AN AMAZING GUY...
I...
...HAVE PEOPLE WHO ARE DEAR TO ME.
LET'S DISCARD ...
ALWAYS...
...OUR SWORDS.
TONOMINE!
QUICKLY, GET ON THE ROCK!
ON THE OTHER HAND ...
...I...

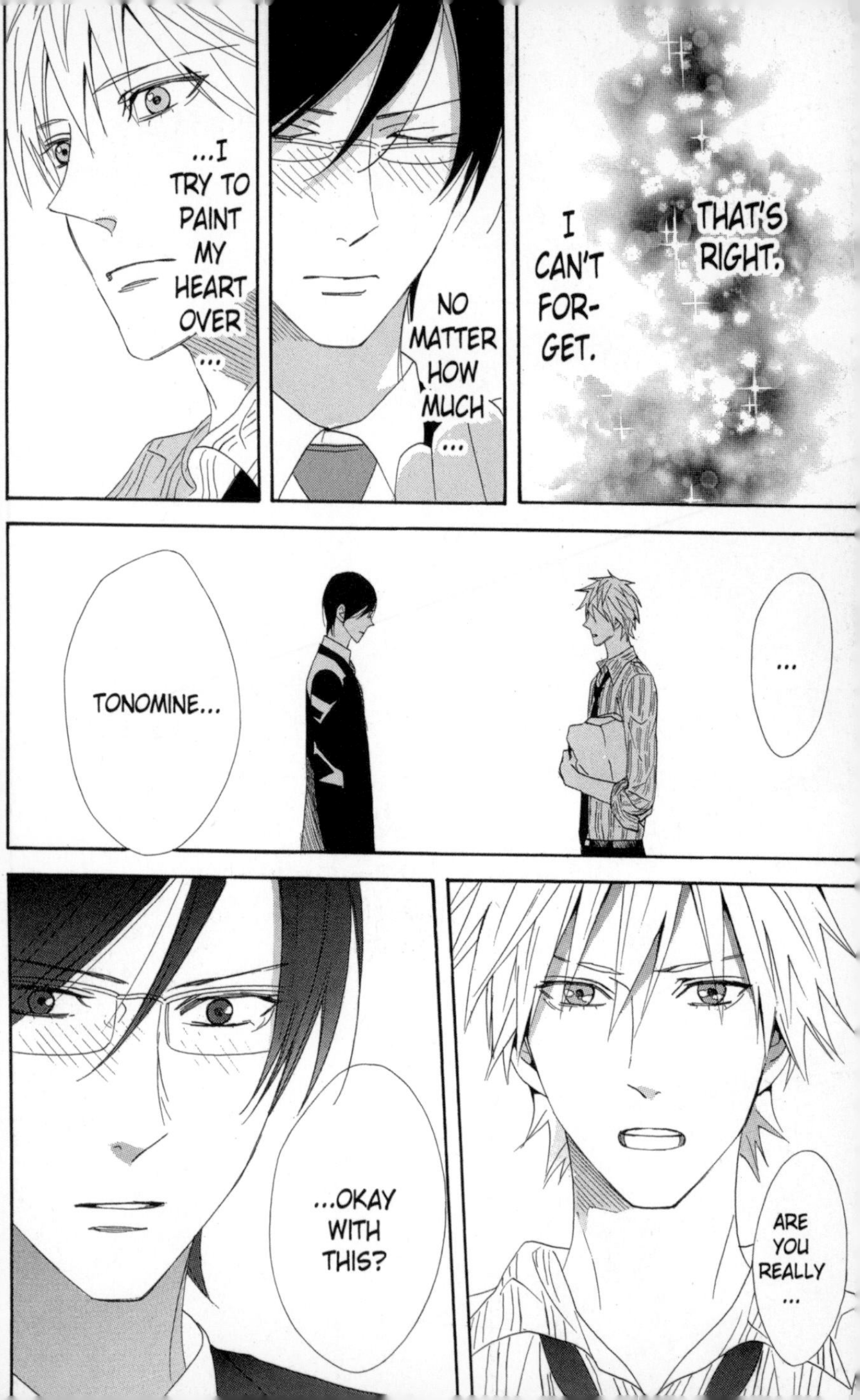
THAT'S RIGHT.
I CAN'T FOR-GET.
NO MATTER HOW MUCH...
...I TRY TO PAINT MY HEART OVER...
...
TONOMINE...
ARE YOU REALLY...
...OKAY WITH THIS?

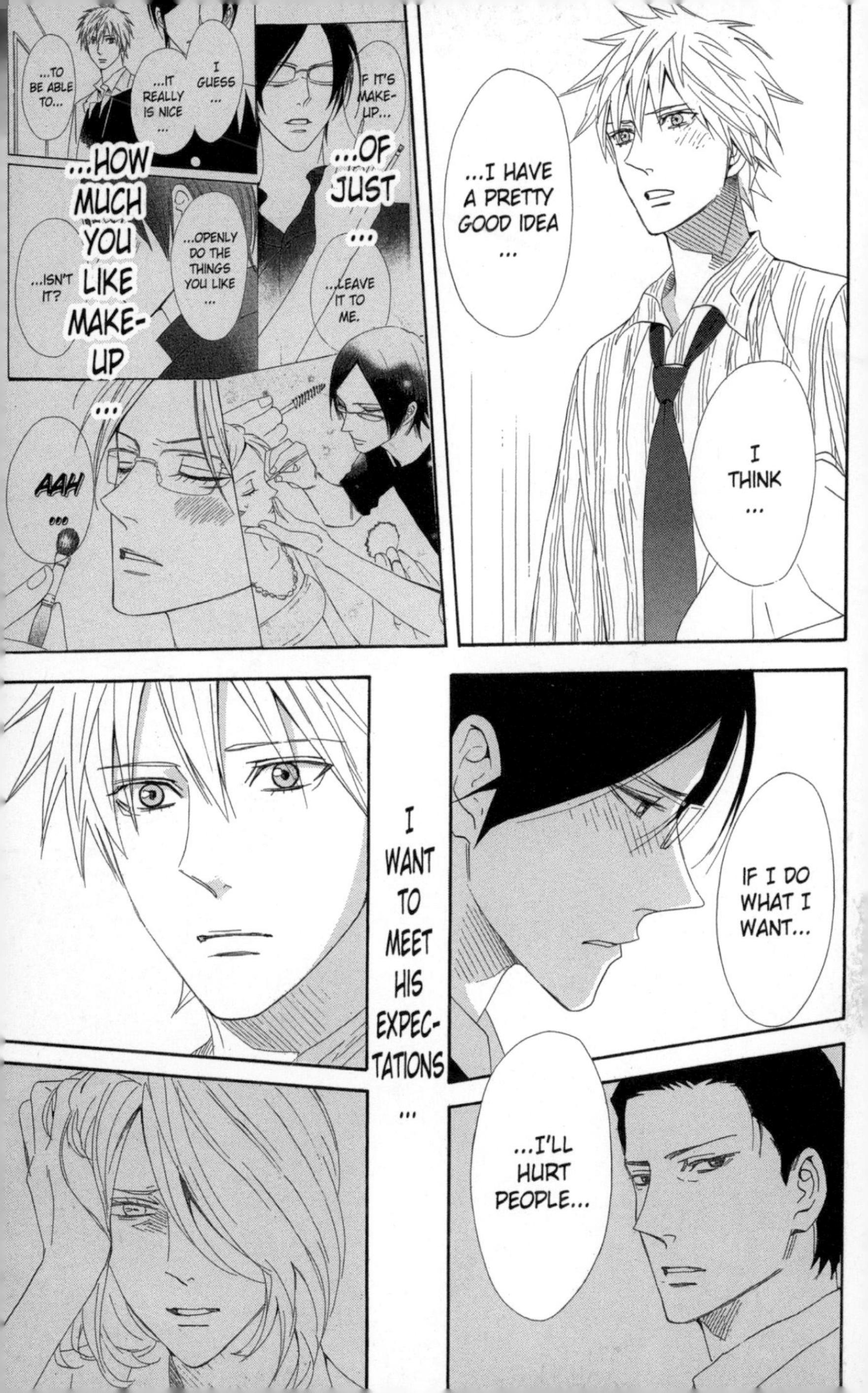
...I HAVE A PRETTY GOOD IDEA ...
I THINK ...
IF IT'S MAKE-UP...
...OF JUST ...
...LEAVE IT TO ME.
I GUESS ...
...IT REALLY IS NICE ...
...TO BE ABLE TO...
...OPENLY DO THE THINGS YOU LIKE ...
...ISN'T IT?
...HOW MUCH YOU LIKE MAKE-UP ...
AAH ...
IF I DO WHAT I WANT...
I WANT TO MEET HIS EXPECTATIONS ...
...I'LL HURT PEOPLE...

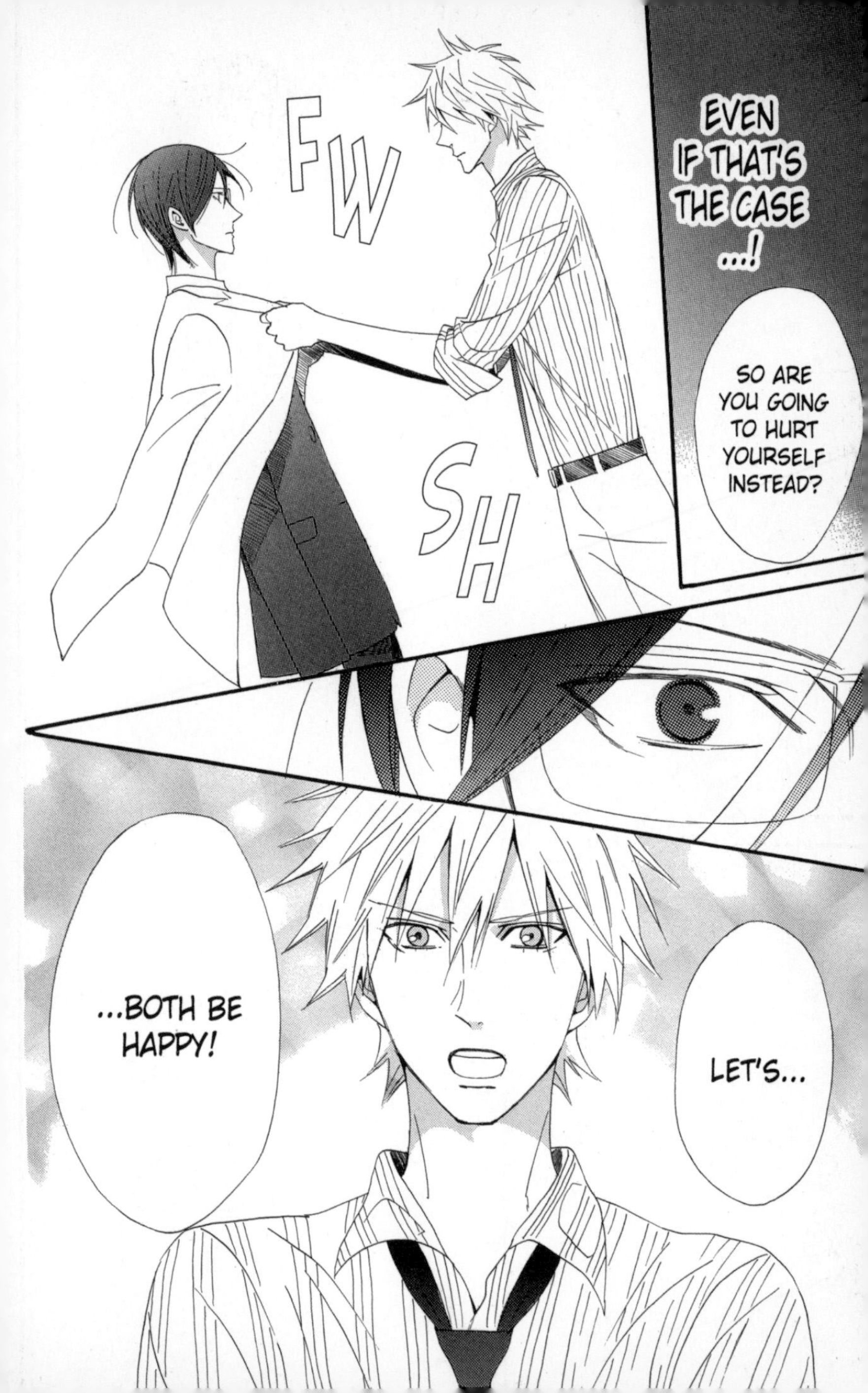
EVEN IF THAT'S THE CASE ...!
SO ARE YOU GOING TO HURT YOURSELF INSTEAD?
FW
SH
LET'S...
...BOTH BE HAPPY!

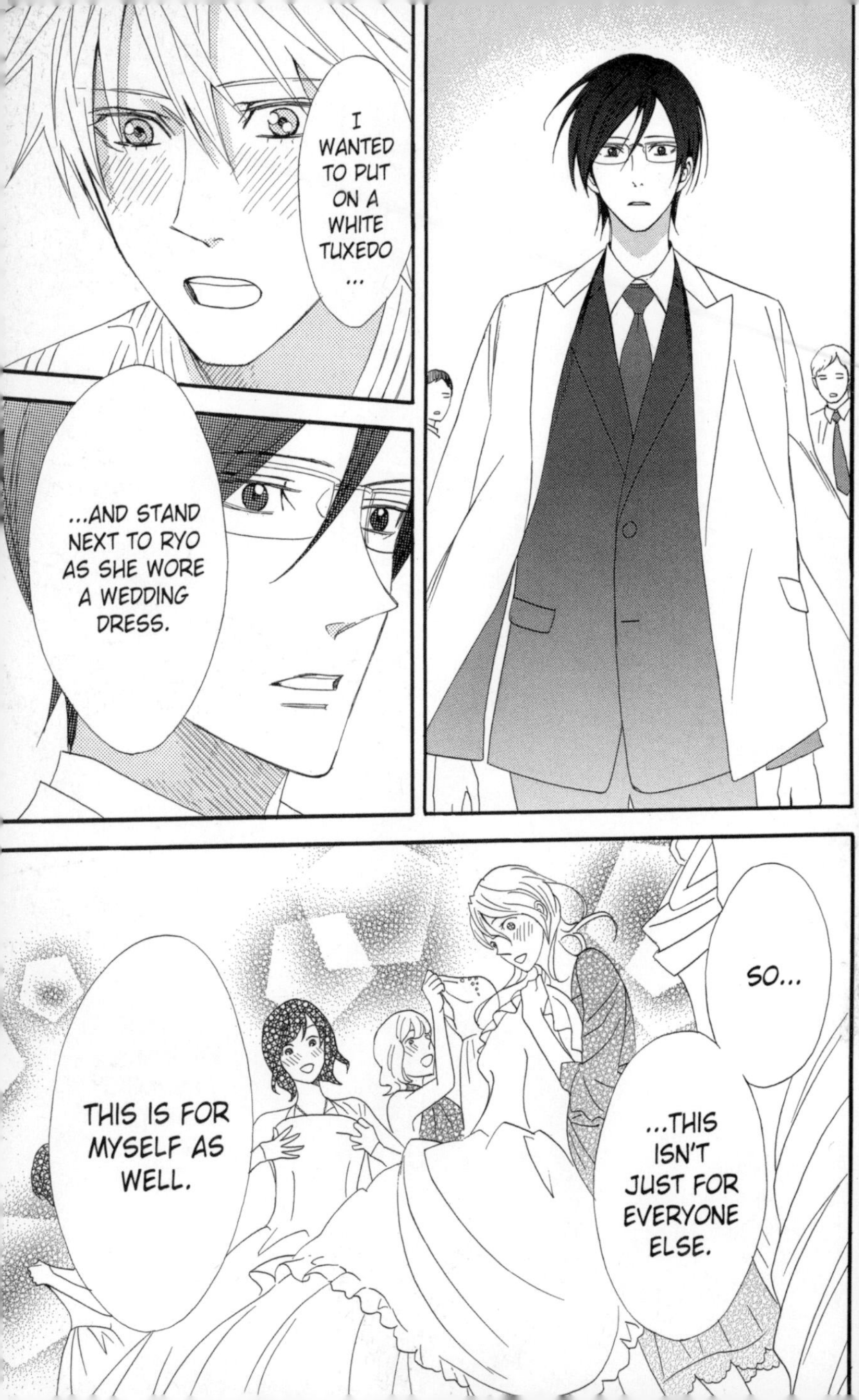
I WANTED TO PUT ON A WHITE TUXEDO ...
...AND STAND NEXT TO RYO AS SHE WORE A WEDDING DRESS.
SO...
...THIS ISN'T JUST FOR EVERYONE ELSE.
THIS IS FOR MYSELF AS WELL.

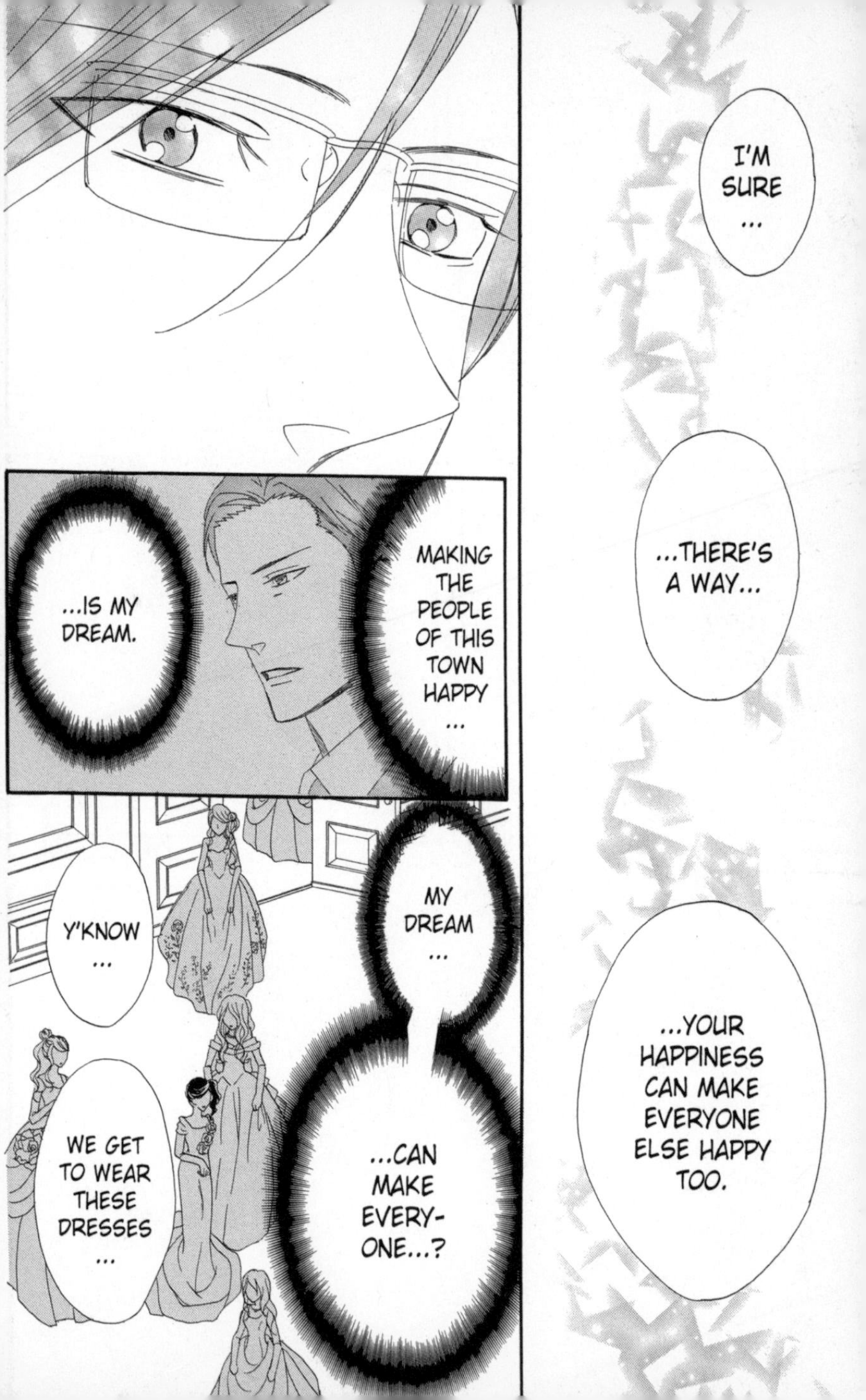
I'M SURE ...
...THERE'S A WAY...
...YOUR HAPPINESS CAN MAKE EVERYONE ELSE HAPPY TOO.
MAKING THE PEOPLE OF THIS TOWN HAPPY ...
...IS MY DREAM.
MY DREAM ...
...CAN MAKE EVERY-ONE...?
Y'KNOW ...
WE GET TO WEAR THESE DRESSES ...

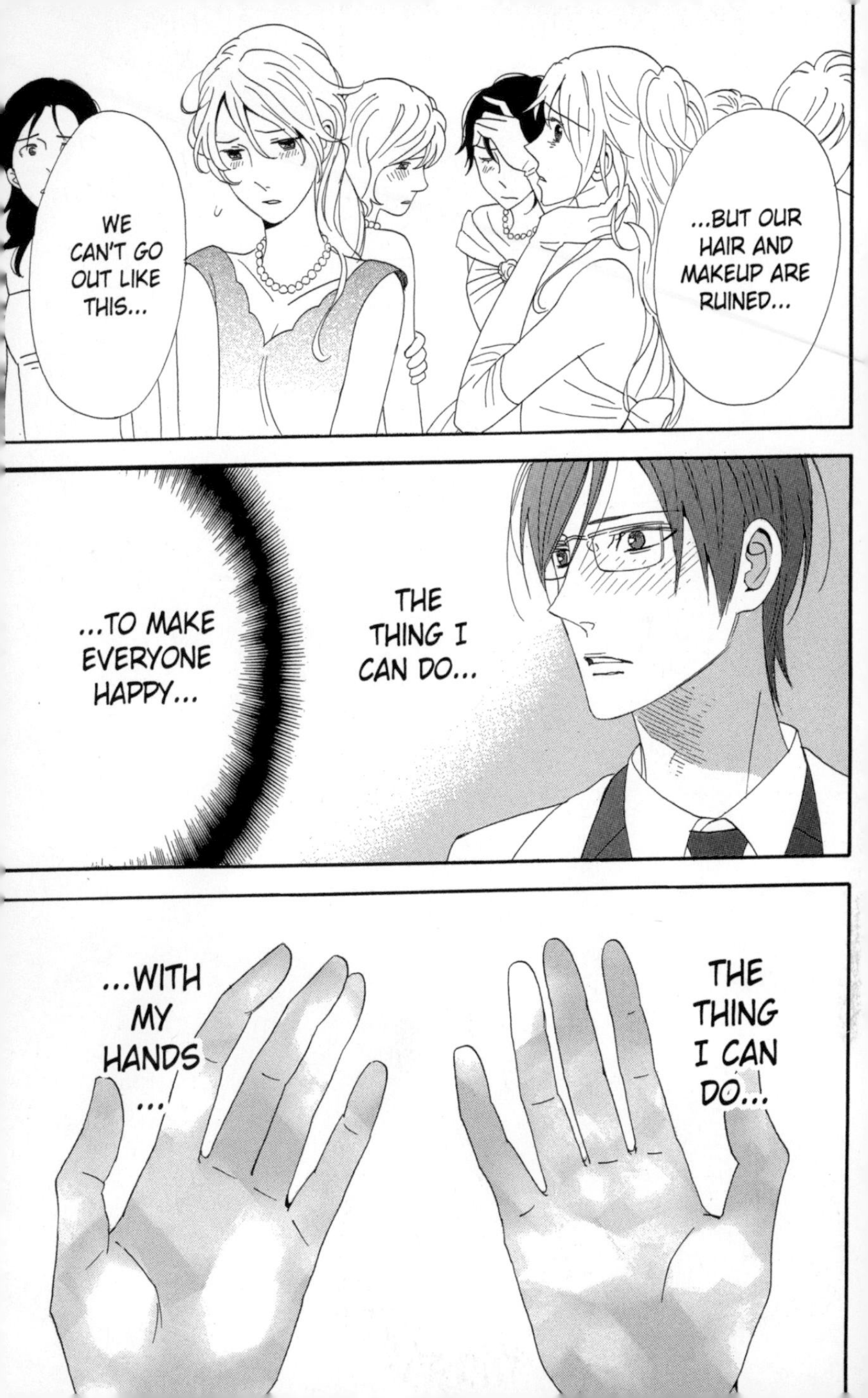
...BUT OUR HAIR AND MAKEUP ARE RUINED...
WE CAN'T GO OUT LIKE THIS...
THE THING I CAN DO...
...TO MAKE EVERYONE HAPPY...
THE THING I CAN DO...
...WITH MY HANDS...

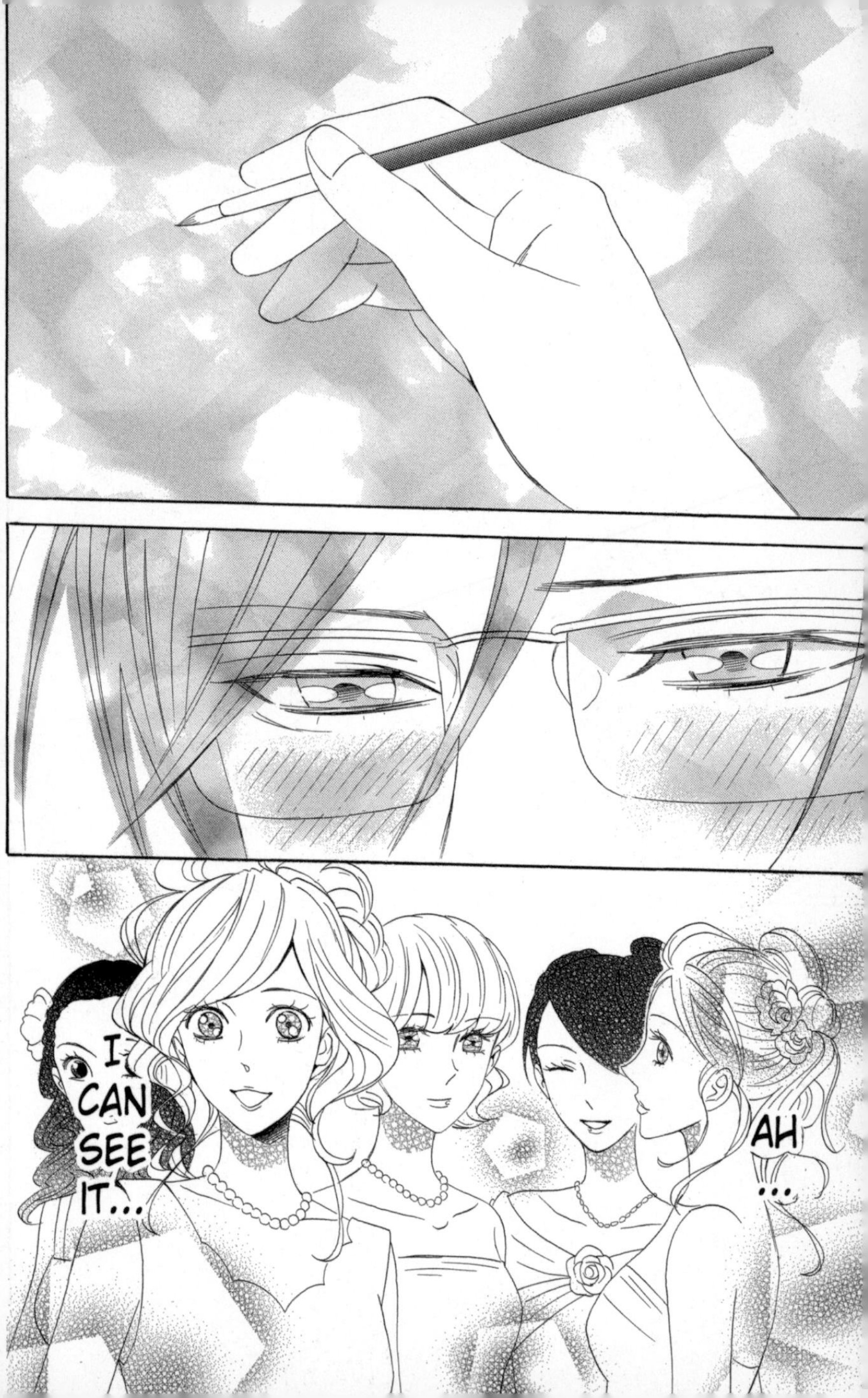
AH...
I CAN SEE IT...

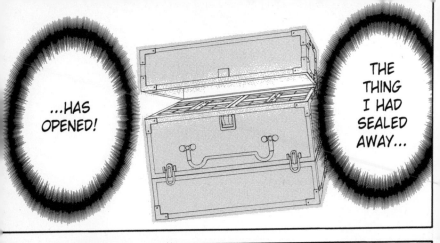

THE THING I HAD SEALED AWAY...
...HAS OPENED!
THAT BEAUTIFUL SENSATION...
THE THRILL...
THE SPARKLES...
I COULD NEVER KEEP IT SHUT.
...
BUT...
...I KNOW NOW...
DAD...
MY HANDS...
...CAN MAKE PEOPLE HAPPY!

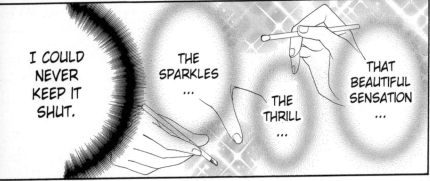

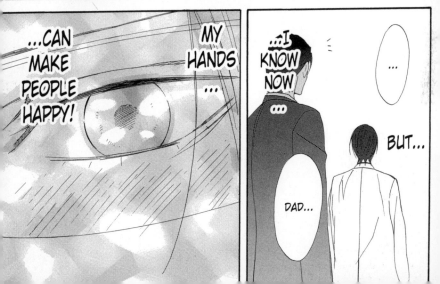

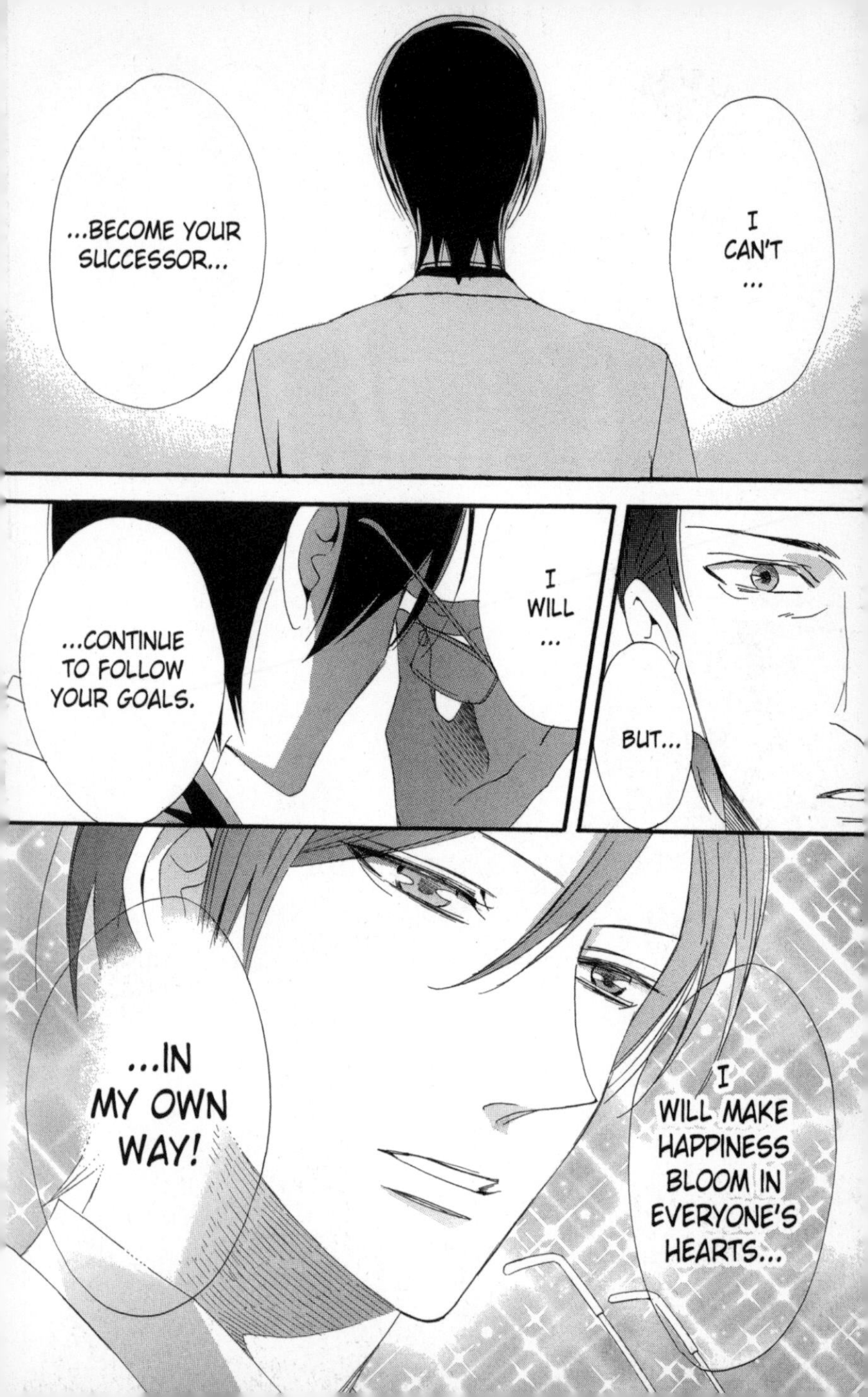
I CAN'T ...
...BECOME YOUR SUCCESSOR...
BUT...
I WILL ...
...CONTINUE TO FOLLOW YOUR GOALS.
I WILL MAKE HAPPINESS BLOOM IN EVERYONE'S HEARTS...
...IN MY OWN WAY!

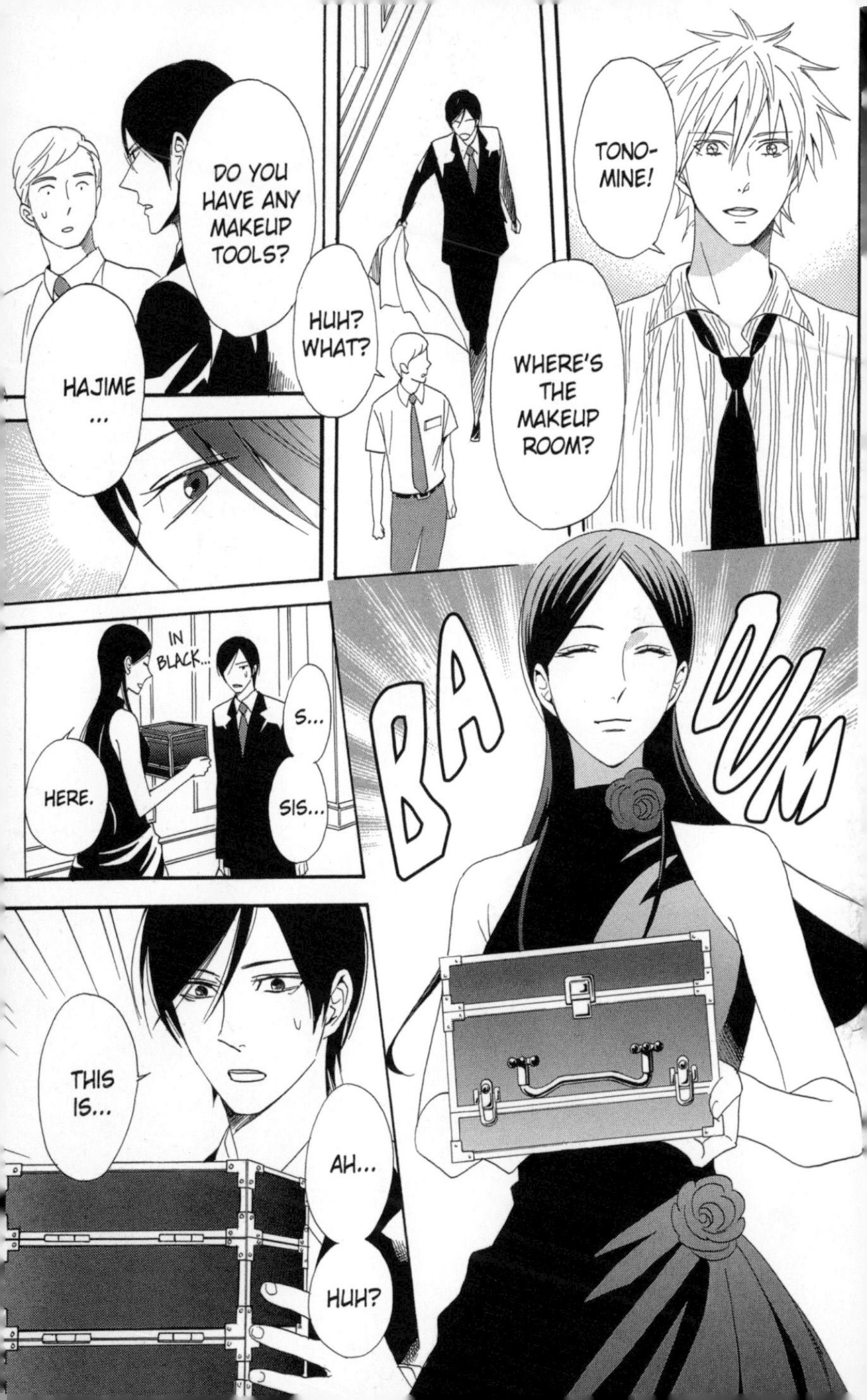
TONO-MINE!
WHERE'S THE MAKEUP ROOM?
HUH? WHAT?
DO YOU HAVE ANY MAKEUP TOOLS?
HAJIME...
BA DUM
IN BLACK...
S...
SIS...
HERE.
THIS IS...
AH...
HUH?

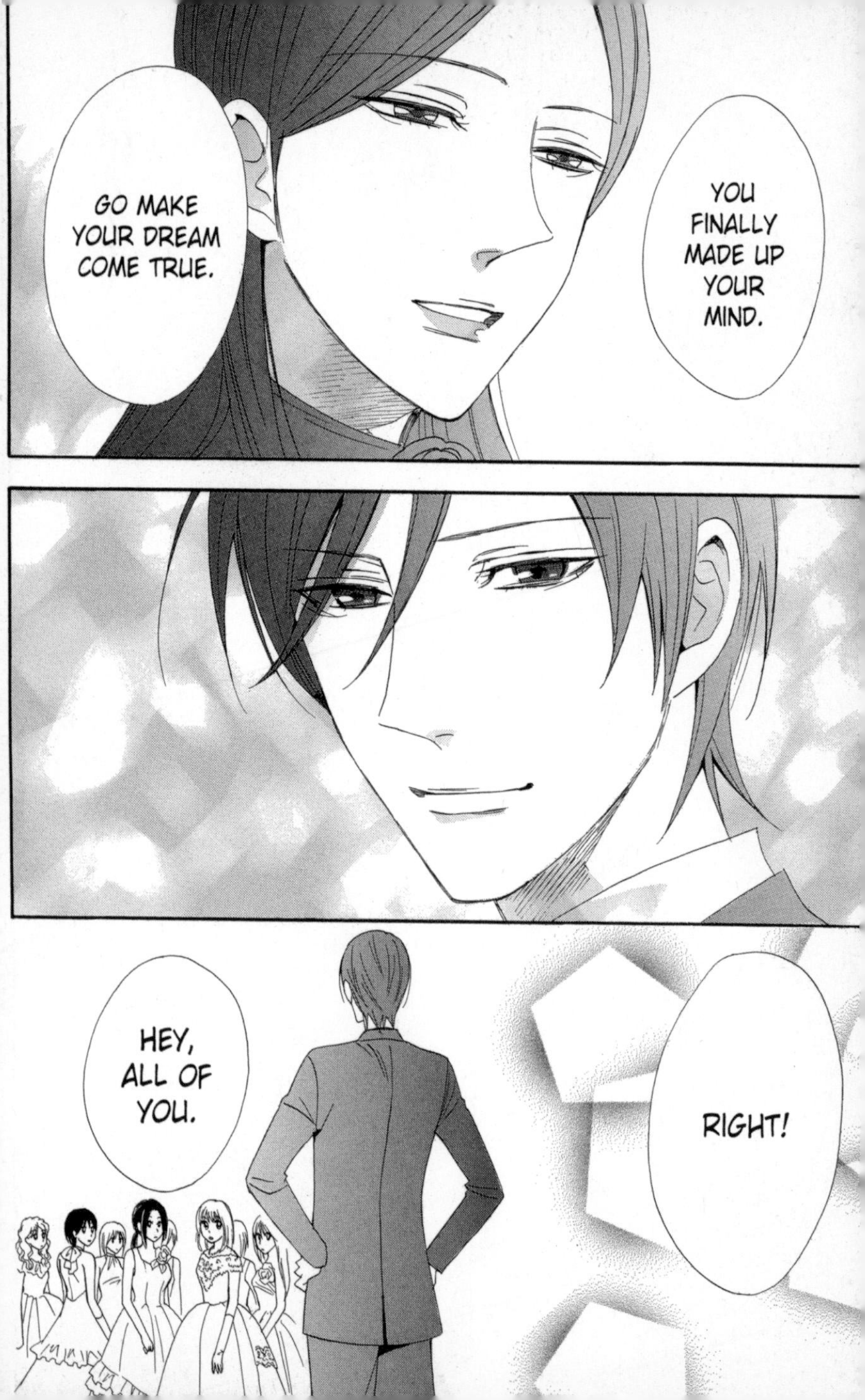
YOU FINALLY MADE UP YOUR MIND.
GO MAKE YOUR DREAM COME TRUE.
RIGHT!
HEY, ALL OF YOU.

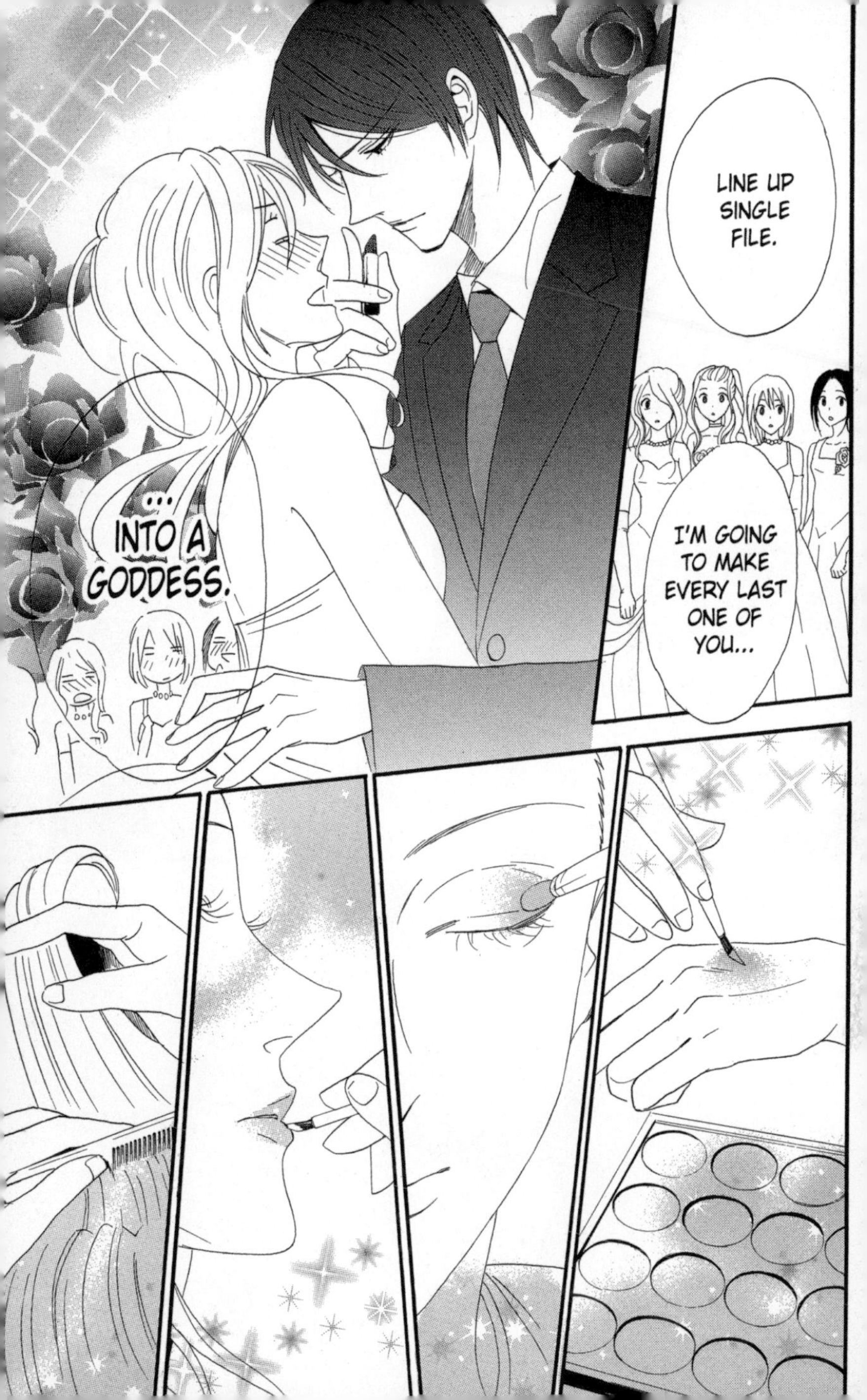
LINE UP SINGLE FILE.
I'M GOING TO MAKE EVERY LAST ONE OF YOU...
... INTO A GODDESS.

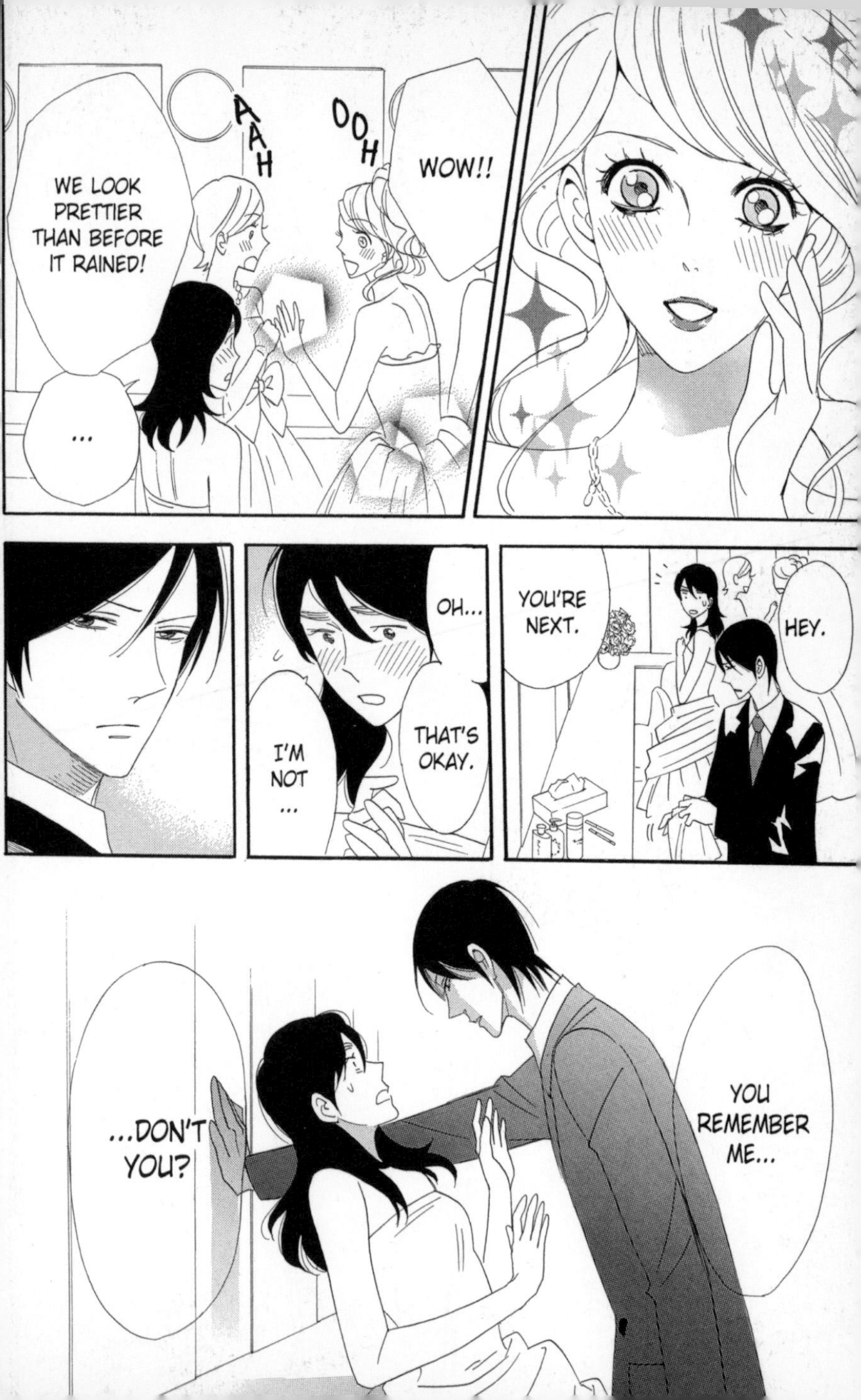
WOW!!
OOH
AAH
WE LOOK PRETTIER THAN BEFORE IT RAINED!
...
HEY.
YOU'RE NEXT.
OH...
THAT'S OKAY.
I'M NOT ...
YOU REMEMBER ME...
...DON'T YOU?

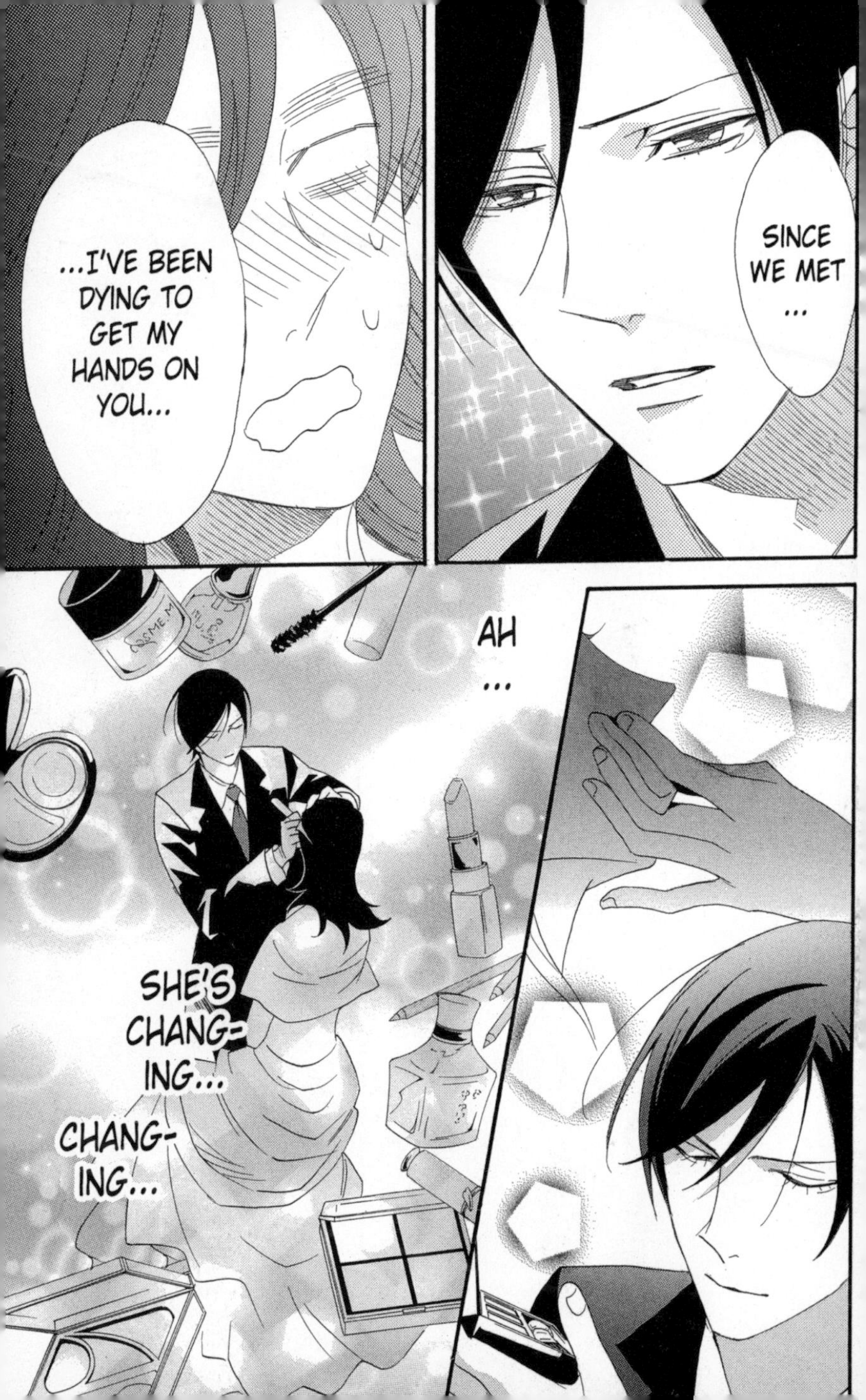
SINCE WE MET ...
...I'VE BEEN DYING TO GET MY HANDS ON YOU...
AH ...
SHE'S CHANG-ING...
CHANG-ING...

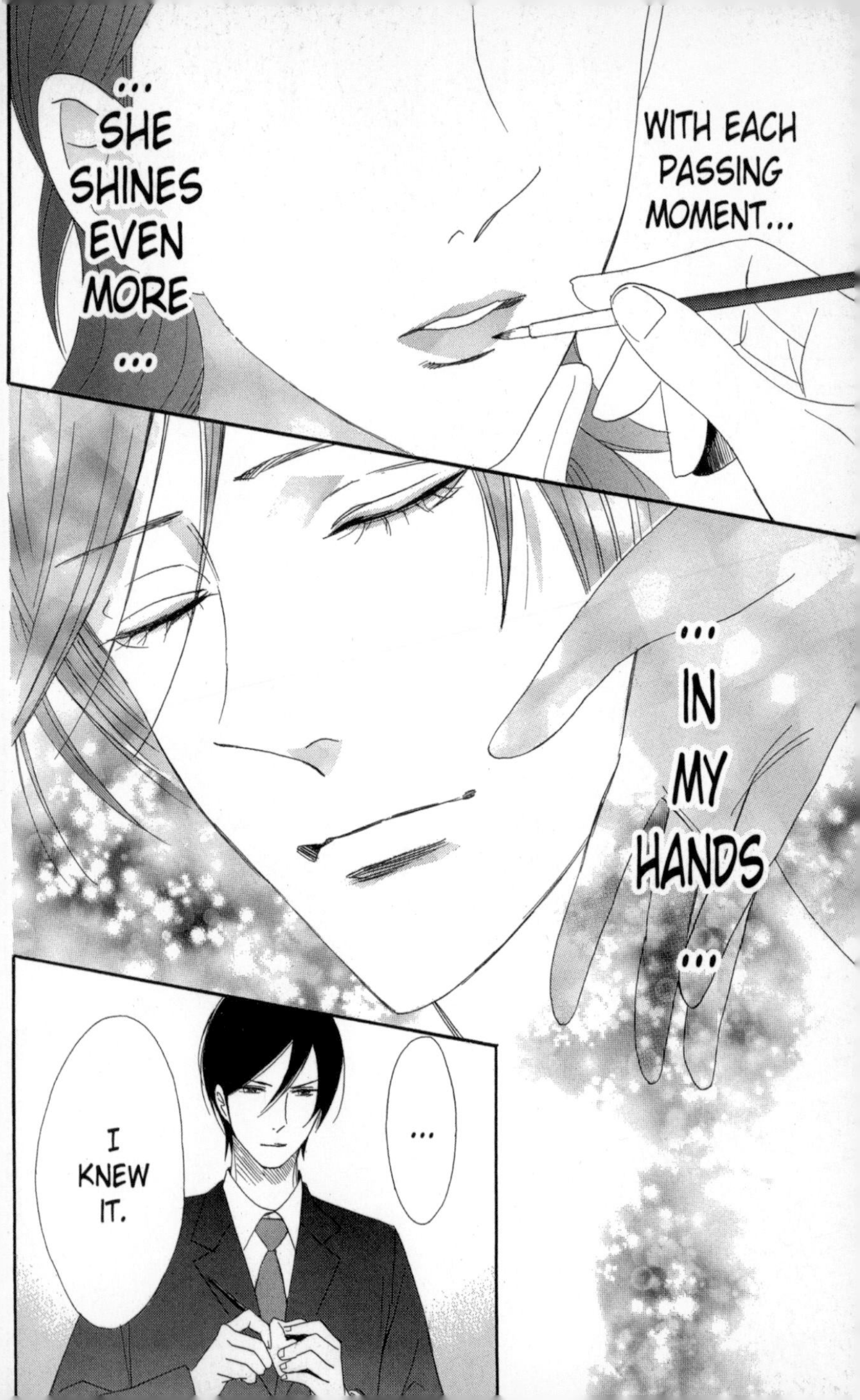
WITH EACH PASSING MOMENT...
...SHE SHINES EVEN MORE...
...IN MY HANDS...
...
I KNEW IT.

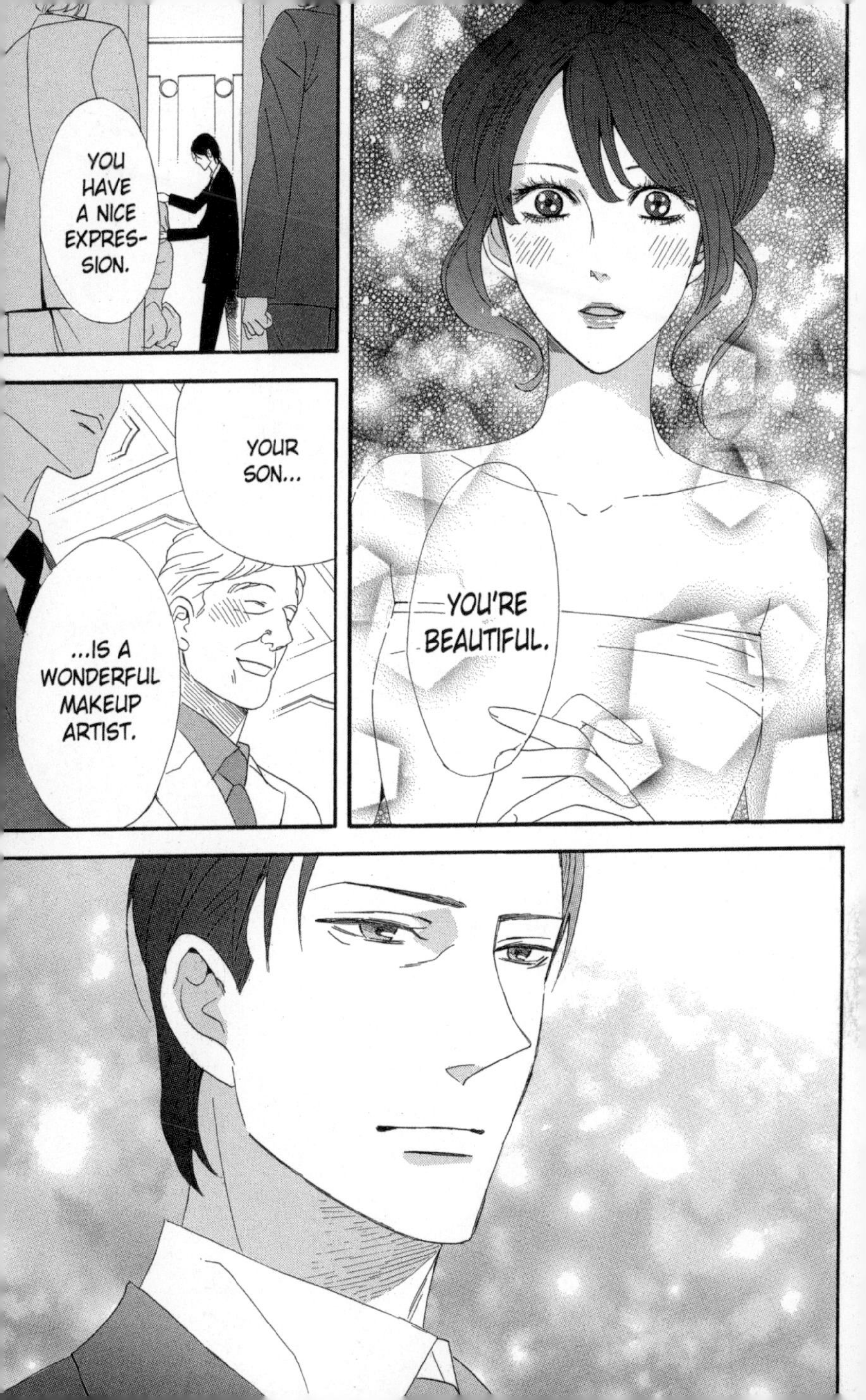
YOU'RE BEAUTIFUL.
YOU HAVE A NICE EXPRES-SION.
YOUR SON...
...IS A WONDERFUL MAKEUP ARTIST.

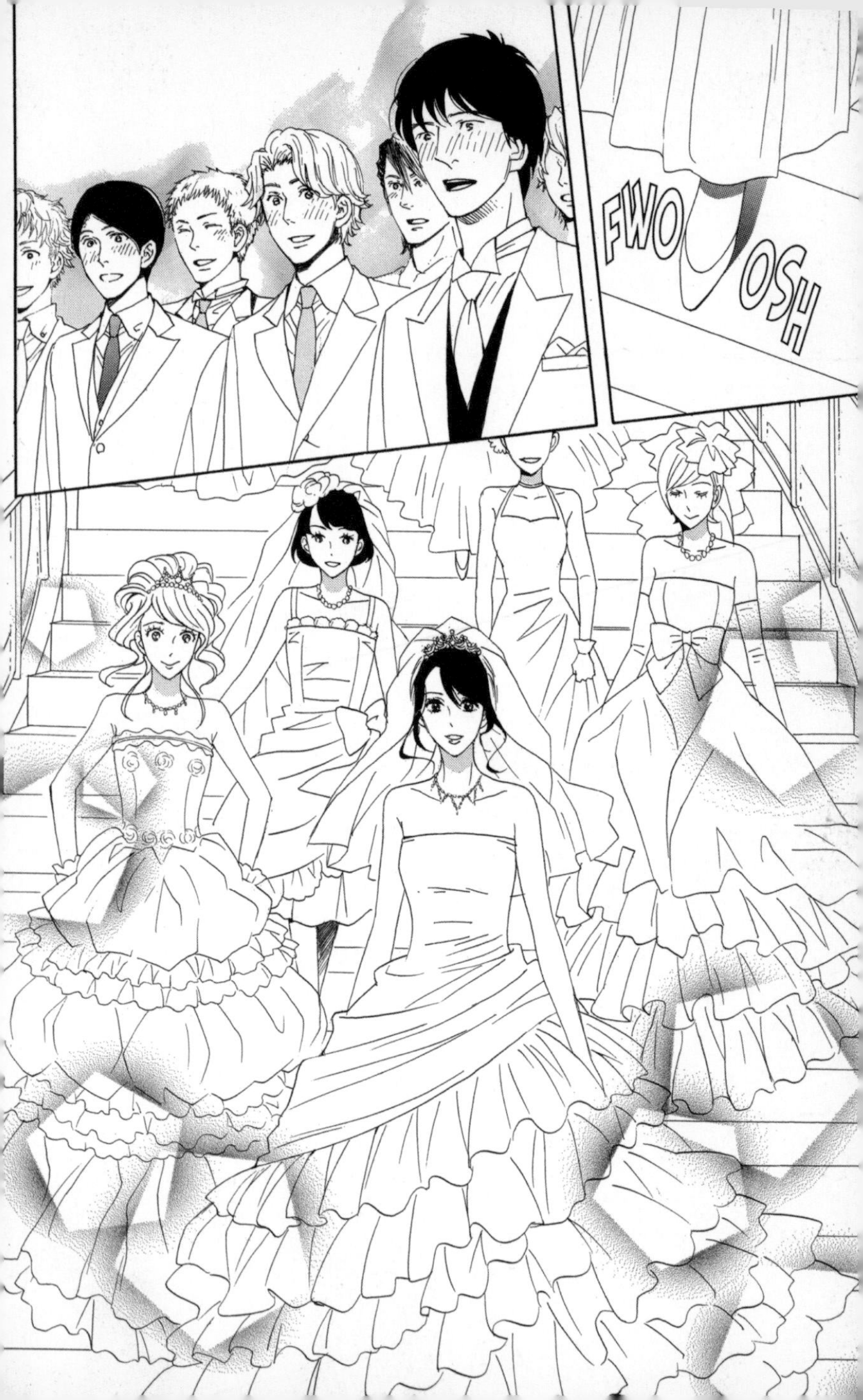
FWOOSH

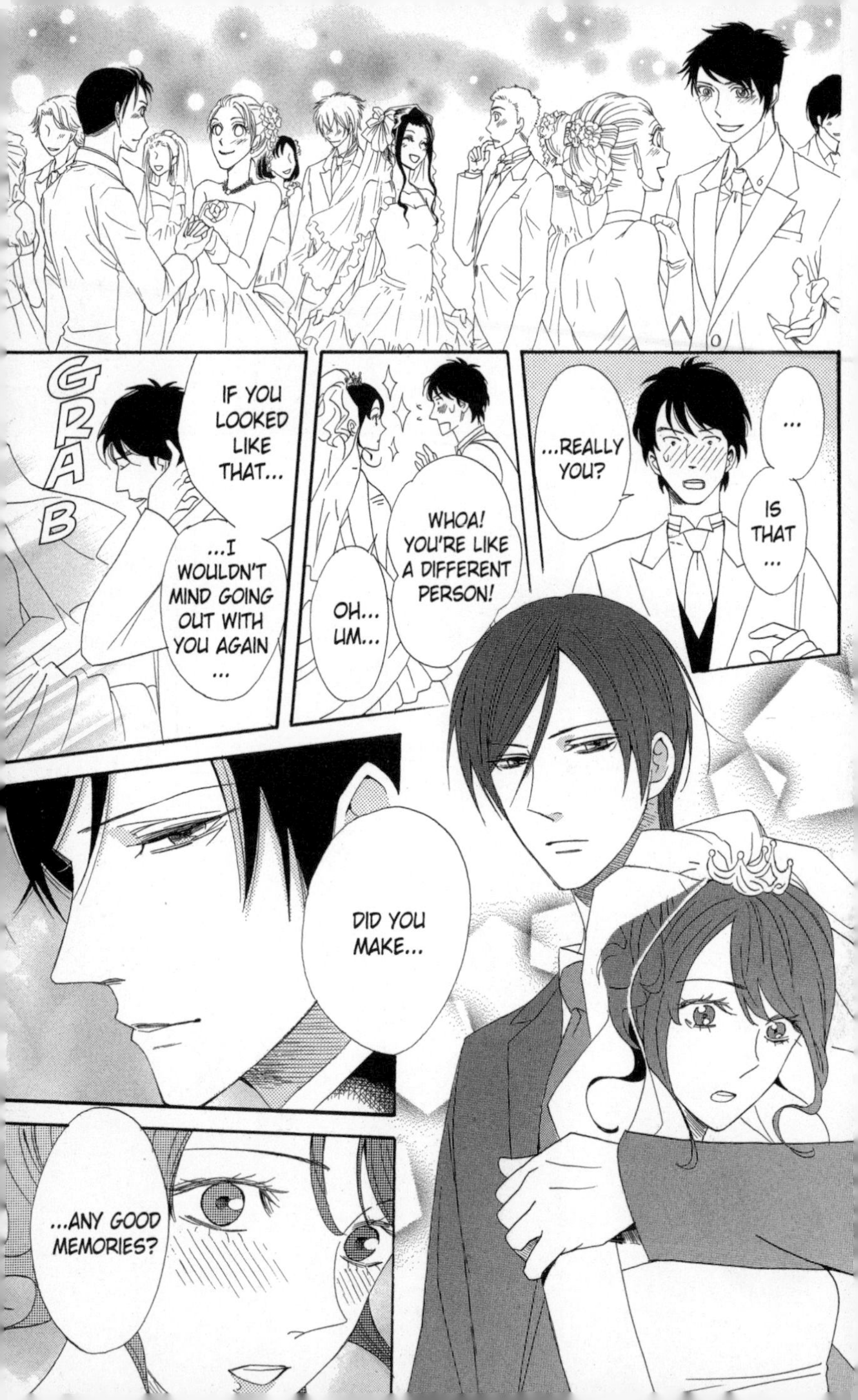
...
IS THAT ...
...REALLY YOU?
WHOA! YOU'RE LIKE A DIFFERENT PERSON!
OH... UM...
IF YOU LOOKED LIKE THAT...
...I WOULDN'T MIND GOING OUT WITH YOU AGAIN ...
GRAB
DID YOU MAKE...
...ANY GOOD MEMORIES?

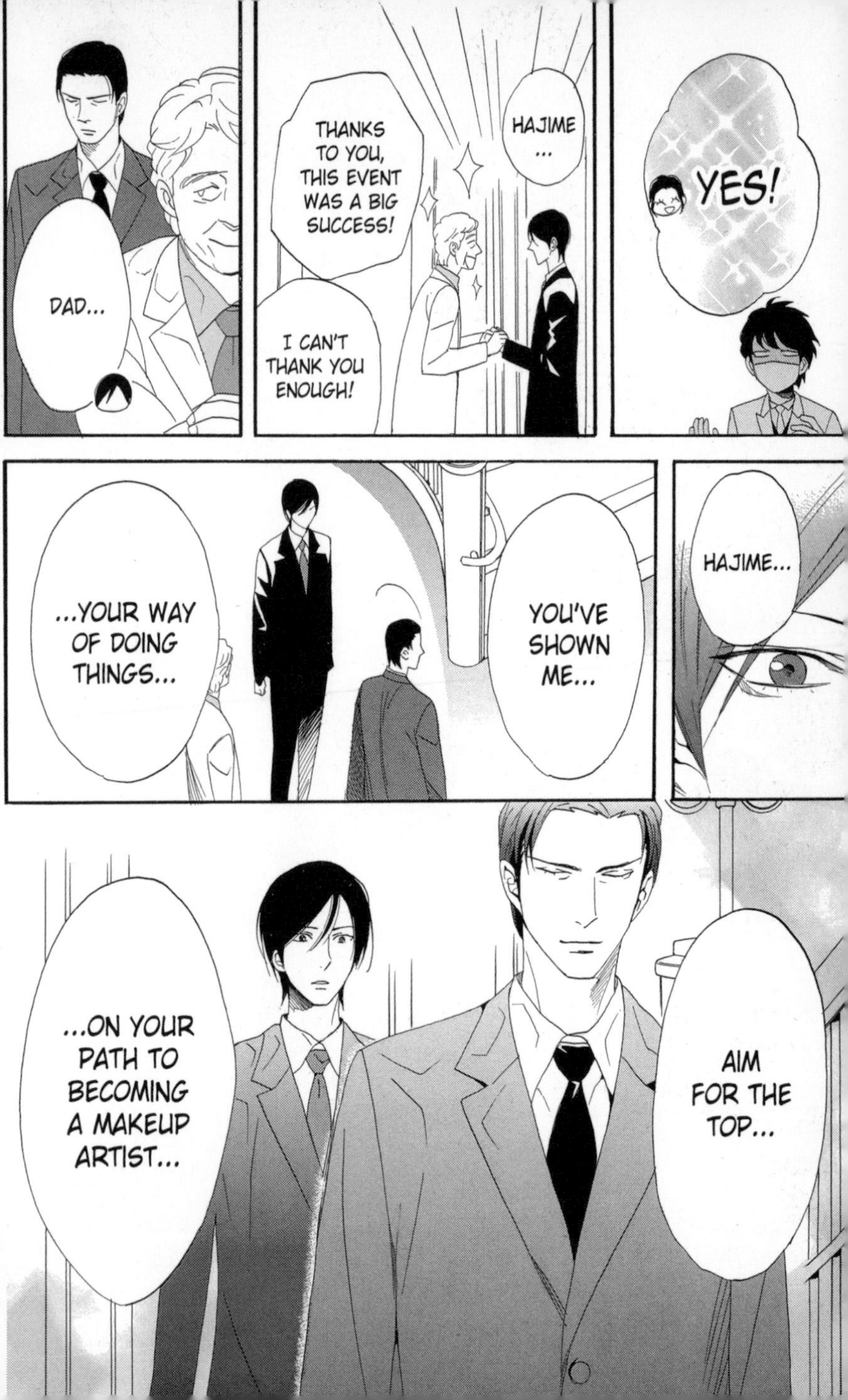
YES!
HAJIME...
THANKS TO YOU, THIS EVENT WAS A BIG SUCCESS!
I CAN'T THANK YOU ENOUGH!
DAD...
HAJIME...
YOU'VE SHOWN ME...
...YOUR WAY OF DOING THINGS...
AIM FOR THE TOP...
...ON YOUR PATH TO BECOMING A MAKEUP ARTIST...

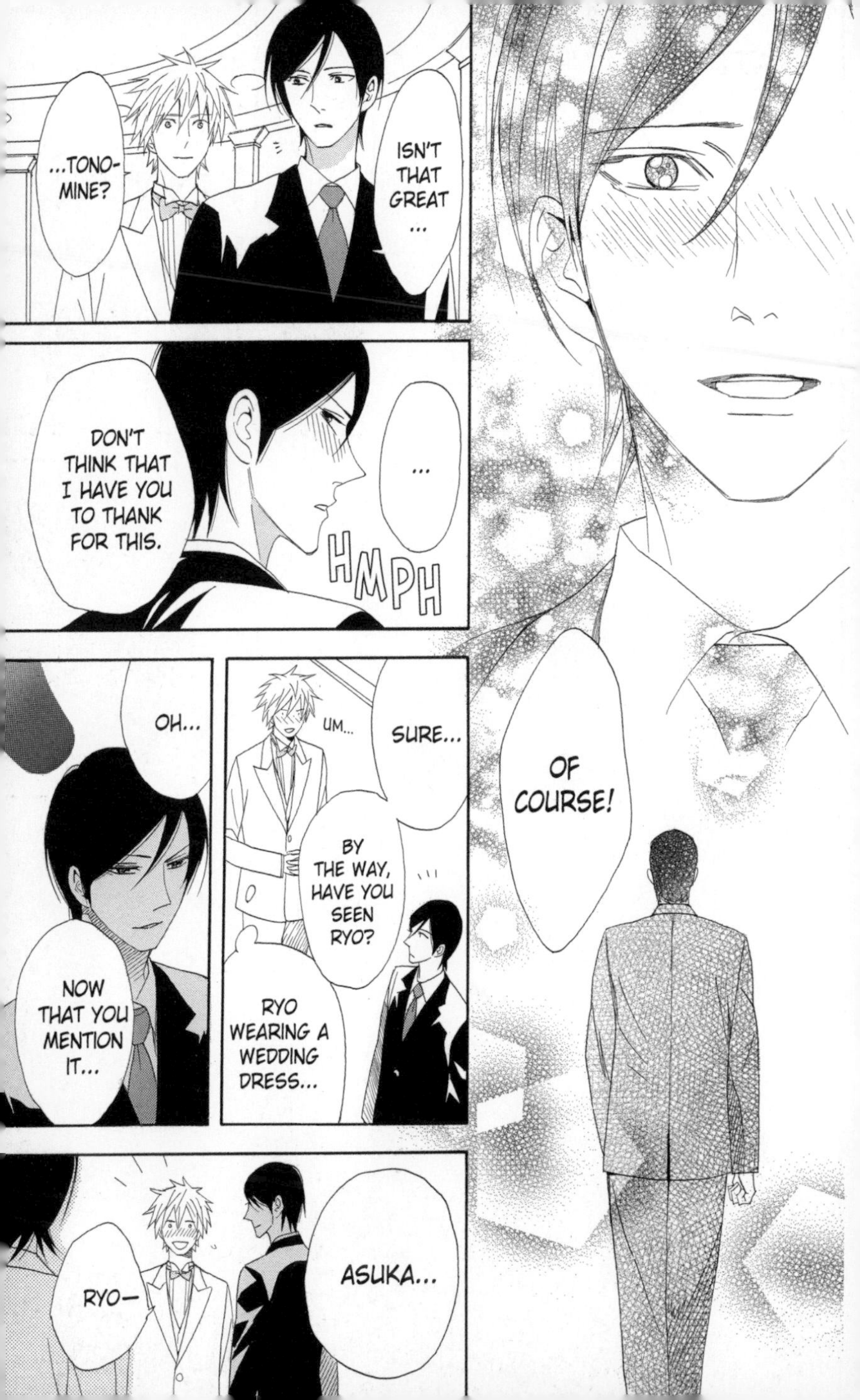
OF COURSE!
ISN'T THAT GREAT...
...TONO-MINE?
...
HMPH
DON'T THINK THAT I HAVE YOU TO THANK FOR THIS.
SURE...
UM...
BY THE WAY, HAVE YOU SEEN RYO?
RYO WEARING A WEDDING DRESS...
OH...
NOW THAT YOU MENTION IT...
ASUKA...
RYO—

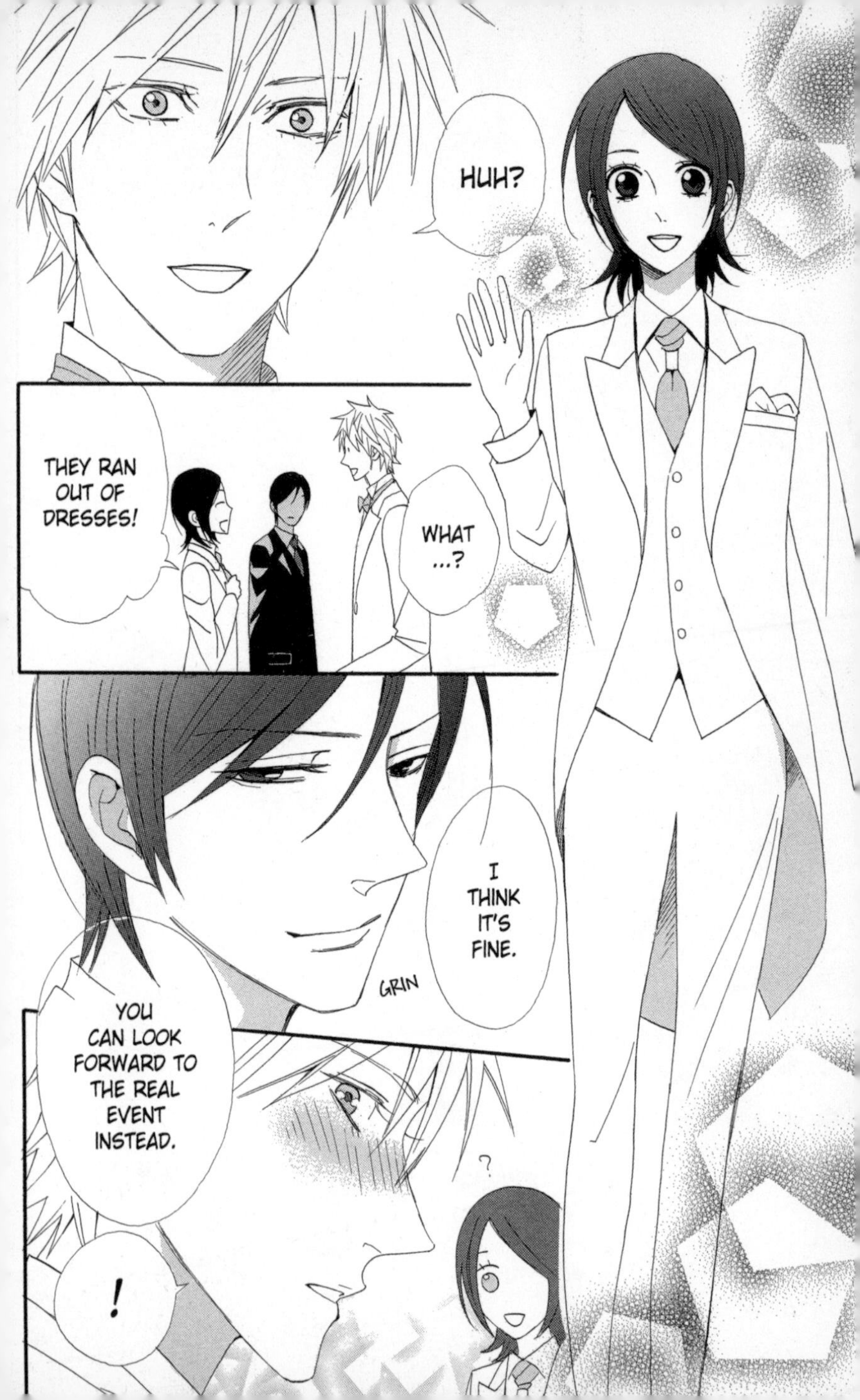
HUH?
THEY RAN OUT OF DRESSES!
WHAT ...?
I THINK IT'S FINE.
GRIN
YOU CAN LOOK FORWARD TO THE REAL EVENT INSTEAD.
!
?

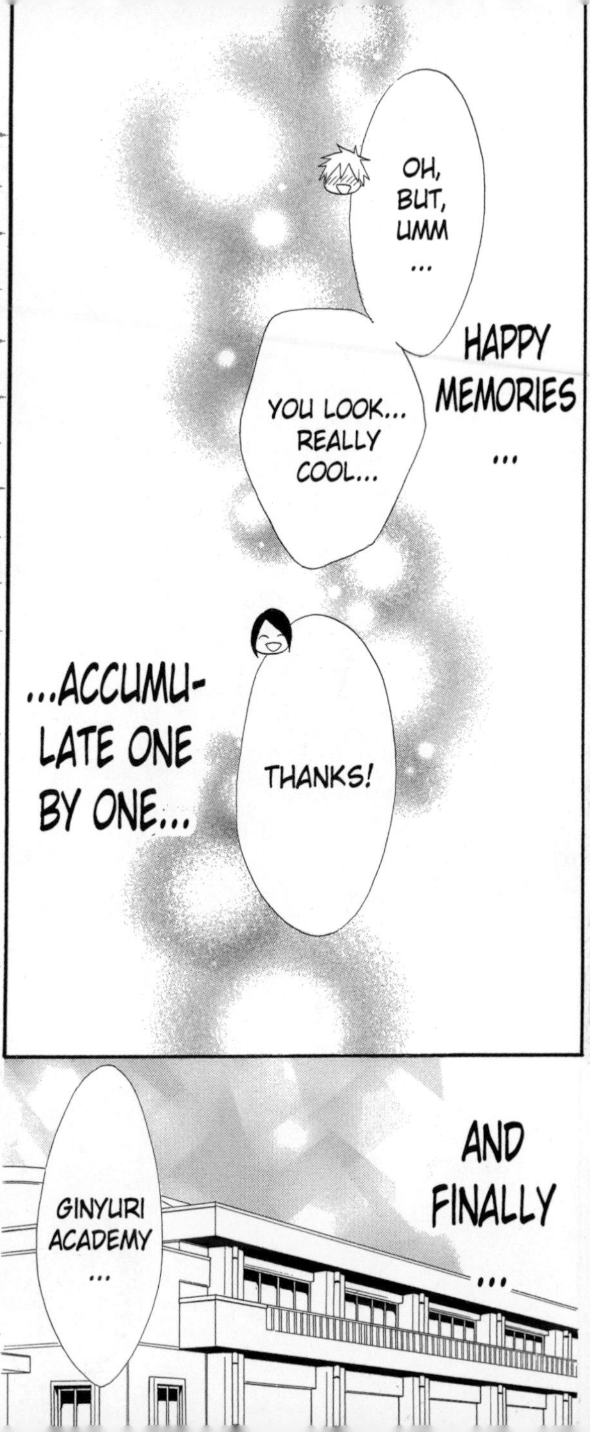
HAPPY MEMORIES ...
OH, BUT, UMM ...
YOU LOOK... REALLY COOL...
THANKS!
...ACCUMU-LATE ONE BY ONE...
AND FINALLY ...
GINYURI ACADEMY ...

It's volume 15!

We're finally at volume 15. Thank you so much for following this long.

I had been aiming for *Otomen* to reach at least fifteen volumes from the beginning.

I was able to continue drawing this long because of all of you readers.

I can't thank you enough.

Thank you from the bottom of my heart.

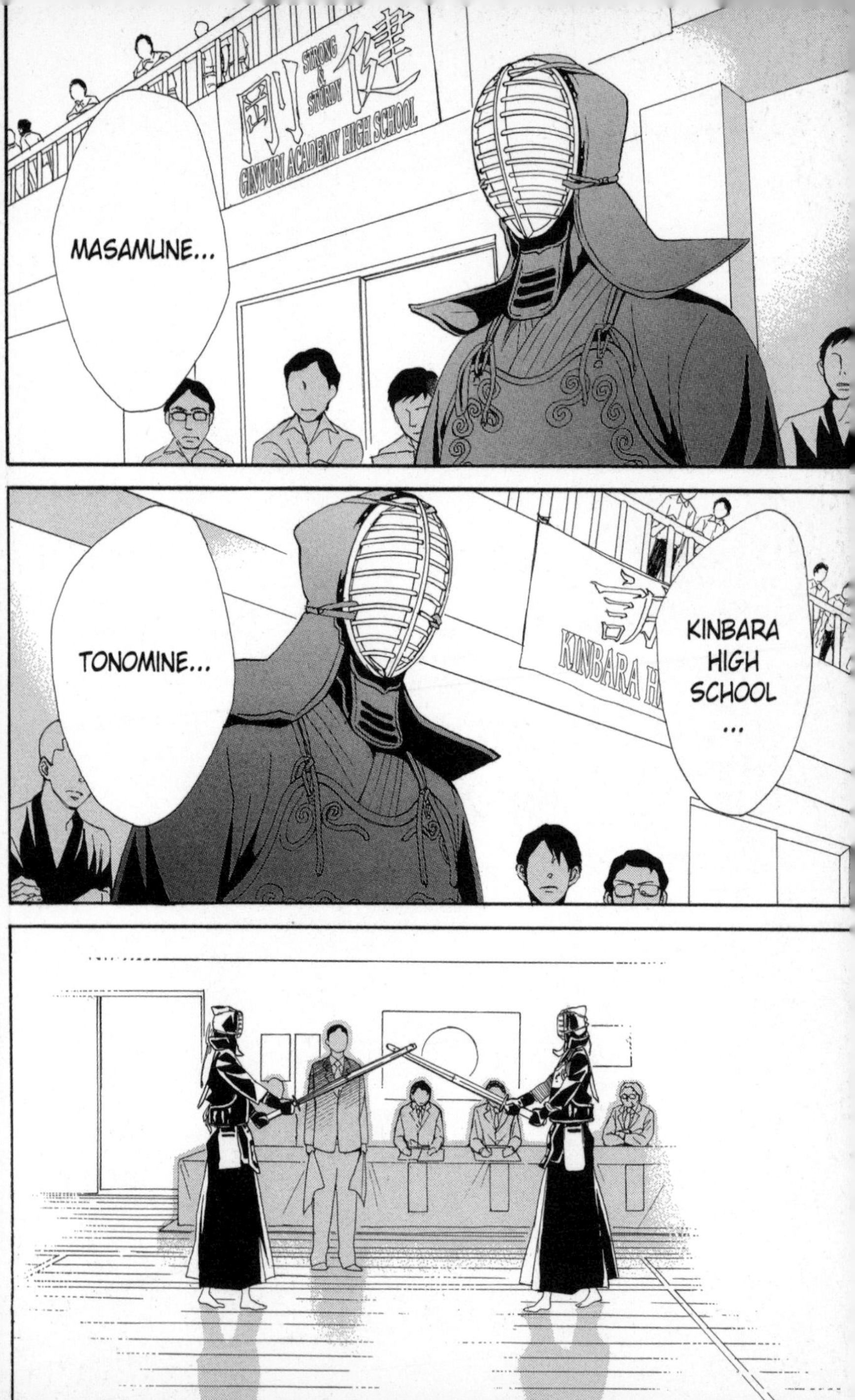
STRONG & STURDY
GINYURI ACADEMY HIGH SCHOOL
MASAMUNE...
KINBARA HIGH SCHOOL ...
TONOMINE...

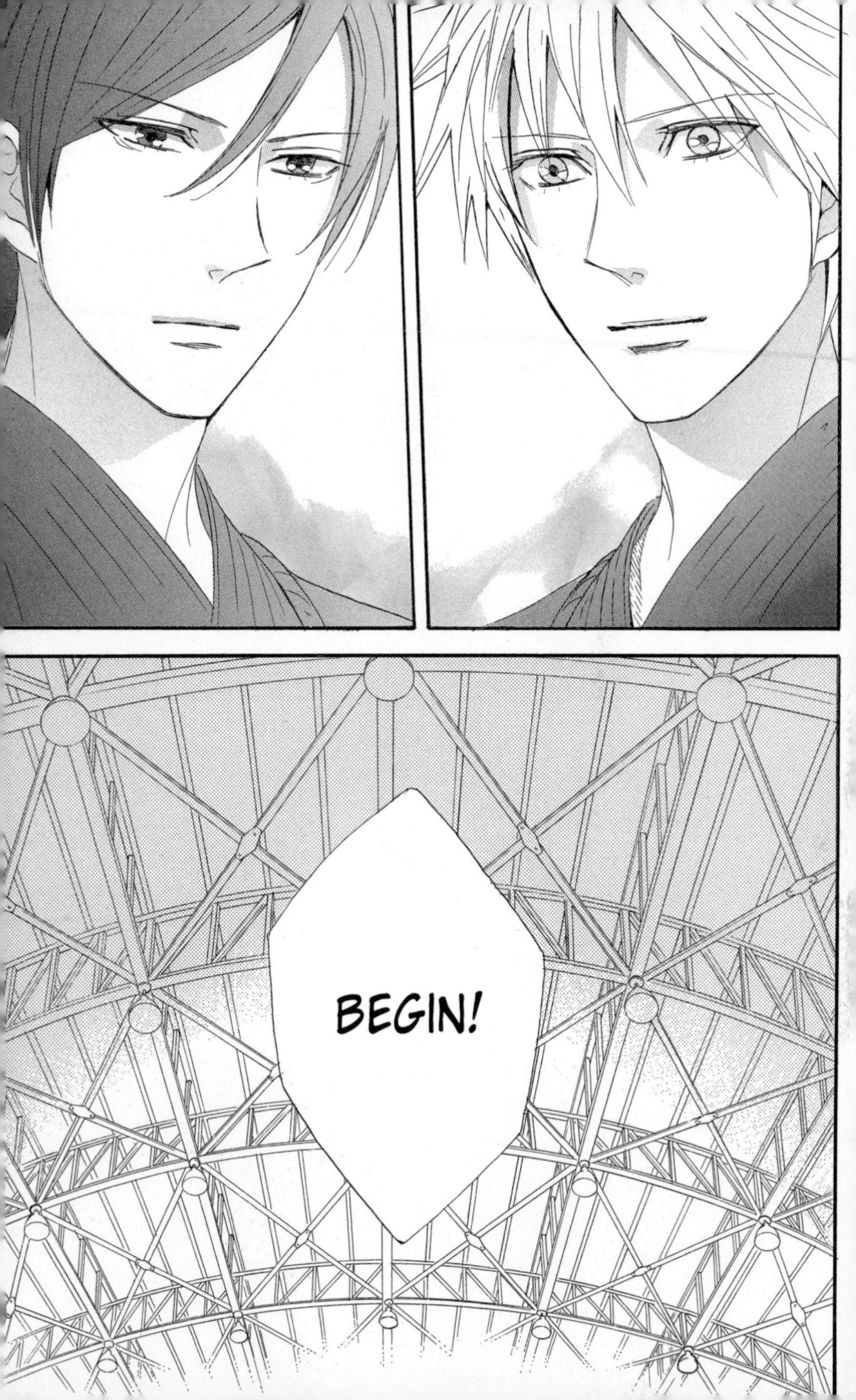
BEGIN!

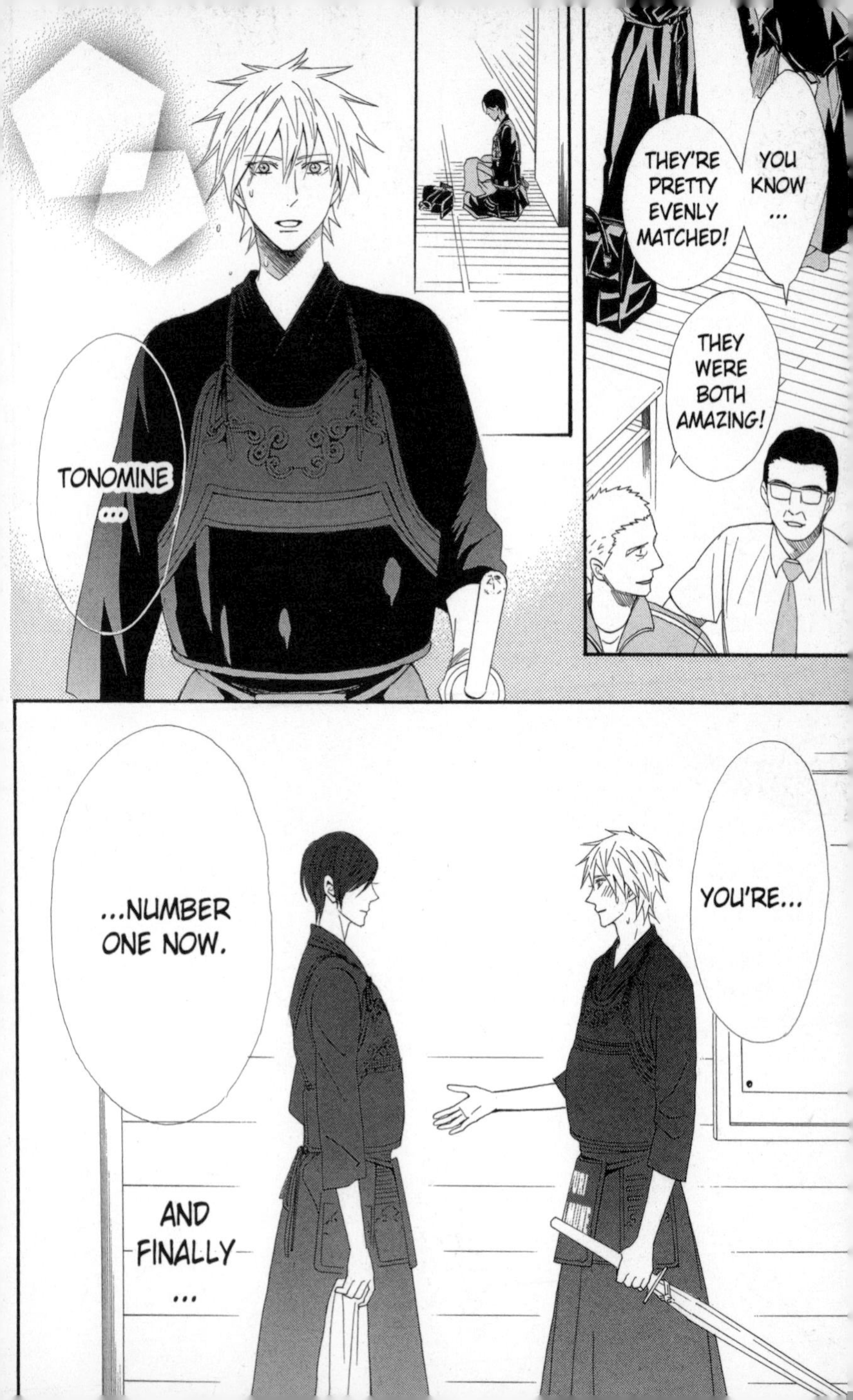
YOU KNOW...
THEY'RE PRETTY EVENLY MATCHED!
THEY WERE BOTH AMAZING!
TONOMINE...
YOU'RE...
...NUMBER ONE NOW.
AND FINALLY...

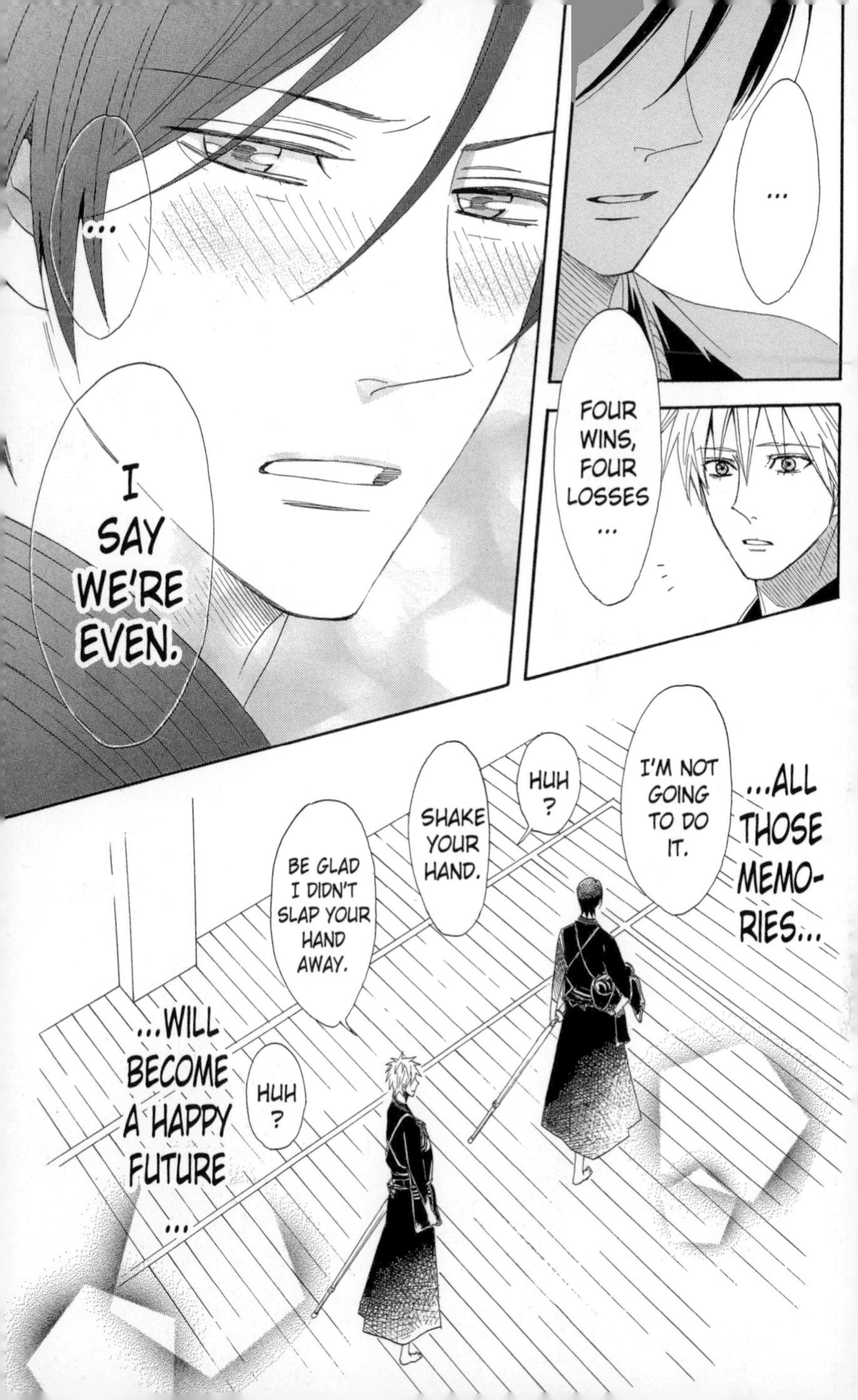
...
FOUR WINS, FOUR LOSSES ...
...
I SAY WE'RE EVEN.
...ALL THOSE MEMORIES...
I'M NOT GOING TO DO IT.
HUH?
SHAKE YOUR HAND.
BE GLAD I DIDN'T SLAP YOUR HAND AWAY.
HUH?
...WILL BECOME A HAPPY FUTURE ...

OTOMEN

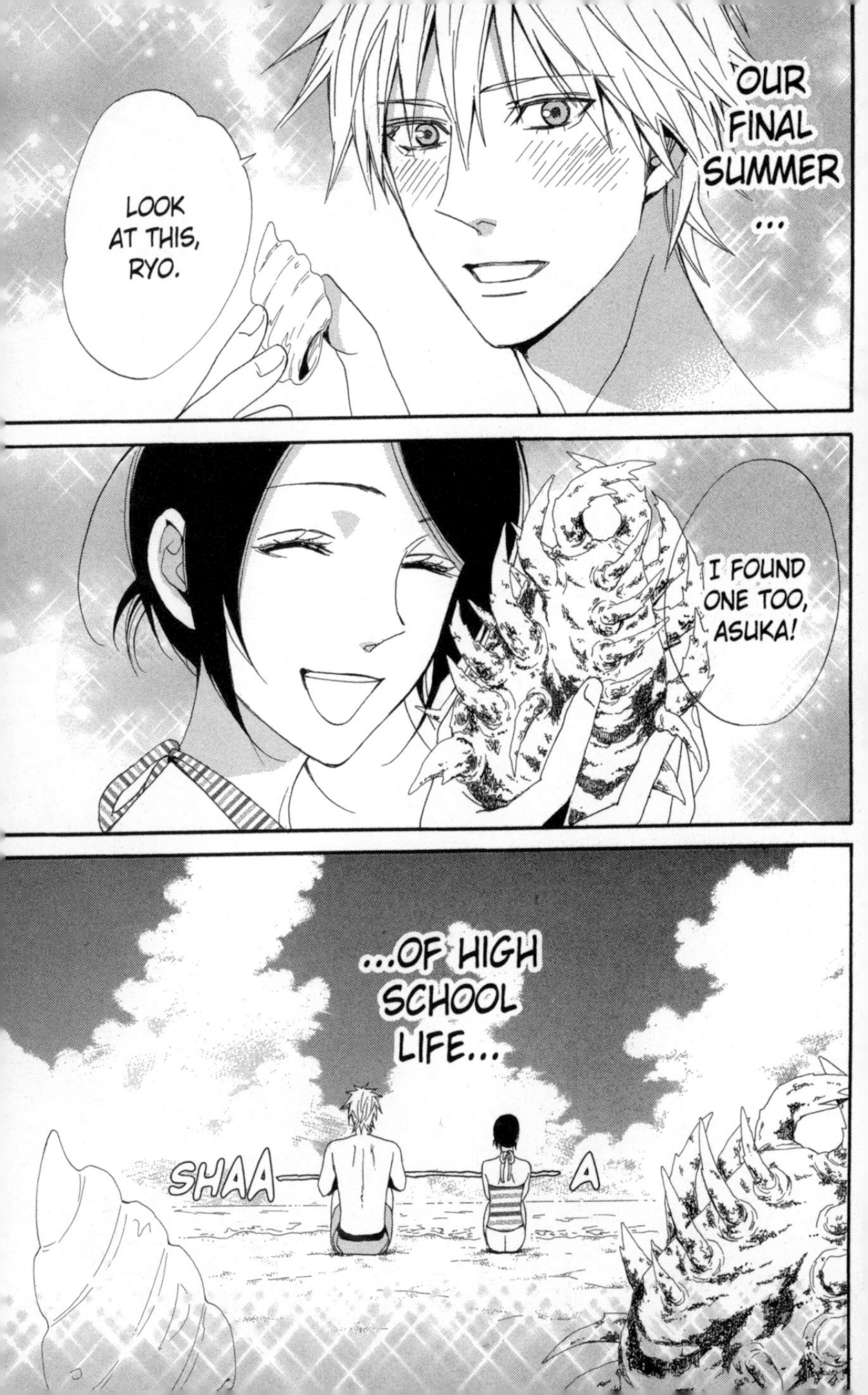
OUR FINAL SUMMER...
LOOK AT THIS, RYO.
I FOUND ONE TOO, ASUKA!
...OF HIGH SCHOOL LIFE...
SHAA A

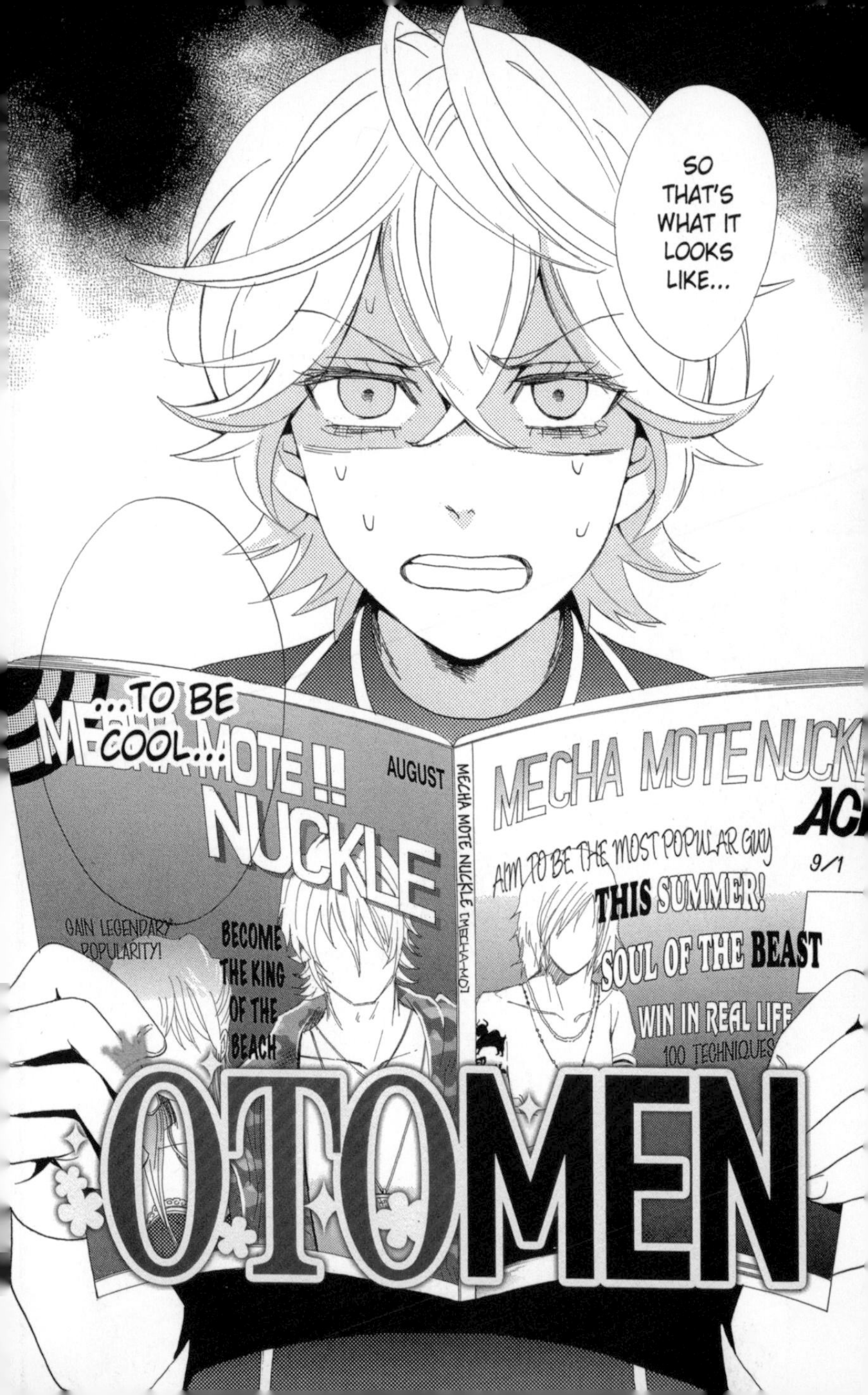
SO THAT'S WHAT IT LOOKS LIKE...
...TO BE COOL...
MECHA MOTE NUCKL
9/1
AIM TO BE THE MOST POPULAR GUY
THIS SUMMER!
SOUL OF THE BEAST
WIN IN REAL LIFE
100 TECHNIQUES
MECHA MOTE NUCKLE
AUGUST
NUCKLE
GAIN LEGENDARY POPULARITY!
BECOME THE KING OF THE BEACH
OTOMEN

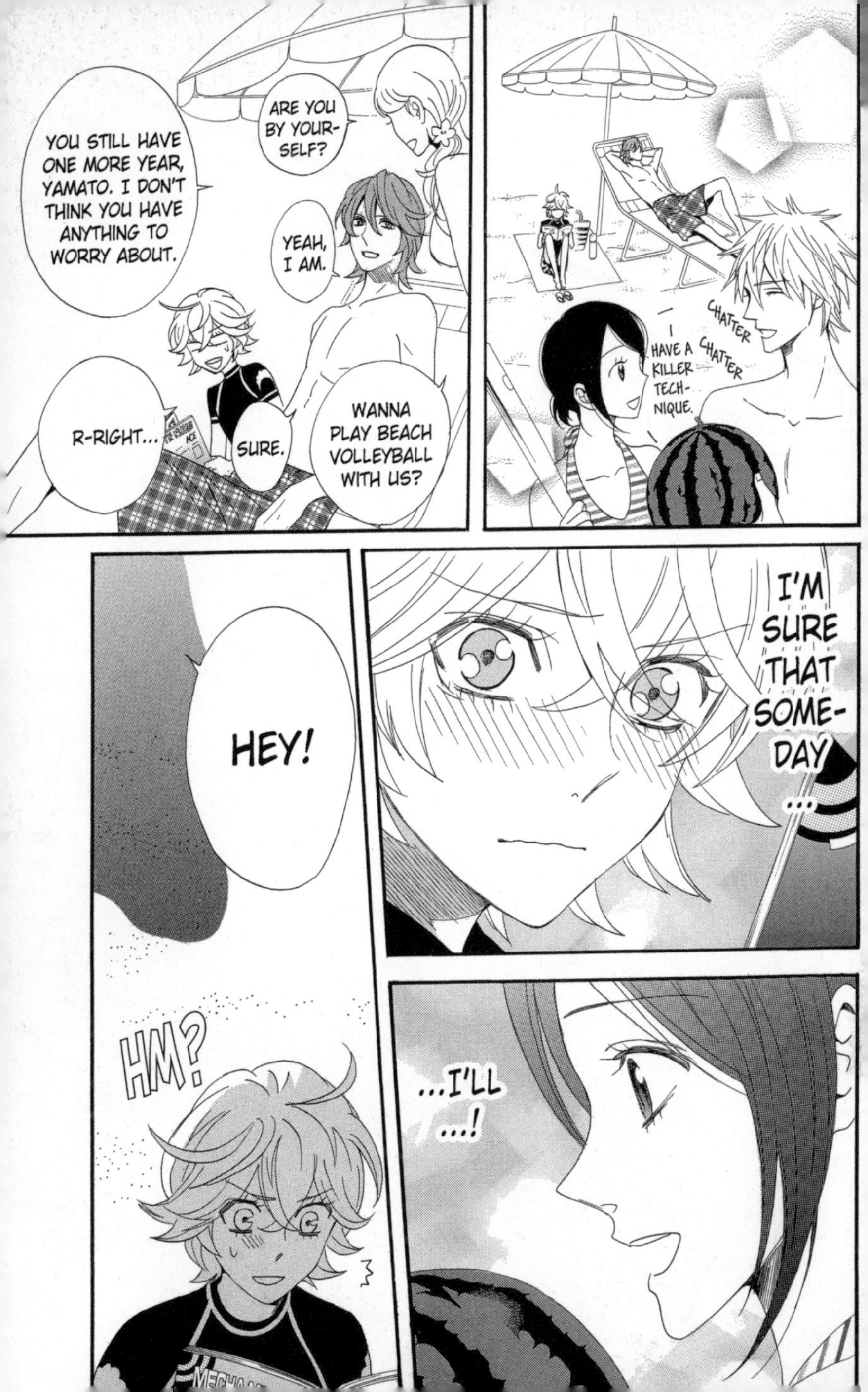
CHATTER CHATTER
I HAVE A KILLER TECH-NIQUE.
ARE YOU BY YOUR-SELF?
YEAH, I AM.
WANNA PLAY BEACH VOLLEYBALL WITH US?
SURE.
YOU STILL HAVE ONE MORE YEAR, YAMATO. I DON'T THINK YOU HAVE ANYTHING TO WORRY ABOUT.
R-RIGHT...
I'M SURE THAT SOME-DAY...
...I'LL ...!
HEY!
HM?

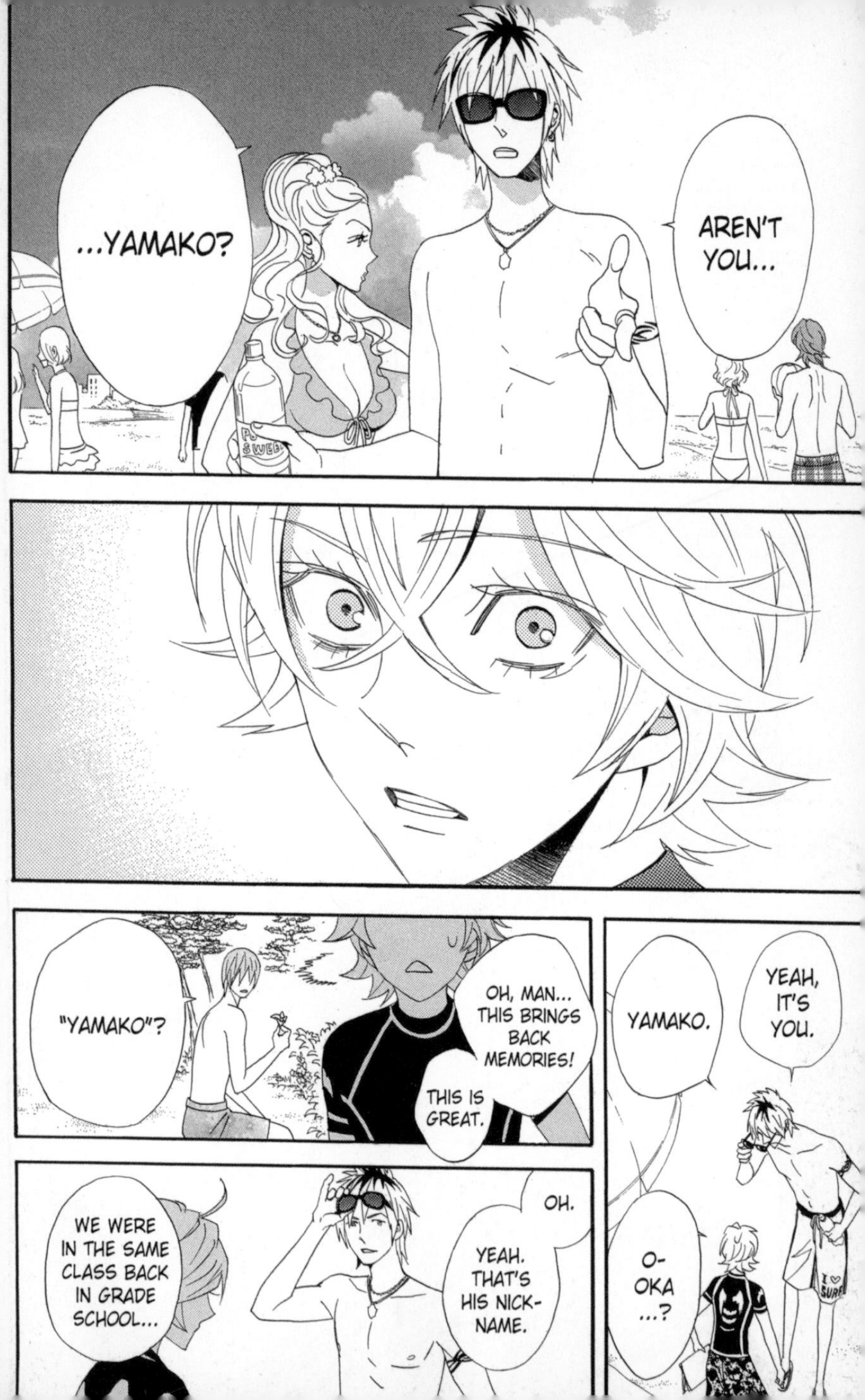
AREN'T YOU...
...YAMAKO?
YEAH, IT'S YOU.
YAMAKO.
O-OKA...?
OH, MAN... THIS BRINGS BACK MEMORIES!
THIS IS GREAT.
"YAMAKO"?
OH.
YEAH. THAT'S HIS NICK-NAME.
WE WERE IN THE SAME CLASS BACK IN GRADE SCHOOL...

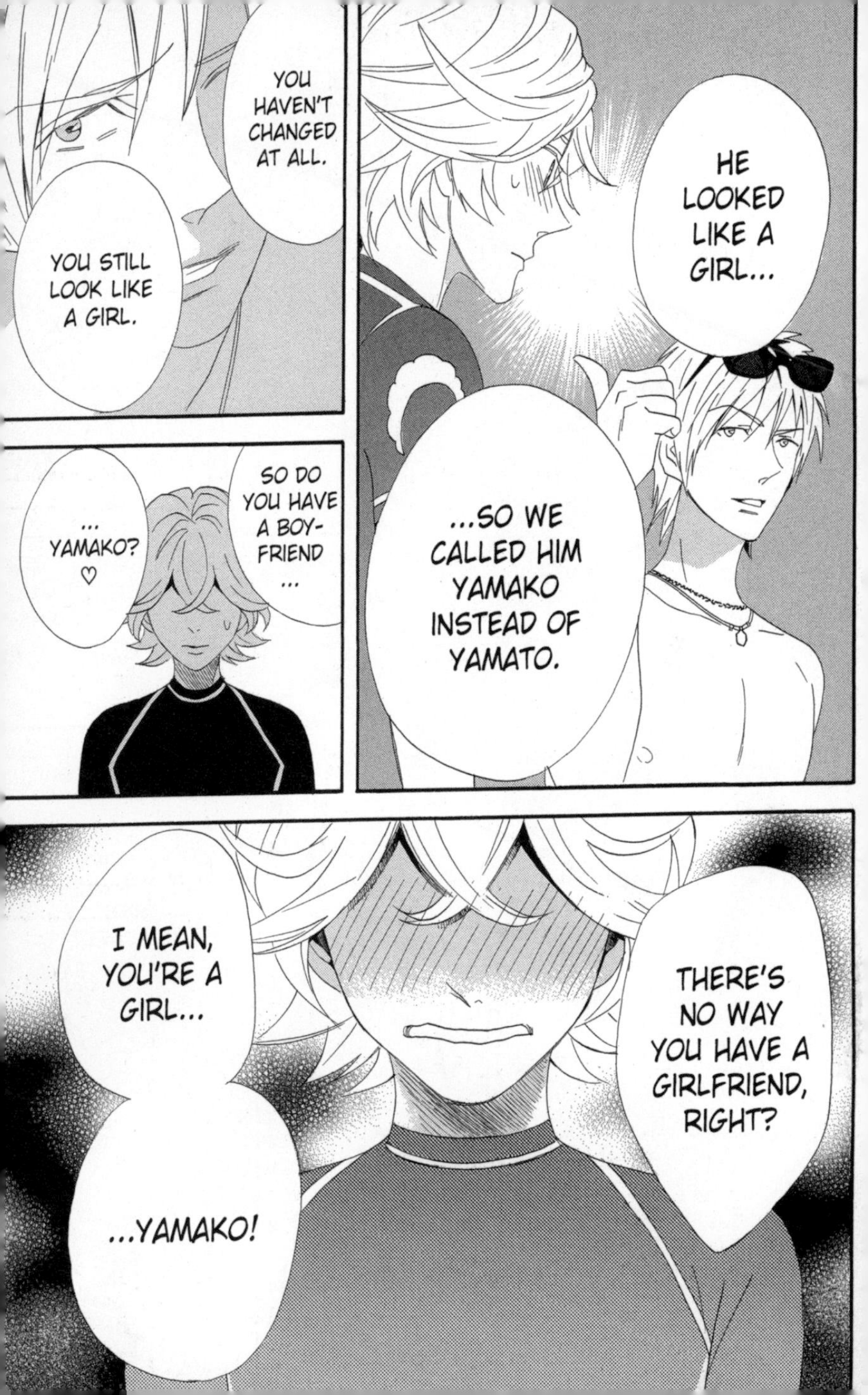
HE LOOKED LIKE A GIRL...
...SO WE CALLED HIM YAMAKO INSTEAD OF YAMATO.
YOU HAVEN'T CHANGED AT ALL.
YOU STILL LOOK LIKE A GIRL.
SO DO YOU HAVE A BOY-FRIEND...
...YAMAKO? ♡
THERE'S NO WAY YOU HAVE A GIRLFRIEND, RIGHT?
I MEAN, YOU'RE A GIRL...
...YAMAKO!

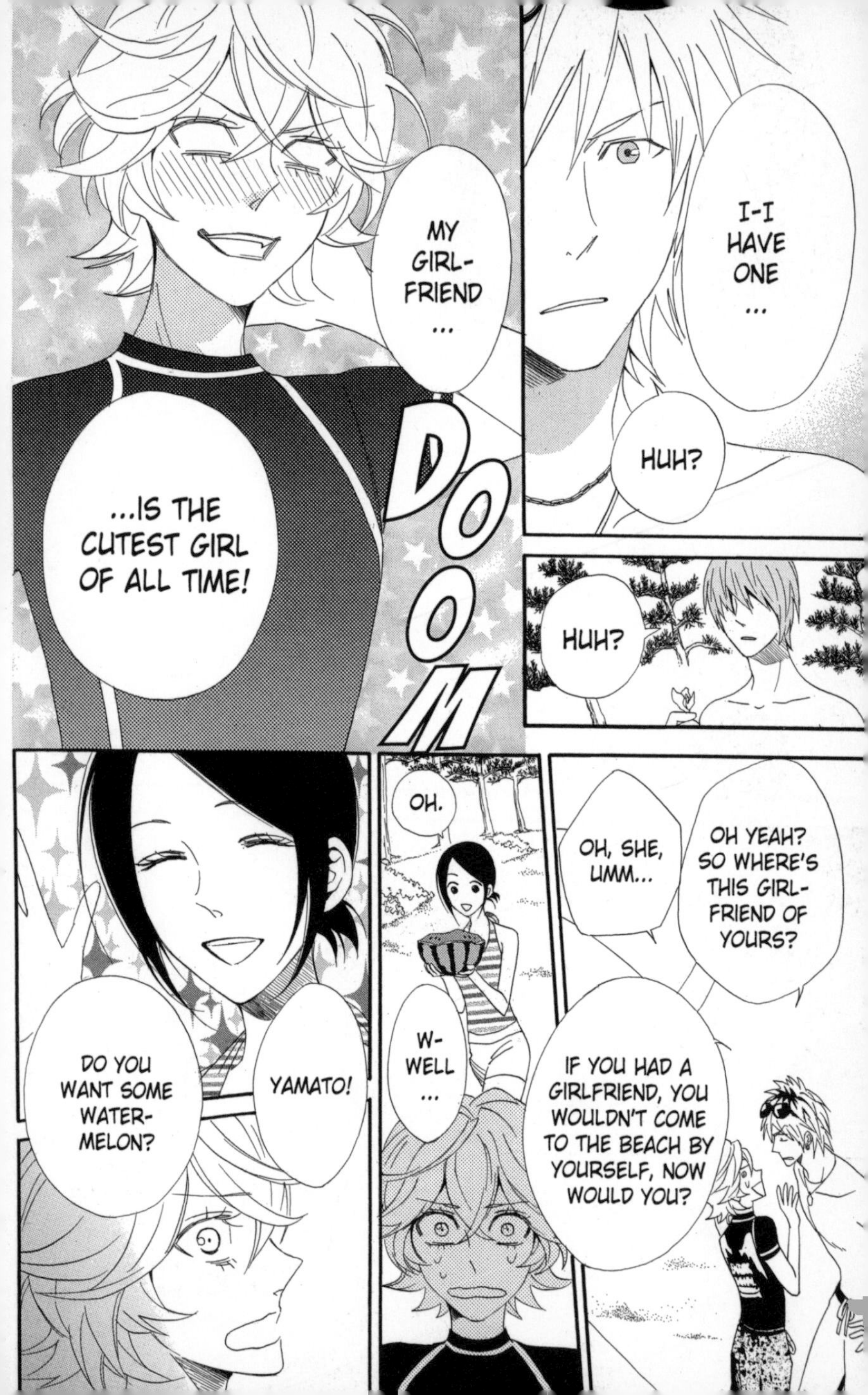
I-I HAVE ONE...
HUH?
HUH?
MY GIRL-FRIEND...
...IS THE CUTEST GIRL OF ALL TIME!
DOOOM
OH YEAH? SO WHERE'S THIS GIRL-FRIEND OF YOURS?
OH, SHE, UMM...
IF YOU HAD A GIRLFRIEND, YOU WOULDN'T COME TO THE BEACH BY YOURSELF, NOW WOULD YOU?
OH.
W-WELL...
YAMATO!
DO YOU WANT SOME WATER-MELON?

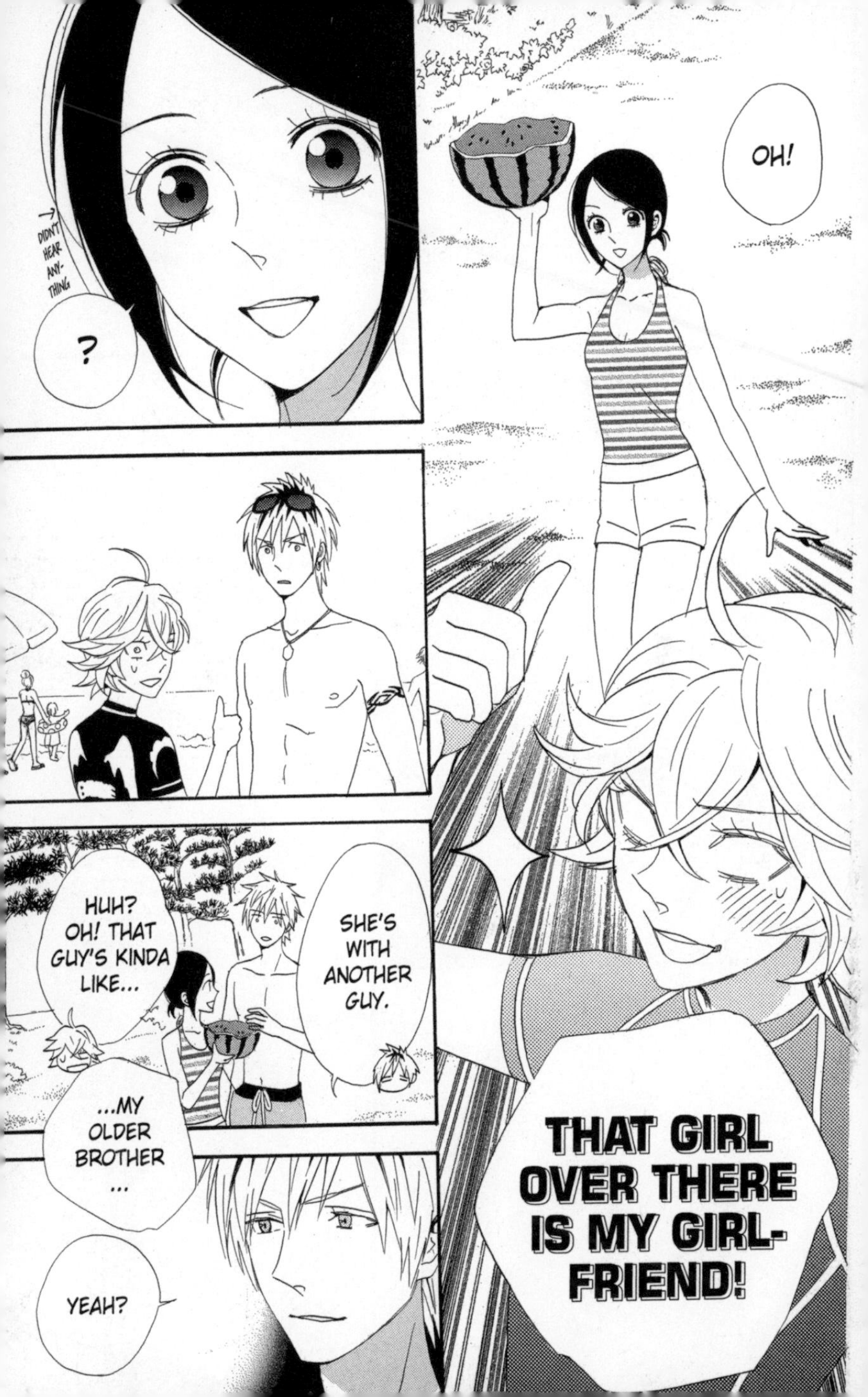
OH!
THAT GIRL OVER THERE IS MY GIRL-FRIEND!
DIDN'T HEAR ANY-THING
?
SHE'S WITH ANOTHER GUY.
HUH? OH! THAT GUY'S KINDA LIKE...
...MY OLDER BROTHER ...
YEAH?

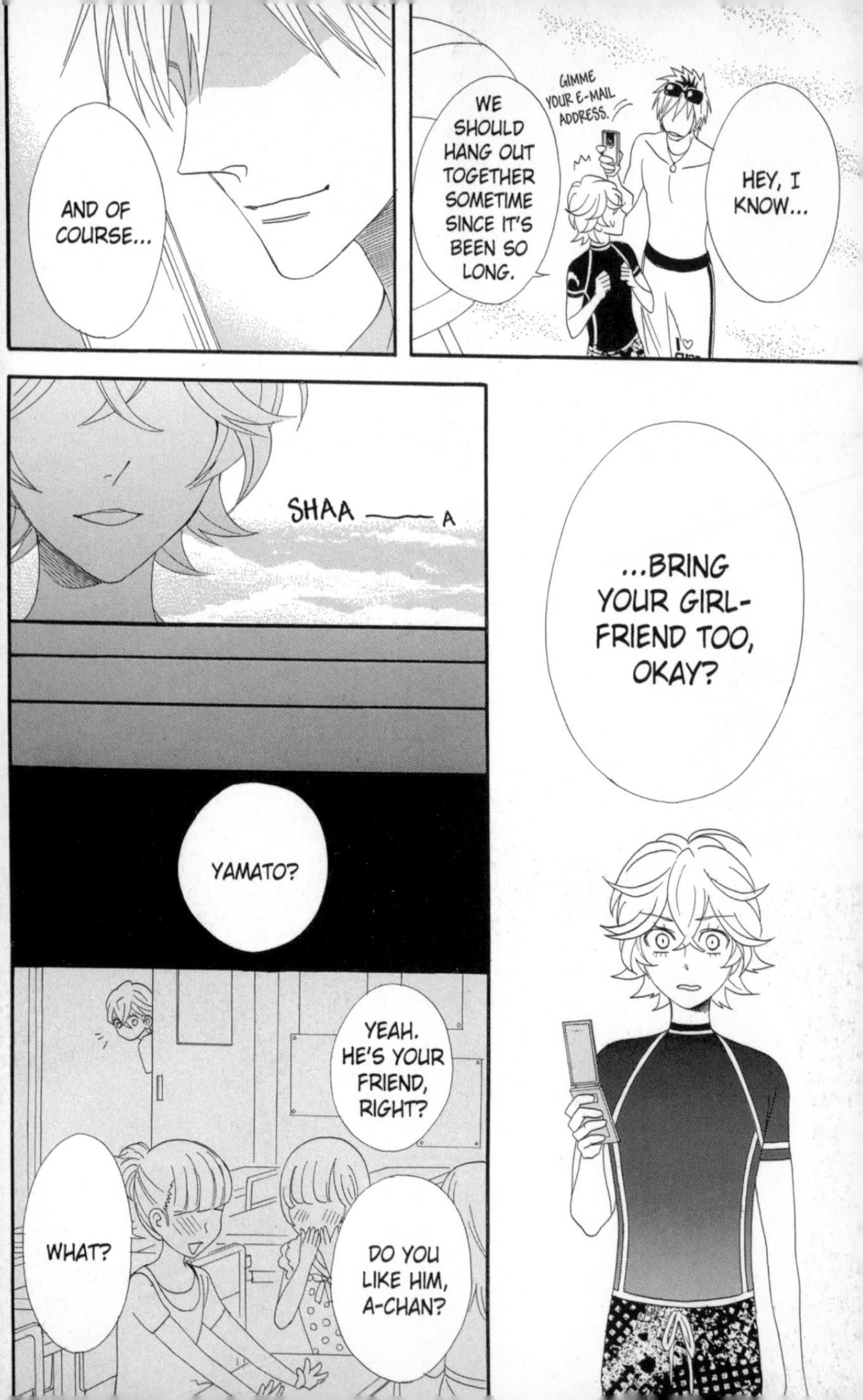
HEY, I KNOW...
GIMME YOUR E-MAIL ADDRESS.
WE SHOULD HANG OUT TOGETHER SOMETIME SINCE IT'S BEEN SO LONG.
AND OF COURSE...
...BRING YOUR GIRL-FRIEND TOO, OKAY?
SHAA——A
YAMATO?
YEAH. HE'S YOUR FRIEND, RIGHT?
DO YOU LIKE HIM, A-CHAN?
WHAT?

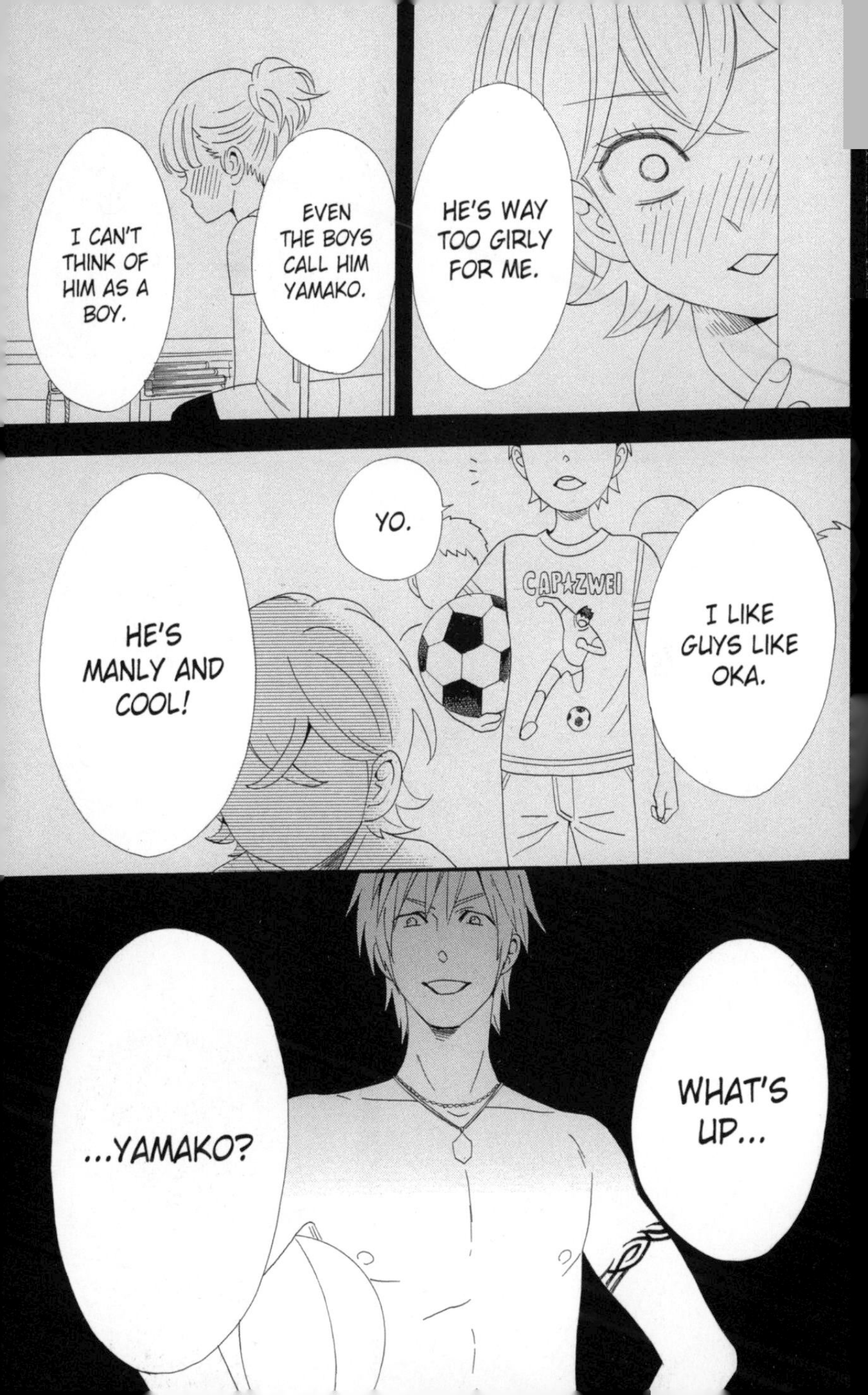
HE'S WAY TOO GIRLY FOR ME.
EVEN THE BOYS CALL HIM YAMAKO.
I CAN'T THINK OF HIM AS A BOY.
I LIKE GUYS LIKE OKA.
YO.
CAP☆ZWEI
HE'S MANLY AND COOL!
WHAT'S UP...
...YAMAKO?

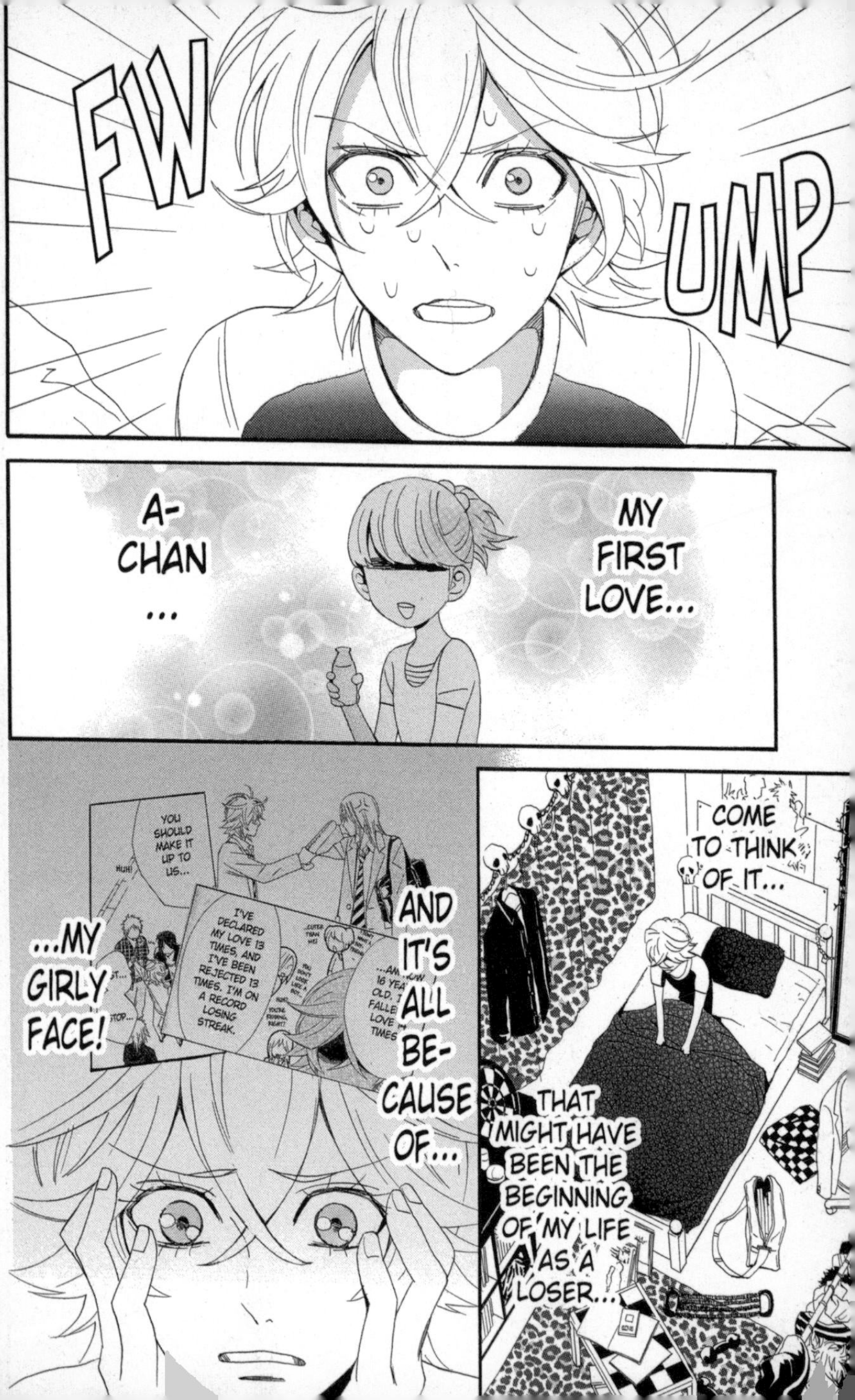
FWUMP
MY FIRST LOVE...
A-CHAN...
COME TO THINK OF IT...
THAT MIGHT HAVE BEEN THE BEGINNING OF MY LIFE AS A LOSER...
YOU SHOULD MAKE IT UP TO US...
HUH!
I'VE DECLARED MY LOVE 13 TIMES, AND I'VE BEEN REJECTED 13 TIMES. I'M ON A RECORD LOSING STREAK.
AND IT'S ALL BE-CAUSE OF...
...MY GIRLY FACE!

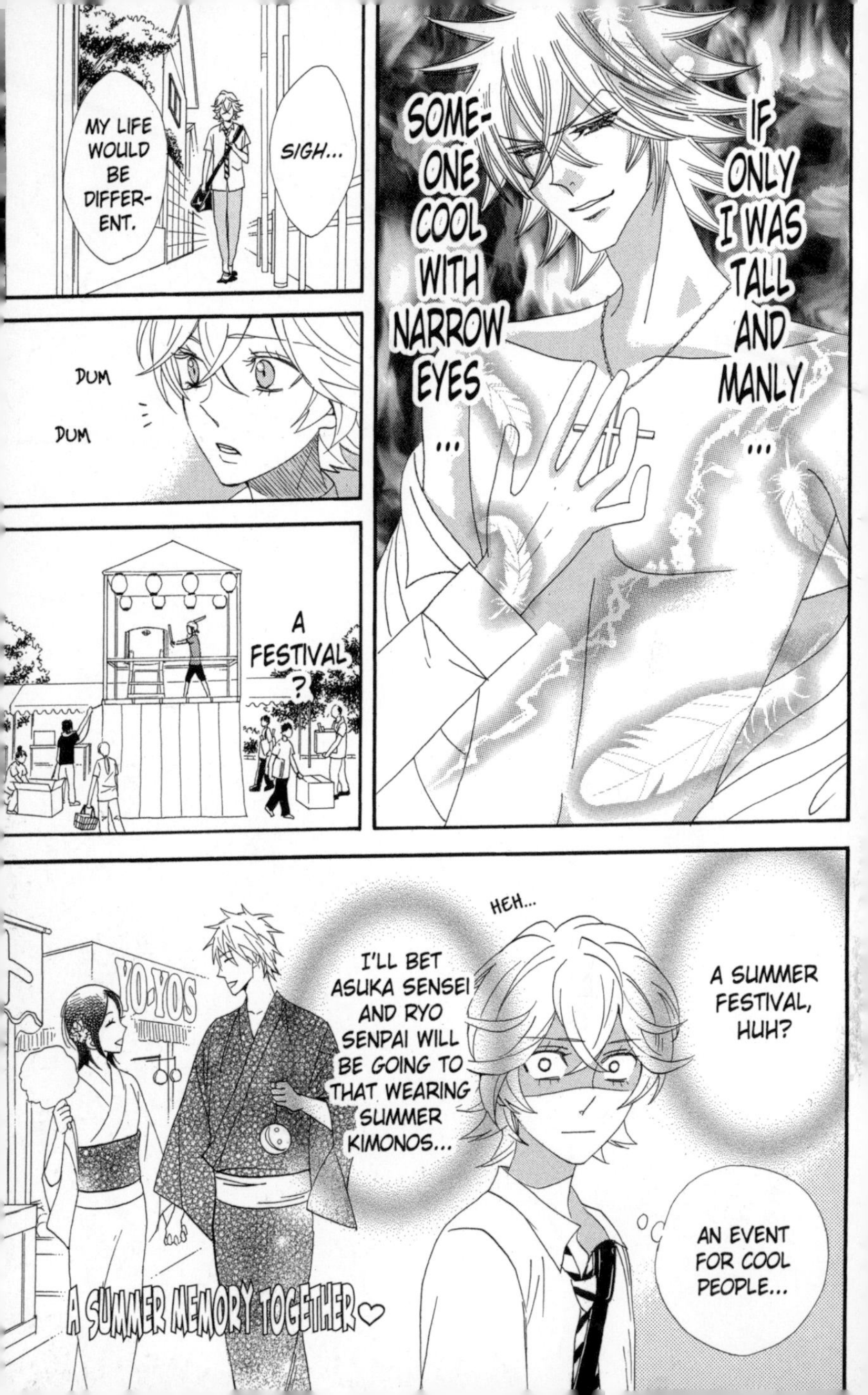
IF ONLY I WAS TALL AND MANLY...
SOME-ONE COOL WITH NARROW EYES...
SIGH...
MY LIFE WOULD BE DIFFER-ENT.
DUM
DUM
A FESTIVAL?
HEH...
A SUMMER FESTIVAL, HUH?
I'LL BET ASUKA SENSEI AND RYO SENPAI WILL BE GOING TO THAT WEARING SUMMER KIMONOS...
AN EVENT FOR COOL PEOPLE...
YO-YOS
A SUMMER MEMORY TOGETHER♡

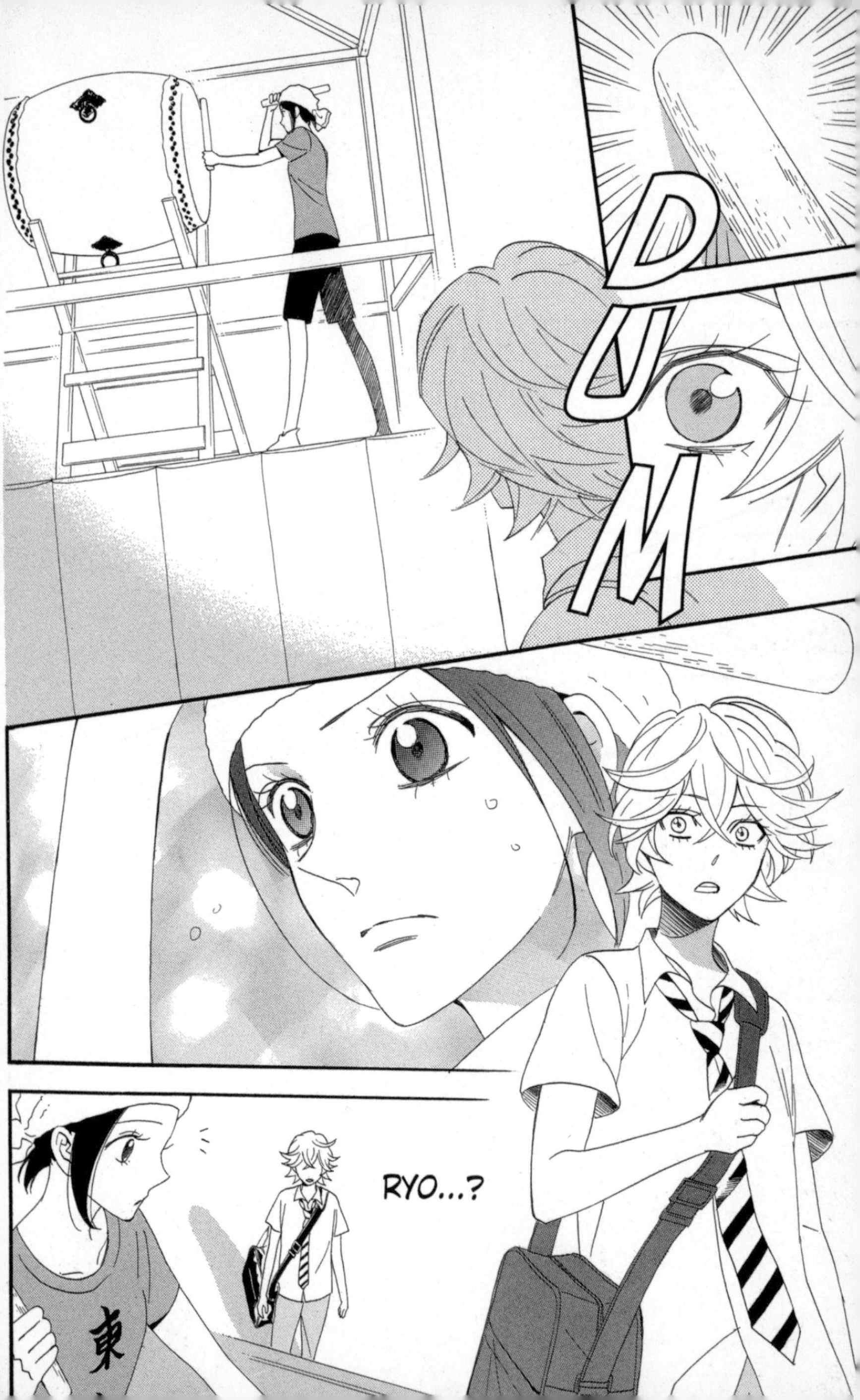
DUM
RYO...?

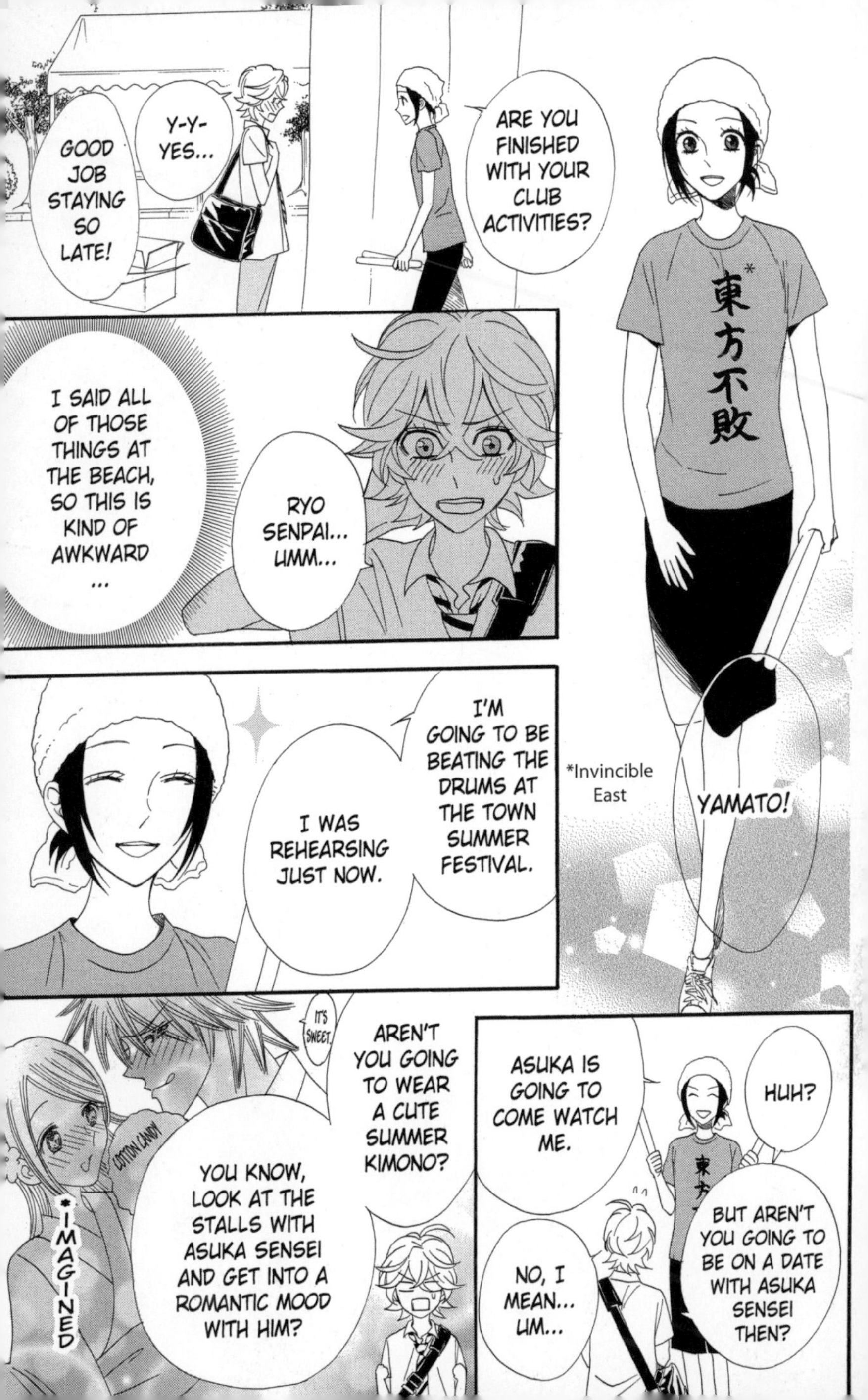
東方不敗*
*Invincible East
YAMATO!
ARE YOU FINISHED WITH YOUR CLUB ACTIVITIES?
Y-Y-YES...
GOOD JOB STAYING SO LATE!
RYO SENPAI... UMM...
I SAID ALL OF THOSE THINGS AT THE BEACH, SO THIS IS KIND OF AWKWARD...
I'M GOING TO BE BEATING THE DRUMS AT THE TOWN SUMMER FESTIVAL.
I WAS REHEARSING JUST NOW.
HUH?
ASUKA IS GOING TO COME WATCH ME.
BUT AREN'T YOU GOING TO BE ON A DATE WITH ASUKA SENSEI THEN?
NO, I MEAN... UM...
AREN'T YOU GOING TO WEAR A CUTE SUMMER KIMONO?
IT'S SWEET.
YOU KNOW, LOOK AT THE STALLS WITH ASUKA SENSEI AND GET INTO A ROMANTIC MOOD WITH HIM?
COTTON CANDY
*IMAGINED

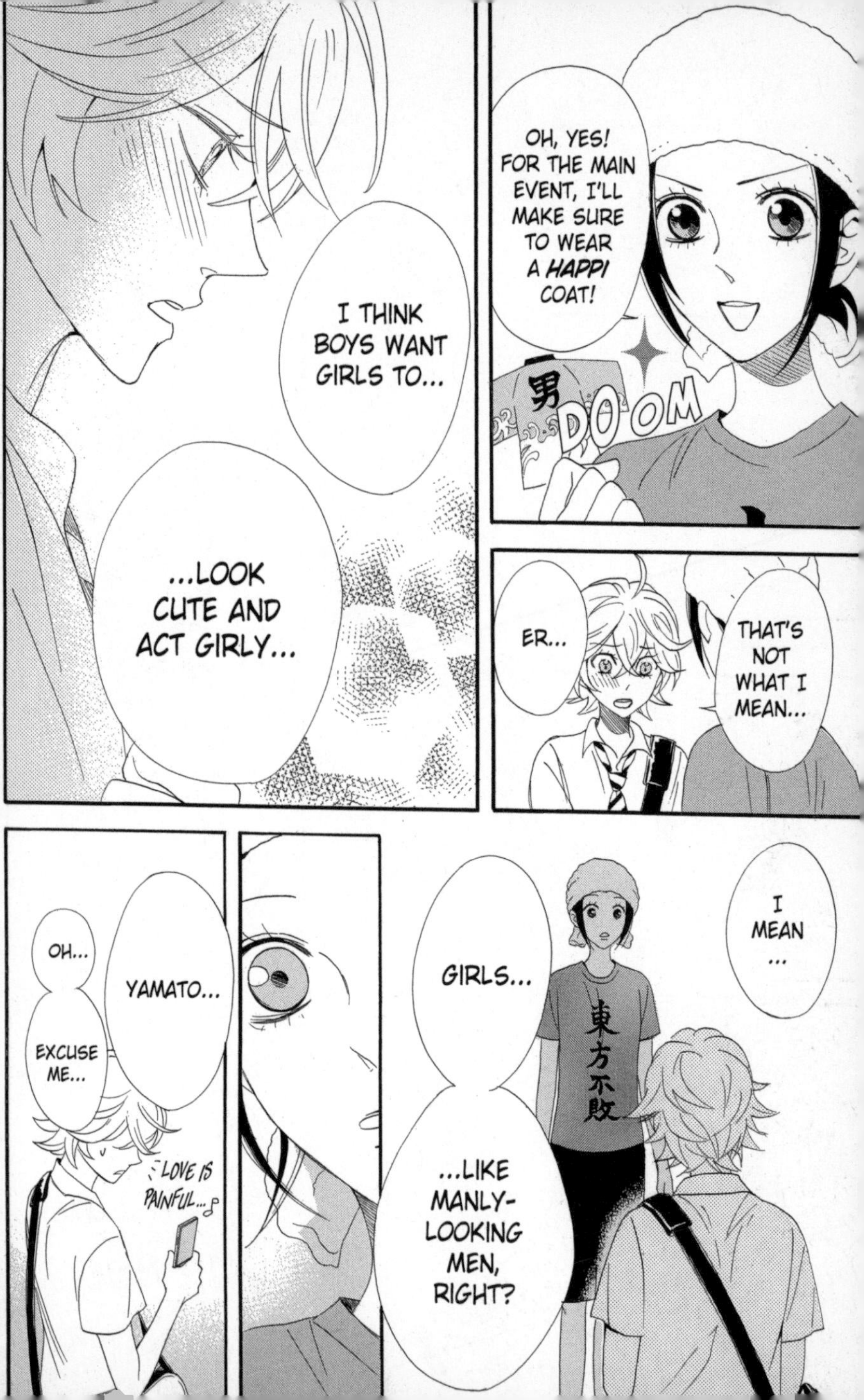
OH, YES! FOR THE MAIN EVENT, I'LL MAKE SURE TO WEAR A *HAPPI* COAT!
男
DOOM
THAT'S NOT WHAT I MEAN...
ER...
I THINK BOYS WANT GIRLS TO...
...LOOK CUTE AND ACT GIRLY...
I MEAN...
GIRLS...
東方不敗
...LIKE MANLY-LOOKING MEN, RIGHT?
YAMATO...
OH...
EXCUSE ME...
LOVE IS PAINFUL...♪

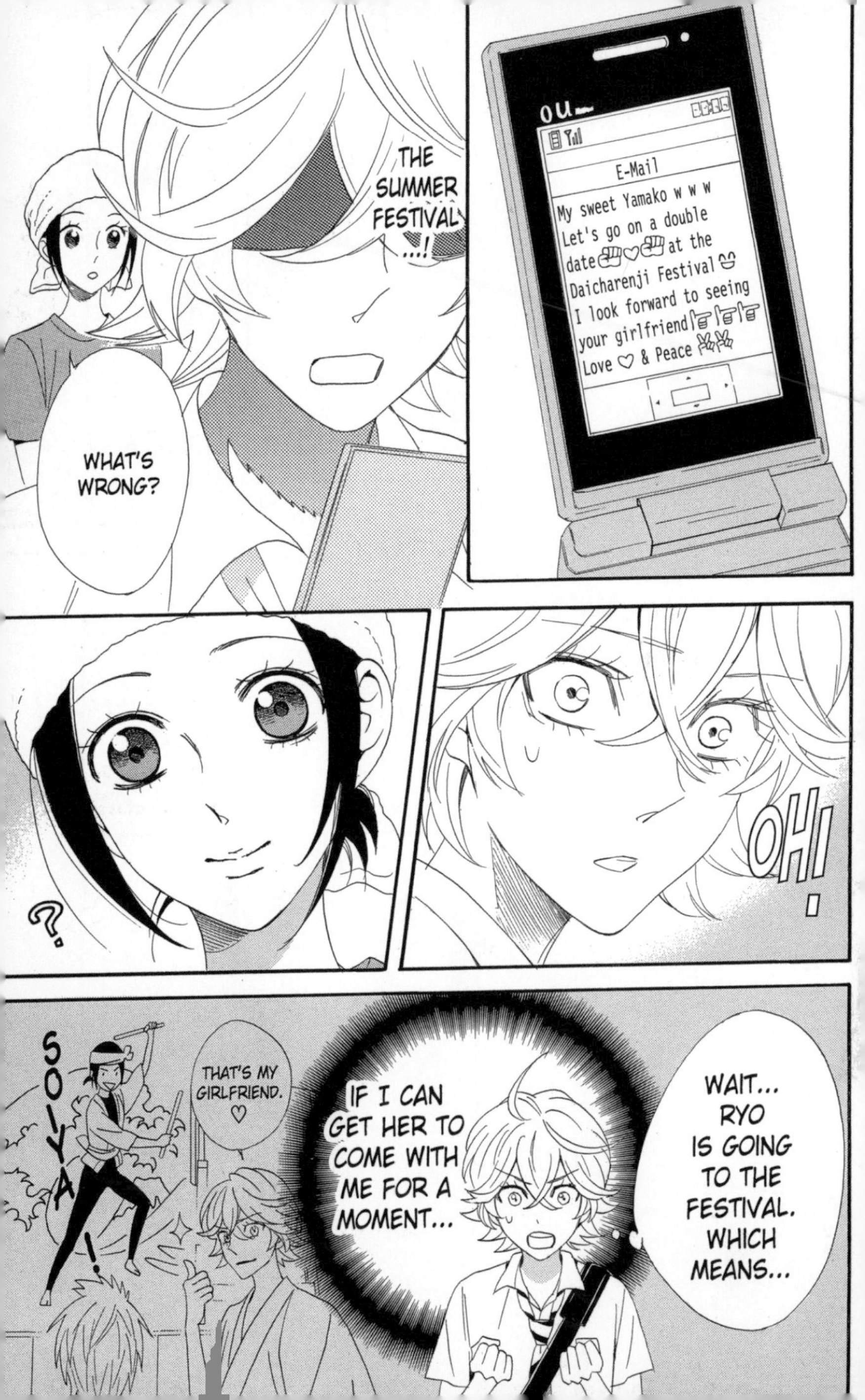
E-Mail
My sweet Yamako w w w
Let's go on a double
date at the
Daicharenji Festival
I look forward to seeing
your girlfriend
Love ♡ & Peace
THE SUMMER FESTIVAL...!
WHAT'S WRONG?
OH!
?
WAIT... RYO IS GOING TO THE FESTIVAL. WHICH MEANS...
IF I CAN GET HER TO COME WITH ME FOR A MOMENT...
THAT'S MY GIRLFRIEND. ♡
SOIYA!

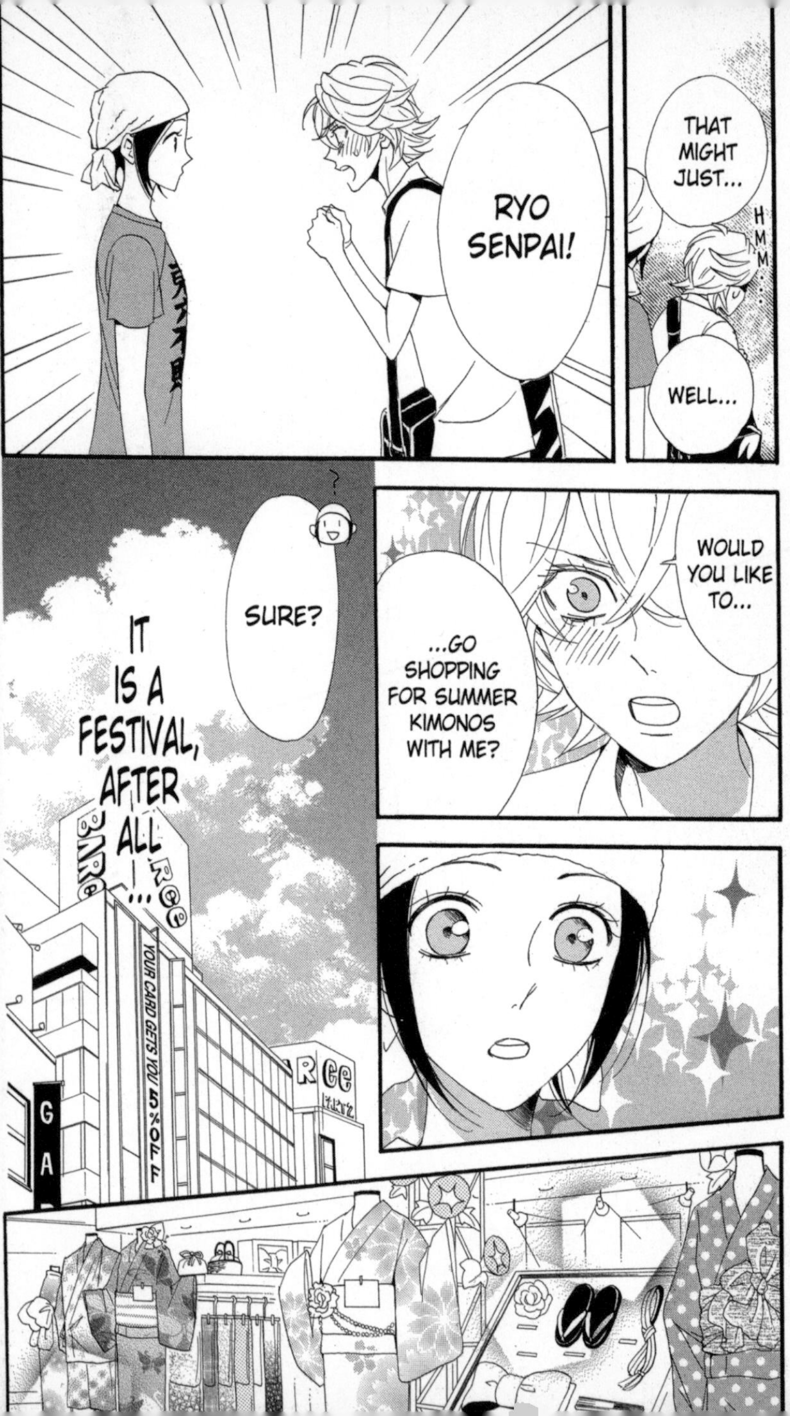
THAT MIGHT JUST...
HMM...
WELL...
RYO SENPAI!
WOULD YOU LIKE TO...
...GO SHOPPING FOR SUMMER KIMONOS WITH ME?
SURE?
IT IS A FESTIVAL, AFTER ALL...!
YOUR CARD GETS YOU 5% OFF

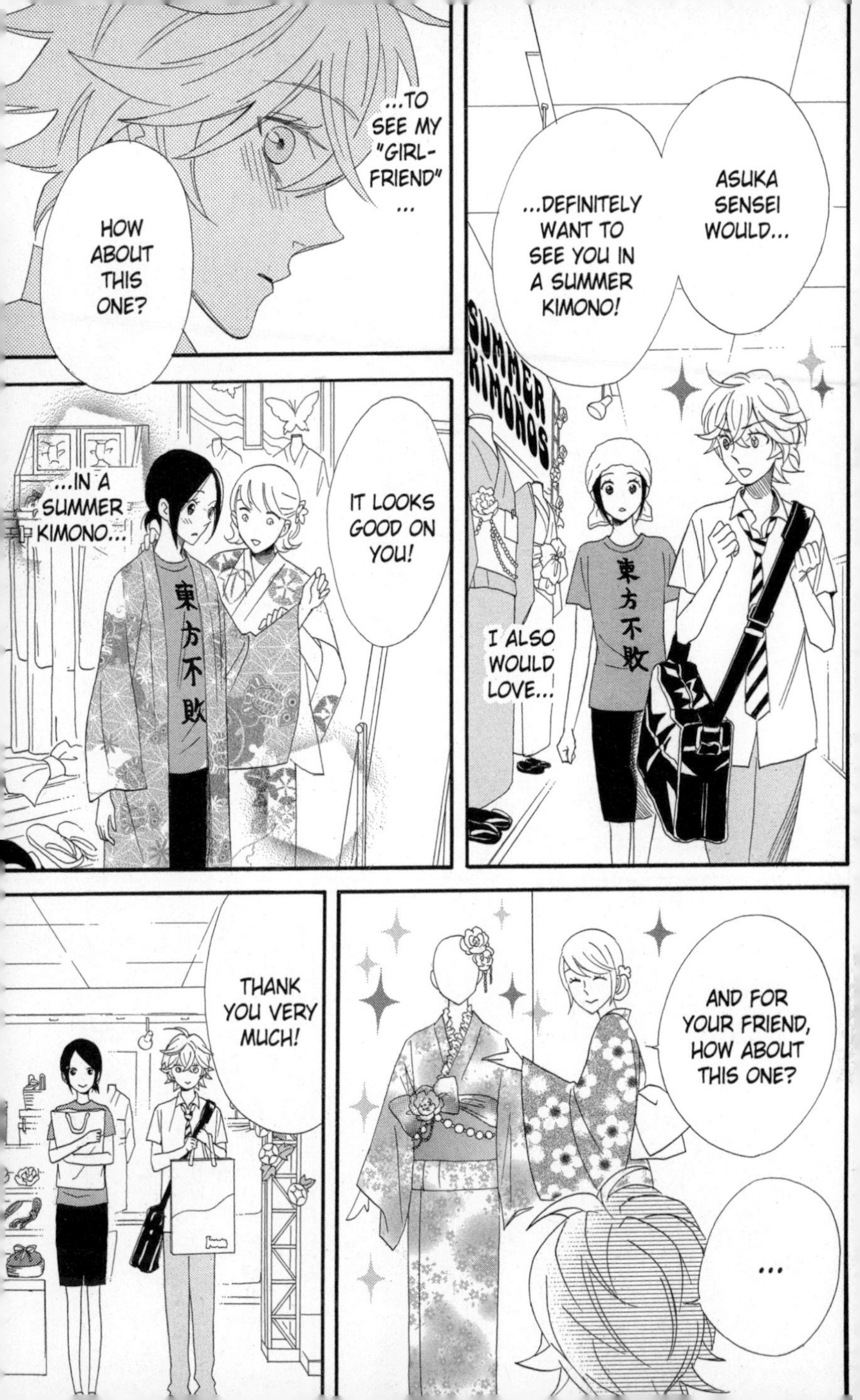
ASUKA SENSEI WOULD...
...DEFINITELY WANT TO SEE YOU IN A SUMMER KIMONO!
SUMMER KIMONOS
I ALSO WOULD LOVE...
...TO SEE MY "GIRL-FRIEND"...
HOW ABOUT THIS ONE?
IT LOOKS GOOD ON YOU!
...IN A SUMMER KIMONO...
AND FOR YOUR FRIEND, HOW ABOUT THIS ONE?
...
THANK YOU VERY MUCH!

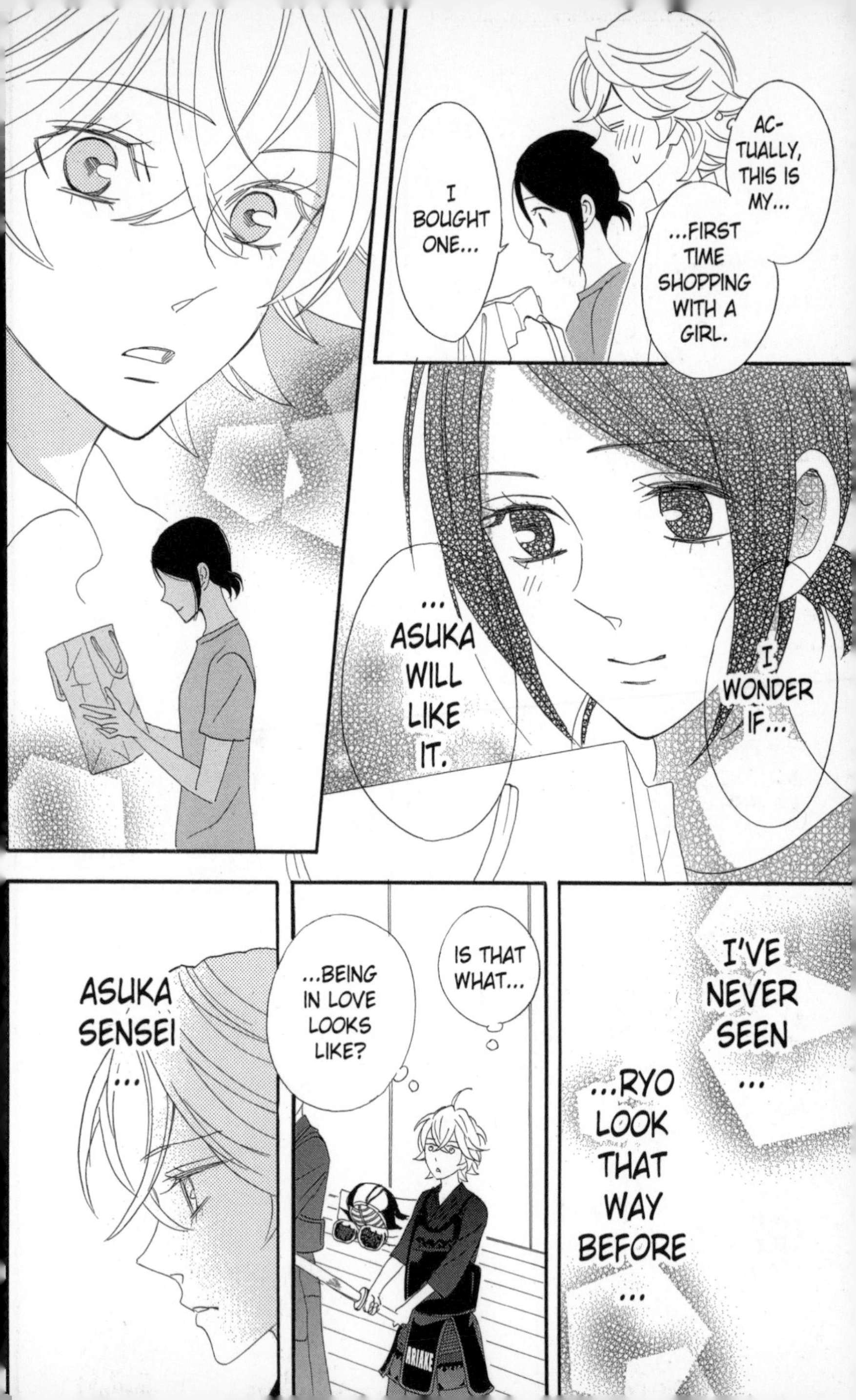
ACTUALLY, THIS IS MY...
...FIRST TIME SHOPPING WITH A GIRL.
I BOUGHT ONE...
I WONDER IF...
...ASUKA WILL LIKE IT.
I'VE NEVER SEEN...
...RYO LOOK THAT WAY BEFORE...
IS THAT WHAT...
...BEING IN LOVE LOOKS LIKE?
ASUKA SENSEI...

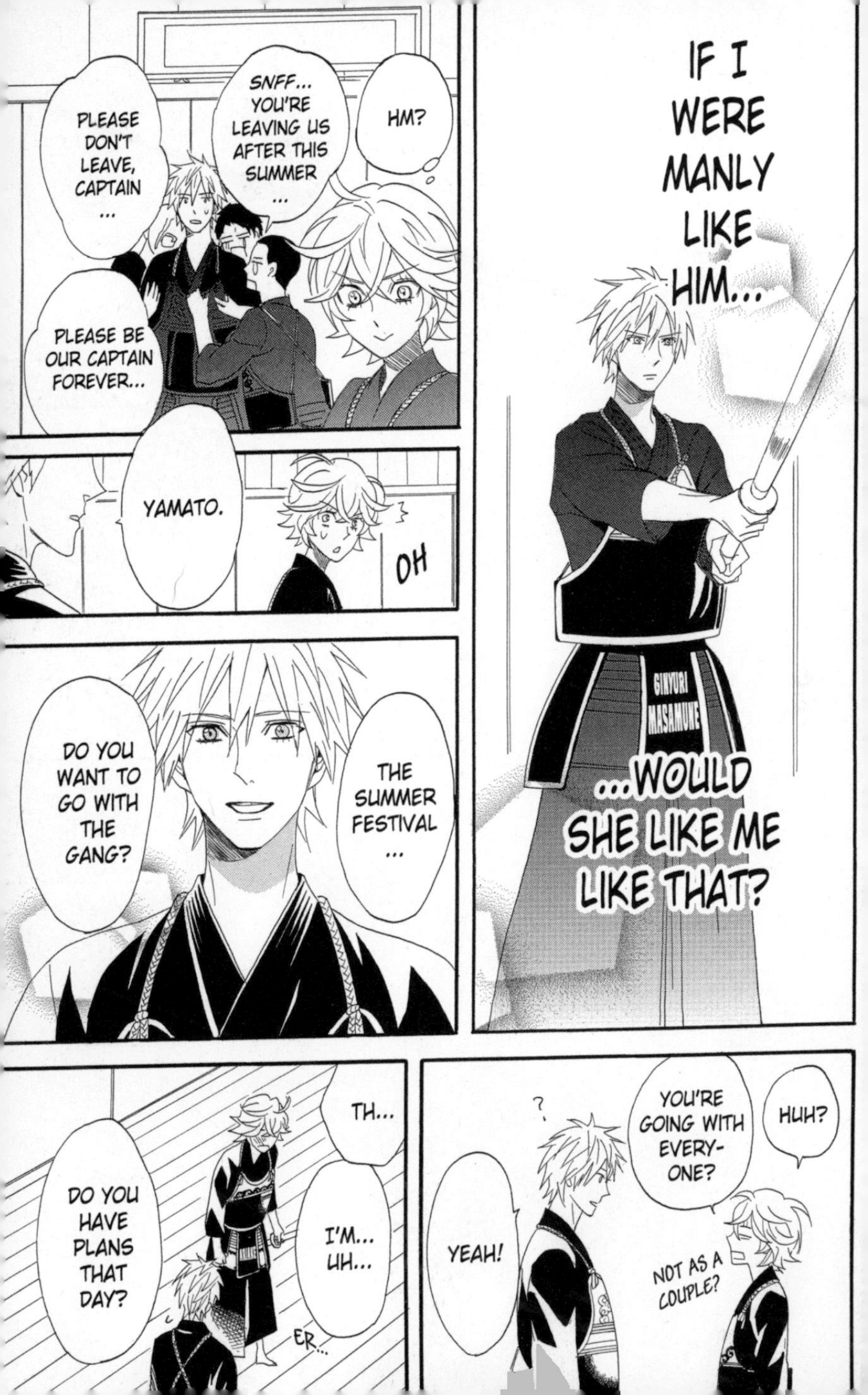
IF I WERE MANLY LIKE HIM...
GINYURI MASAMUNE
...WOULD SHE LIKE ME LIKE THAT?
HM?
SNFF... YOU'RE LEAVING US AFTER THIS SUMMER ...
PLEASE DON'T LEAVE, CAPTAIN ...
PLEASE BE OUR CAPTAIN FOREVER...
OH
YAMATO.
THE SUMMER FESTIVAL ...
DO YOU WANT TO GO WITH THE GANG?
HUH?
YOU'RE GOING WITH EVERY-ONE?
?
YEAH!
NOT AS A COUPLE?
TH...
I'M... UH...
DO YOU HAVE PLANS THAT DAY?
ER...

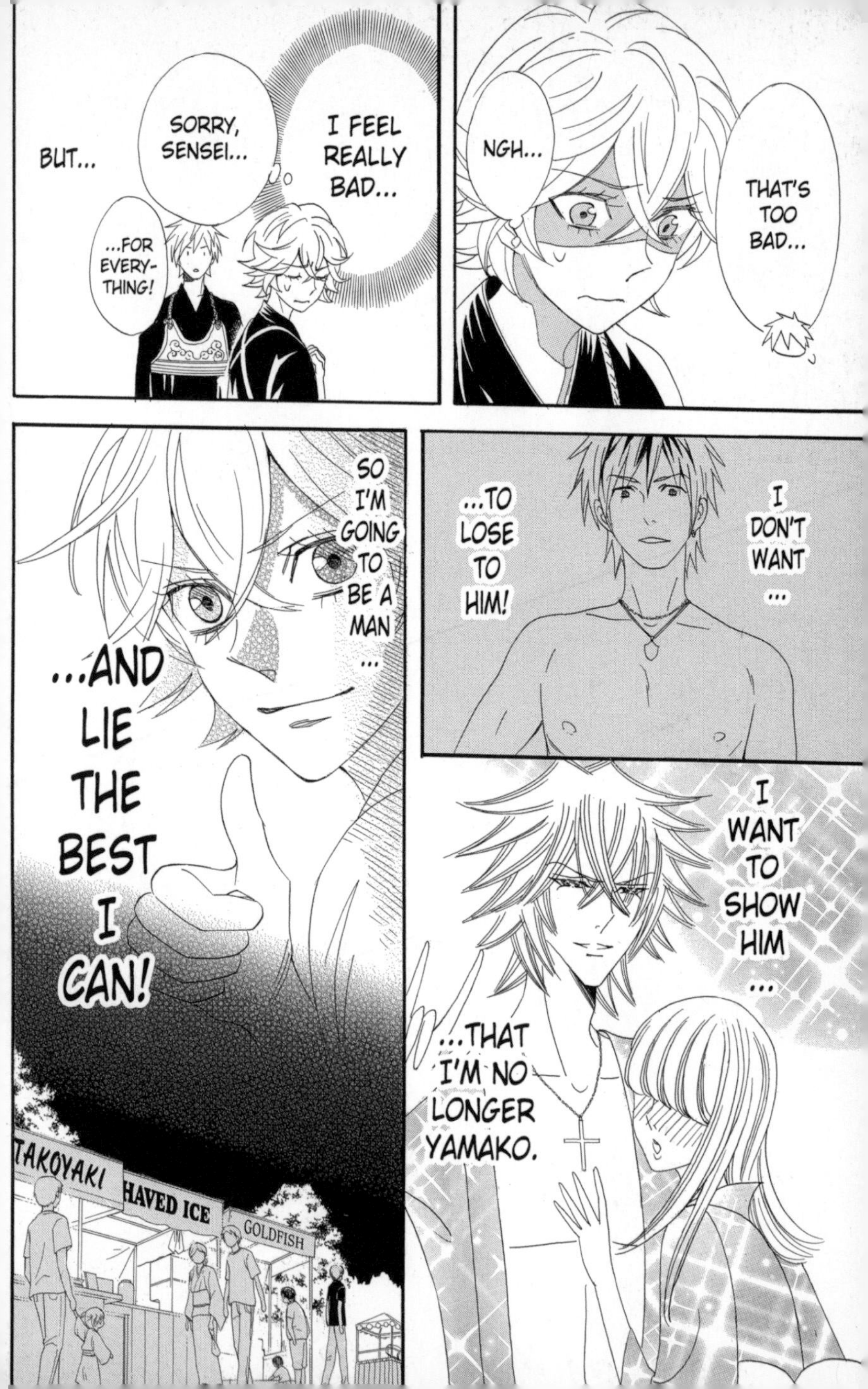
THAT'S TOO BAD...
NGH...
I FEEL REALLY BAD...
SORRY, SENSEI...
...FOR EVERYTHING!
BUT...
I DON'T WANT...
...TO LOSE TO HIM!
I WANT TO SHOW HIM...
...THAT I'M NO LONGER YAMAKO.
SO I'M GOING TO BE A MAN...
...AND LIE THE BEST I CAN!
TAKOYAKI
HAVED ICE
GOLDFISH

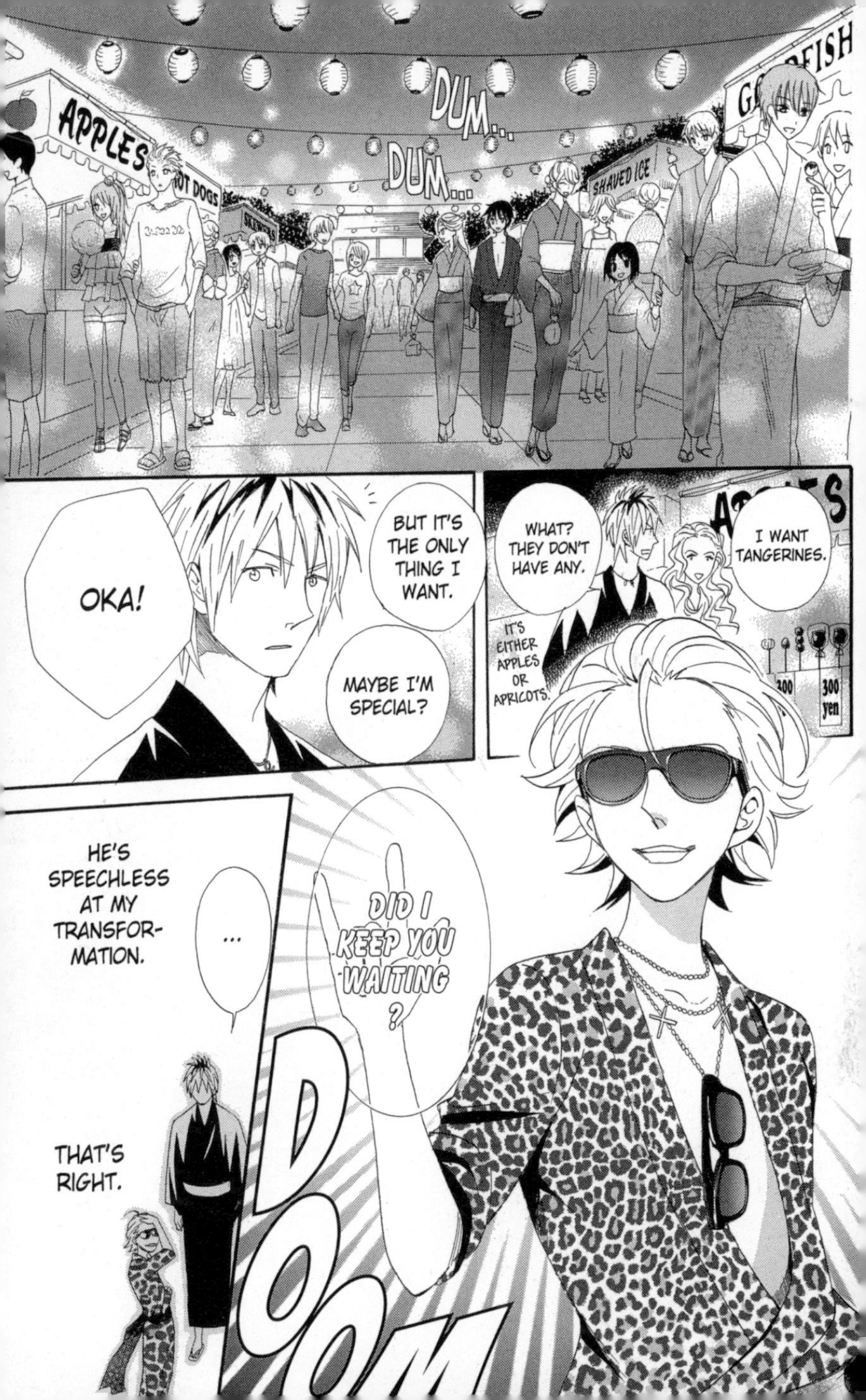
DUM...
DUM...
APPLES
HOT DOGS
SHAVED ICE
I WANT TANGERINES.
WHAT? THEY DON'T HAVE ANY.
IT'S EITHER APPLES OR APRICOTS.
300
300 yen
BUT IT'S THE ONLY THING I WANT.
MAYBE I'M SPECIAL?
OKA!
DID I KEEP YOU WAITING?
DOOOM
...
HE'S SPEECHLESS AT MY TRANSFOR-MATION.
THAT'S RIGHT.

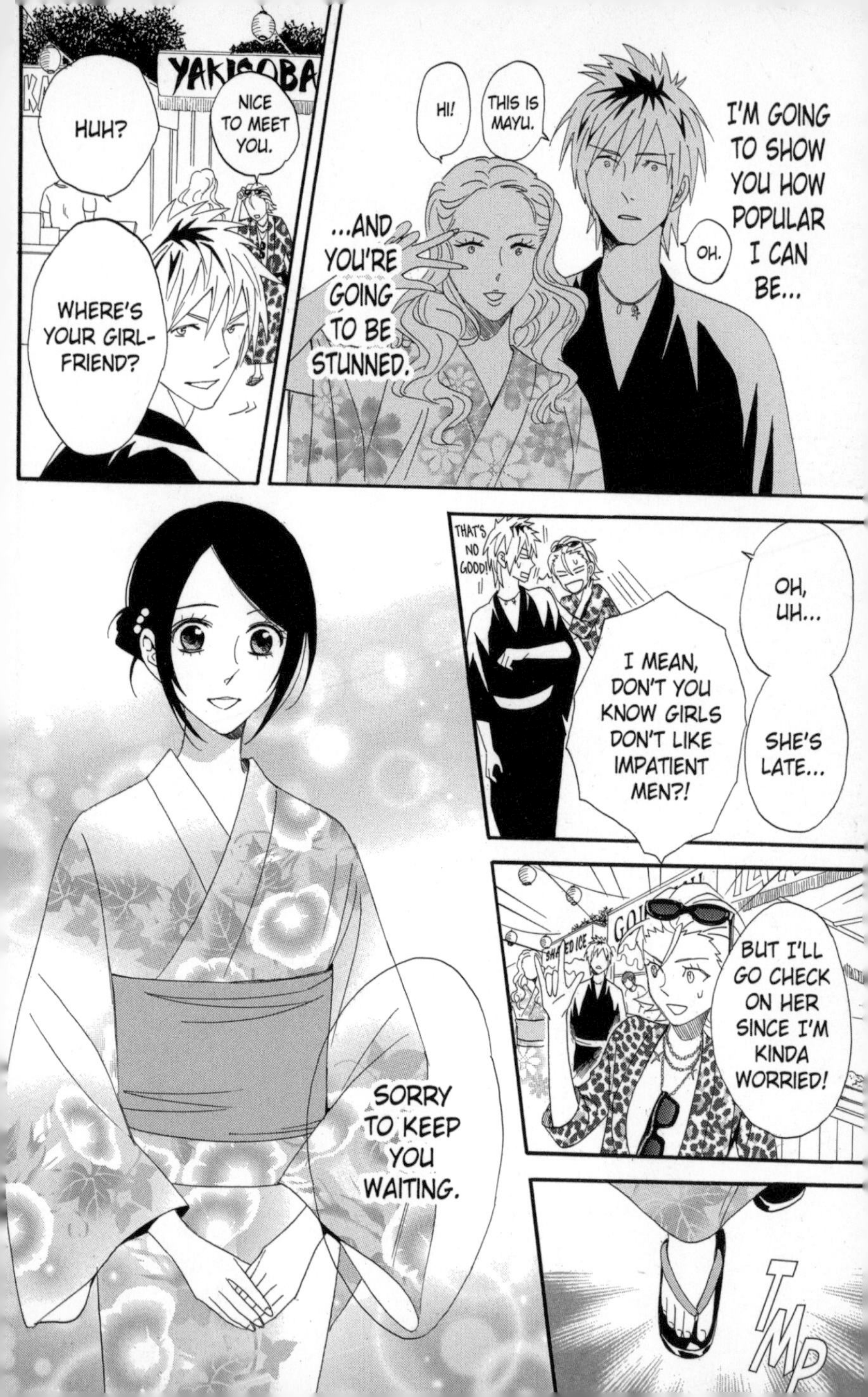
I'M GOING TO SHOW YOU HOW POPULAR I CAN BE...
OH.
THIS IS MAYU.
HI!
...AND YOU'RE GOING TO BE STUNNED.
YAKISOBA
NICE TO MEET YOU.
HUH?
WHERE'S YOUR GIRL-FRIEND?
OH, UH...
SHE'S LATE...
THAT'S NO GOOD!!
I MEAN, DON'T YOU KNOW GIRLS DON'T LIKE IMPATIENT MEN?!
BUT I'LL GO CHECK ON HER SINCE I'M KINDA WORRIED!
TMP
SORRY TO KEEP YOU WAITING.

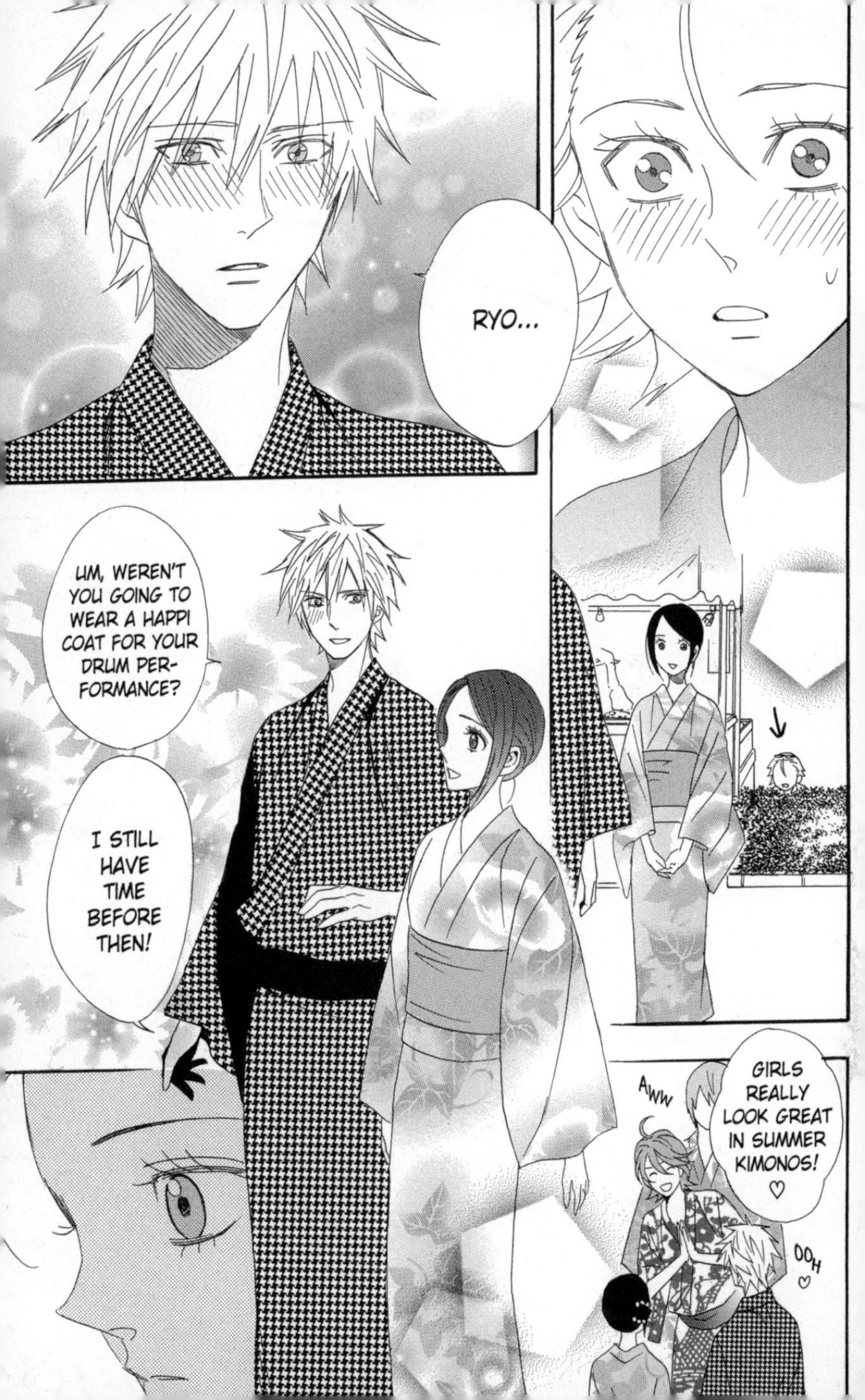
RYO...
UM, WEREN'T YOU GOING TO WEAR A HAPPI COAT FOR YOUR DRUM PER-FORMANCE?
I STILL HAVE TIME BEFORE THEN!
GIRLS REALLY LOOK GREAT IN SUMMER KIMONOS! ♡
AWW
OOH ♡

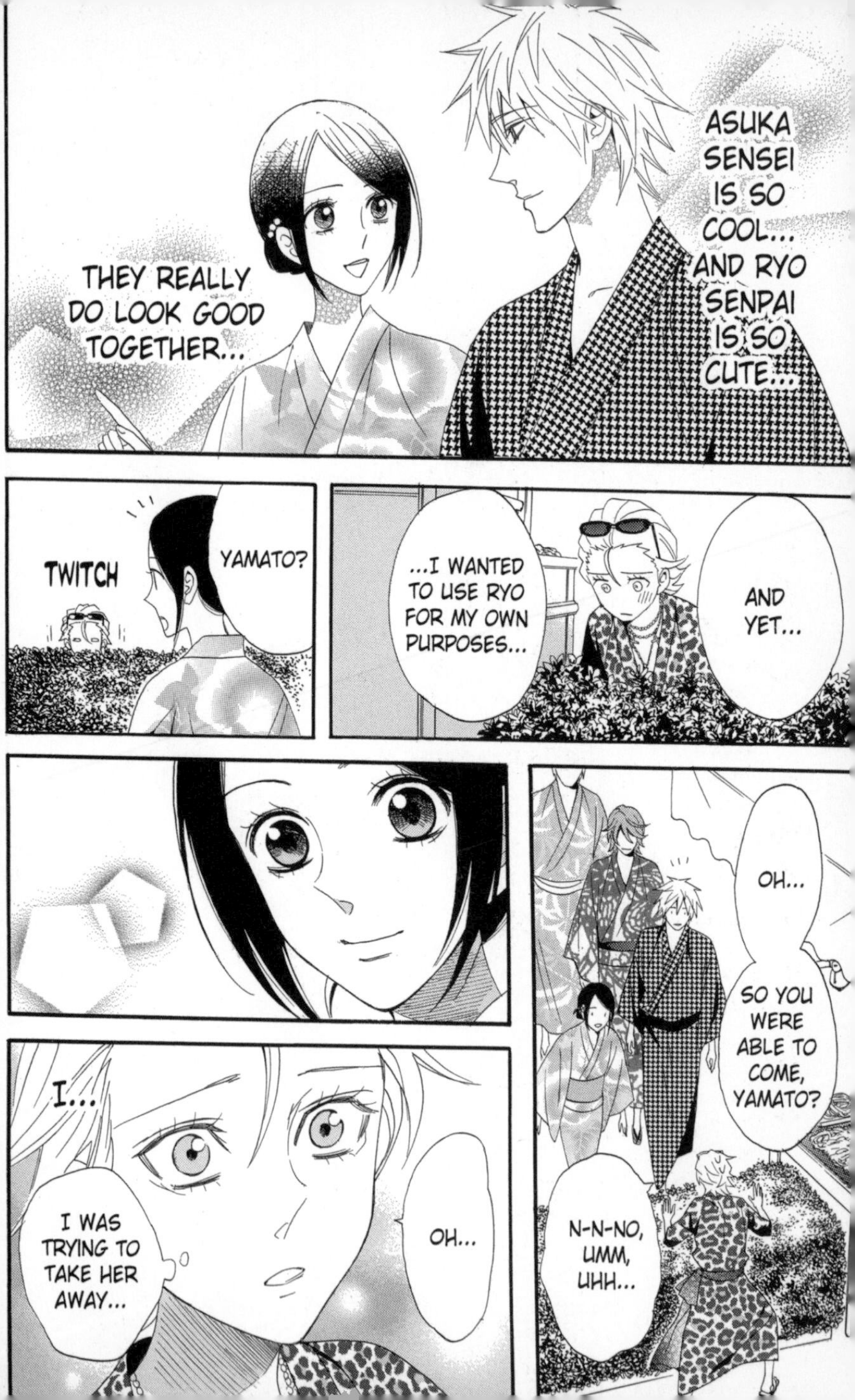

ASUKA SENSEI IS SO COOL... AND RYO SENPAI IS SO CUTE...
THEY REALLY DO LOOK GOOD TOGETHER...
AND YET...
...I WANTED TO USE RYO FOR MY OWN PURPOSES...
YAMATO?
TWITCH
OH...
SO YOU WERE ABLE TO COME, YAMATO?
N-N-NO, UMM, UHH...
OH...
I...
I WAS TRYING TO TAKE HER AWAY...

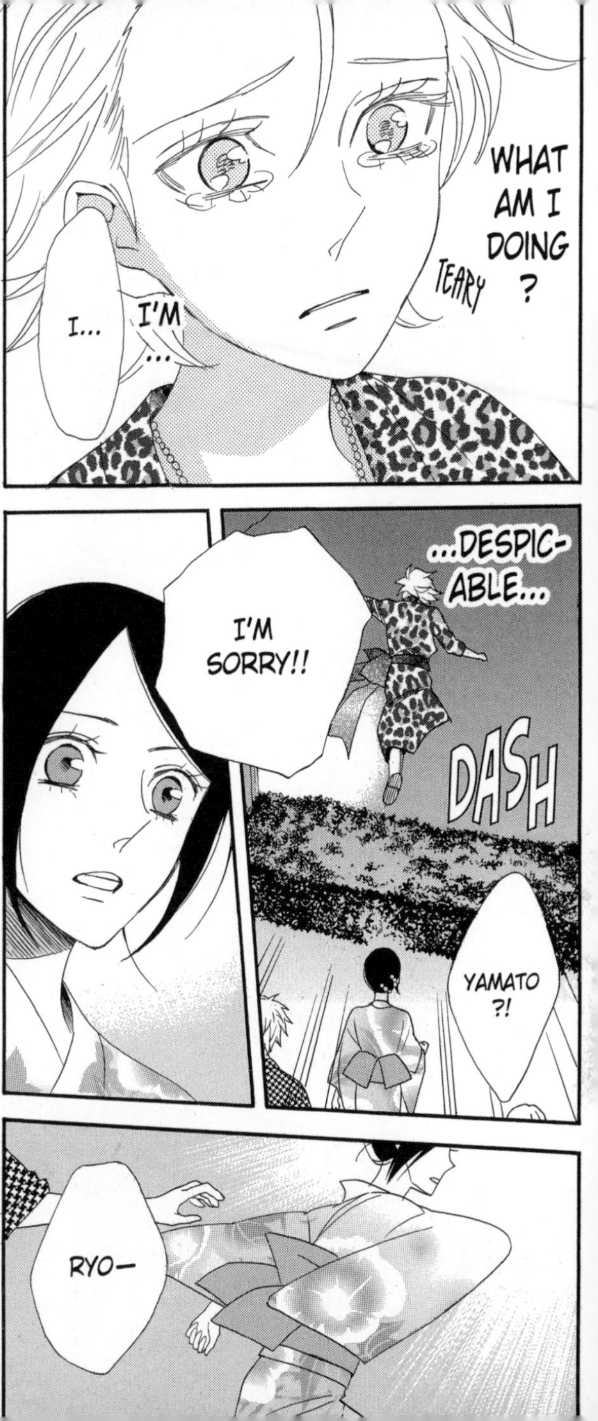
WHAT AM I DOING?
TEARY
I'M...
I...
...DESPICABLE...
I'M SORRY!!
DASH
YAMATO?!
RYO—

The last of the stories that feature a main character is about Yamato.

I really hadn't planned on writing this story at all. Or rather, I hadn't planned on making Yamato the main character of any story... Ha ha.

I was thinking of stories I hadn't had a chance to tell yet, and I felt like making one more story where Yamato was the main character.

I make him excessively cute and treat him very horribly, but I really do love him.

He's a nice guy.

He's annoying, though. Ha ha.

He's a cute kid.

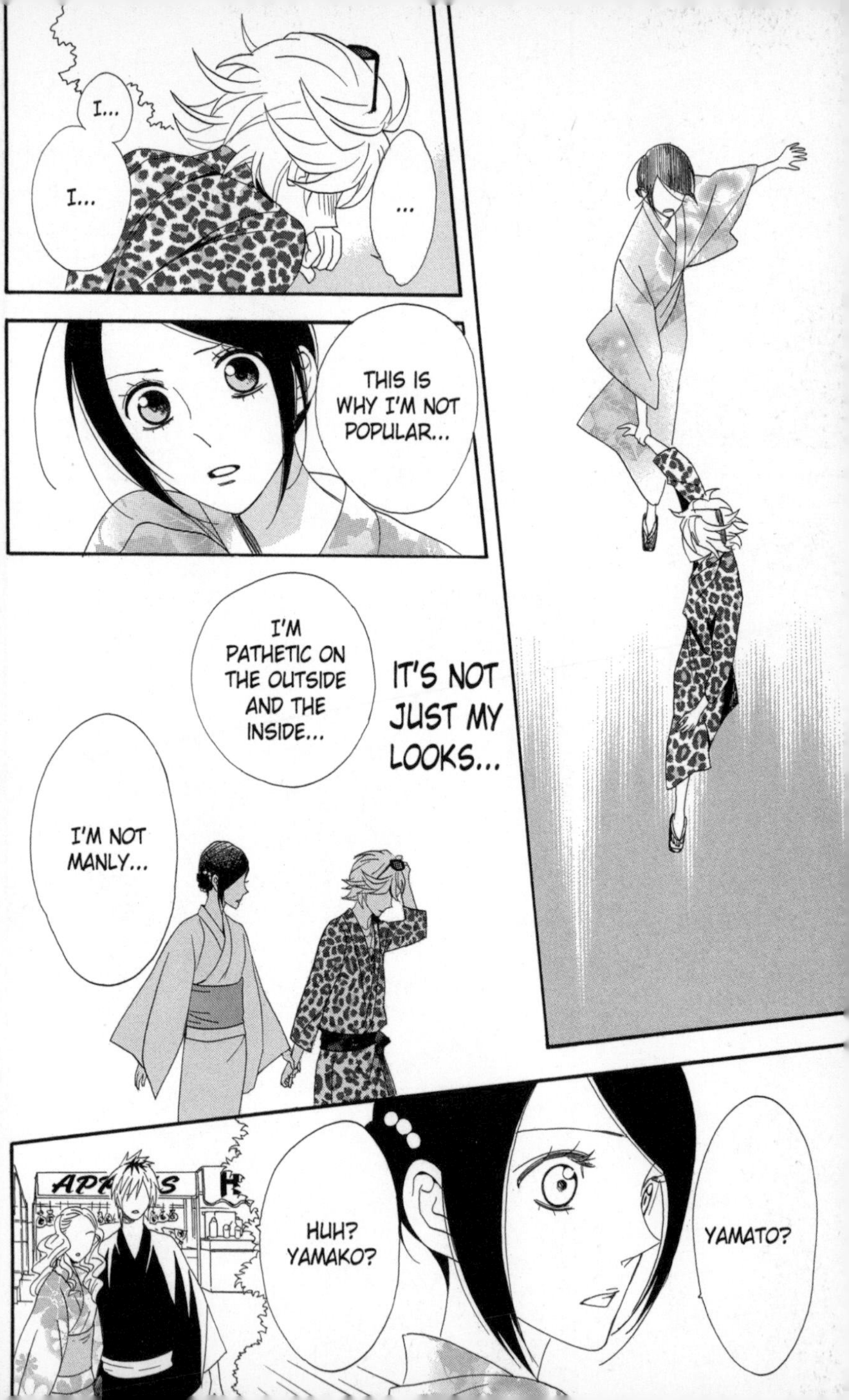
...
I...
I...
THIS IS WHY I'M NOT POPULAR...
IT'S NOT JUST MY LOOKS...
I'M PATHETIC ON THE OUTSIDE AND THE INSIDE...
I'M NOT MANLY...
YAMATO?
HUH? YAMAKO?

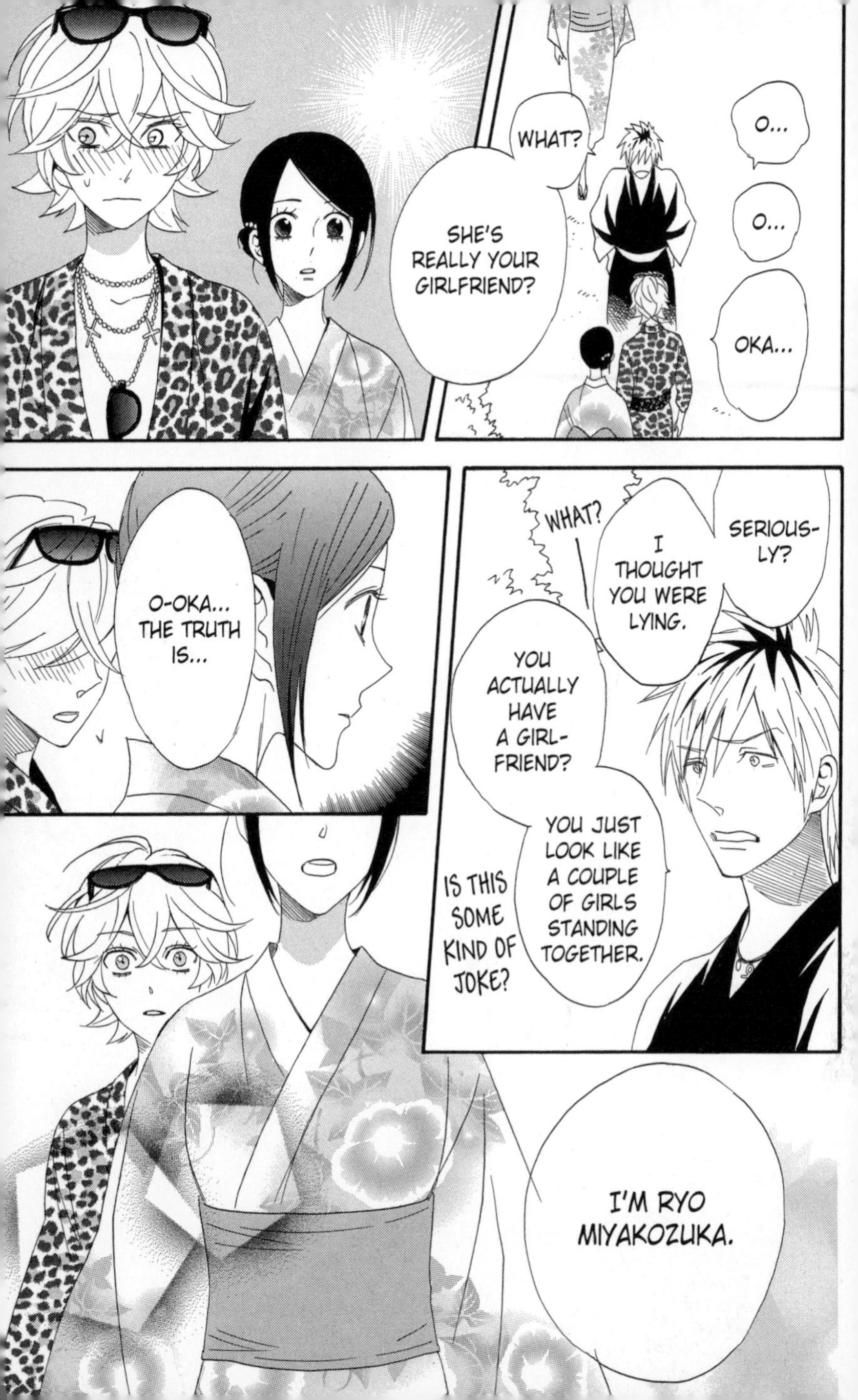
O...
O...
OKA...
WHAT?
SHE'S REALLY YOUR GIRLFRIEND?
SERIOUS-LY?
I THOUGHT YOU WERE LYING.
WHAT?
YOU ACTUALLY HAVE A GIRL-FRIEND?
YOU JUST LOOK LIKE A COUPLE OF GIRLS STANDING TOGETHER.
IS THIS SOME KIND OF JOKE?
O-OKA... THE TRUTH IS...
I'M RYO MIYAKOZUKA.

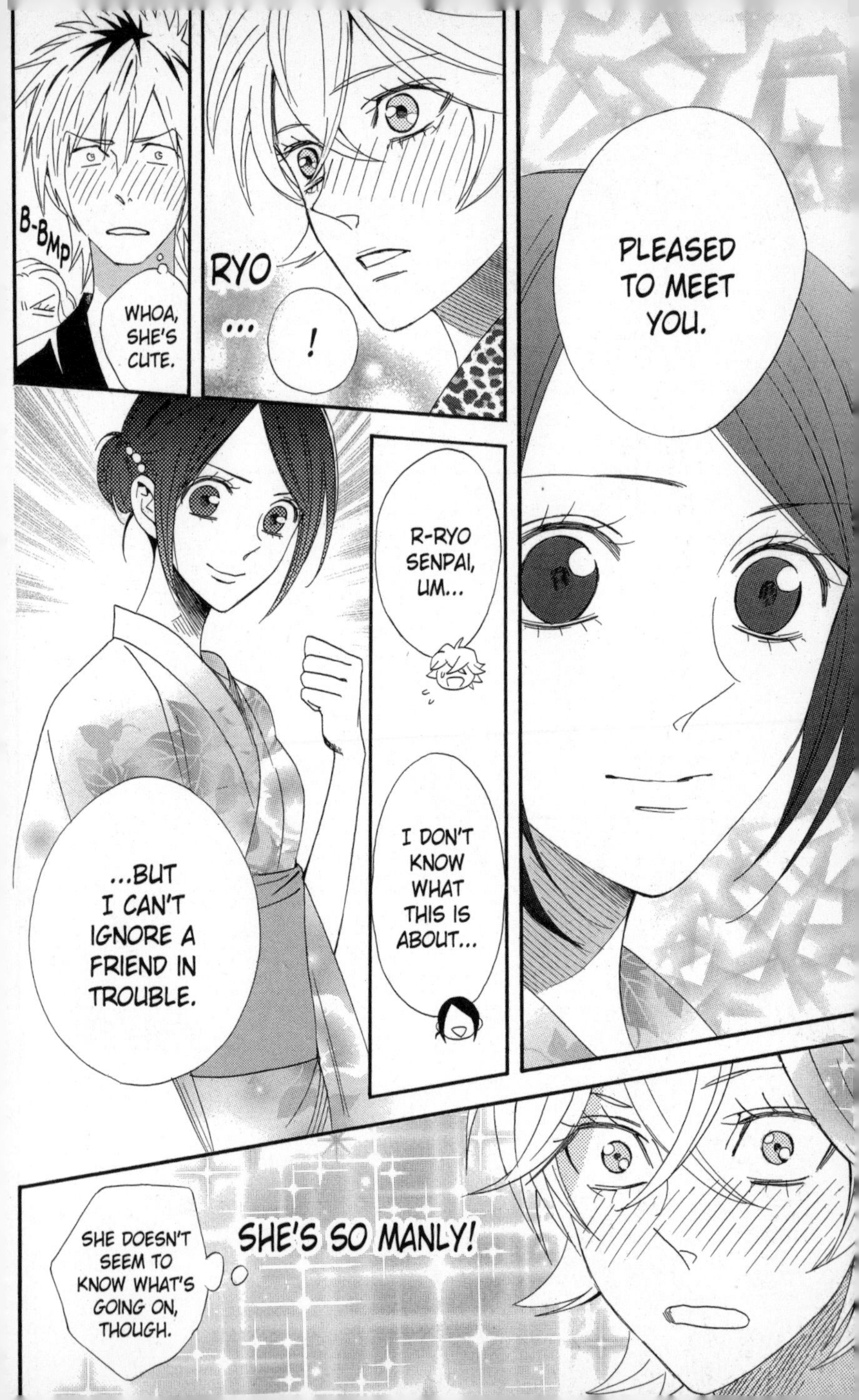
PLEASED TO MEET YOU.
RYO...
!
B-BMP
WHOA, SHE'S CUTE.
R-RYO SENPAI, UM...
I DON'T KNOW WHAT THIS IS ABOUT...
...BUT I CAN'T IGNORE A FRIEND IN TROUBLE.
SHE'S SO MANLY!
SHE DOESN'T SEEM TO KNOW WHAT'S GOING ON, THOUGH.

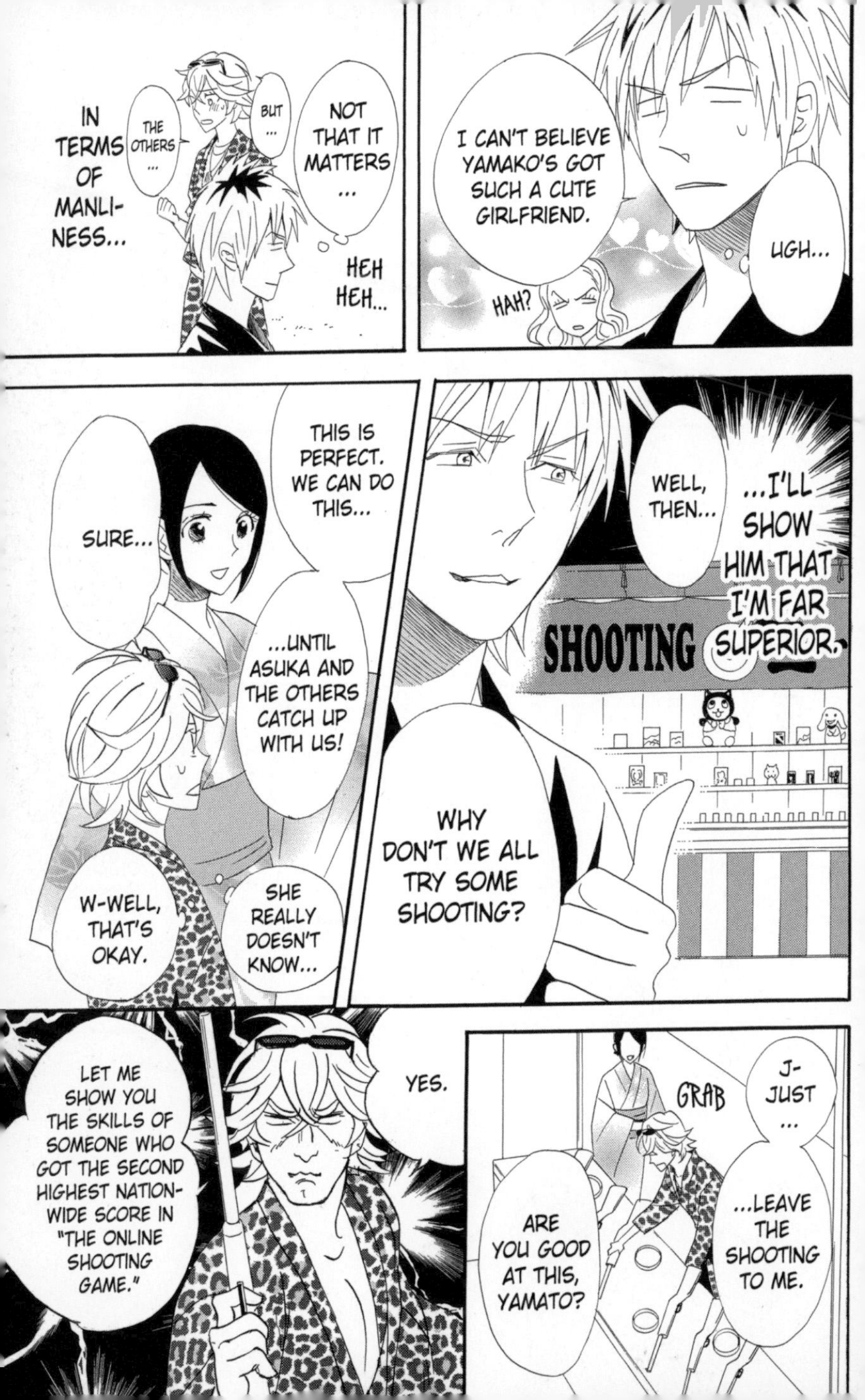
I CAN'T BELIEVE YAMAKO'S GOT SUCH A CUTE GIRLFRIEND.
UGH...
HAH?
NOT THAT IT MATTERS...
BUT...
THE OTHERS...
IN TERMS OF MANLINESS...
HEH HEH...
WELL, THEN...
...I'LL SHOW HIM THAT I'M FAR SUPERIOR.
SHOOTING
WHY DON'T WE ALL TRY SOME SHOOTING?
THIS IS PERFECT. WE CAN DO THIS...
...UNTIL ASUKA AND THE OTHERS CATCH UP WITH US!
SURE...
SHE REALLY DOESN'T KNOW...
W-WELL, THAT'S OKAY.
J-JUST...
GRAB
...LEAVE THE SHOOTING TO ME.
ARE YOU GOOD AT THIS, YAMATO?
YES.
LET ME SHOW YOU THE SKILLS OF SOMEONE WHO GOT THE SECOND HIGHEST NATION-WIDE SCORE IN "THE ONLINE SHOOTING GAME."

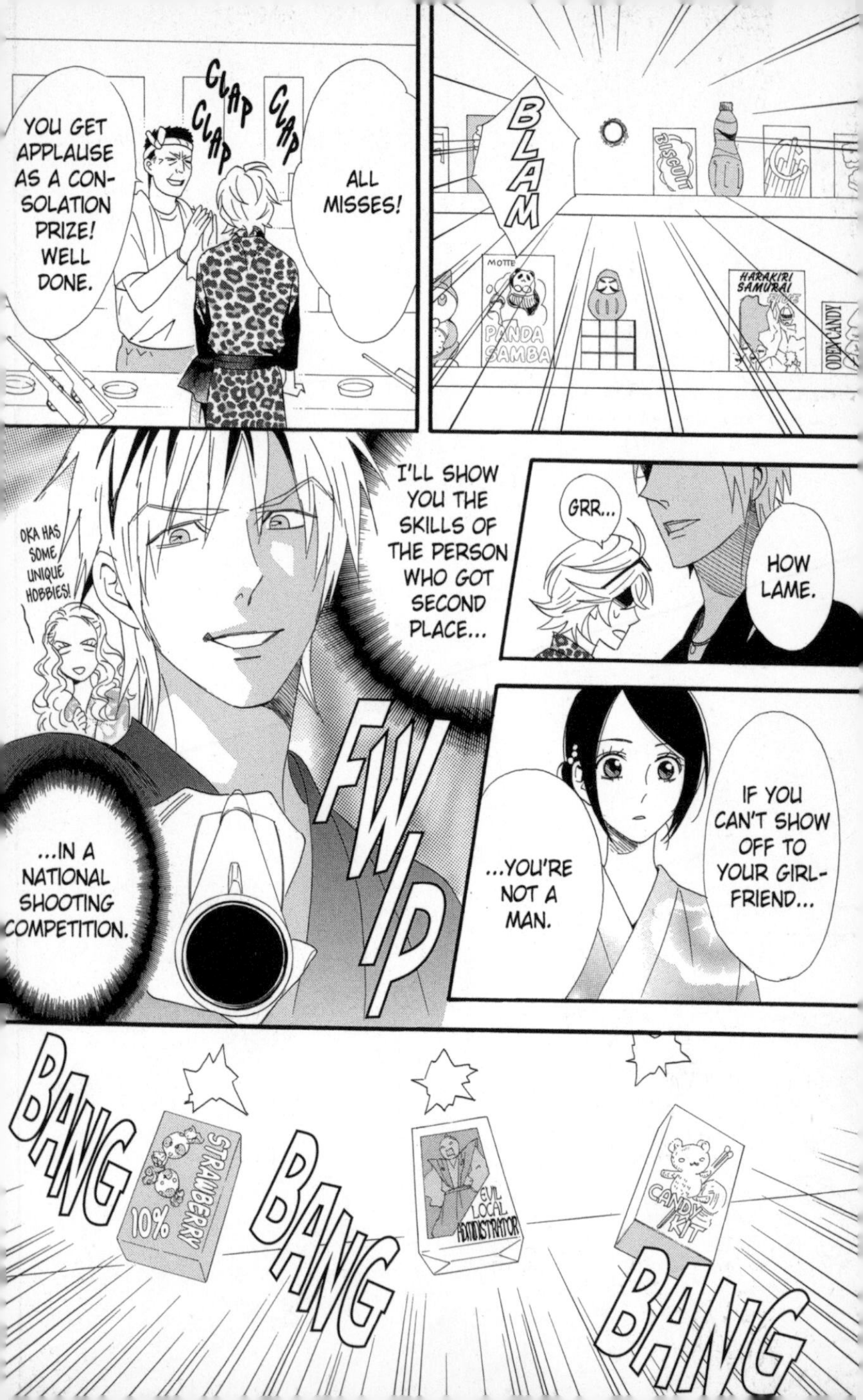
BLAM
BISCUIT
MOTTE
HARAKIRI SAMURAI
ODEN CANDY
PANDA SAMBA
ALL MISSES!
CLAP CLAP CLAP
YOU GET APPLAUSE AS A CONSOLATION PRIZE! WELL DONE.
HOW LAME.
GRR...
IF YOU CAN'T SHOW OFF TO YOUR GIRLFRIEND...
...YOU'RE NOT A MAN.
I'LL SHOW YOU THE SKILLS OF THE PERSON WHO GOT SECOND PLACE...
OKA HAS SOME UNIQUE HOBBIES!
FWIP
...IN A NATIONAL SHOOTING COMPETITION.
BANG
CANDY KIT
BANG
EVIL LOCAL ADMINISTRATOR
BANG
STRAWBERRY 10%

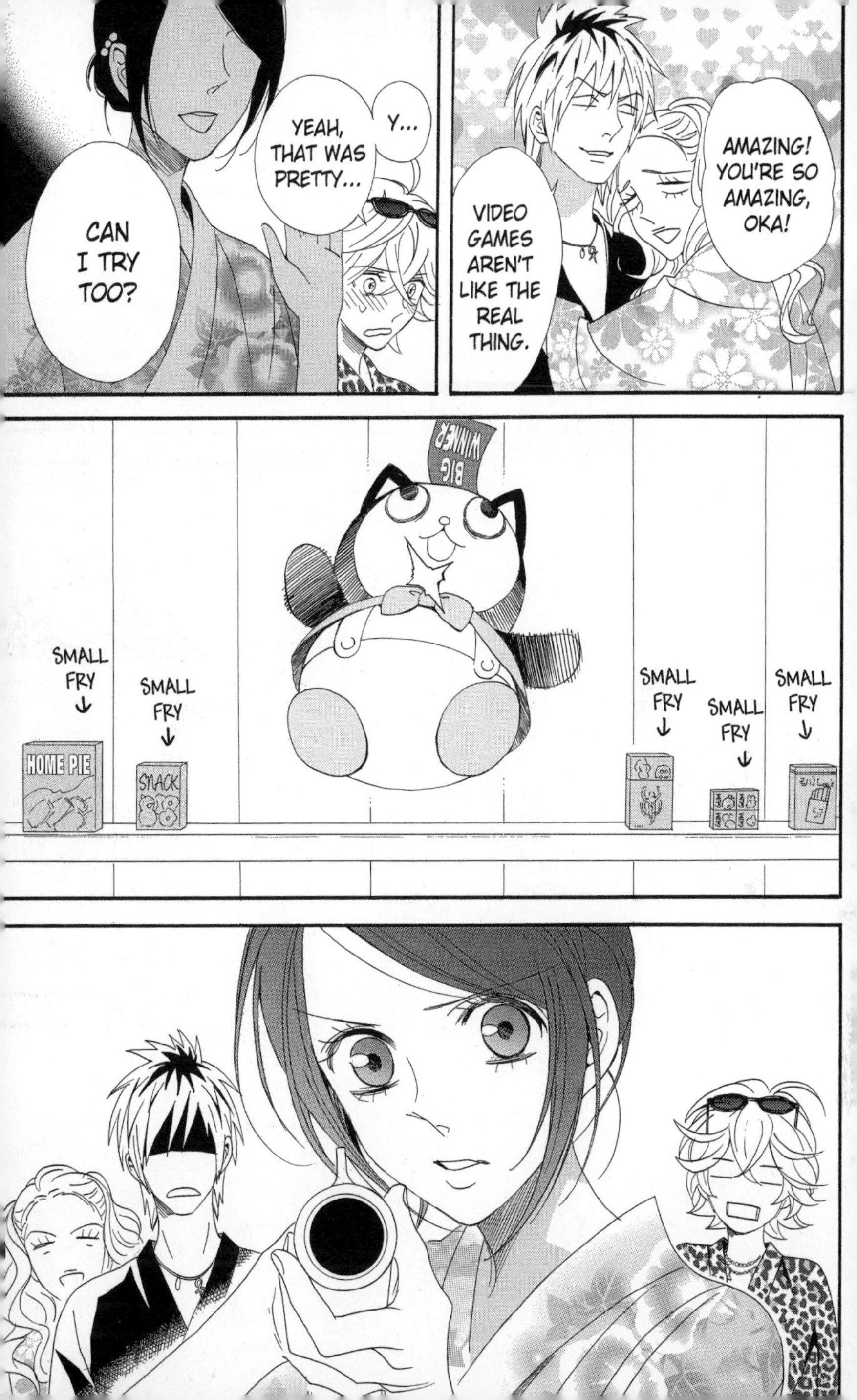
AMAZING! YOU'RE SO AMAZING, OKA!
VIDEO GAMES AREN'T LIKE THE REAL THING.
Y...
YEAH, THAT WAS PRETTY...
CAN I TRY TOO?
BIG WINNER
SMALL FRY
SMALL FRY
SMALL FRY
SMALL FRY
SMALL FRY
HOME PIE
SNACK

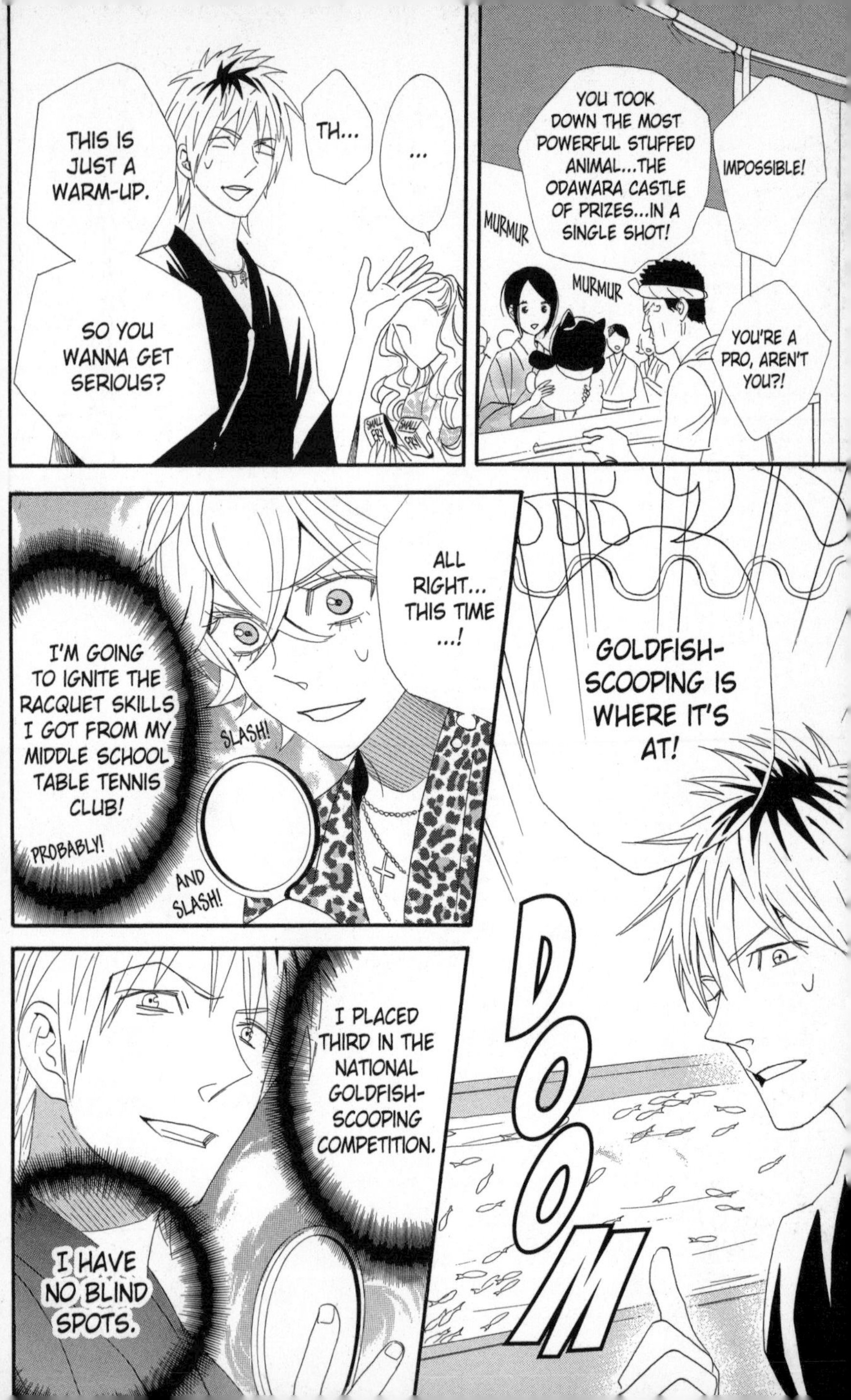
IMPOSSIBLE!
YOU TOOK DOWN THE MOST POWERFUL STUFFED ANIMAL...THE ODAWARA CASTLE OF PRIZES...IN A SINGLE SHOT!
MURMUR
MURMUR
YOU'RE A PRO, AREN'T YOU?!
...
TH...
THIS IS JUST A WARM-UP.
SO YOU WANNA GET SERIOUS?
SMALL FRY
SMALL FRY
GOLDFISH-SCOOPING IS WHERE IT'S AT!
DOOOM
ALL RIGHT... THIS TIME ...!
I'M GOING TO IGNITE THE RACQUET SKILLS I GOT FROM MY MIDDLE SCHOOL TABLE TENNIS CLUB!
SLASH!
AND SLASH!
PROBABLY!
I PLACED THIRD IN THE NATIONAL GOLDFISH-SCOOPING COMPETITION.
I HAVE NO BLIND SPOTS.

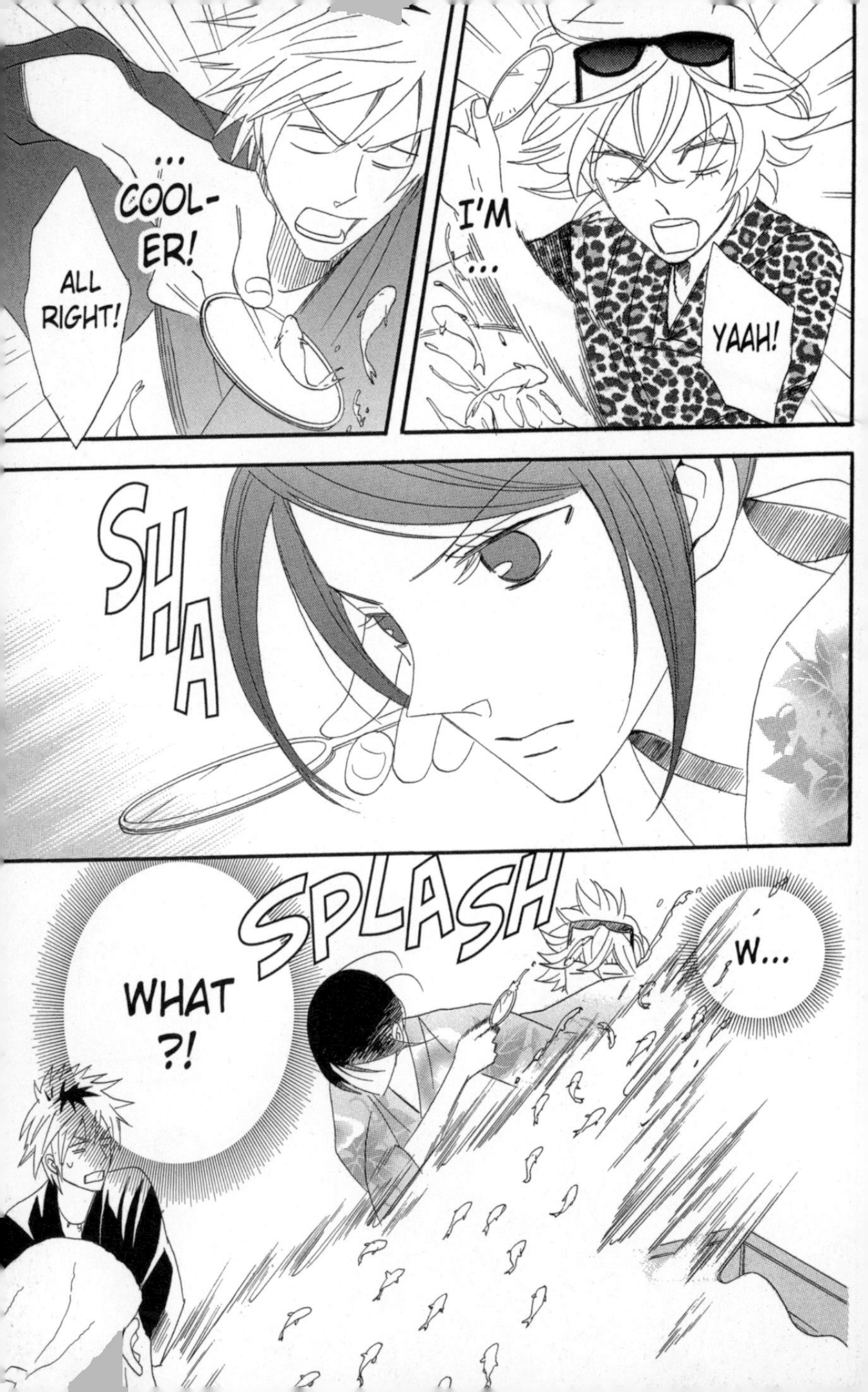
YAAH!
I'M ...
... COOL-ER!
ALL RIGHT!
SHA
SPLASH
W...
WHAT ?!

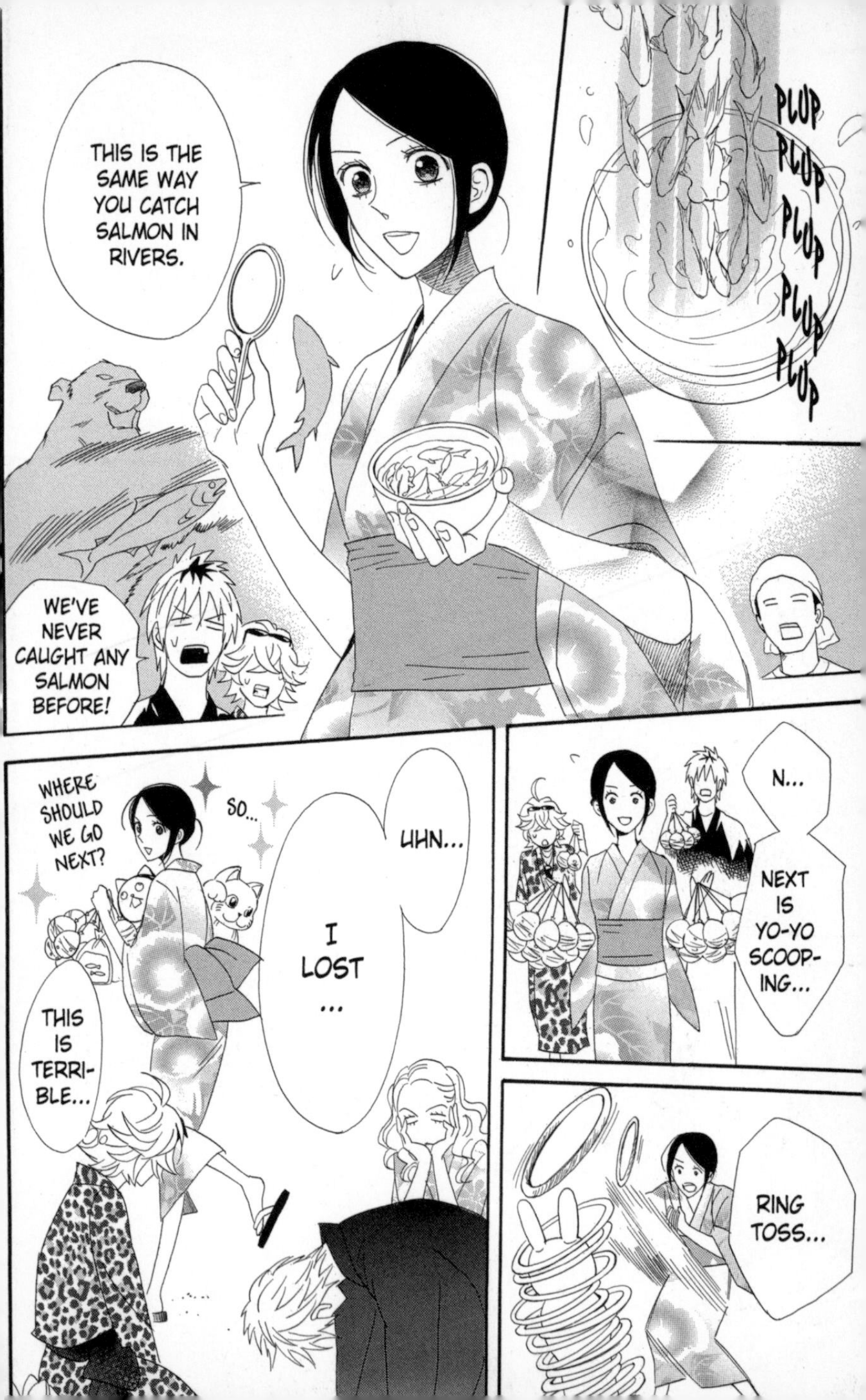
PLUP PLUP PLUP PLUP PLUP
THIS IS THE SAME WAY YOU CATCH SALMON IN RIVERS.
WE'VE NEVER CAUGHT ANY SALMON BEFORE!
N... NEXT IS YO-YO SCOOP-ING...
RING TOSS...
UHN... I LOST...
SO...
WHERE SHOULD WE GO NEXT?
THIS IS TERRI-BLE...

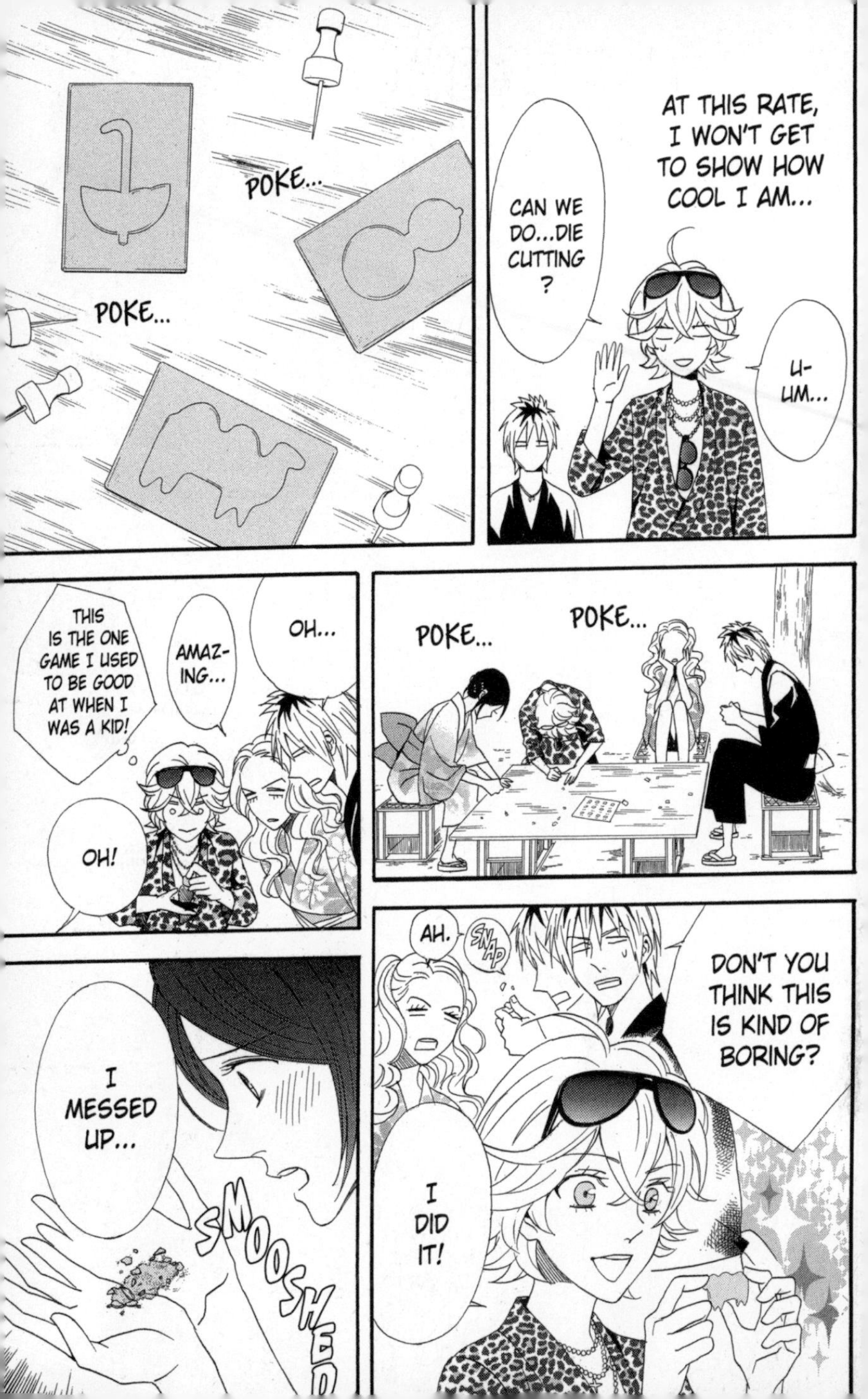
AT THIS RATE, I WON'T GET TO SHOW HOW COOL I AM...
CAN WE DO...DIE CUTTING ?
U-UM...
POKE...
POKE...
POKE...
POKE...
OH...
AMAZ-ING...
THIS IS THE ONE GAME I USED TO BE GOOD AT WHEN I WAS A KID!
OH!
DON'T YOU THINK THIS IS KIND OF BORING?
SNAP
AH.
I DID IT!
I MESSED UP...
SMOOSHED

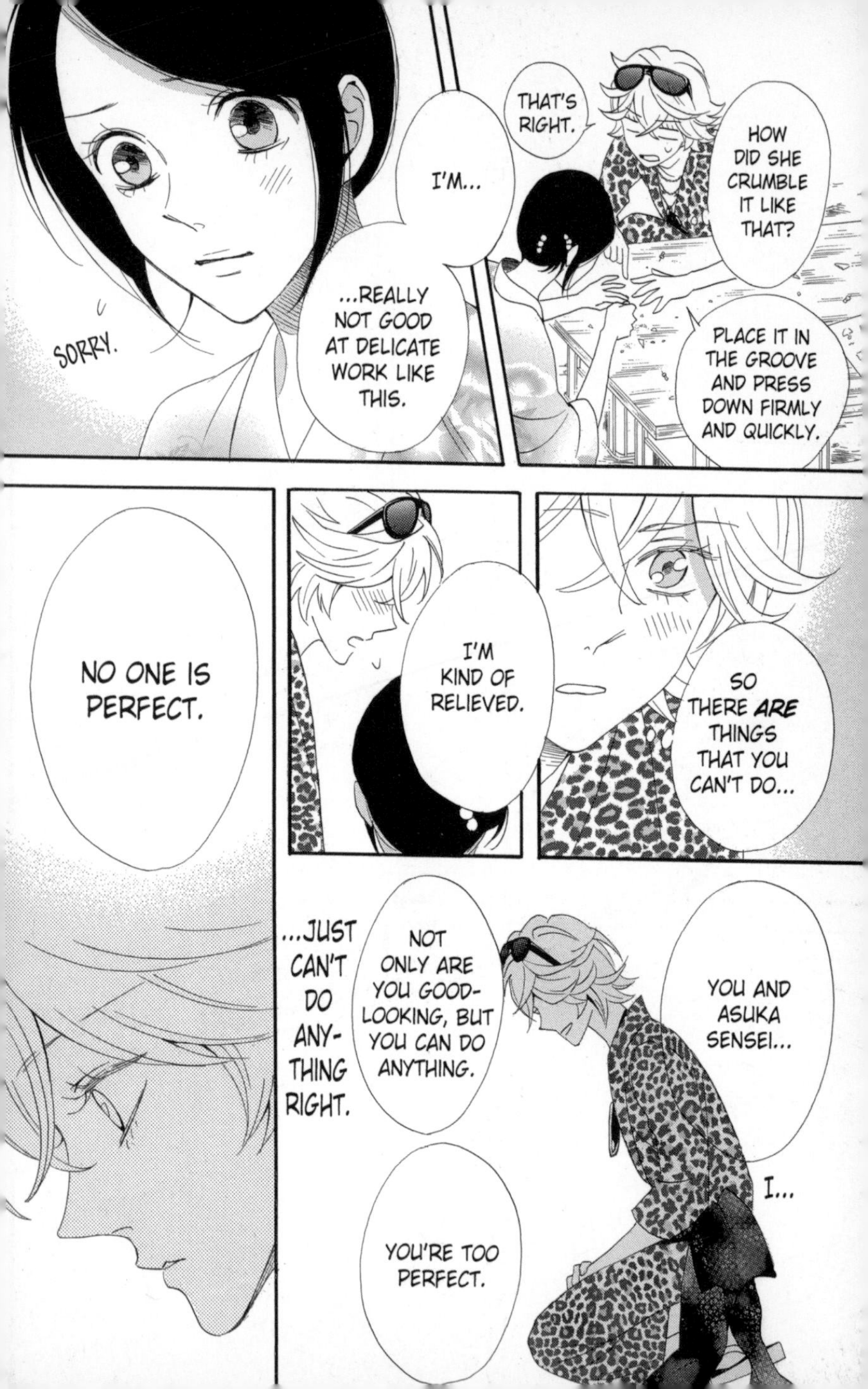
HOW DID SHE CRUMBLE IT LIKE THAT?
THAT'S RIGHT.
PLACE IT IN THE GROOVE AND PRESS DOWN FIRMLY AND QUICKLY.
I'M...
...REALLY NOT GOOD AT DELICATE WORK LIKE THIS.
SORRY.
SO THERE ARE THINGS THAT YOU CAN'T DO...
I'M KIND OF RELIEVED.
YOU AND ASUKA SENSEI...
NOT ONLY ARE YOU GOOD-LOOKING, BUT YOU CAN DO ANYTHING.
I...
...JUST CAN'T DO ANY-THING RIGHT.
YOU'RE TOO PERFECT.
NO ONE IS PERFECT.

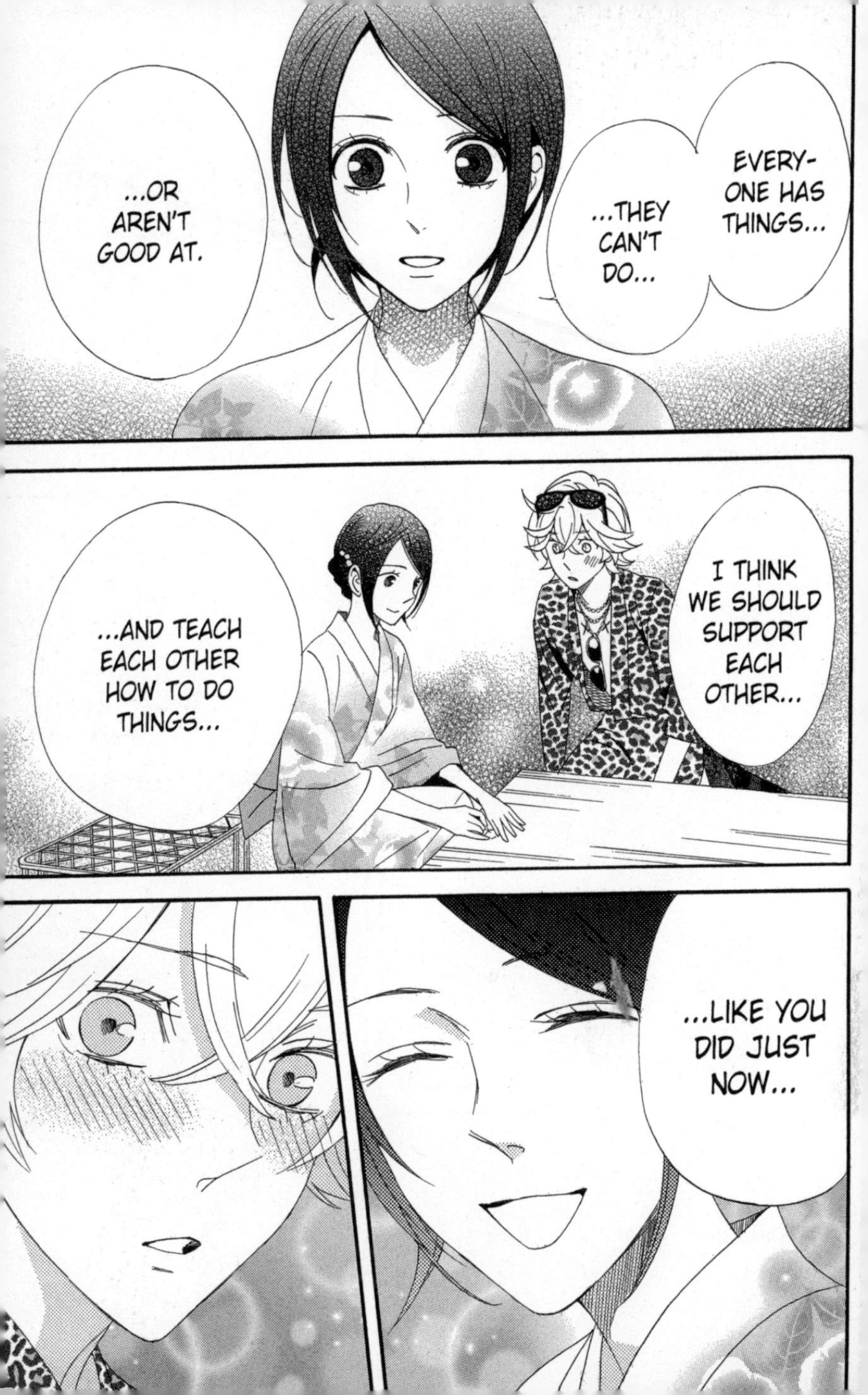
EVERY-ONE HAS THINGS...
...THEY CAN'T DO...
...OR AREN'T GOOD AT.
I THINK WE SHOULD SUPPORT EACH OTHER...
...AND TEACH EACH OTHER HOW TO DO THINGS...
...LIKE YOU DID JUST NOW...

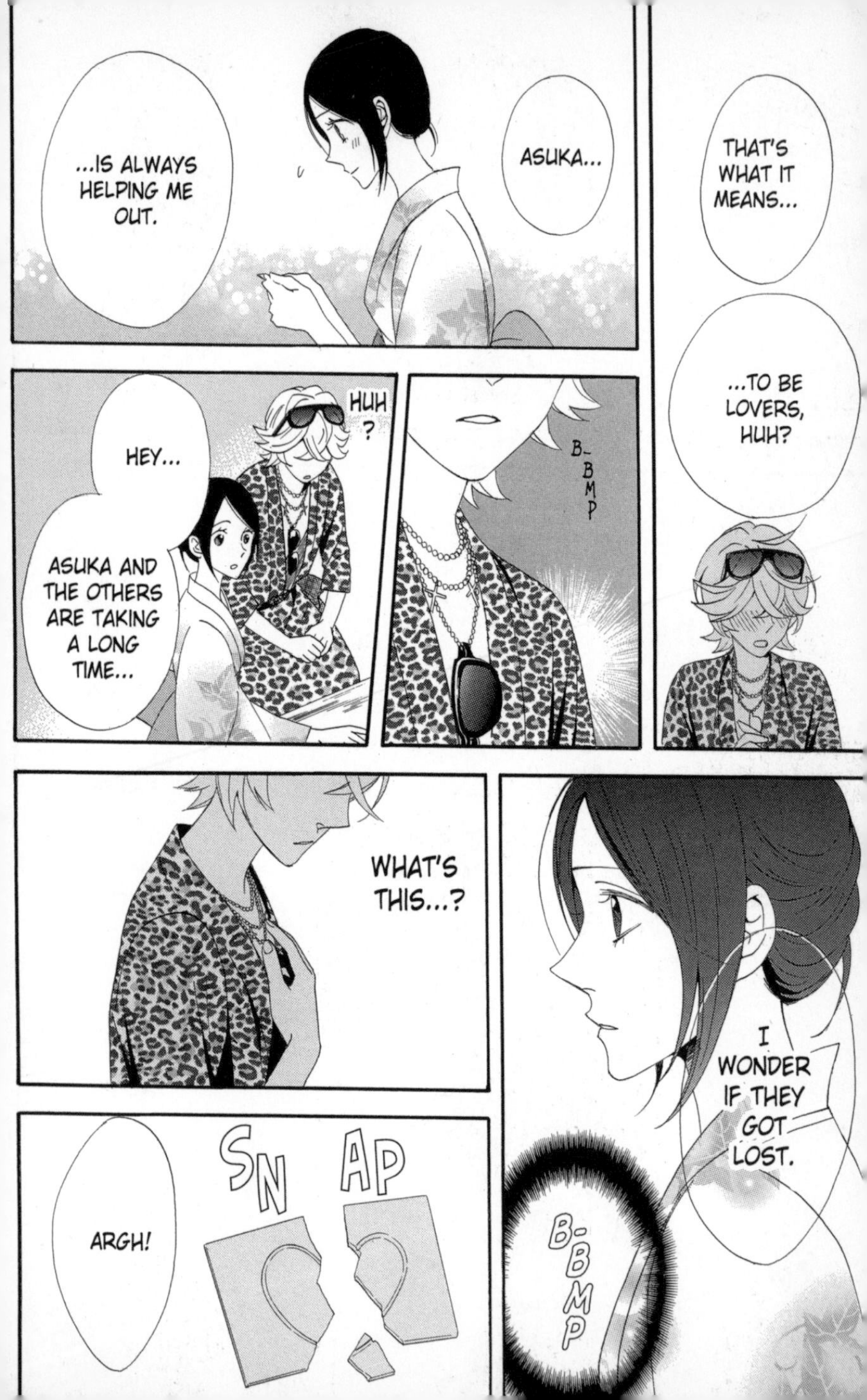
THAT'S WHAT IT MEANS...
...TO BE LOVERS, HUH?
ASUKA...
...IS ALWAYS HELPING ME OUT.
B-BMP
HUH?
HEY...
ASUKA AND THE OTHERS ARE TAKING A LONG TIME...
I WONDER IF THEY GOT LOST.
B-BMP
WHAT'S THIS...?
SNAP
ARGH!

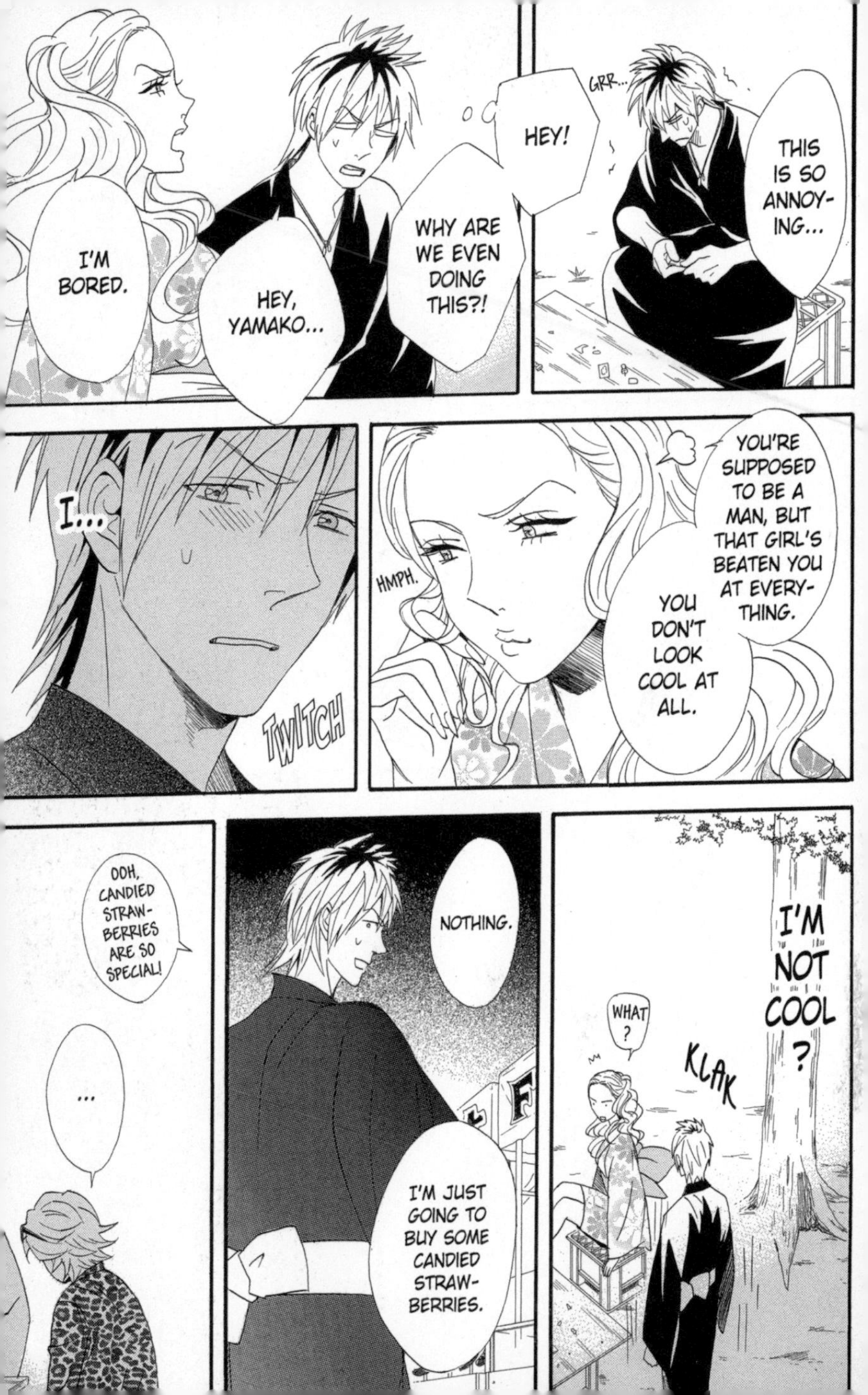
GRR...
THIS IS SO ANNOYING...
HEY!
WHY ARE WE EVEN DOING THIS?!
HEY, YAMAKO...
I'M BORED.
YOU'RE SUPPOSED TO BE A MAN, BUT THAT GIRL'S BEATEN YOU AT EVERYTHING.
HMPH.
YOU DON'T LOOK COOL AT ALL.
I...
TWITCH
I'M NOT COOL?
WHAT?
KLAK
NOTHING.
I'M JUST GOING TO BUY SOME CANDIED STRAWBERRIES.
OOH, CANDIED STRAWBERRIES ARE SO SPECIAL!
...

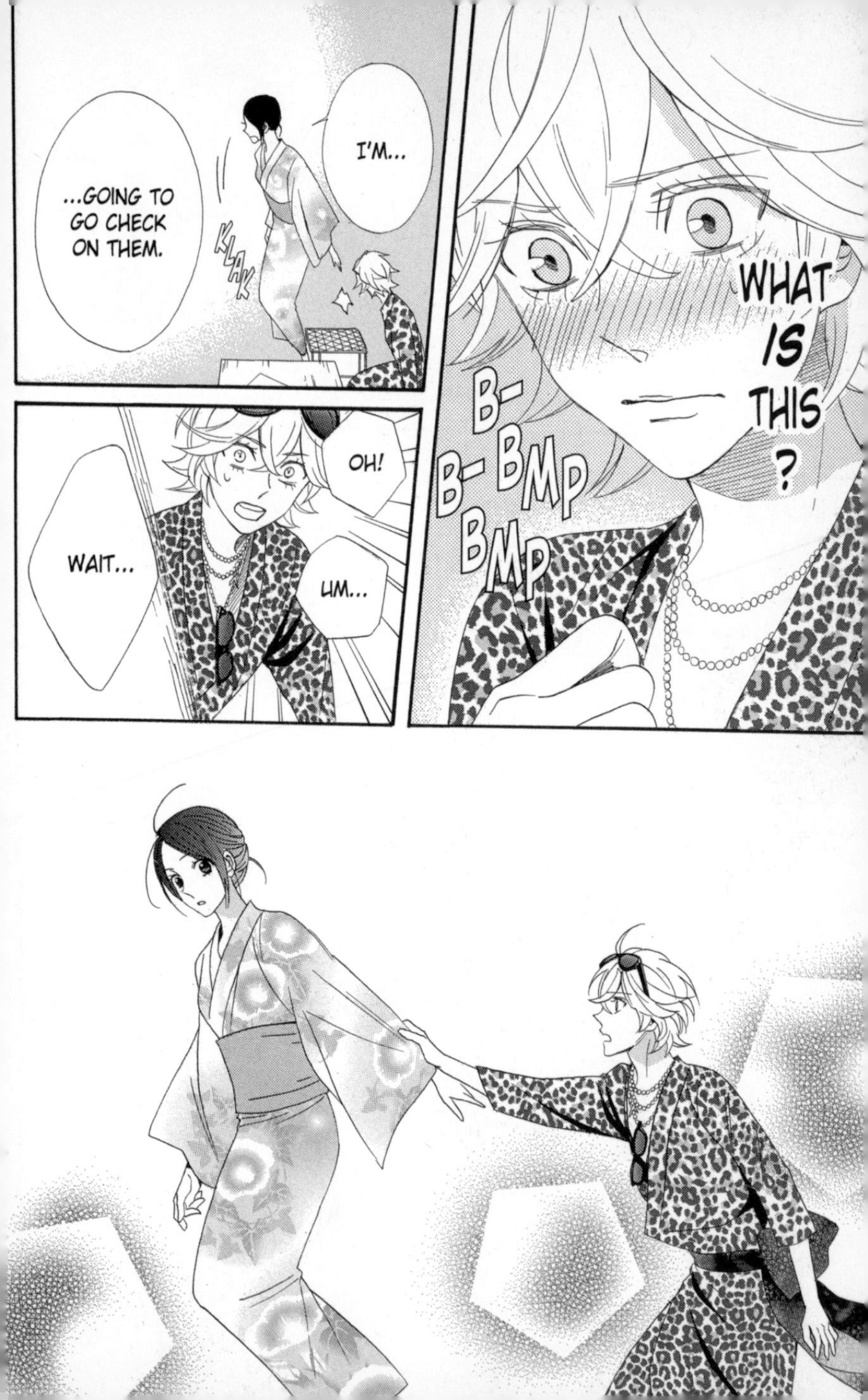
WHAT IS THIS?
B-B-BMP BMP
I'M...
...GOING TO GO CHECK ON THEM.
KLAK
OH!
UM...
WAIT...

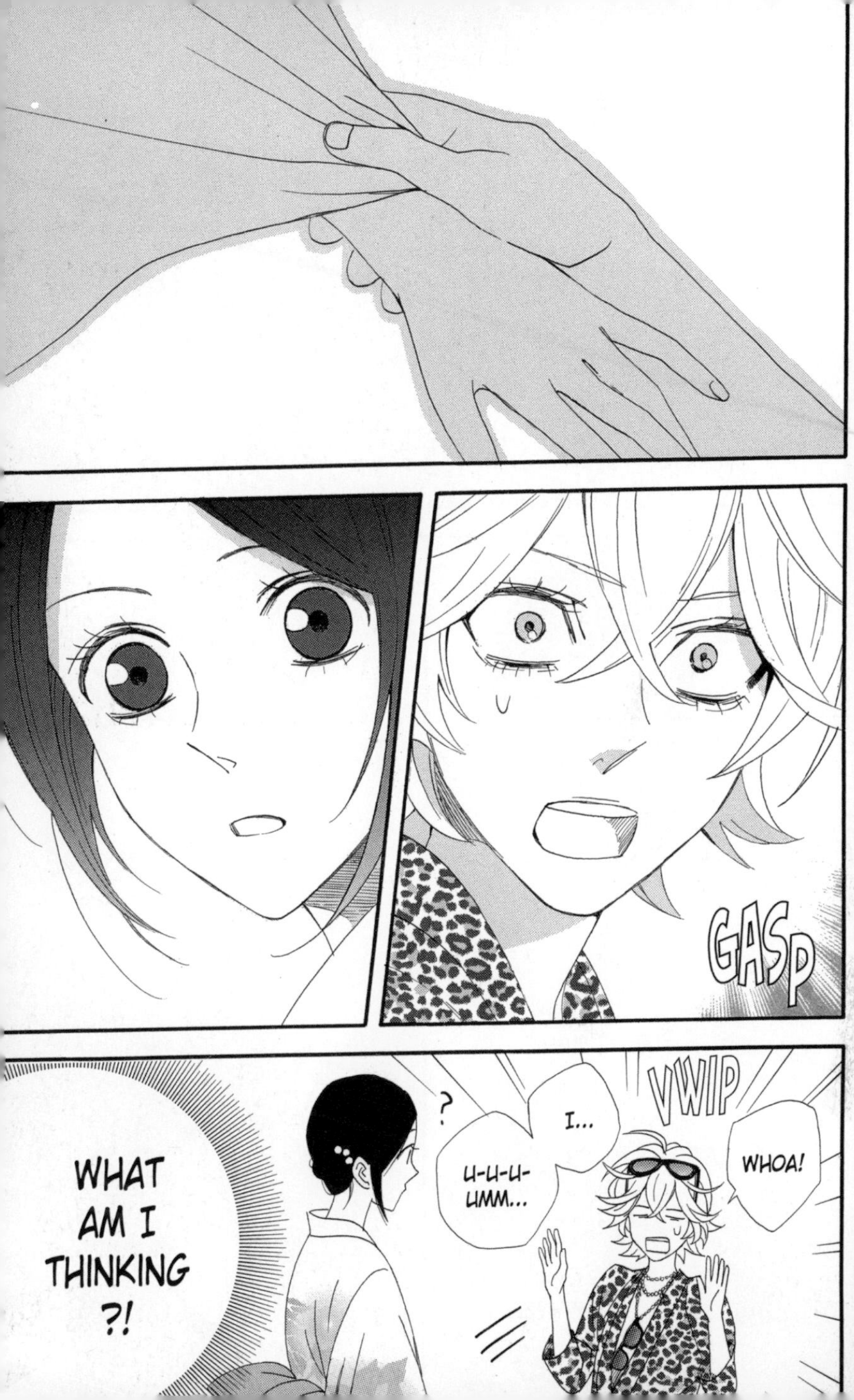
GASP
VWIP
WHOA!
I...
U-U-U-UMM...
?
WHAT AM I THINKING?!

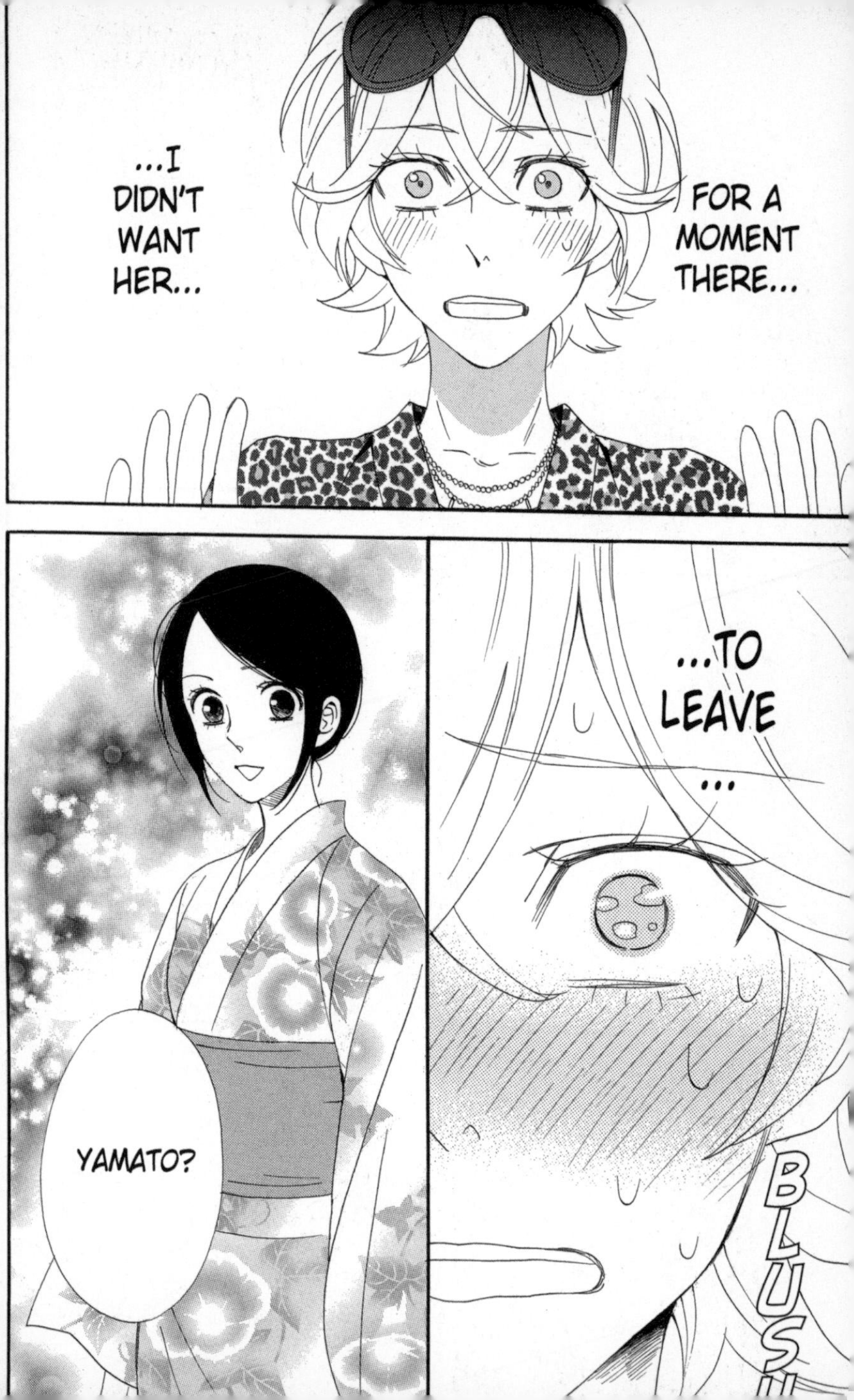
FOR A MOMENT THERE...
...I DIDN'T WANT HER...
...TO LEAVE ...
BLUSH
YAMATO?

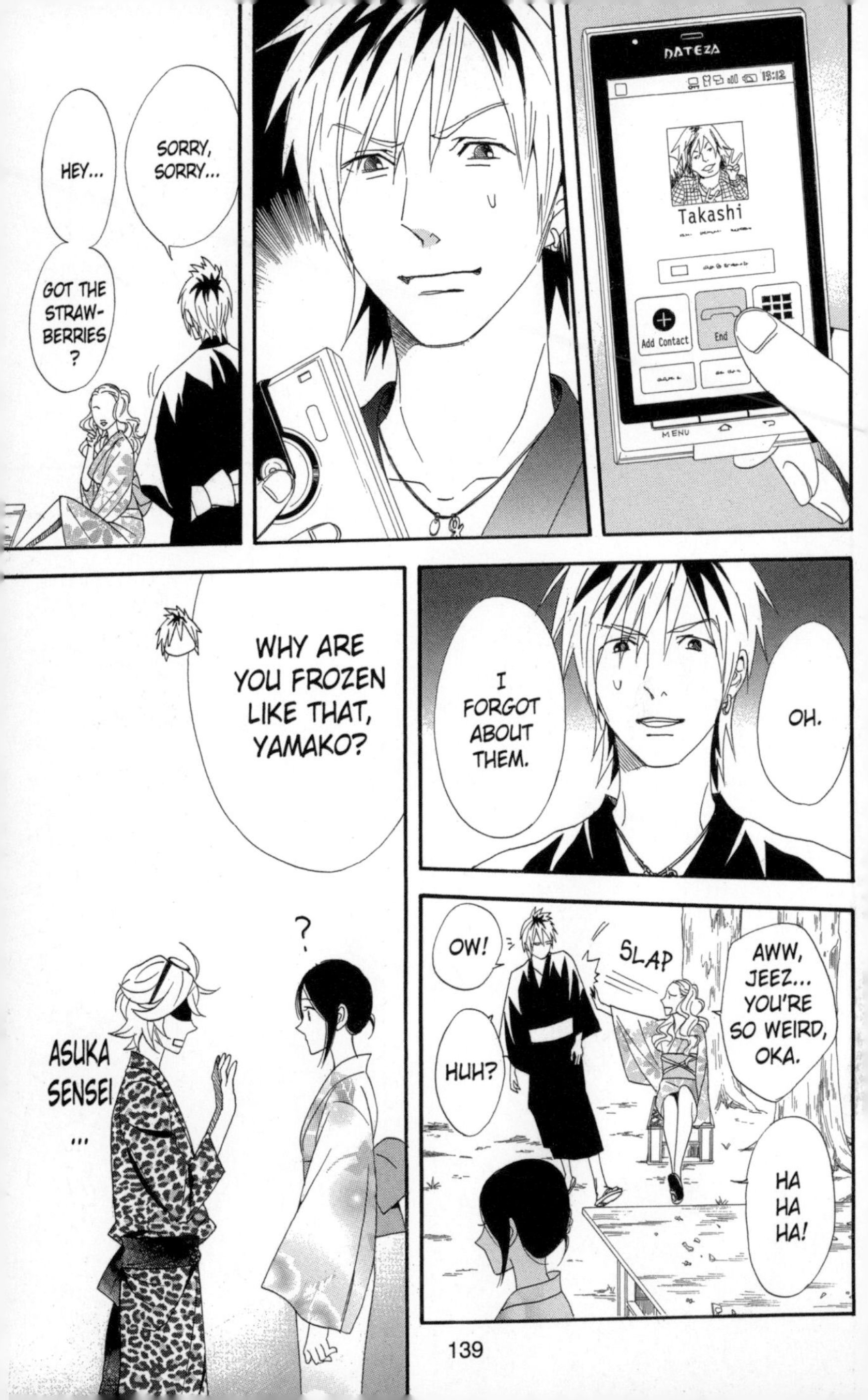
DATEZA
Takashi
Add Contact
End
MENU
SORRY, SORRY...
HEY...
GOT THE STRAW-BERRIES?
OH.
I FORGOT ABOUT THEM.
AWW, JEEZ... YOU'RE SO WEIRD, OKA.
SLAP
OW!
HUH?
HA HA HA!
WHY ARE YOU FROZEN LIKE THAT, YAMAKO?
?
ASUKA SENSEI ...

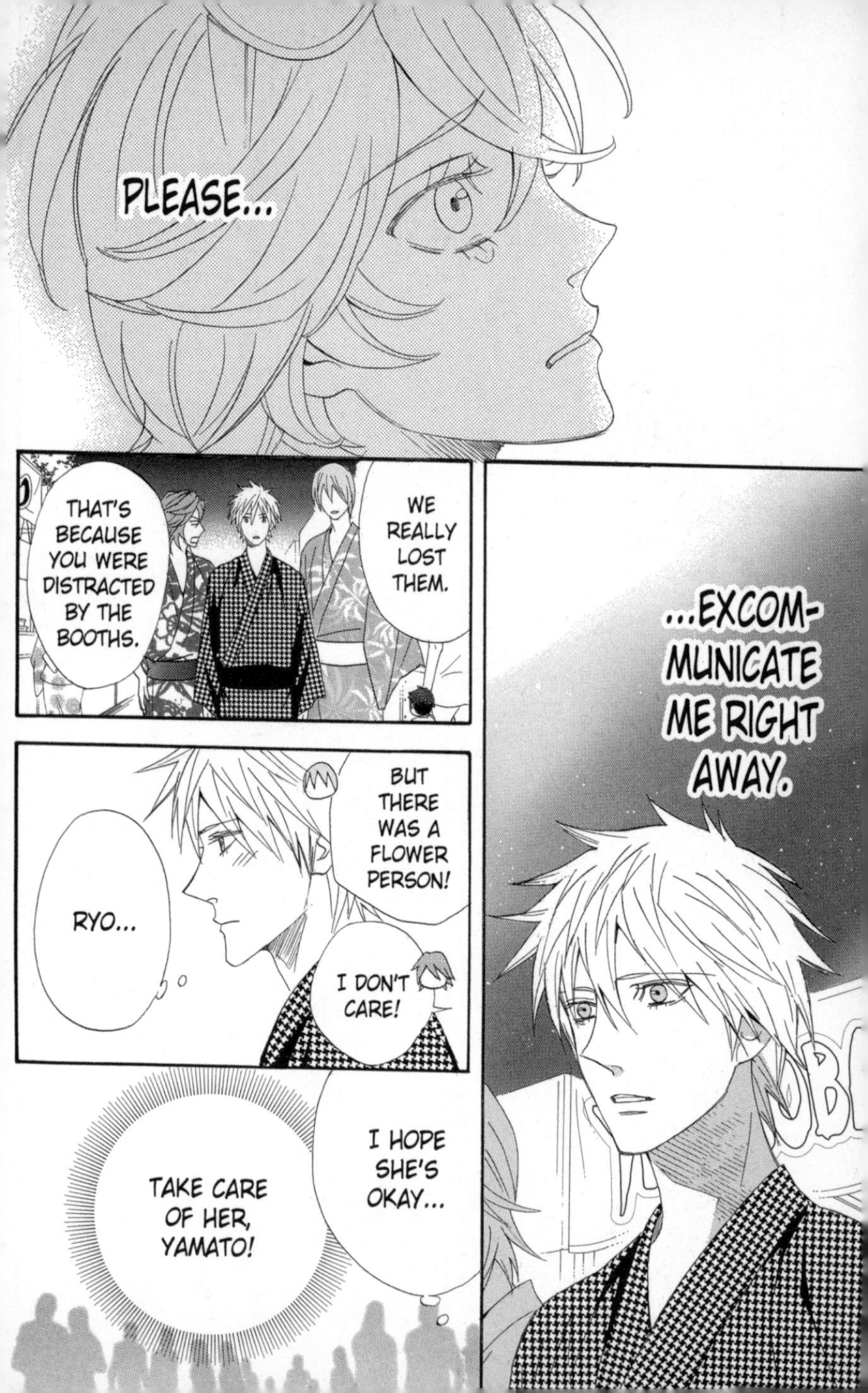
PLEASE...
...EXCOM-MUNICATE ME RIGHT AWAY.
WE REALLY LOST THEM.
THAT'S BECAUSE YOU WERE DISTRACTED BY THE BOOTHS.
BUT THERE WAS A FLOWER PERSON!
I DON'T CARE!
RYO...
I HOPE SHE'S OKAY...
TAKE CARE OF HER, YAMATO!

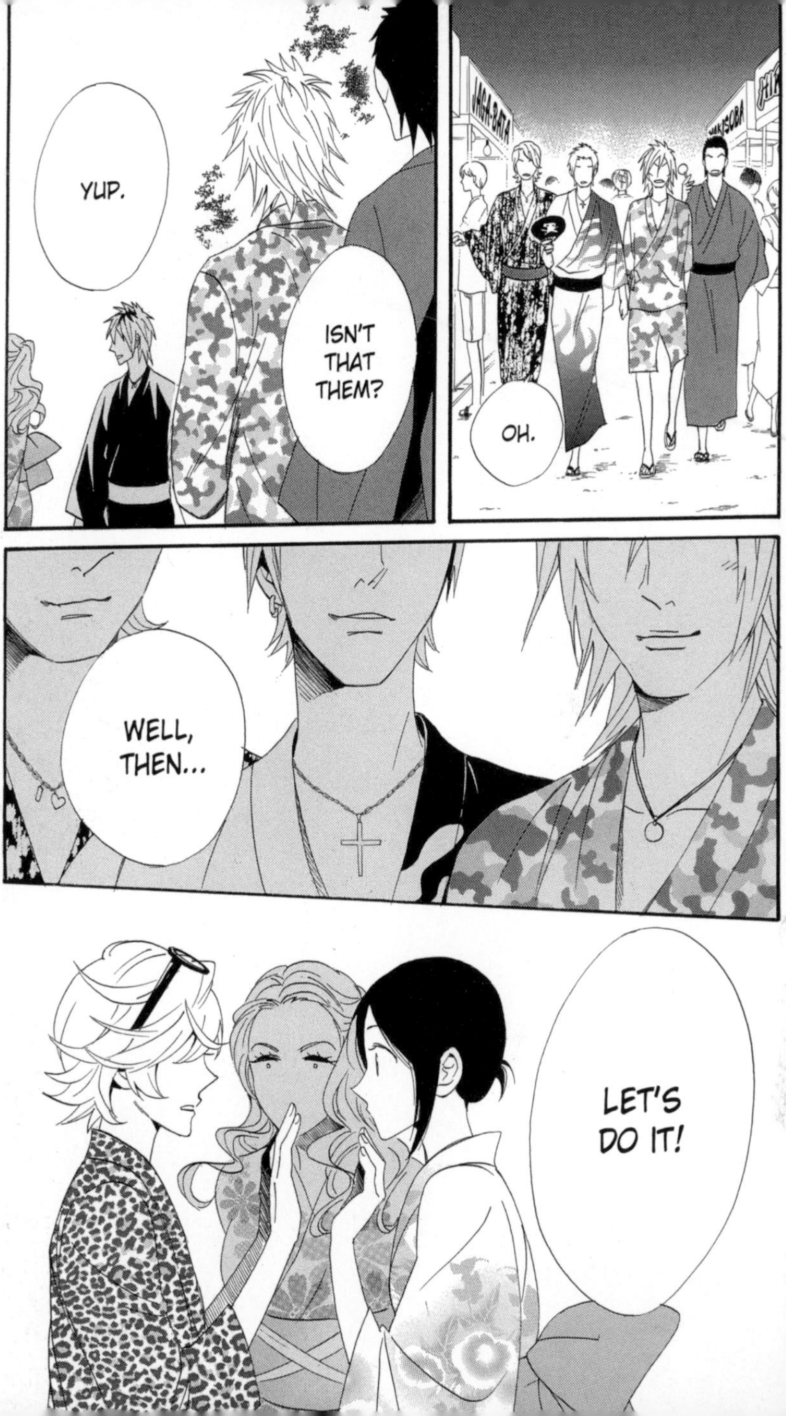
OH.
ISN'T THAT THEM?
YUP.
WELL, THEN...
LET'S DO IT!

OTOMEN

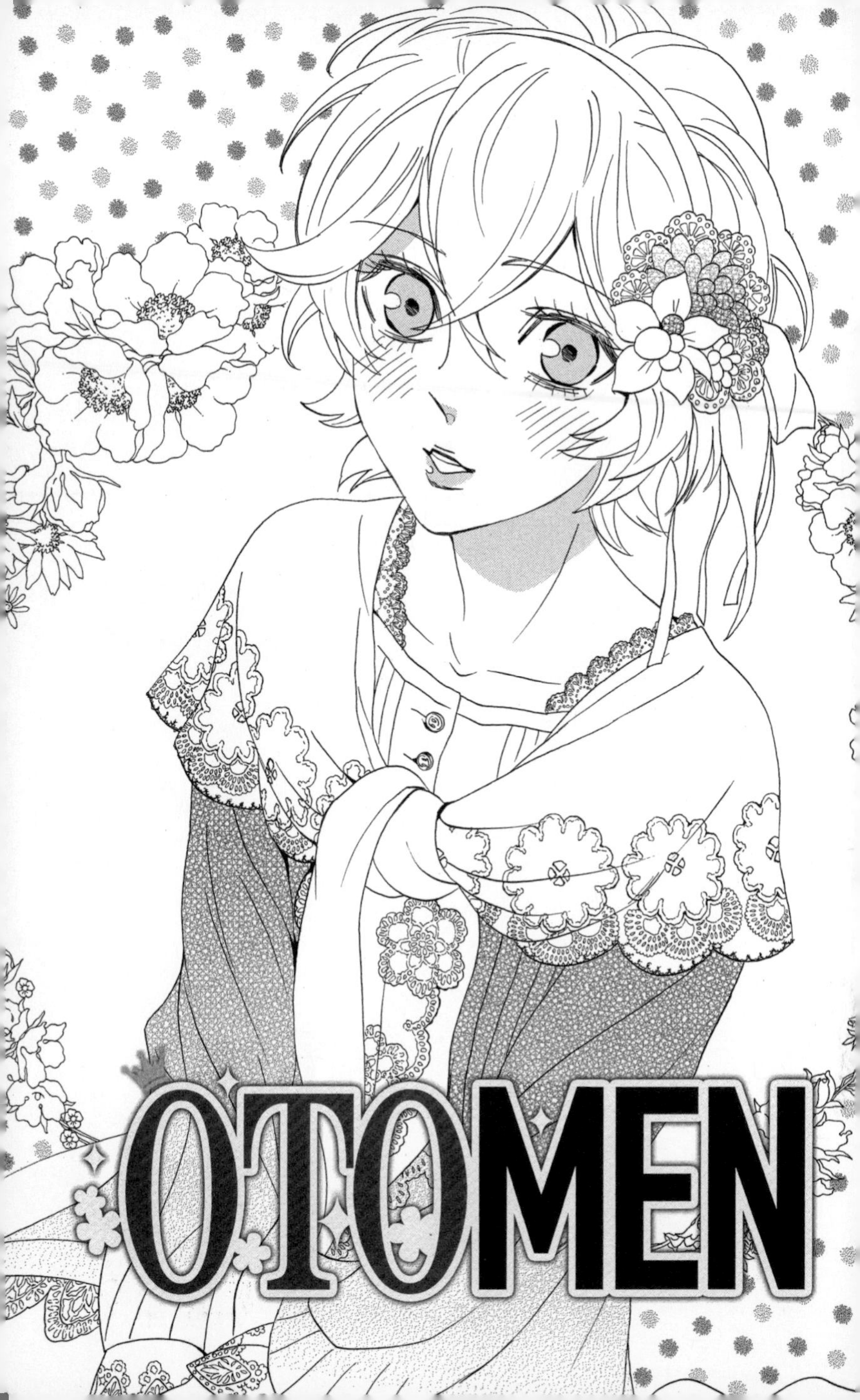
OTOMEN

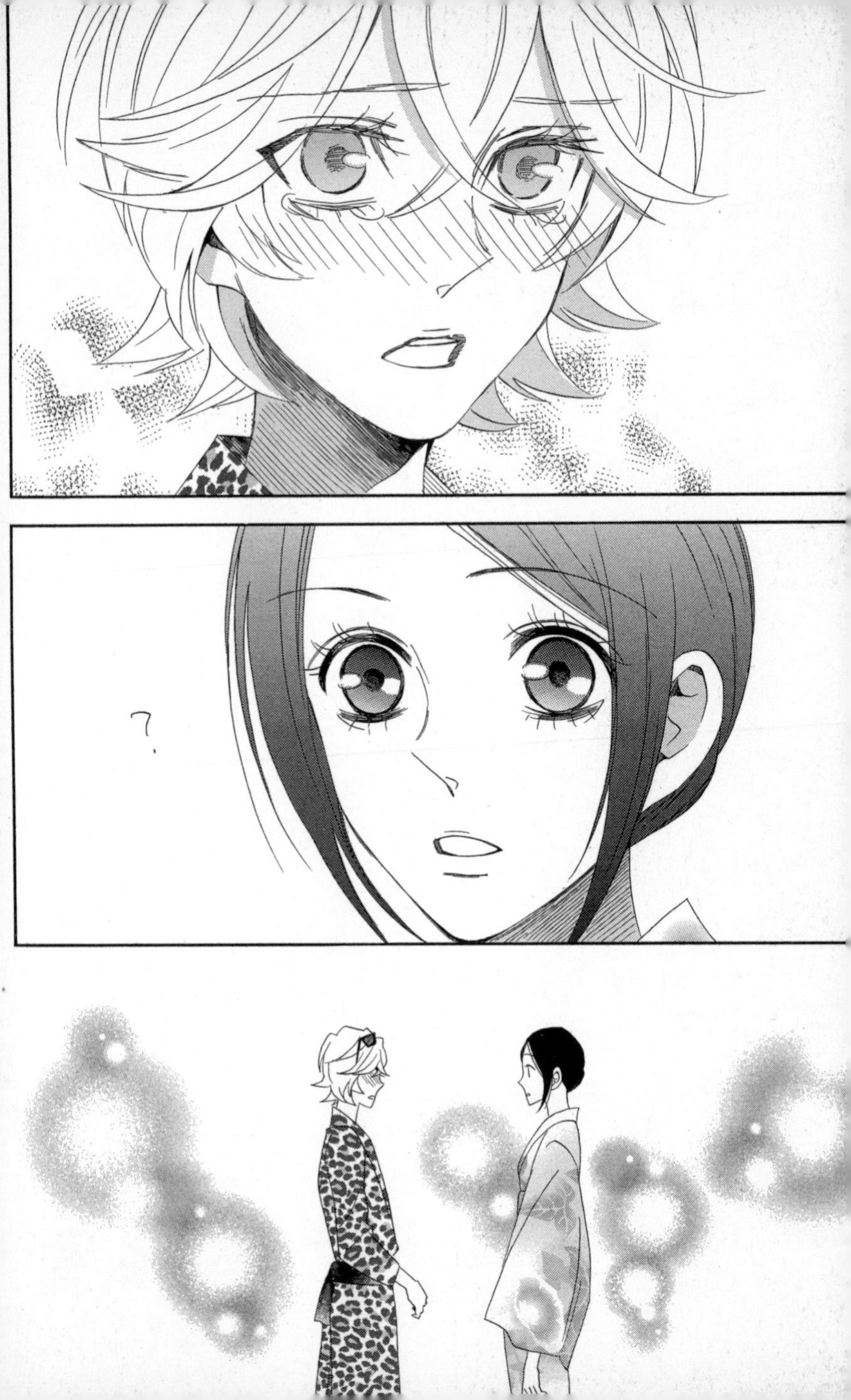
?

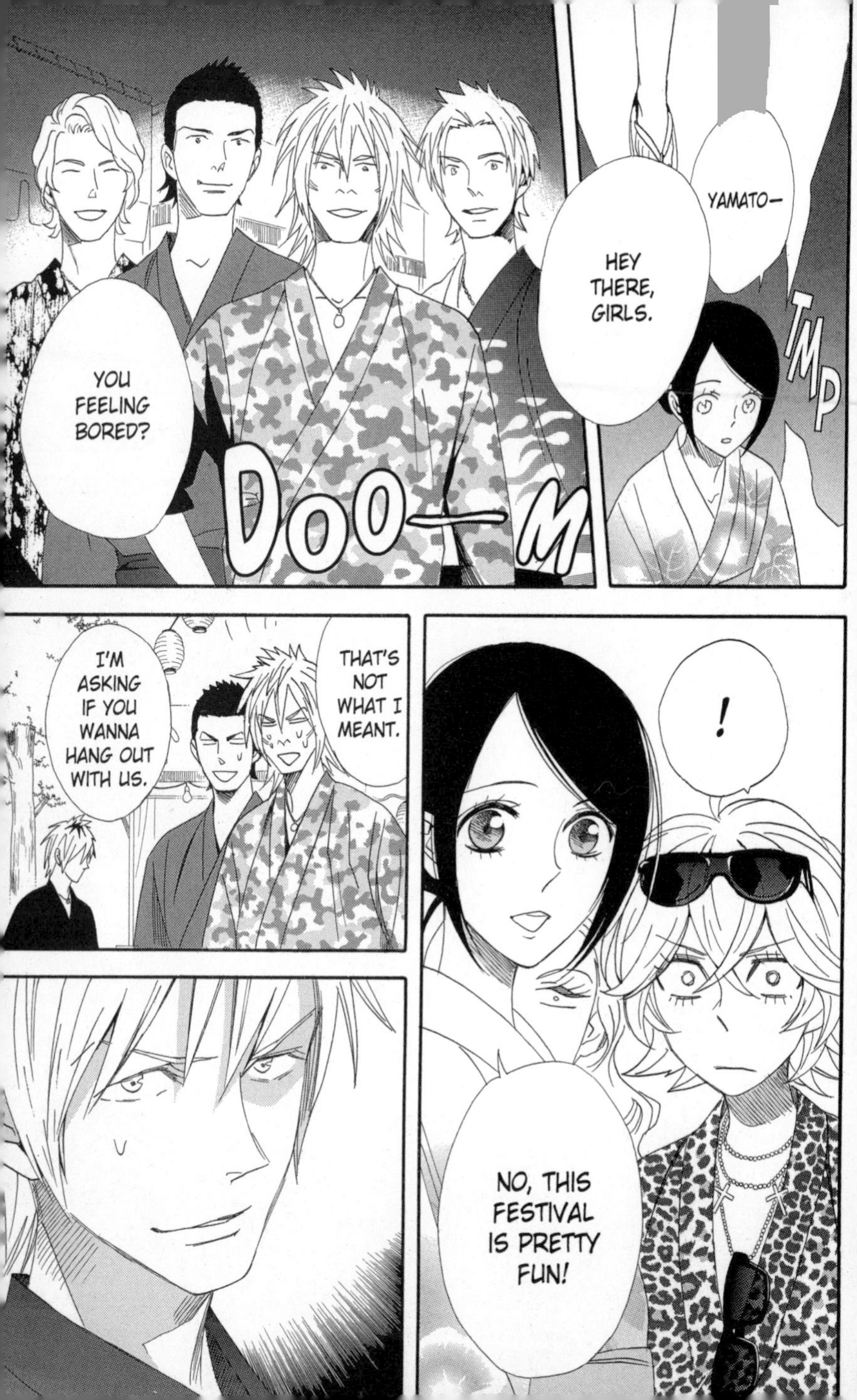
YAMATO—
TMP
HEY THERE, GIRLS.
YOU FEELING BORED?
DOO—M
!
NO, THIS FESTIVAL IS PRETTY FUN!
THAT'S NOT WHAT I MEANT.
I'M ASKING IF YOU WANNA HANG OUT WITH US.

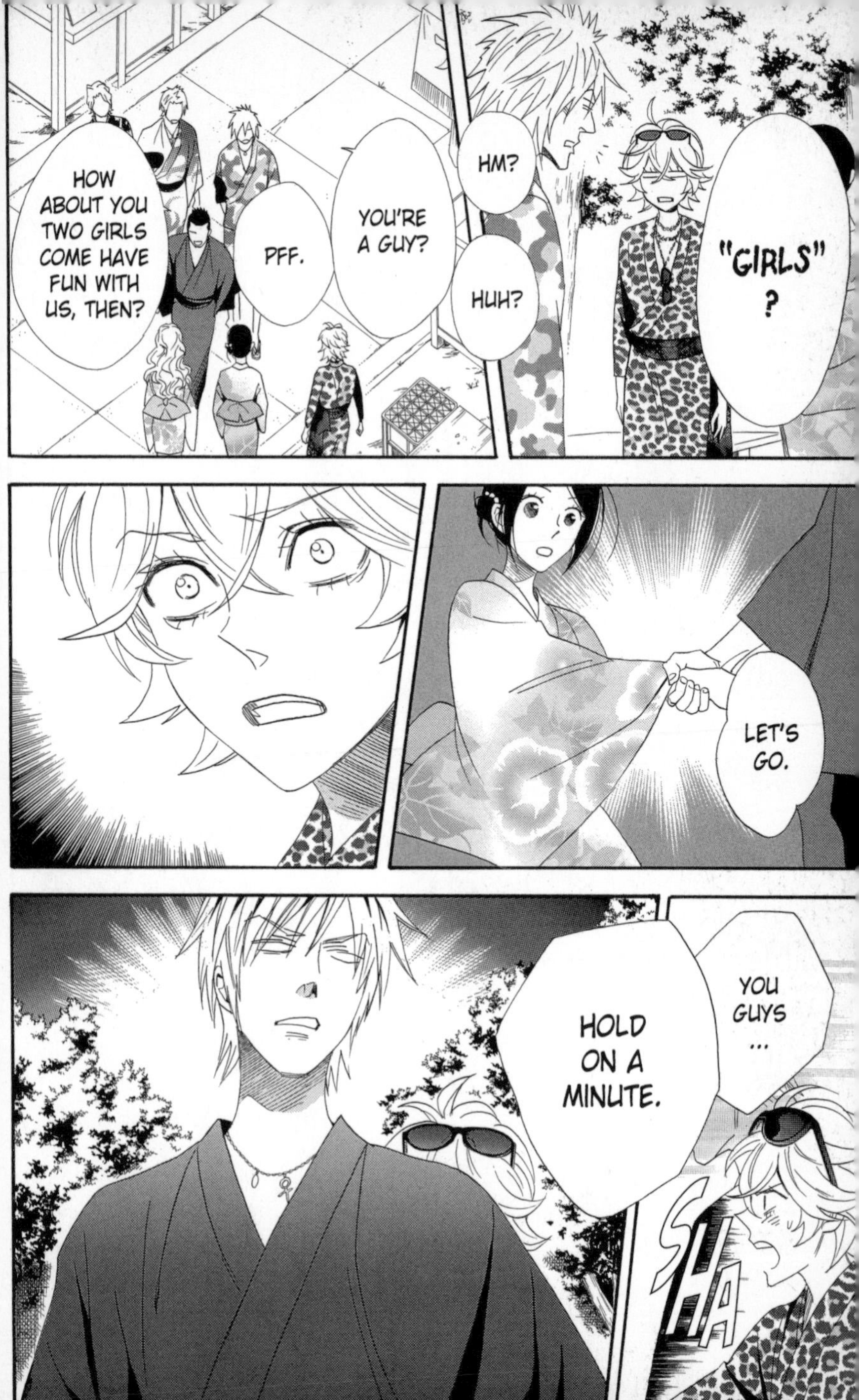
"GIRLS"?
HM?
HUH?
YOU'RE A GUY?
PFF.
HOW ABOUT YOU TWO GIRLS COME HAVE FUN WITH US, THEN?
LET'S GO.
YOU GUYS...
SHA
HOLD ON A MINUTE.

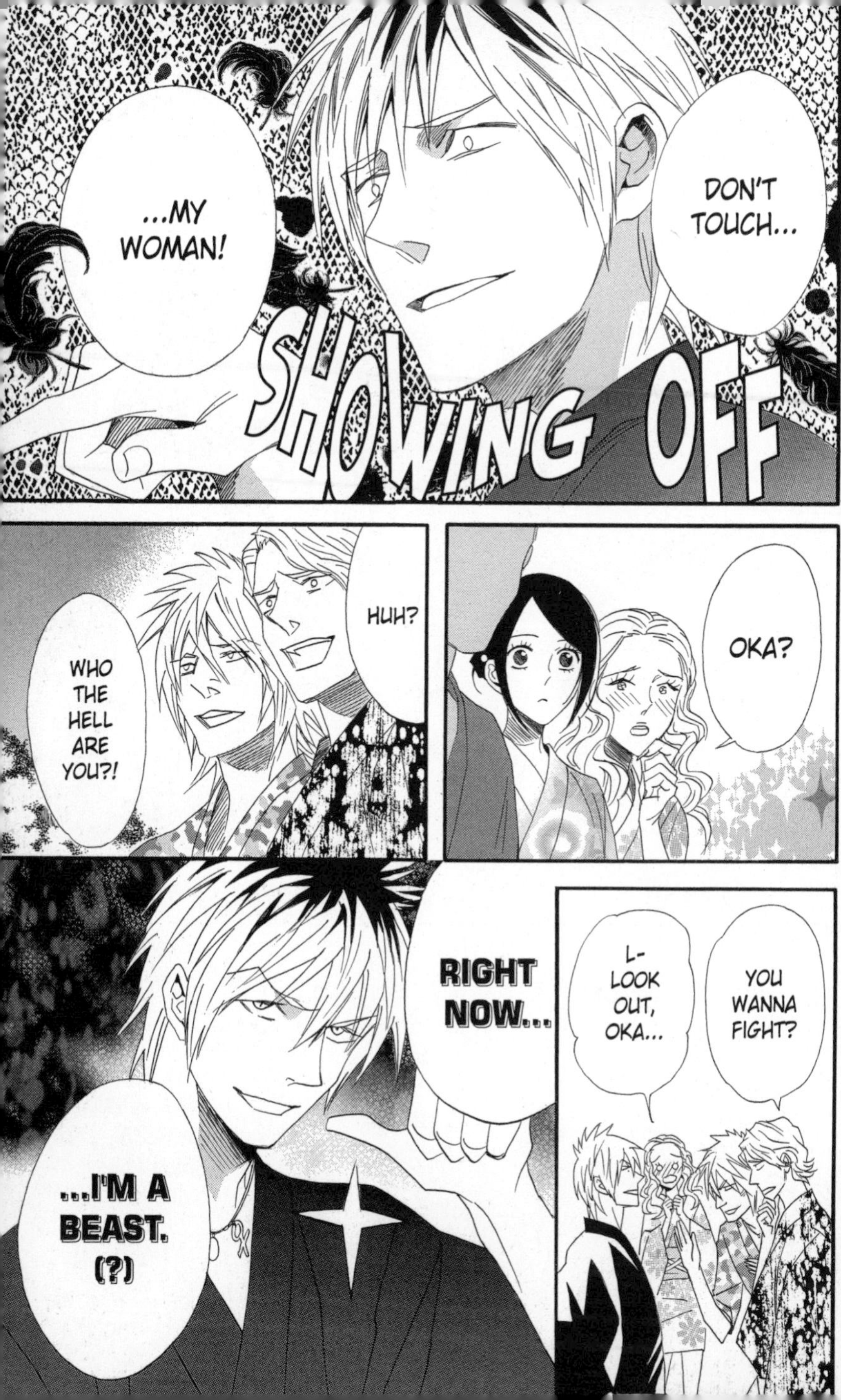
DON'T TOUCH...
...MY WOMAN!
SHOWING OFF
OKA?
HUH?
WHO THE HELL ARE YOU?!
YOU WANNA FIGHT?
L-LOOK OUT, OKA...
RIGHT NOW...
...I'M A BEAST. (?)

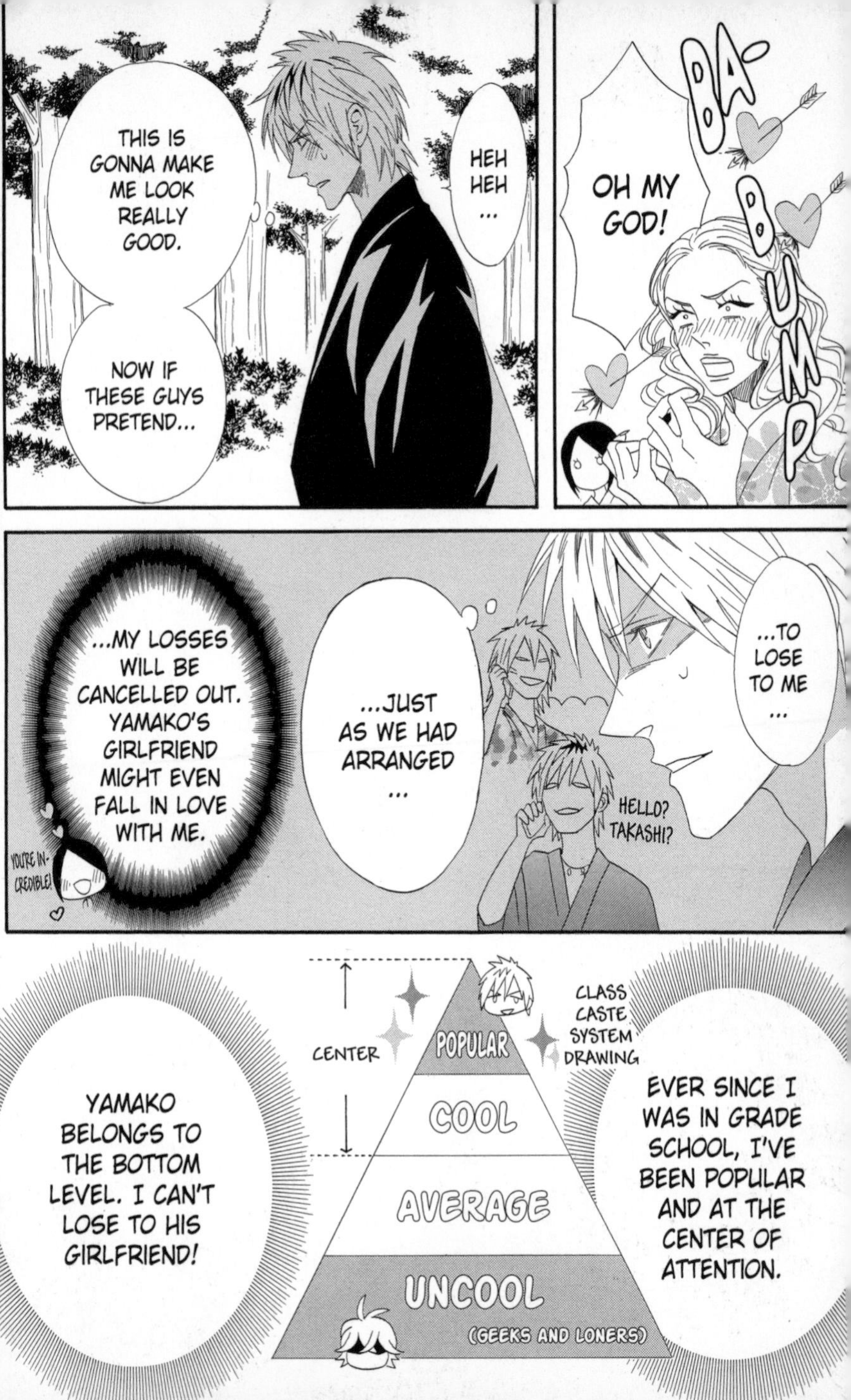
OH MY GOD!
BA-BUMP
HEH HEH ...
THIS IS GONNA MAKE ME LOOK REALLY GOOD.
NOW IF THESE GUYS PRETEND...
...TO LOSE TO ME ...
HELLO? TAKASHI?
...JUST AS WE HAD ARRANGED ...
...MY LOSSES WILL BE CANCELLED OUT. YAMAKO'S GIRLFRIEND MIGHT EVEN FALL IN LOVE WITH ME.
YOU'RE IN-CREDIBLE!
EVER SINCE I WAS IN GRADE SCHOOL, I'VE BEEN POPULAR AND AT THE CENTER OF ATTENTION.
CLASS CASTE SYSTEM DRAWING
CENTER
POPULAR
COOL
AVERAGE
UNCOOL
(GEEKS AND LONERS)
YAMAKO BELONGS TO THE BOTTOM LEVEL. I CAN'T LOSE TO HIS GIRLFRIEND!

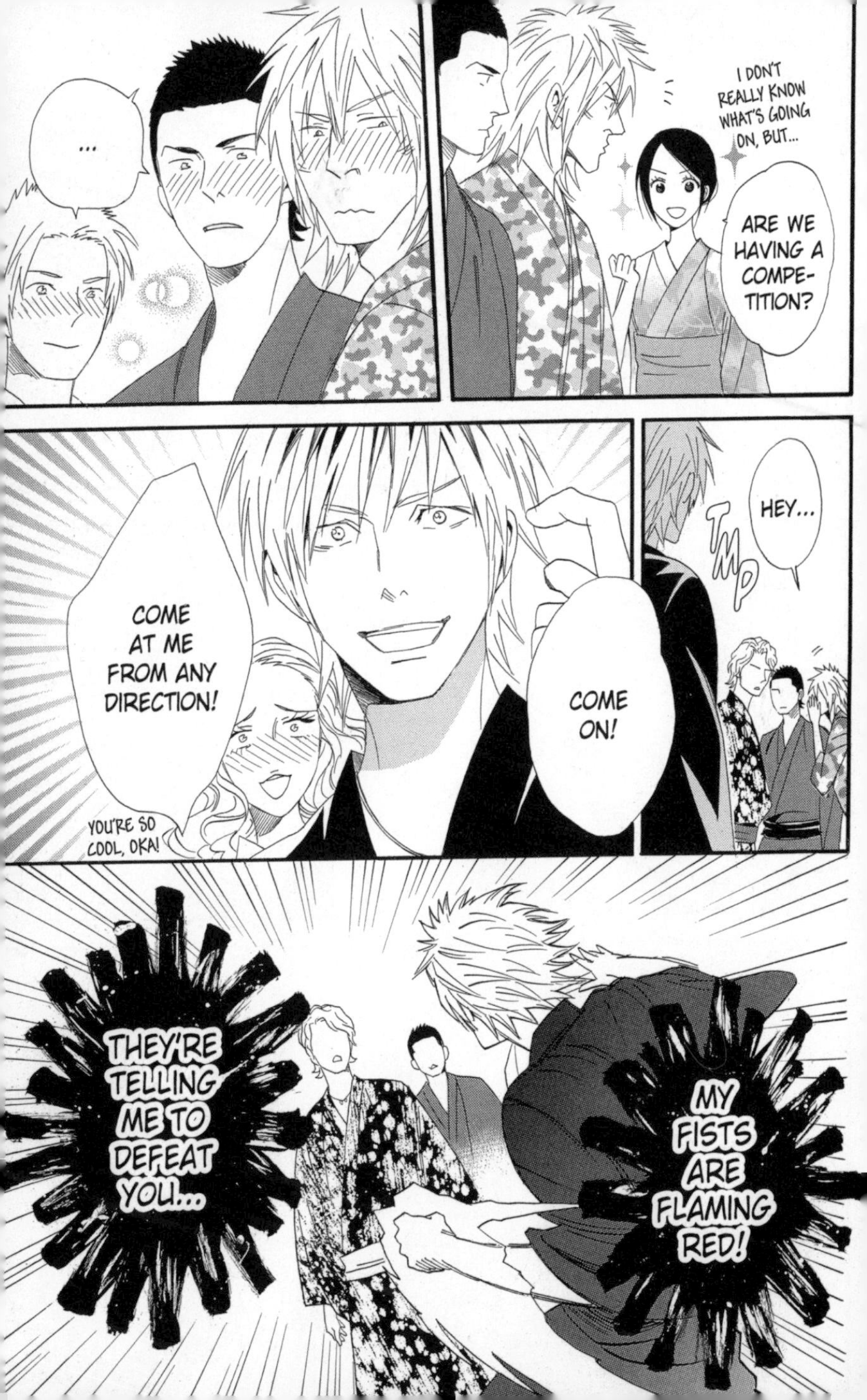
I DON'T REALLY KNOW WHAT'S GOING ON, BUT...
ARE WE HAVING A COMPETITION?
...
HEY...
TMP
COME ON!
COME AT ME FROM ANY DIRECTION!
YOU'RE SO COOL, OKA!
MY FISTS ARE FLAMING RED!
THEY'RE TELLING ME TO DEFEAT YOU...

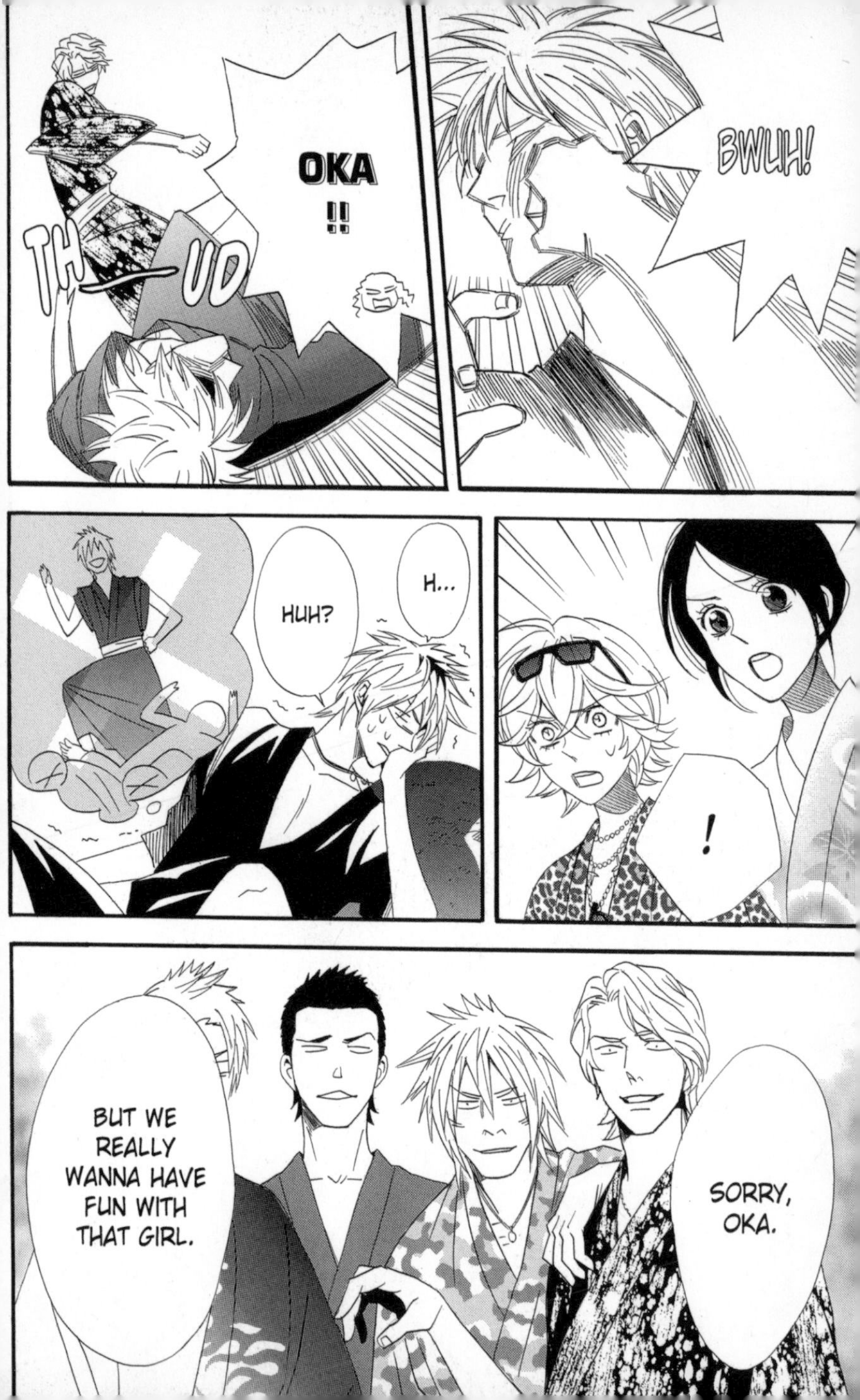
BWUH!
OKA!!
TH—UD
!
H...
HUH?
SORRY, OKA.
BUT WE REALLY WANNA HAVE FUN WITH THAT GIRL.

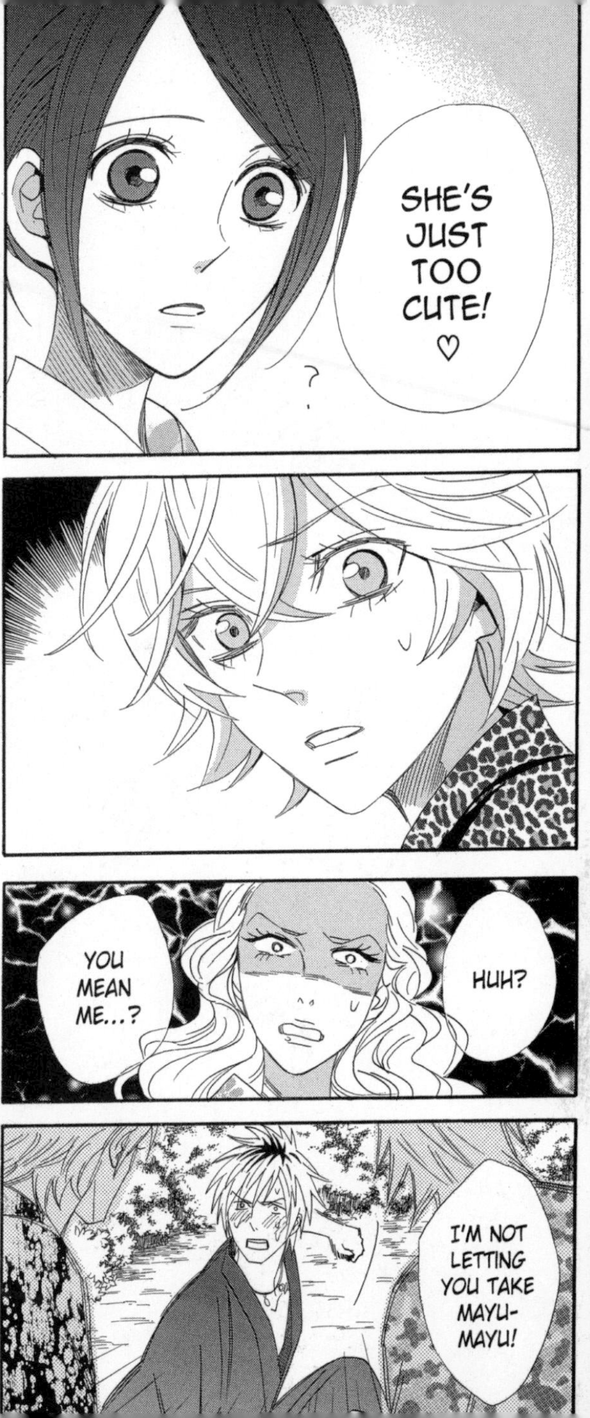
SHE'S JUST TOO CUTE! ♥
?
HUH?
YOU MEAN ME...?
I'M NOT LETTING YOU TAKE MAYU-MAYU!

Production Assistance:

Shimada-san
Kuwana-san
Kaneko-san
Sakurai-san
Takowa-san
Nakazawa-san
Tanaka-san
Kawashima-san
Sayaka-san
Yone-yan

Special Thanks:

Abe-san
All My Readers
My Family

Starting next volume, Otomen will be heading toward its finale. I hope you continue to read the next few volumes until the end.

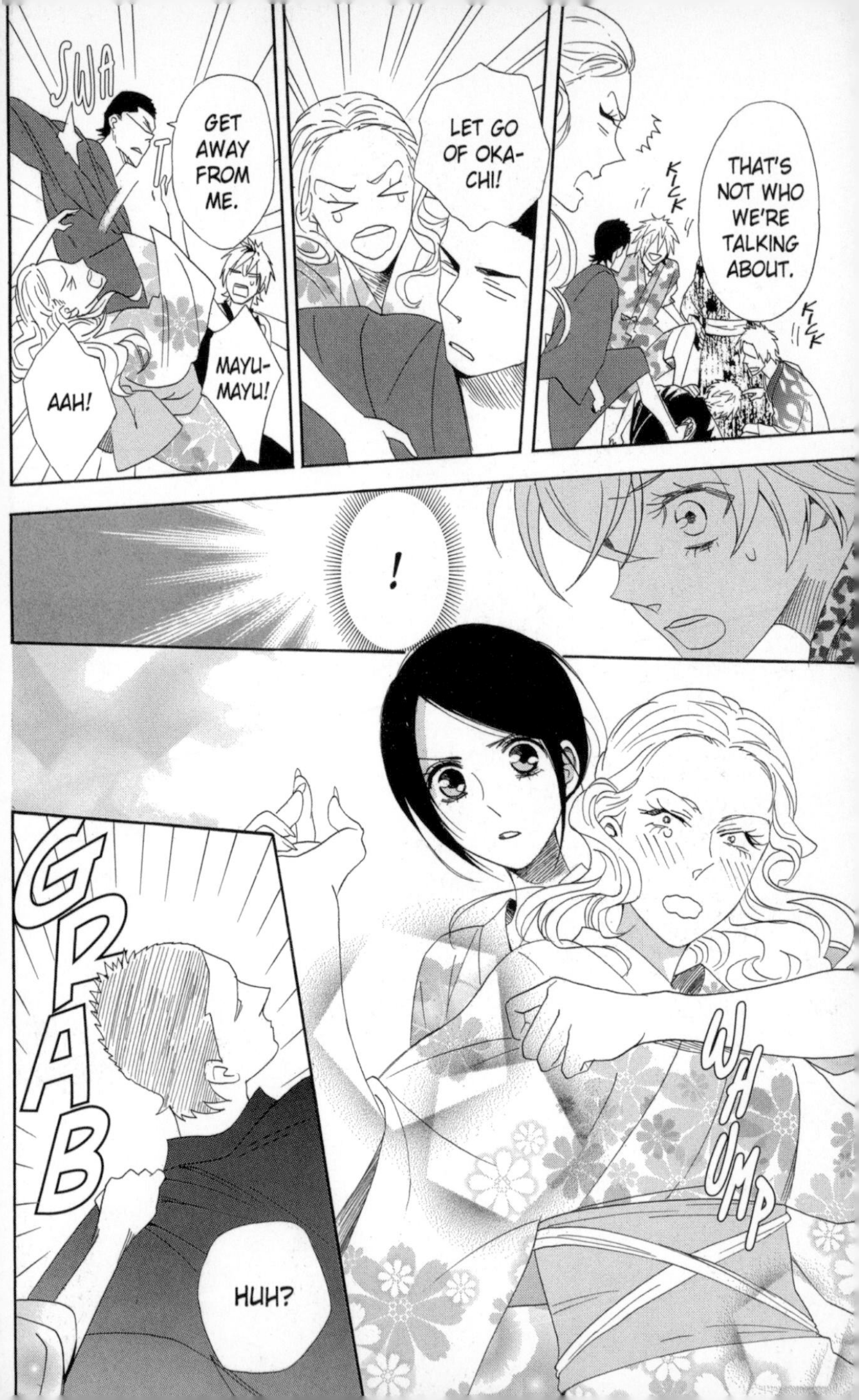
THAT'S NOT WHO WE'RE TALKING ABOUT.
KICK
KICK
LET GO OF OKA-CHI!
GET AWAY FROM ME.
SWA
MAYU-MAYU!
AAH!
!
WHUMP
GRAB
HUH?

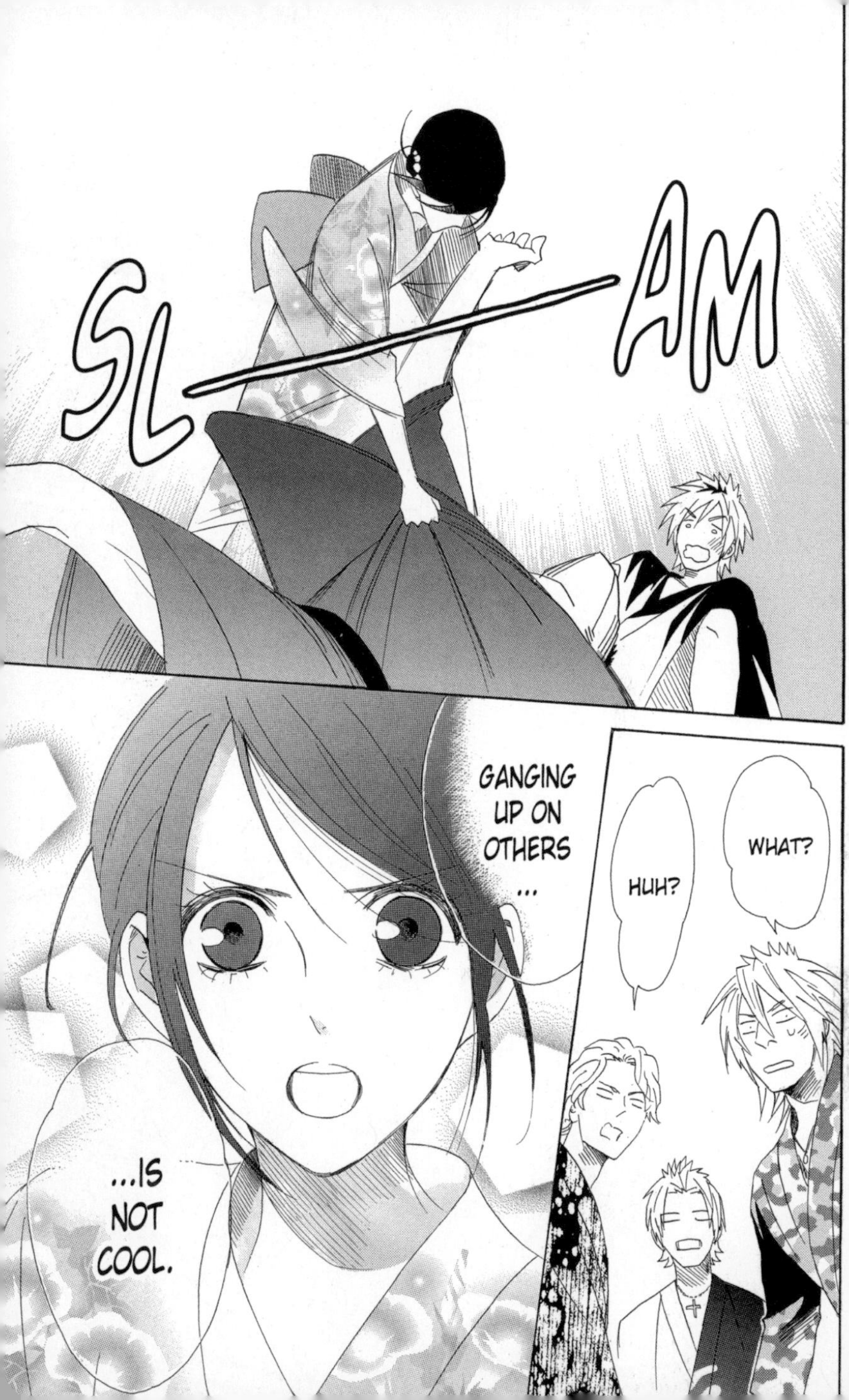
SL
AM
WHAT?
HUH?
GANGING UP ON OTHERS ...
...IS NOT COOL.

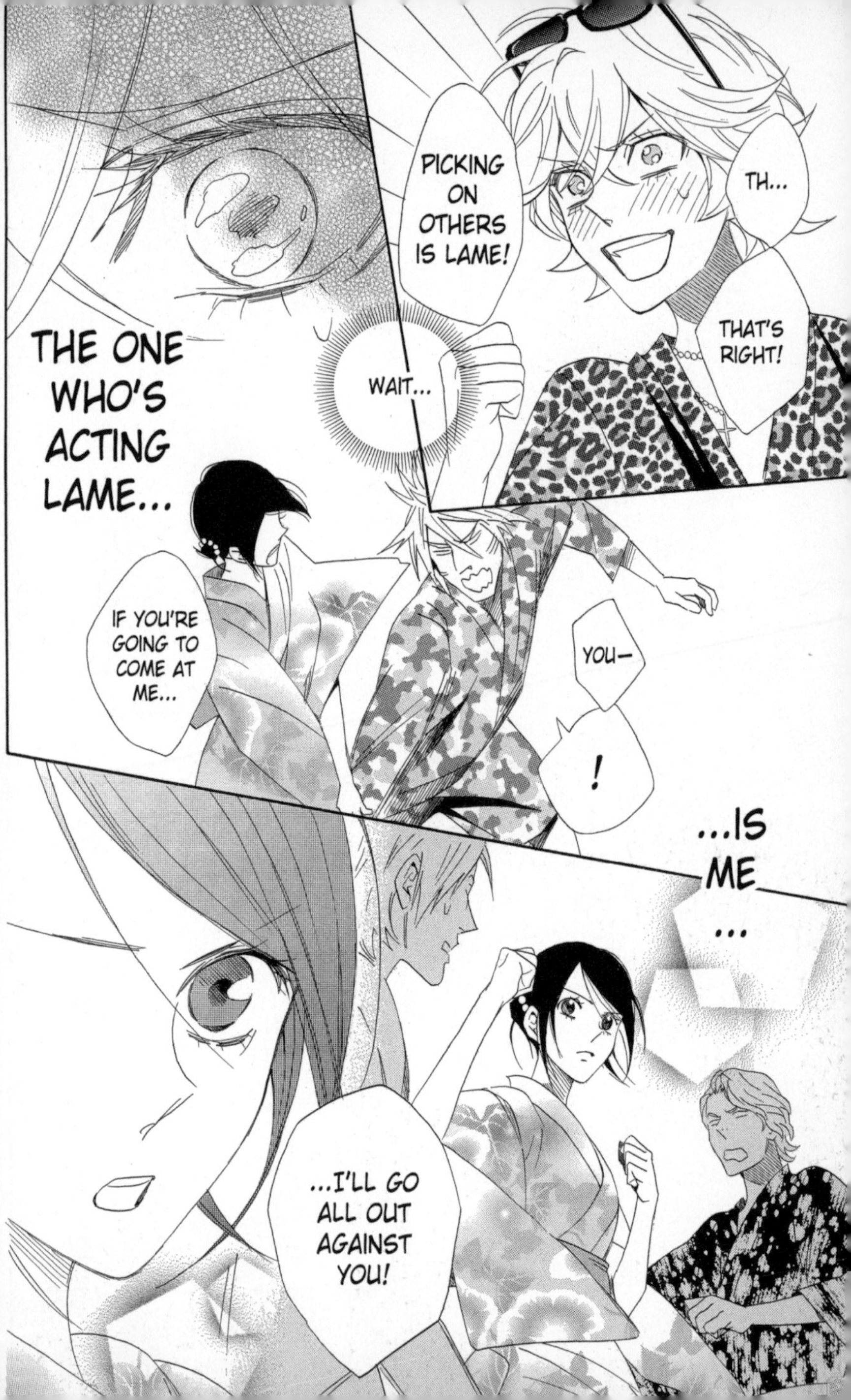
PICKING ON OTHERS IS LAME!
TH...
THAT'S RIGHT!
WAIT...
THE ONE WHO'S ACTING LAME...
YOU—
!
IF YOU'RE GOING TO COME AT ME...
...IS ME...
...I'LL GO ALL OUT AGAINST YOU!

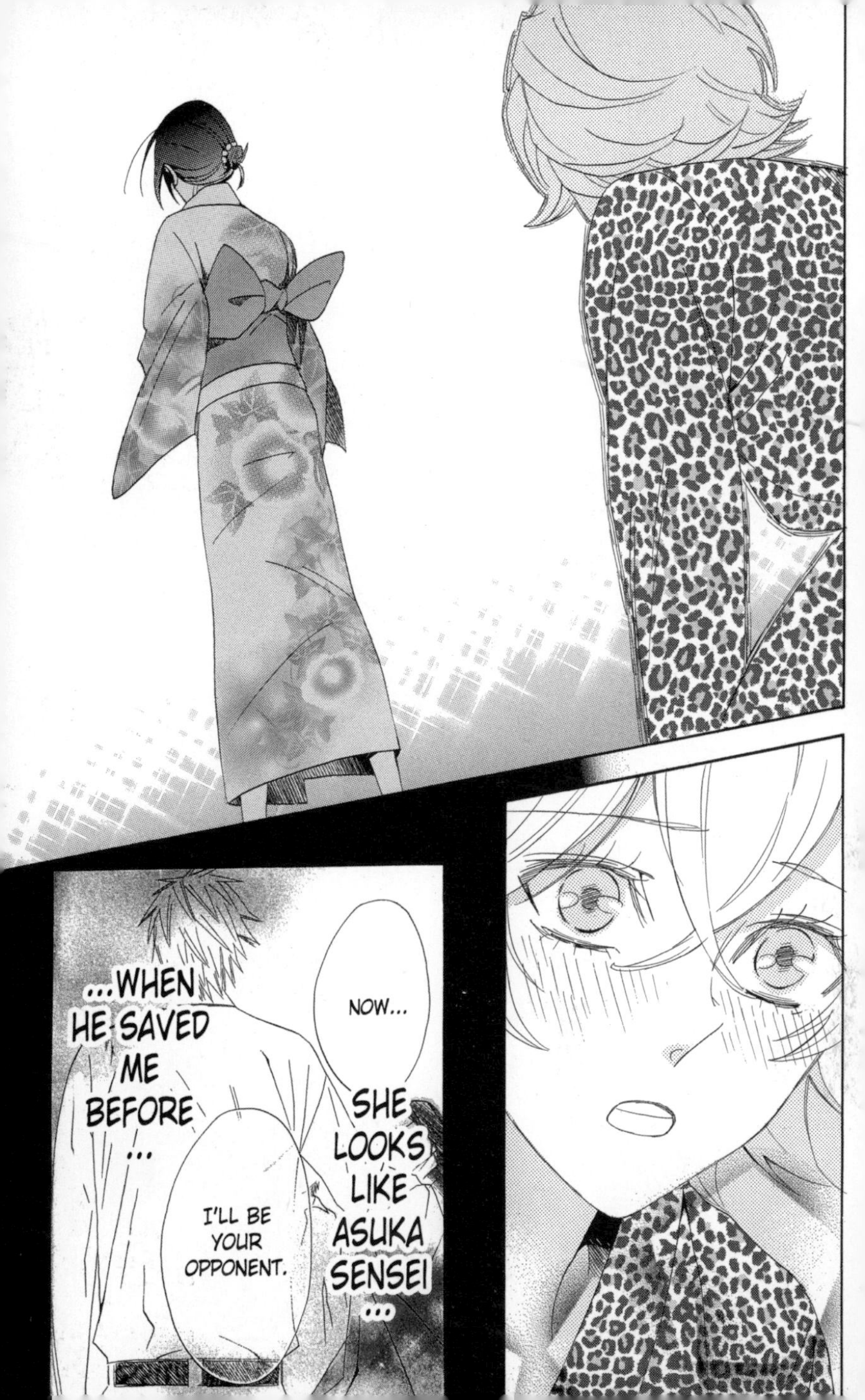
NOW...
SHE LOOKS LIKE ASUKA SENSEI...
...WHEN HE SAVED ME BEFORE...
I'LL BE YOUR OPPONENT.

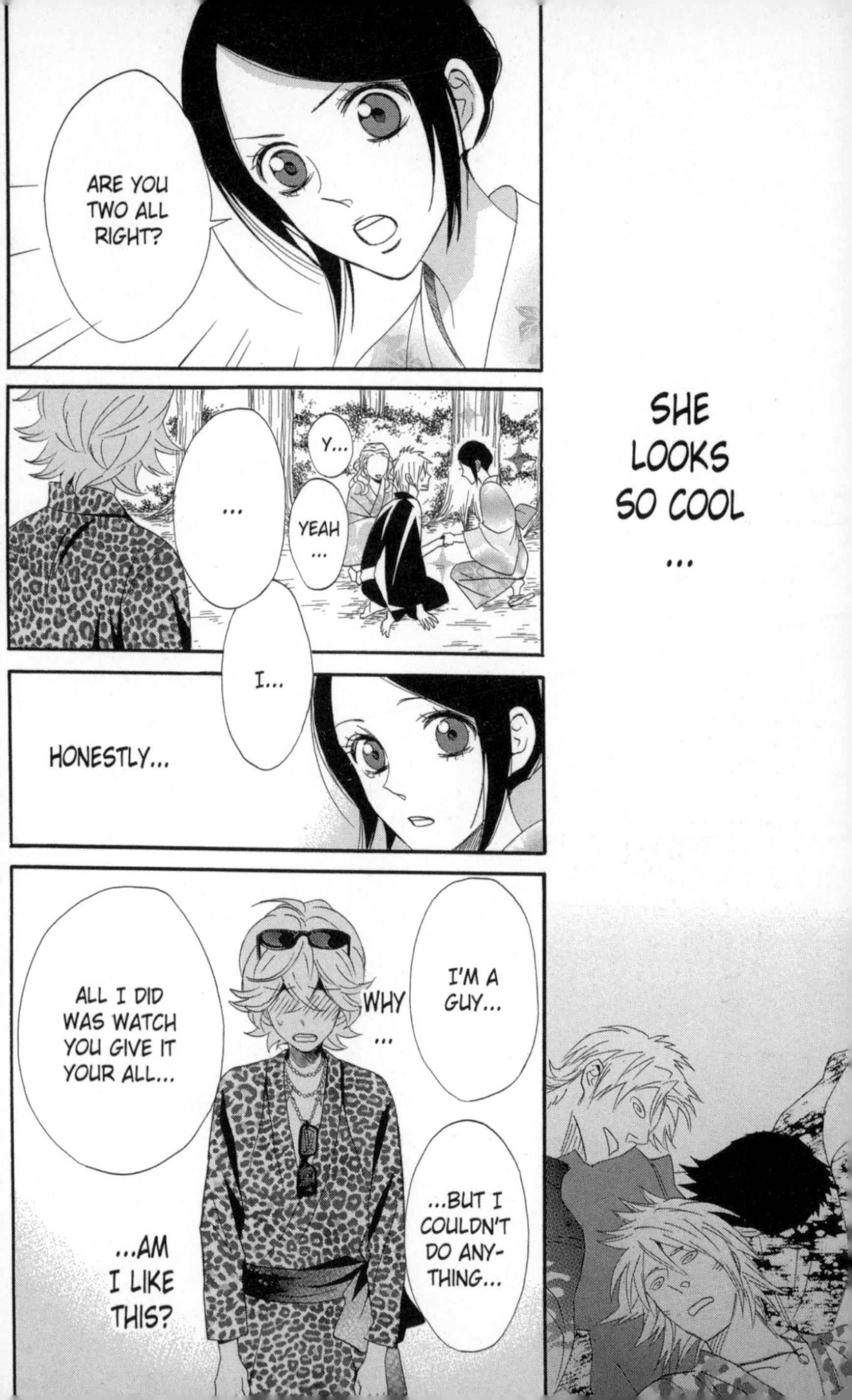
ARE YOU TWO ALL RIGHT?
SHE LOOKS SO COOL ...
Y...
YEAH ...
...
I...
HONESTLY...
I'M A GUY...
WHY ...
ALL I DID WAS WATCH YOU GIVE IT YOUR ALL...
...BUT I COULDN'T DO ANY-THING...
...AM I LIKE THIS?

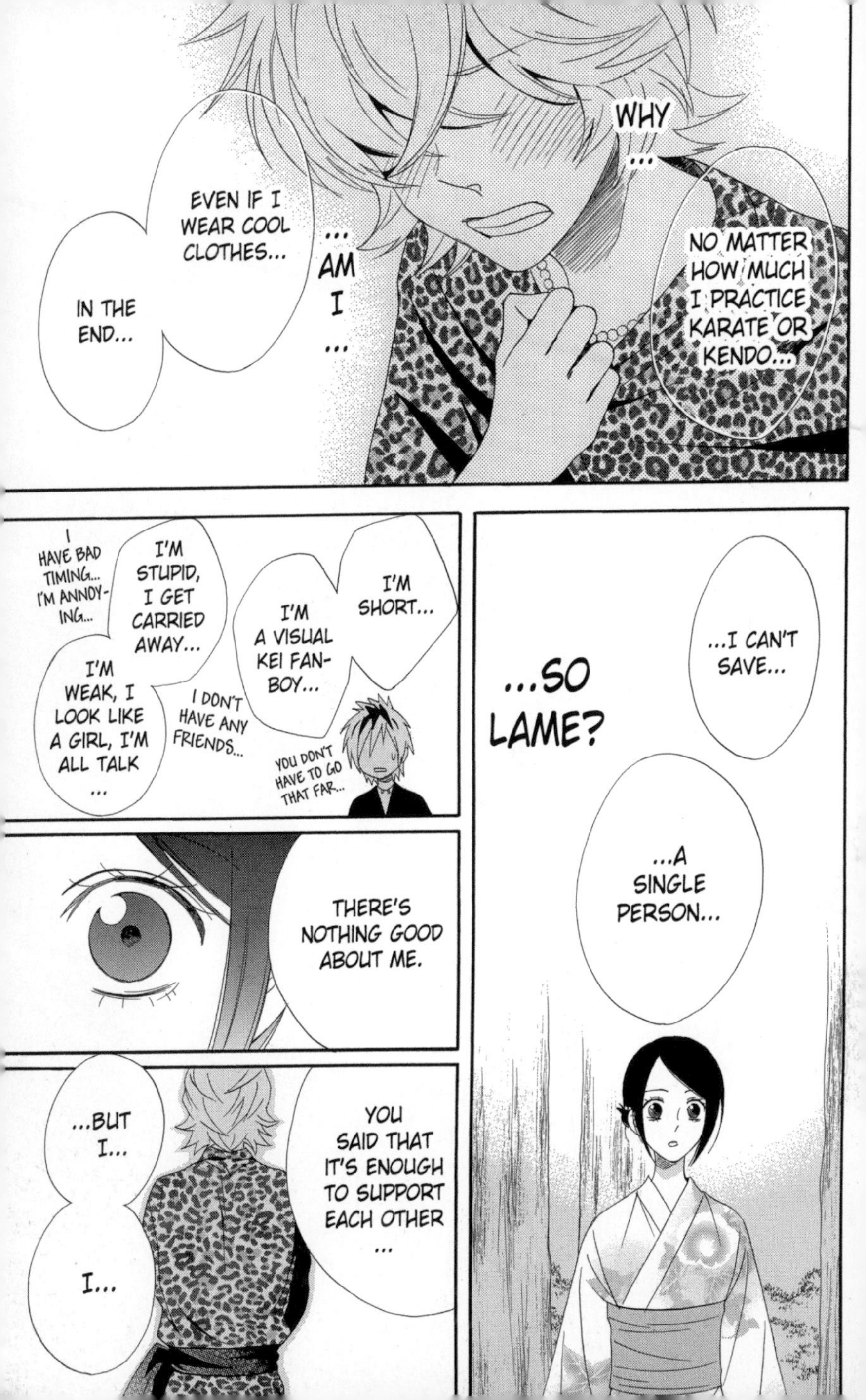
WHY ...
NO MATTER HOW MUCH I PRACTICE KARATE OR KENDO...
...AM I ...
EVEN IF I WEAR COOL CLOTHES...
IN THE END...
...I CAN'T SAVE...
...SO LAME?
...A SINGLE PERSON...
I'M SHORT...
I'M A VISUAL KEI FAN-BOY...
I'M STUPID, I GET CARRIED AWAY...
I HAVE BAD TIMING... I'M ANNOY-ING...
I DON'T HAVE ANY FRIENDS...
I'M WEAK, I LOOK LIKE A GIRL, I'M ALL TALK ...
YOU DON'T HAVE TO GO THAT FAR...
THERE'S NOTHING GOOD ABOUT ME.
YOU SAID THAT IT'S ENOUGH TO SUPPORT EACH OTHER ...
...BUT I...
I...

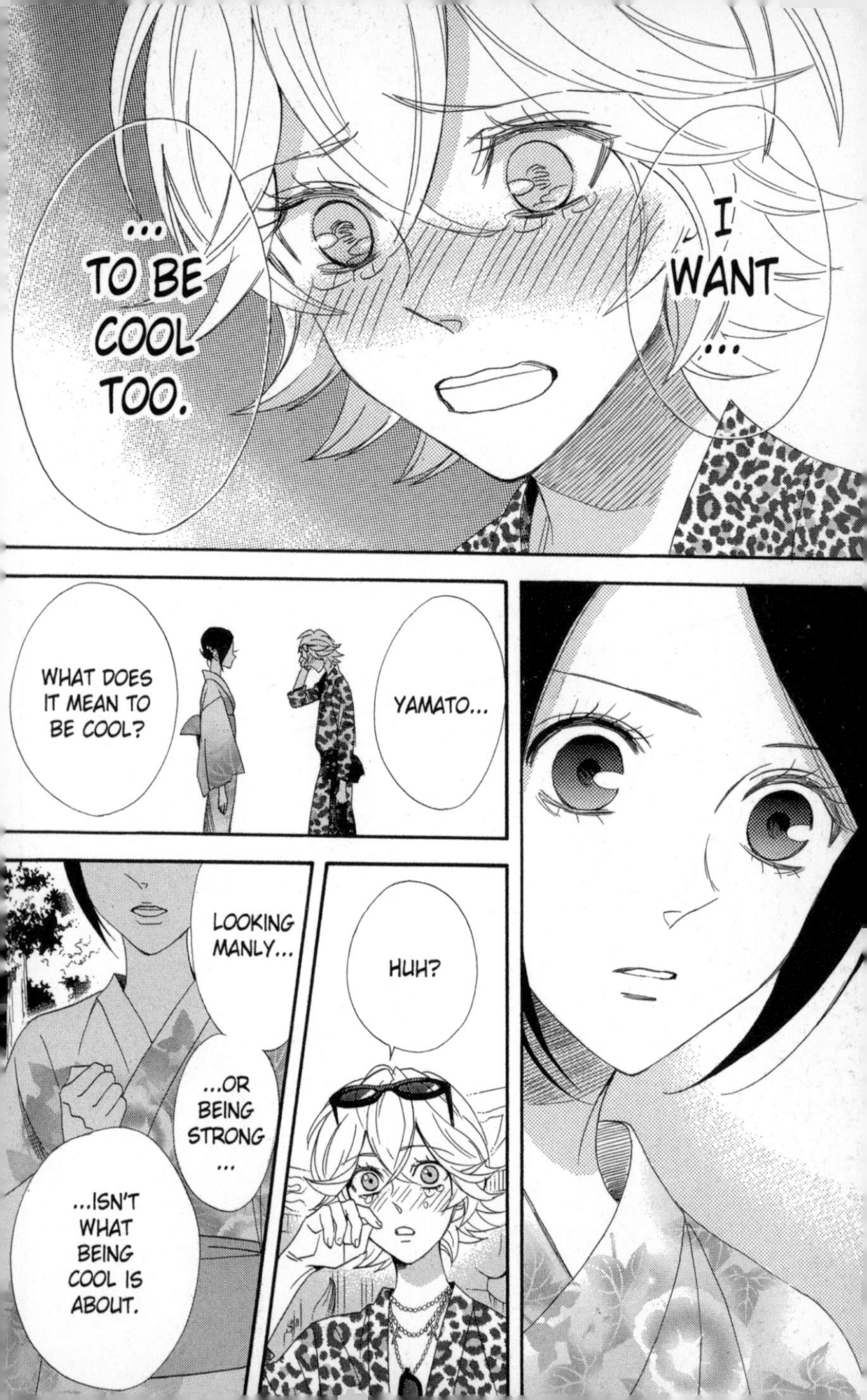
I WANT...
...TO BE COOL TOO.
YAMATO...
WHAT DOES IT MEAN TO BE COOL?
HUH?
LOOKING MANLY...
...OR BEING STRONG ...
...ISN'T WHAT BEING COOL IS ABOUT.

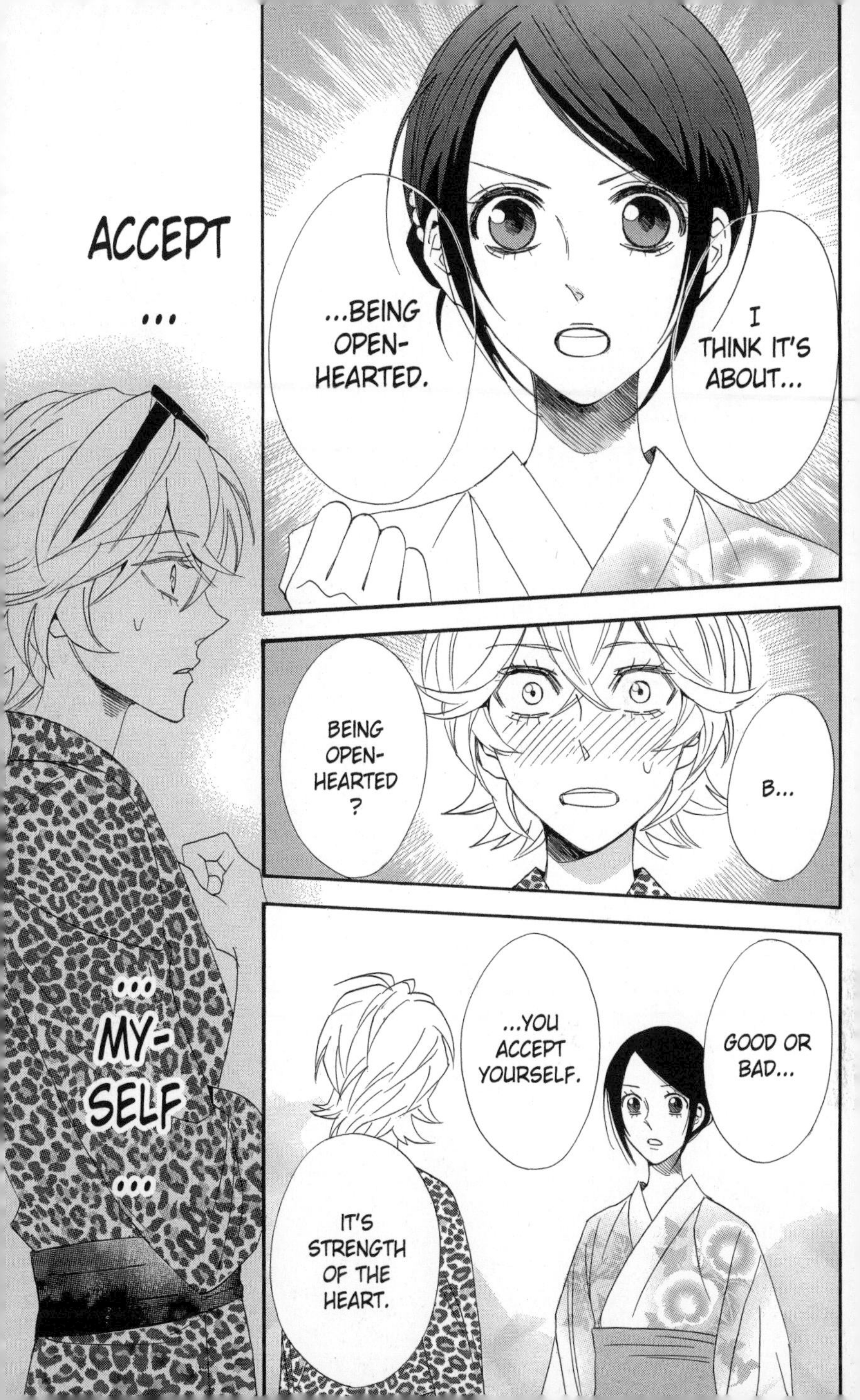
I THINK IT'S ABOUT...
...BEING OPEN-HEARTED.
B...
BEING OPEN-HEARTED?
GOOD OR BAD...
...YOU ACCEPT YOURSELF.
IT'S STRENGTH OF THE HEART.
ACCEPT ...
...MY-SELF...

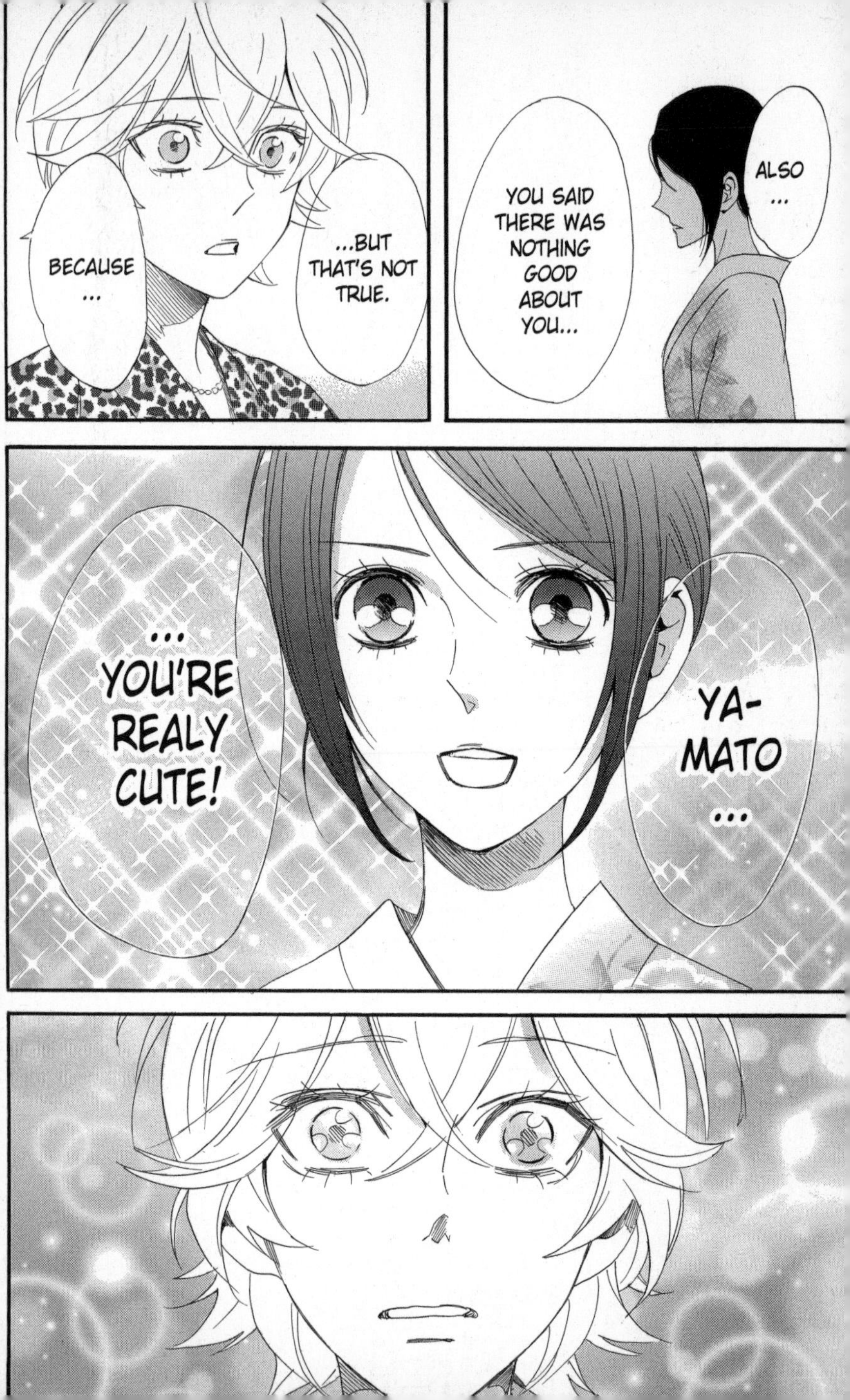
ALSO ...
YOU SAID THERE WAS NOTHING GOOD ABOUT YOU...
...BUT THAT'S NOT TRUE.
BECAUSE ...
YA-MATO ...
... YOU'RE REALY CUTE!

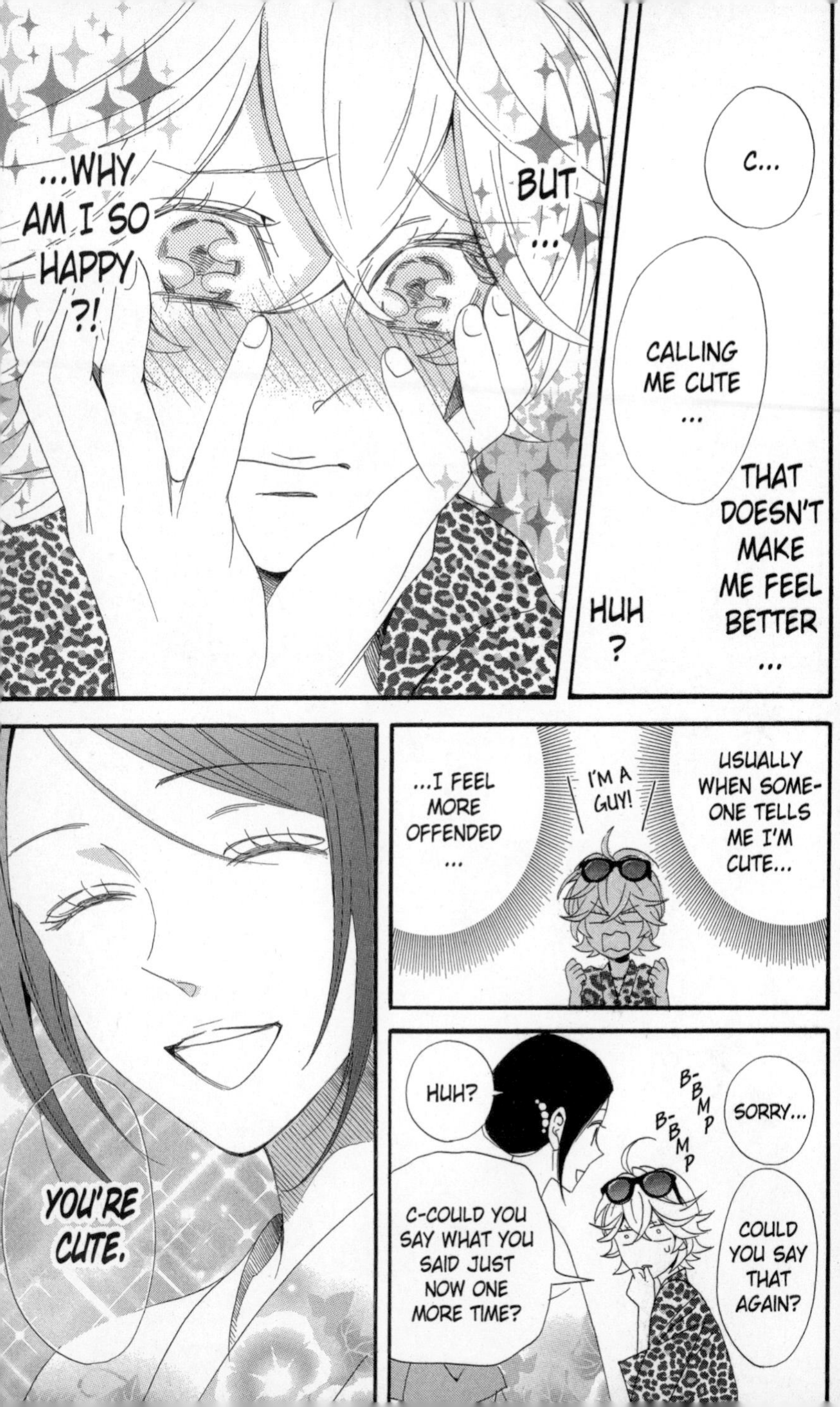
C...
CALLING ME CUTE ...
THAT DOESN'T MAKE ME FEEL BETTER ...
HUH ?
BUT ...
...WHY AM I SO HAPPY ?!
USUALLY WHEN SOME-ONE TELLS ME I'M CUTE...
I'M A GUY!
...I FEEL MORE OFFENDED ...
SORRY...
COULD YOU SAY THAT AGAIN?
B-BMP
B-BMP
HUH?
C-COULD YOU SAY WHAT YOU SAID JUST NOW ONE MORE TIME?
YOU'RE CUTE.

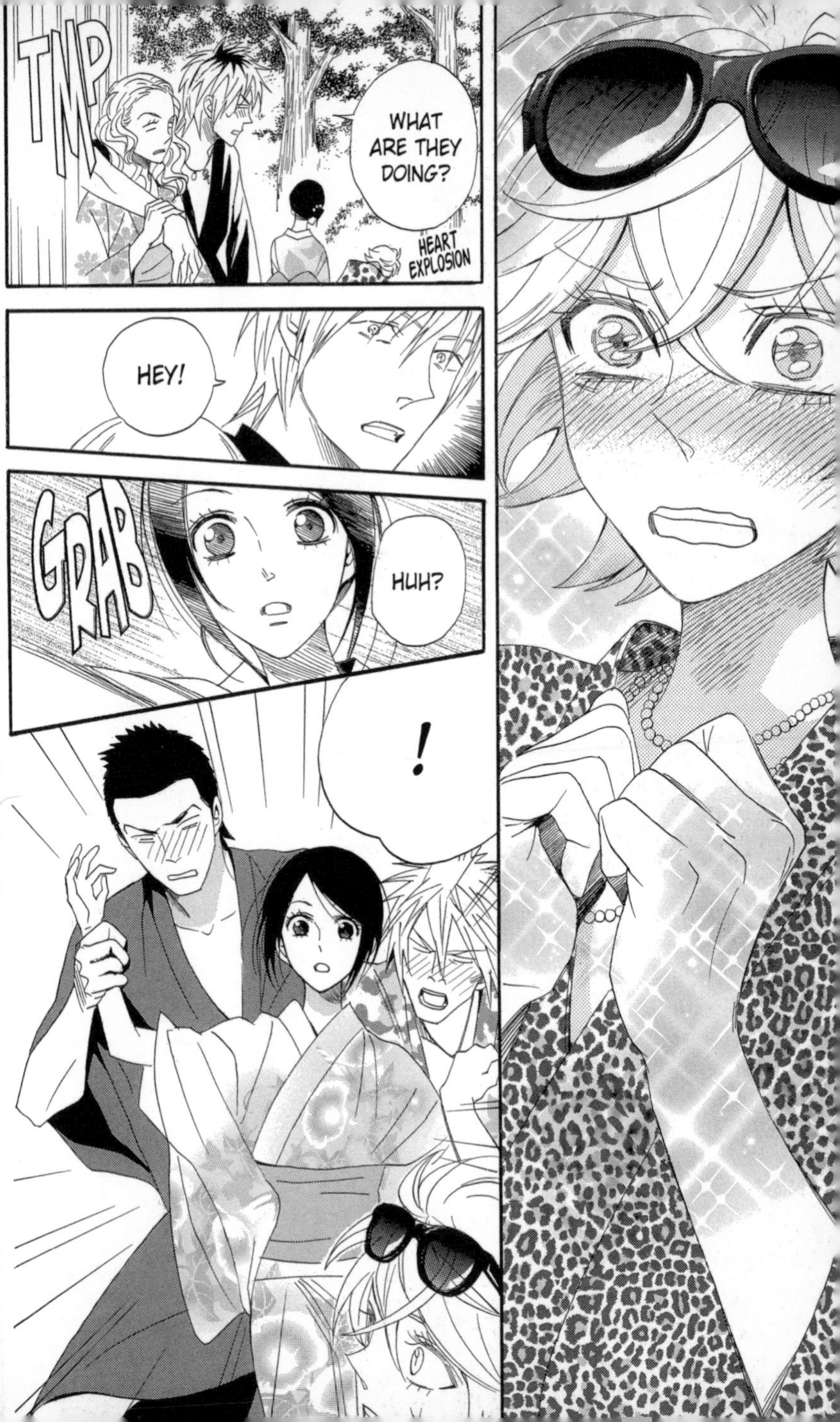
WHAT ARE THEY DOING?
HEART EXPLOSION
TMP
HEY!
HUH?
GRAB
!

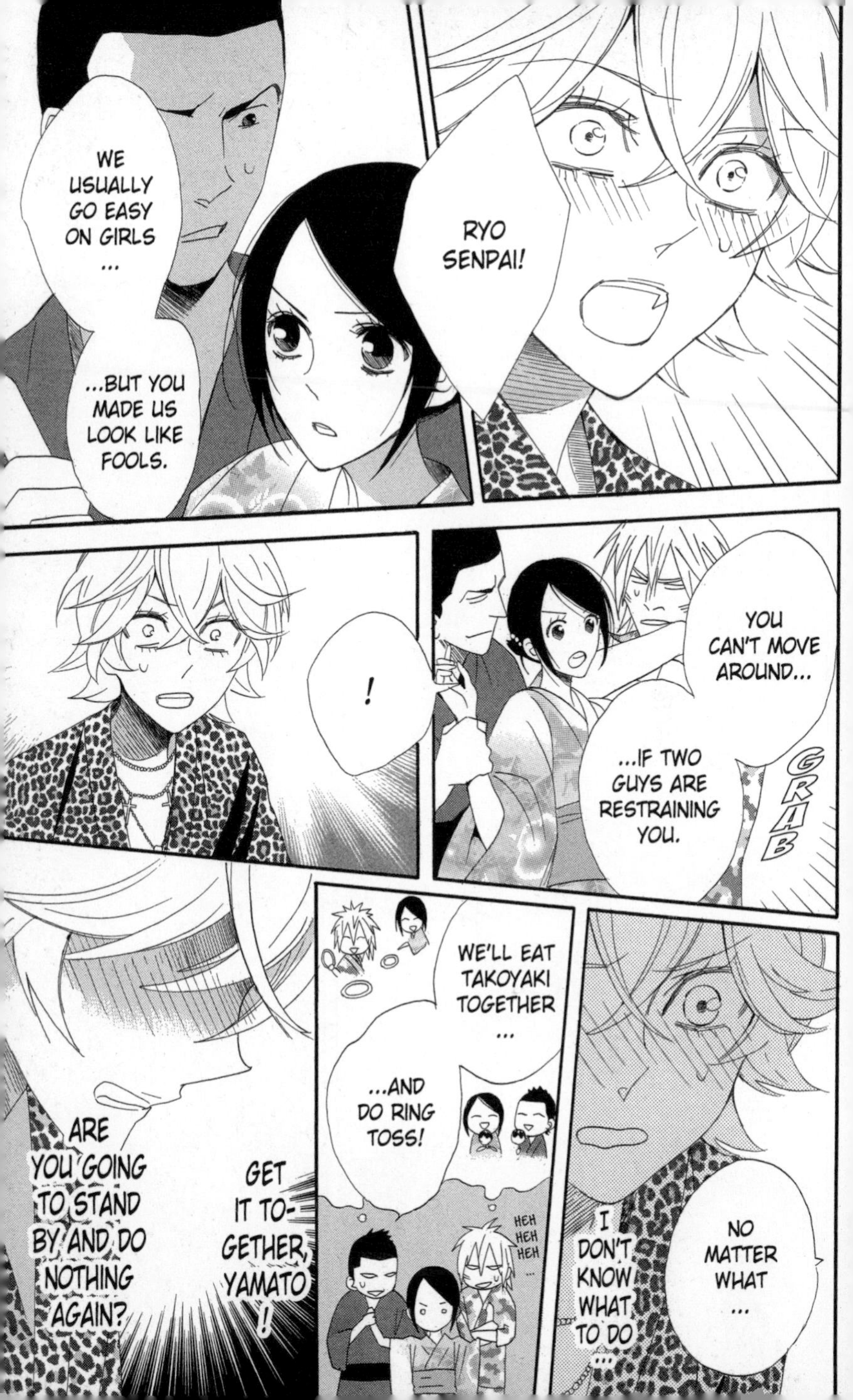
RYO SENPAI!
WE USUALLY GO EASY ON GIRLS ...
...BUT YOU MADE US LOOK LIKE FOOLS.
YOU CAN'T MOVE AROUND...
...IF TWO GUYS ARE RESTRAINING YOU.
GRAB
!
NO MATTER WHAT ...
I DON'T KNOW WHAT TO DO ...
WE'LL EAT TAKOYAKI TOGETHER ...
...AND DO RING TOSS!
HEH HEH HEH ...
GET IT TO-GETHER, YAMATO !
ARE YOU GOING TO STAND BY AND DO NOTHING AGAIN?

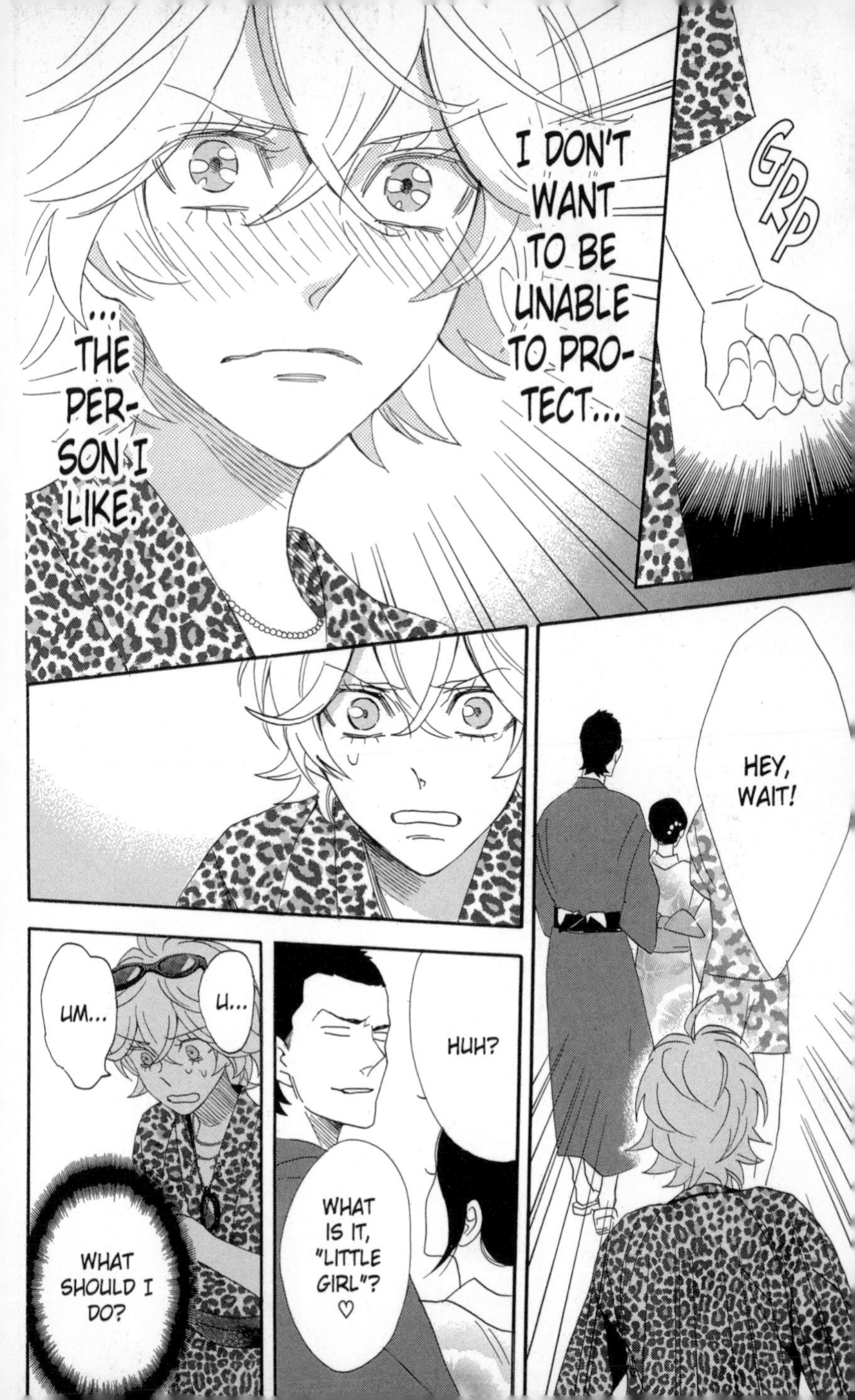
GRP
I DON'T WANT TO BE UNABLE TO PROTECT...
...THE PERSON I LIKE.
HEY, WAIT!
HUH?
WHAT IS IT, "LITTLE GIRL"? ♡
U...
UM...
WHAT SHOULD I DO?

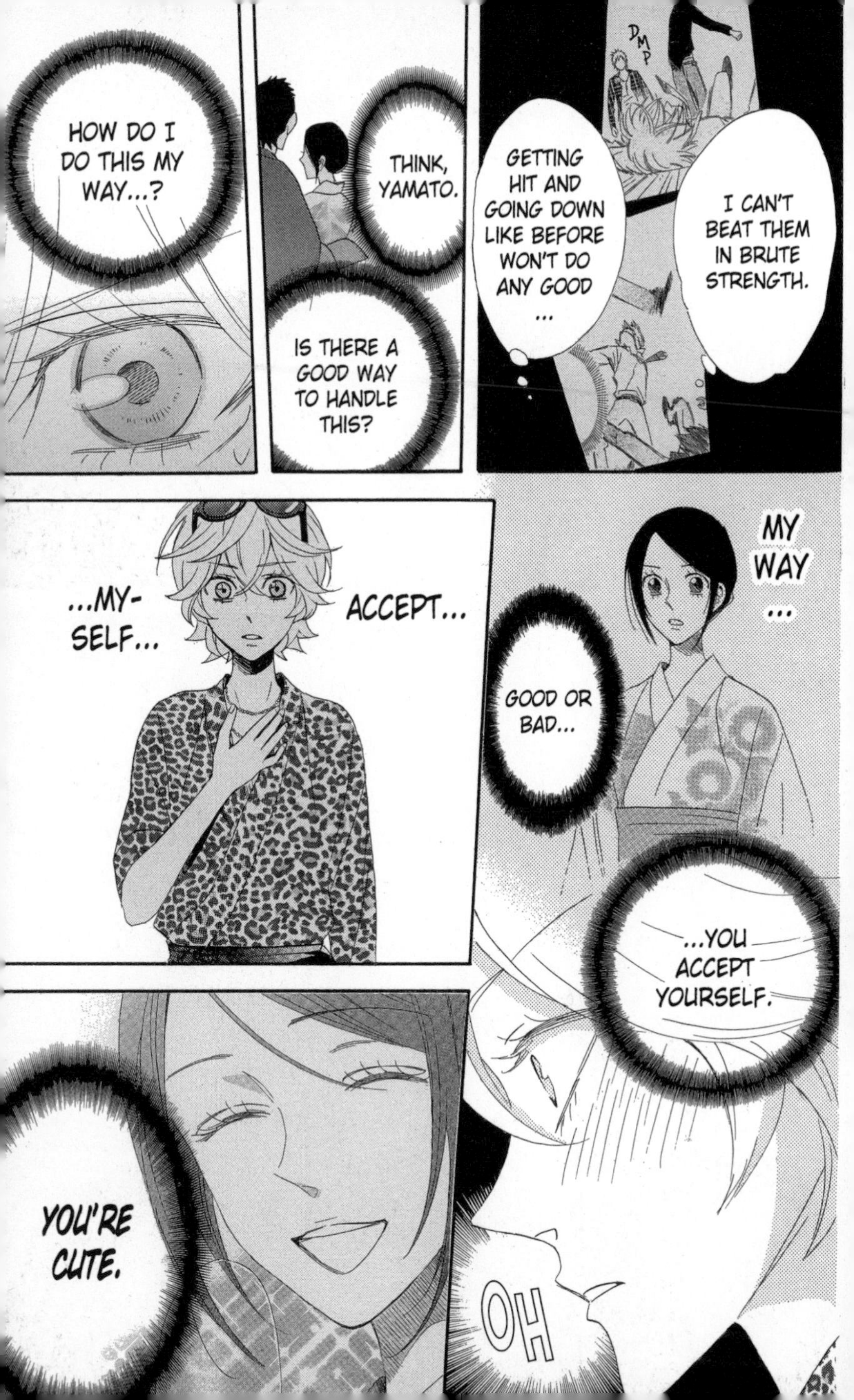
DMP
I CAN'T BEAT THEM IN BRUTE STRENGTH.
GETTING HIT AND GOING DOWN LIKE BEFORE WON'T DO ANY GOOD ...
THINK, YAMATO.
IS THERE A GOOD WAY TO HANDLE THIS?
HOW DO I DO THIS MY WAY...?
MY WAY ...
GOOD OR BAD...
ACCEPT...
...MY-SELF...
...YOU ACCEPT YOURSELF.
OH
YOU'RE CUTE.

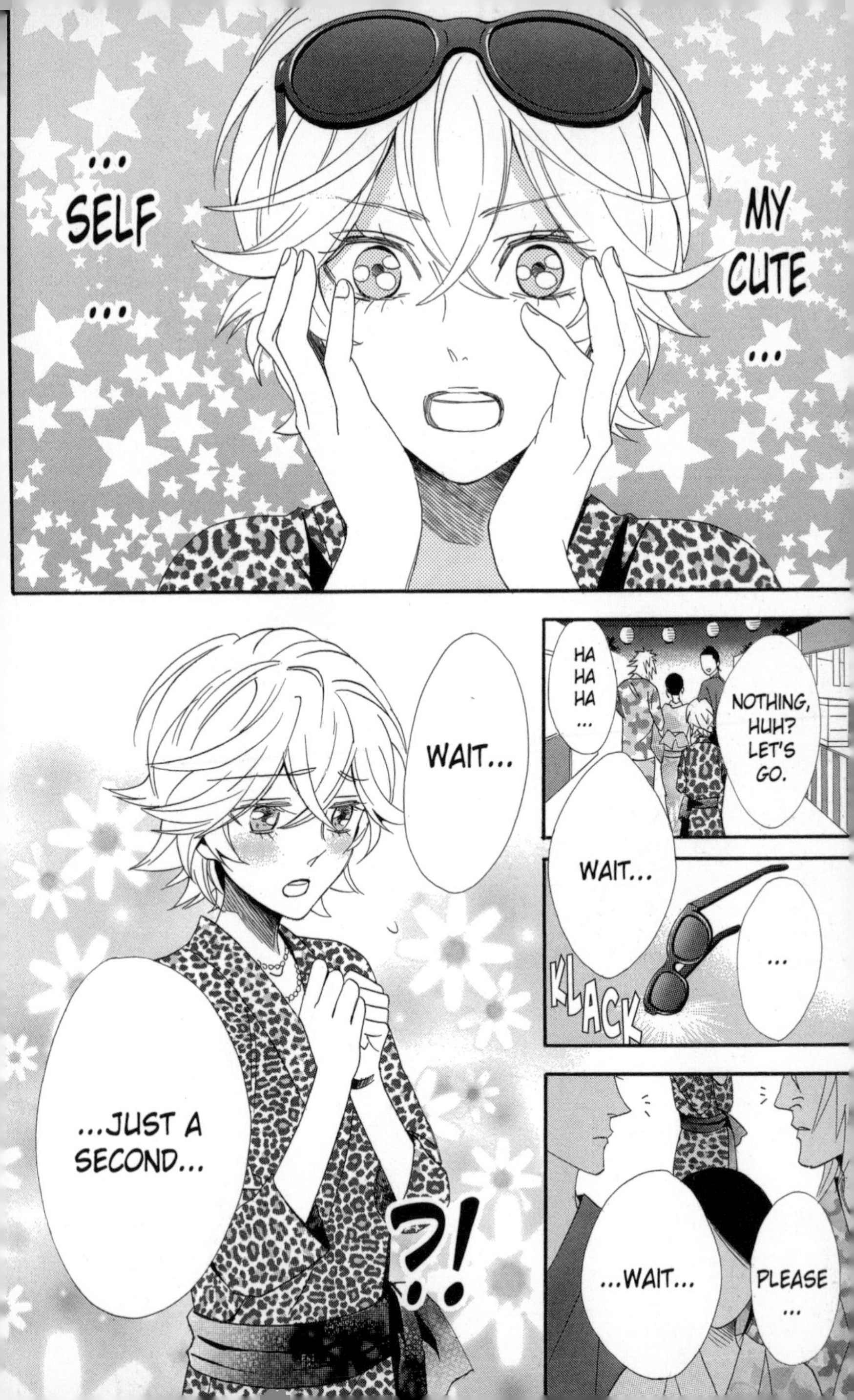
MY CUTE ...
... SELF ...
NOTHING, HUH? LET'S GO.
HA HA HA ...
WAIT...
...
KLACK
PLEASE ...
...WAIT...
WAIT...
...JUST A SECOND...
?!

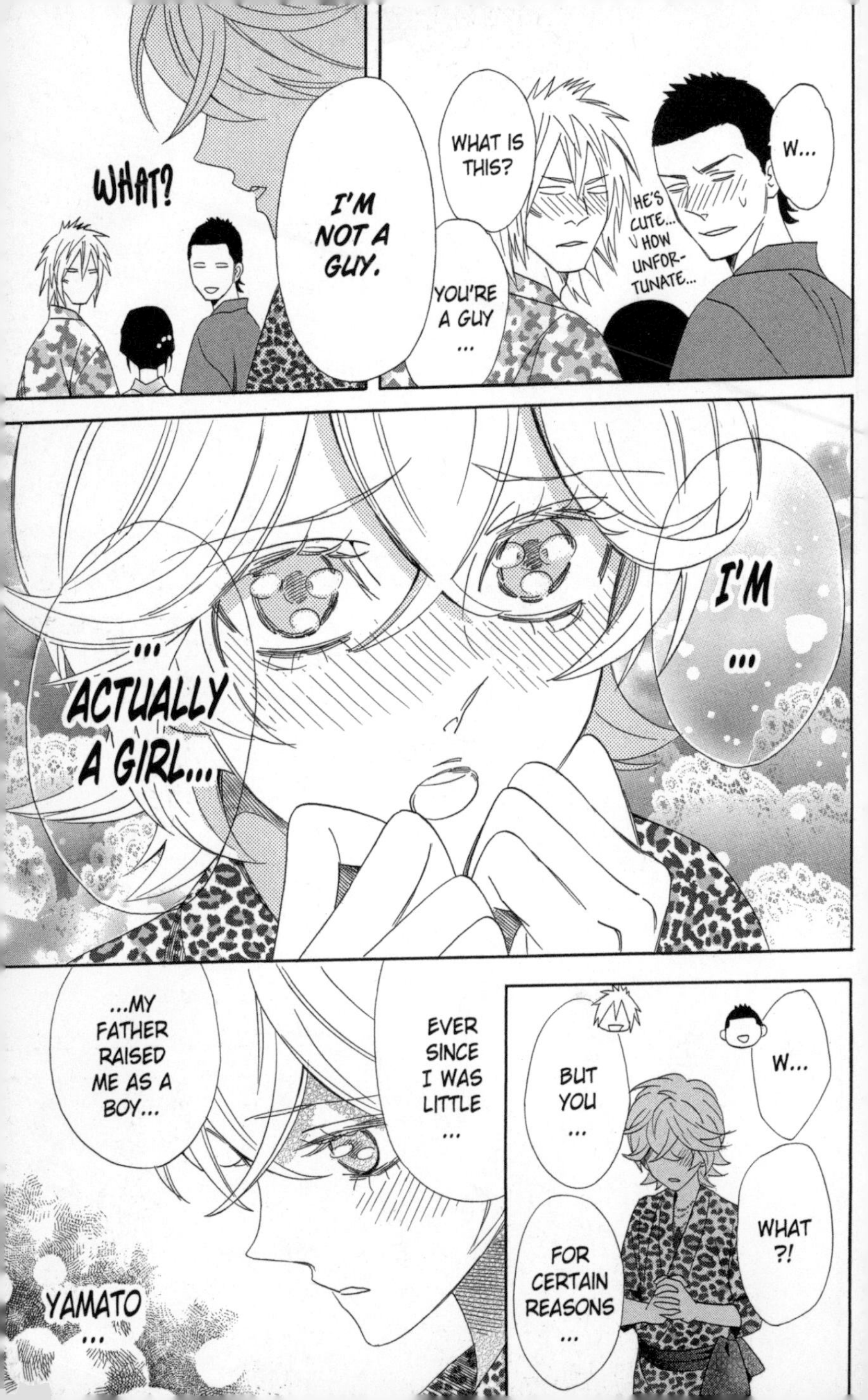
W...
HE'S CUTE... HOW UNFOR-TUNATE...
WHAT IS THIS?
YOU'RE A GUY ...
I'M NOT A GUY.
WHAT?
I'M ...
... ACTUALLY A GIRL...
W...
BUT YOU ...
WHAT ?!
FOR CERTAIN REASONS ...
EVER SINCE I WAS LITTLE ...
...MY FATHER RAISED ME AS A BOY...
YAMATO ...

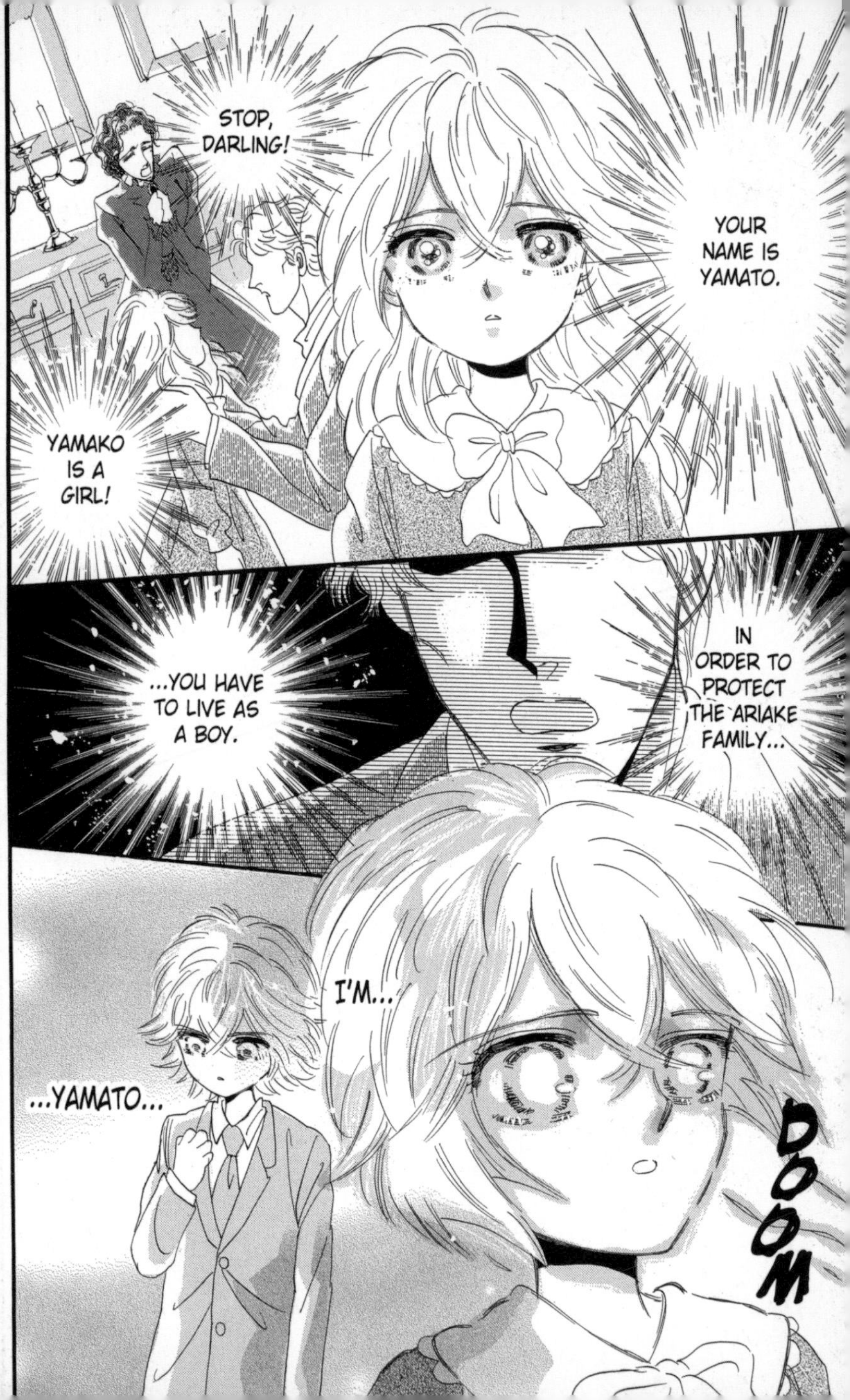
YOUR NAME IS YAMATO.
STOP, DARLING!
YAMAKO IS A GIRL!
IN ORDER TO PROTECT THE ARIAKE FAMILY...
...YOU HAVE TO LIVE AS A BOY.
DOOM
I'M...
...YAMATO...

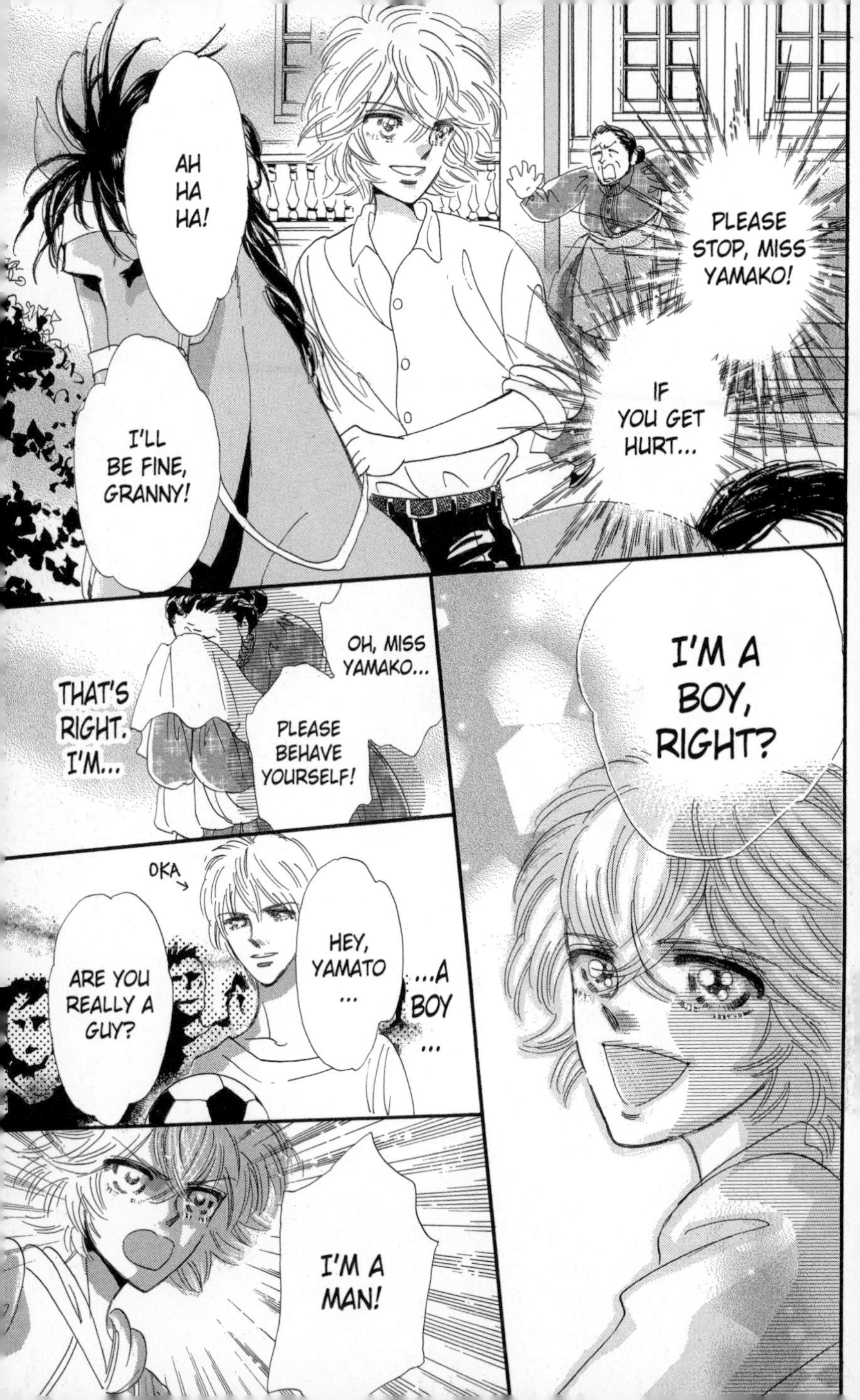
PLEASE STOP, MISS YAMAKO!
IF YOU GET HURT...
AH HA HA!
I'LL BE FINE, GRANNY!
I'M A BOY, RIGHT?
OH, MISS YAMAKO...
PLEASE BEHAVE YOURSELF!
THAT'S RIGHT. I'M...
...A BOY ...
HEY, YAMATO ...
OKA
ARE YOU REALLY A GUY?
I'M A MAN!

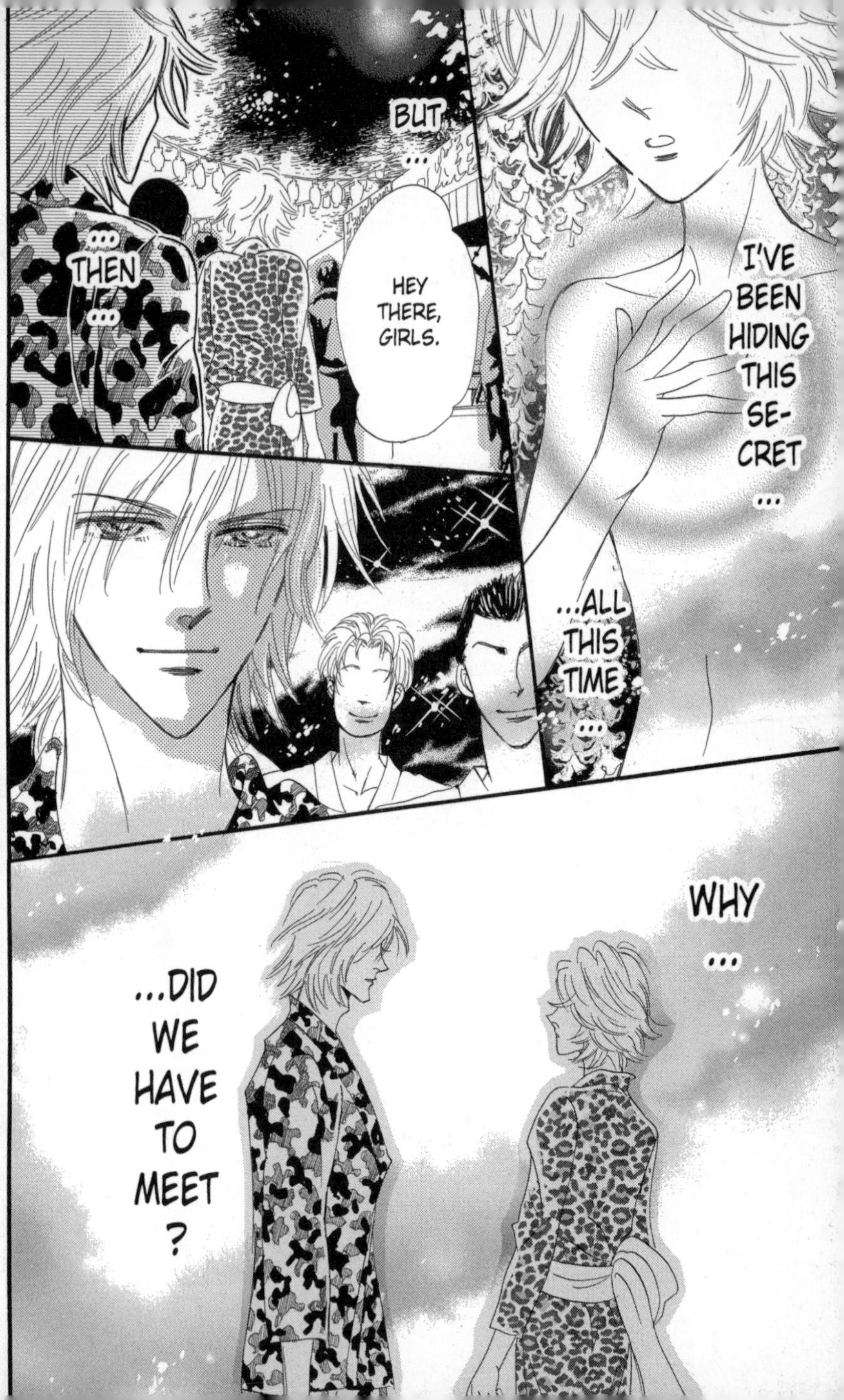
I'VE BEEN HIDING THIS SE-CRET...
...ALL THIS TIME...
BUT...
HEY THERE, GIRLS.
...THEN...
WHY...
...DID WE HAVE TO MEET?

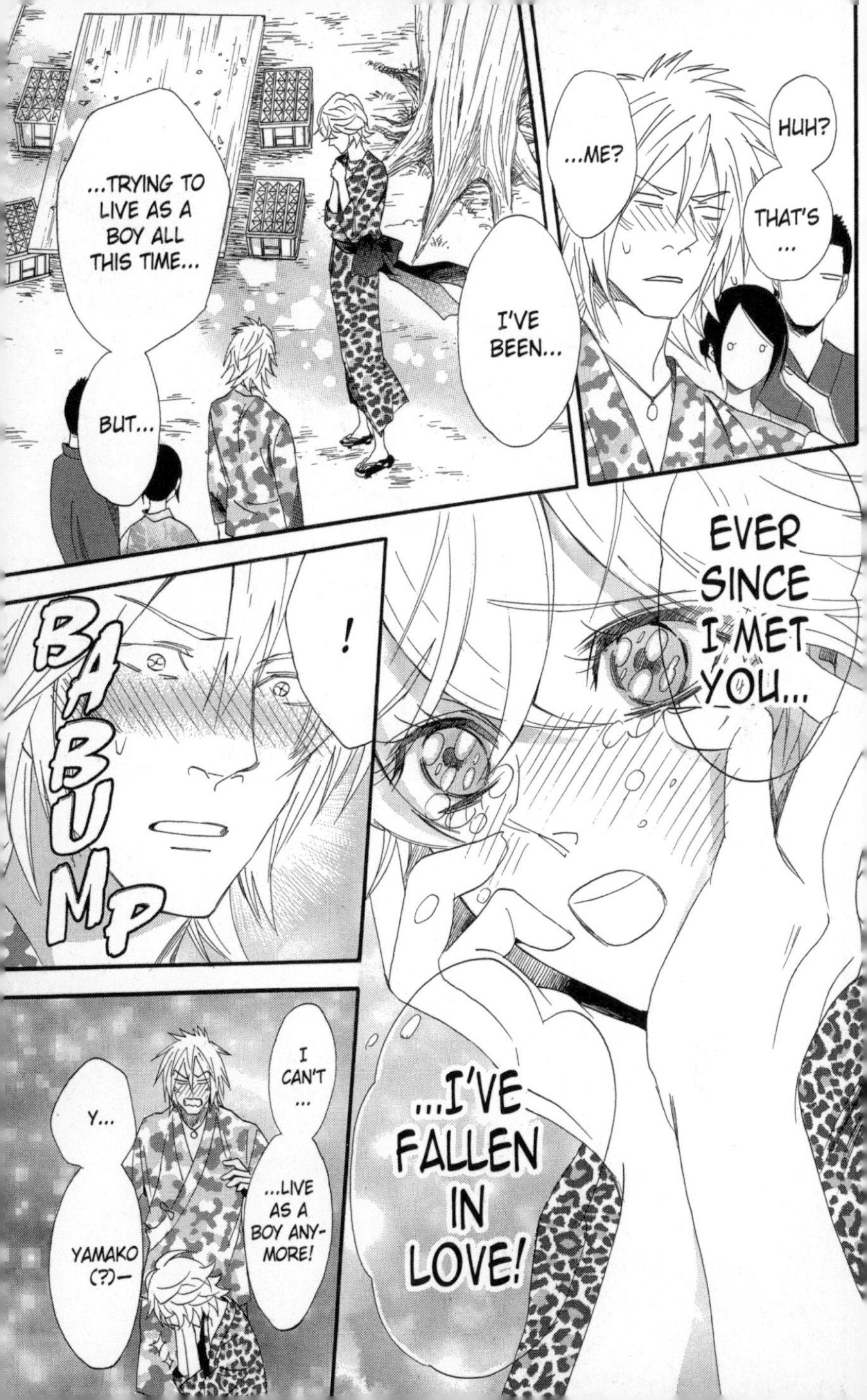
HUH?
THAT'S ...
...ME?
I'VE BEEN...
...TRYING TO LIVE AS A BOY ALL THIS TIME...
BUT...
EVER SINCE I MET YOU...
...I'VE FALLEN IN LOVE!
!
BABUMP
I CAN'T ...
...LIVE AS A BOY ANY-MORE!
Y...
YAMAKO (?)—

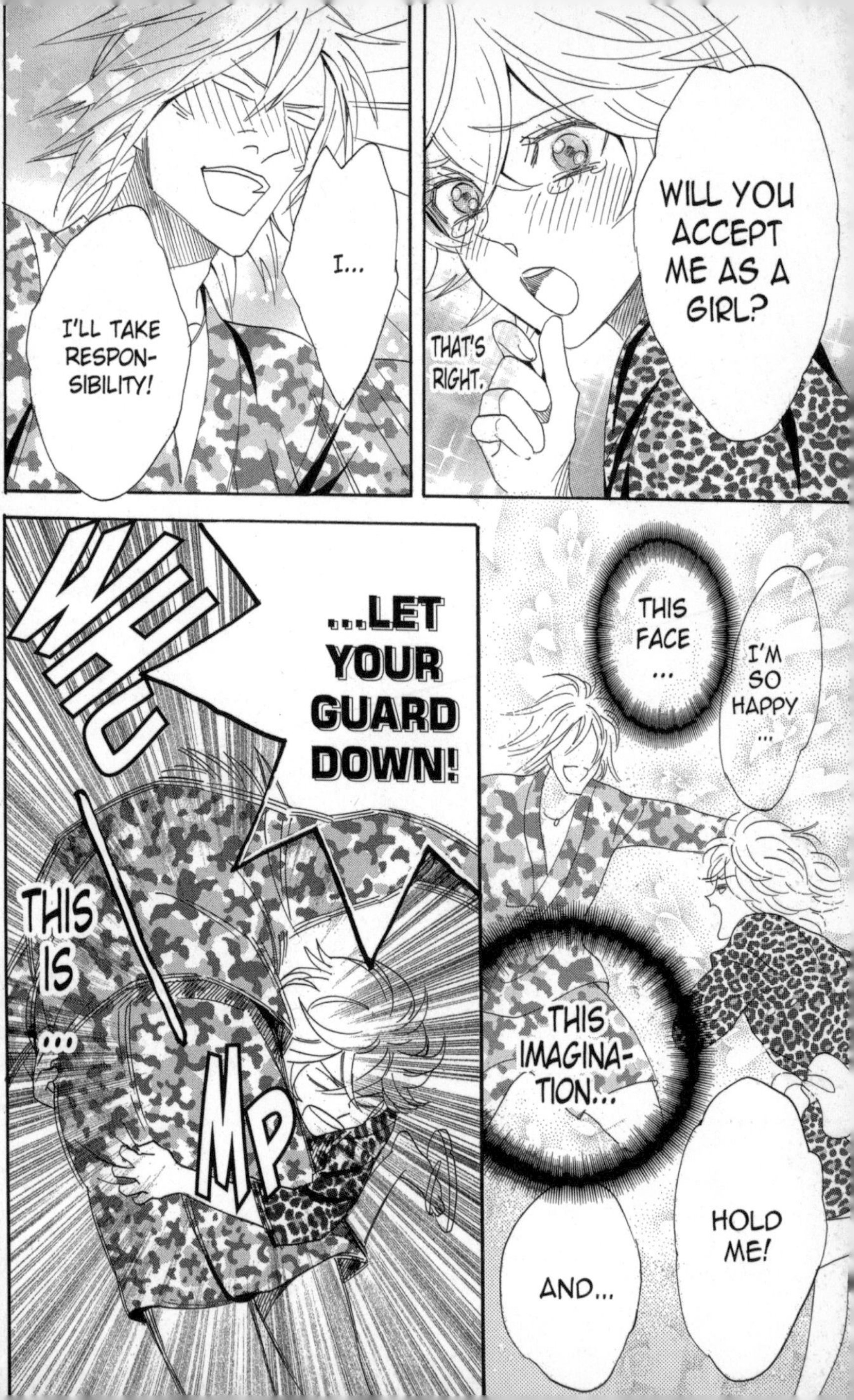
WILL YOU ACCEPT ME AS A GIRL?
THAT'S RIGHT.
I...
I'LL TAKE RESPON-SIBILITY!
I'M SO HAPPY...
THIS FACE...
THIS IMAGINA-TION...
HOLD ME!
AND...
...LET YOUR GUARD DOWN!
WHU
THIS IS...
MP

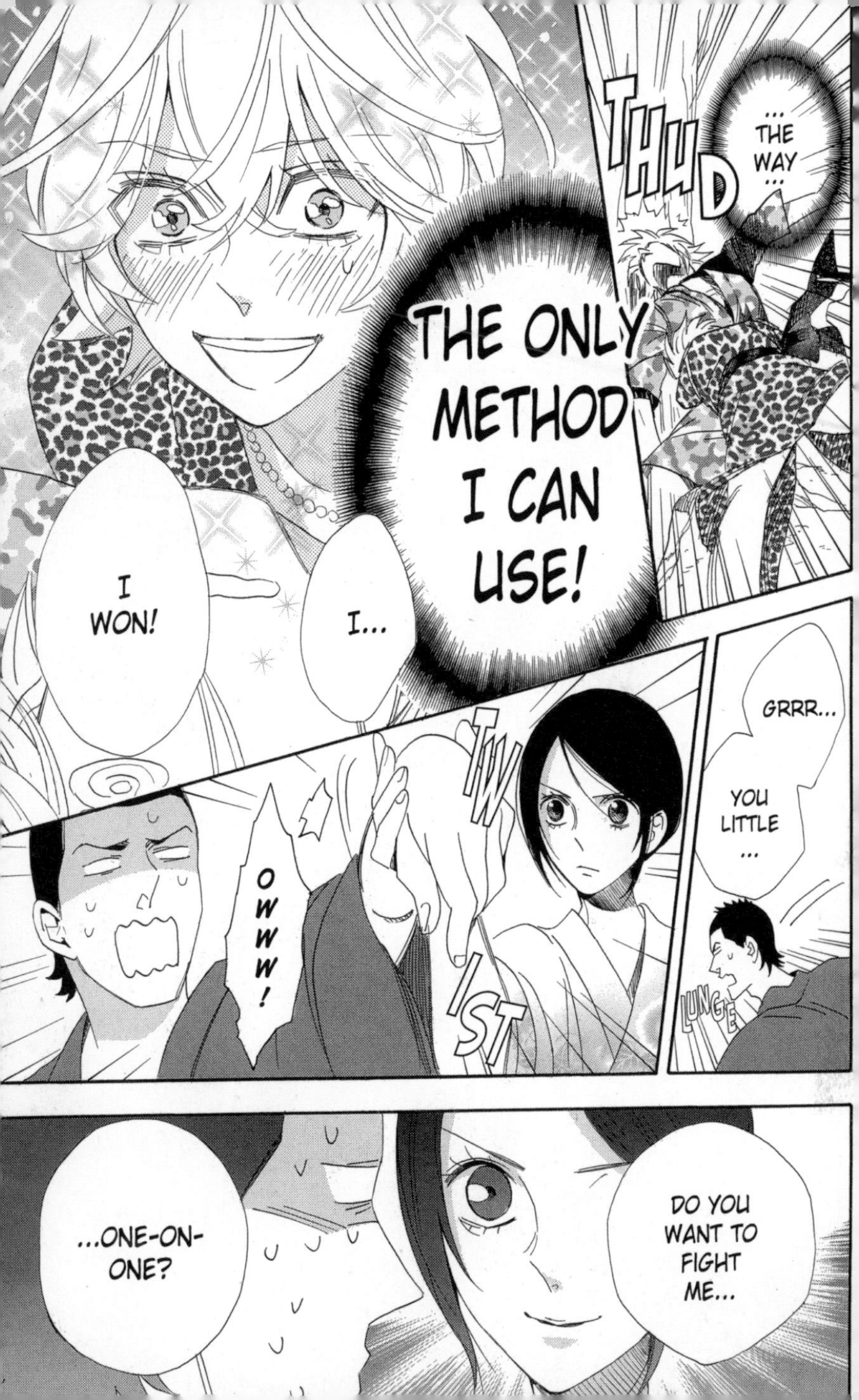
THUD
...THE WAY...
THE ONLY METHOD I CAN USE!
I...
I WON!
GRRR...
YOU LITTLE...
LUNGE
TWIST
OWWW!
DO YOU WANT TO FIGHT ME...
...ONE-ON-ONE?

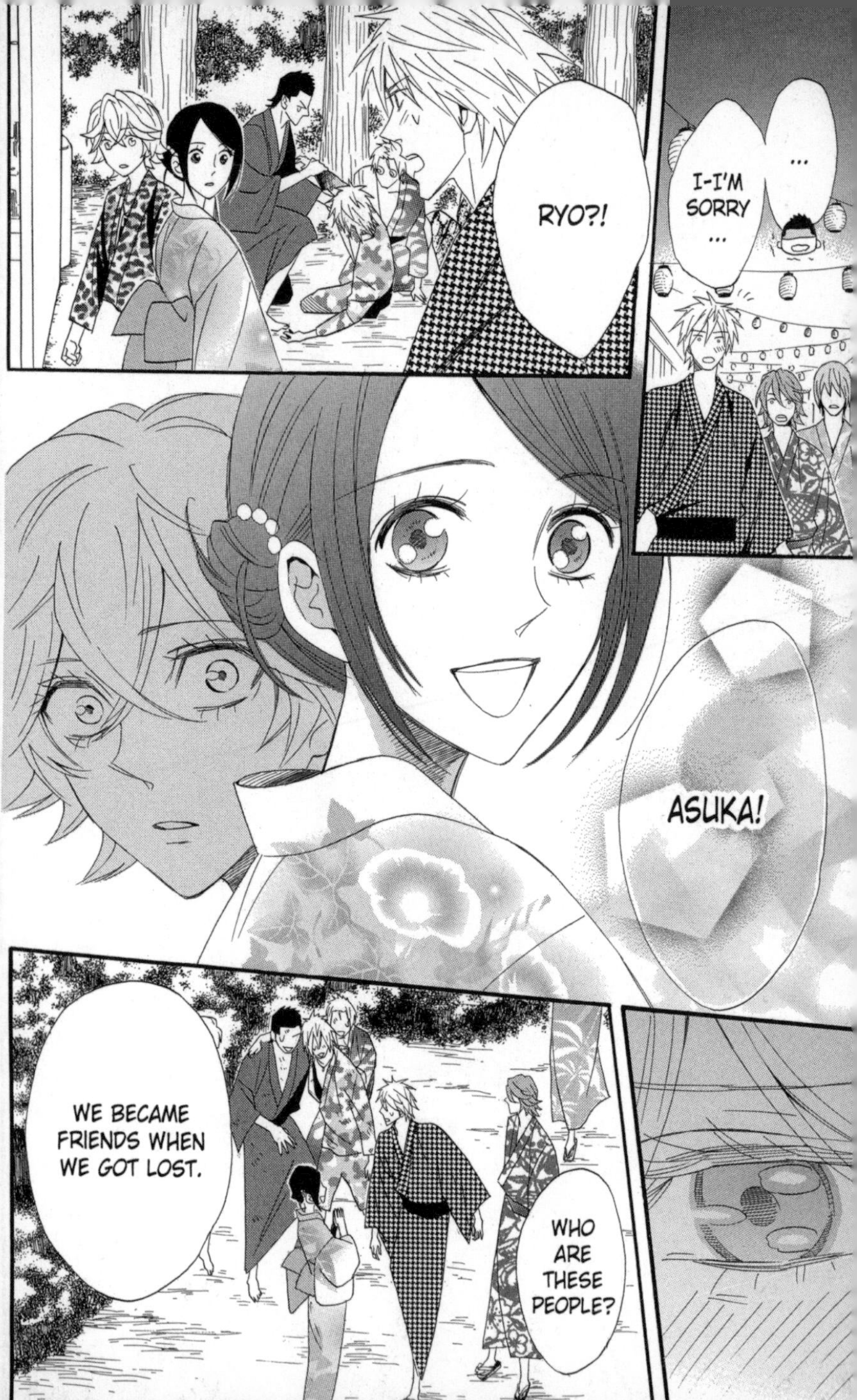
...
I-I'M SORRY ...
RYO?!
ASUKA!
WHO ARE THESE PEOPLE?
WE BECAME FRIENDS WHEN WE GOT LOST.

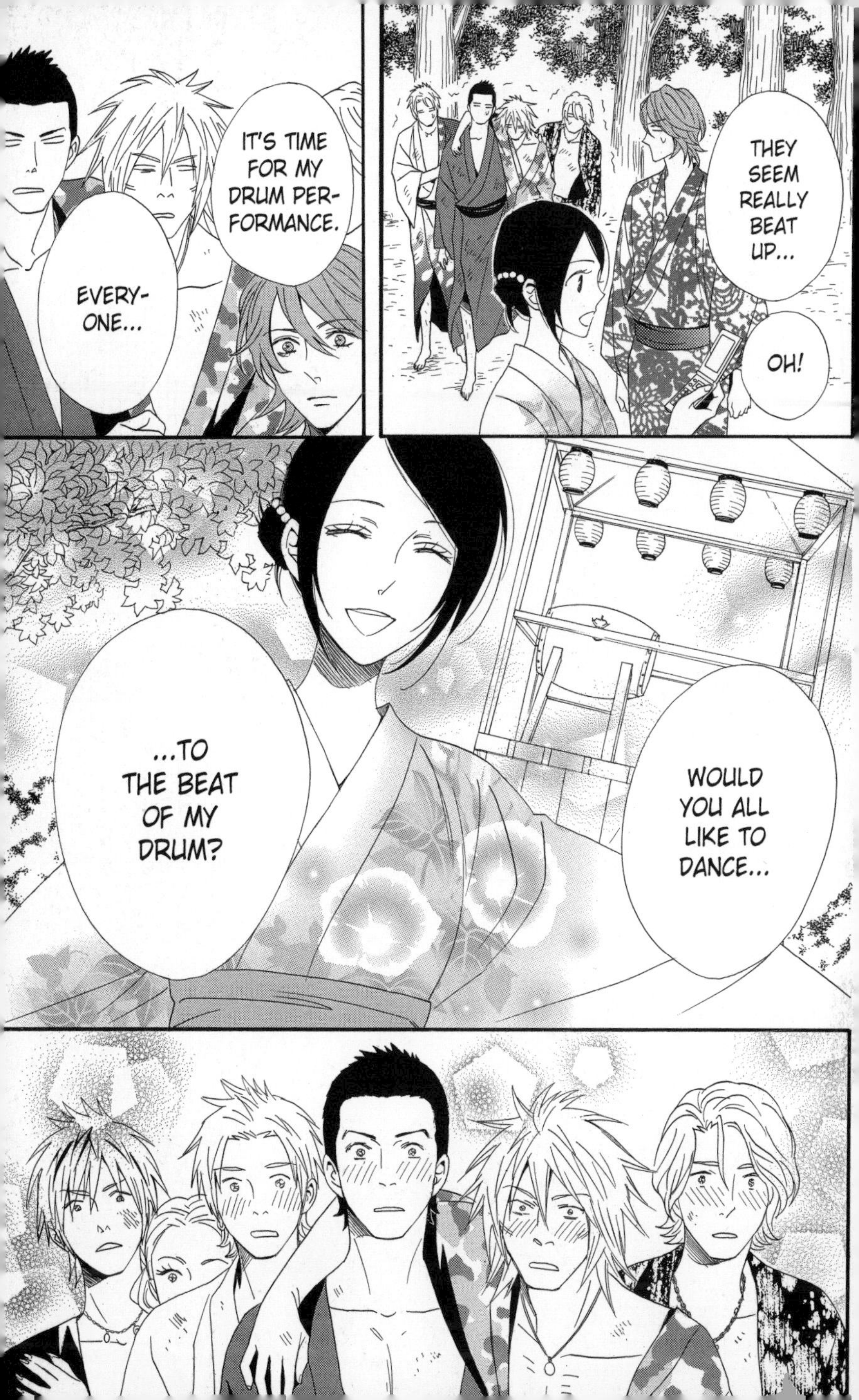
THEY SEEM REALLY BEAT UP...
OH!
IT'S TIME FOR MY DRUM PERFORMANCE.
EVERYONE...
WOULD YOU ALL LIKE TO DANCE...
...TO THE BEAT OF MY DRUM?

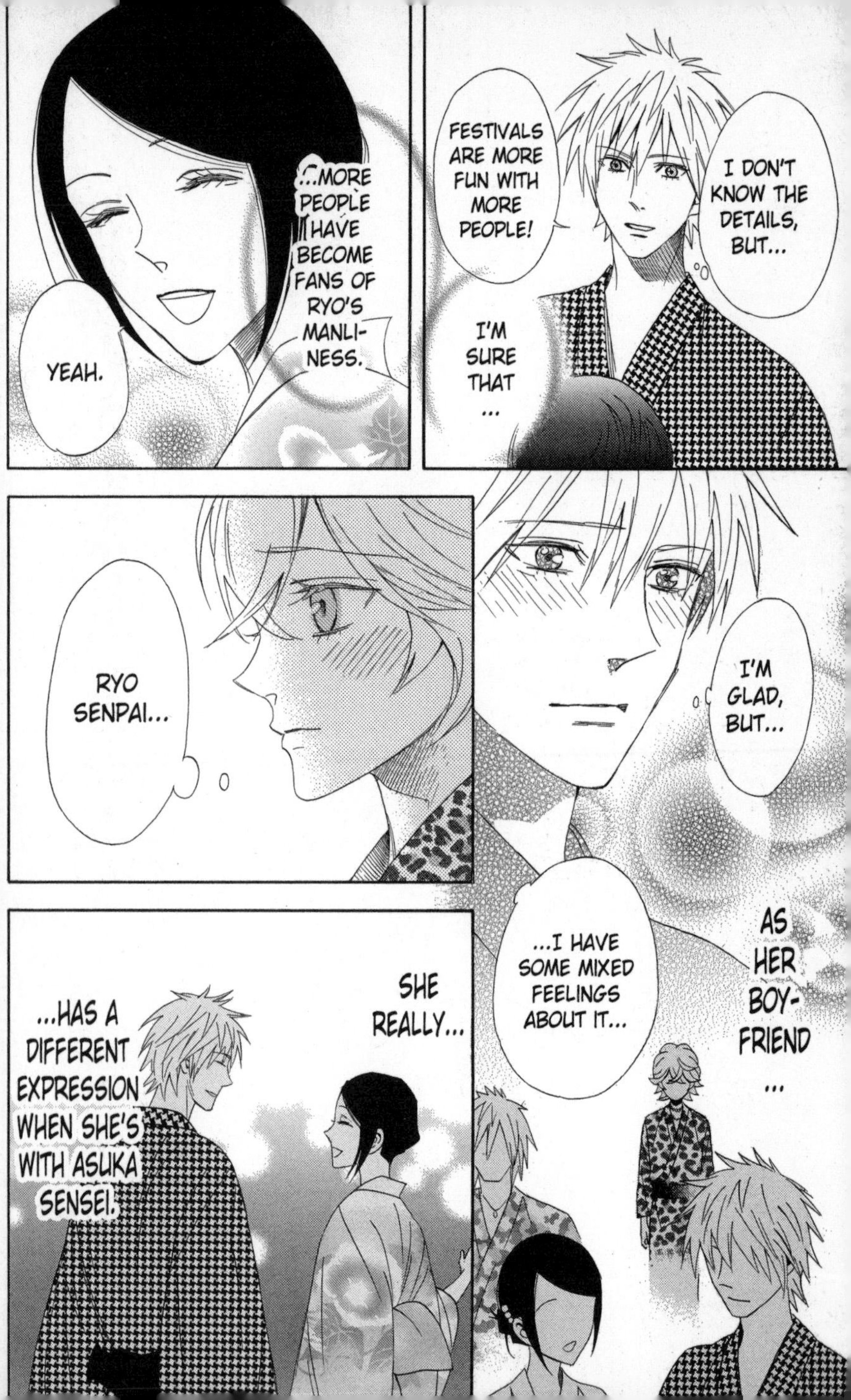
I DON'T KNOW THE DETAILS, BUT...
FESTIVALS ARE MORE FUN WITH MORE PEOPLE!
I'M SURE THAT...
...MORE PEOPLE HAVE BECOME FANS OF RYO'S MANLINESS.
YEAH.
I'M GLAD, BUT...
...I HAVE SOME MIXED FEELINGS ABOUT IT...
AS HER BOYFRIEND...
RYO SENPAI...
SHE REALLY...
...HAS A DIFFERENT EXPRESSION WHEN SHE'S WITH ASUKA SENSEI.

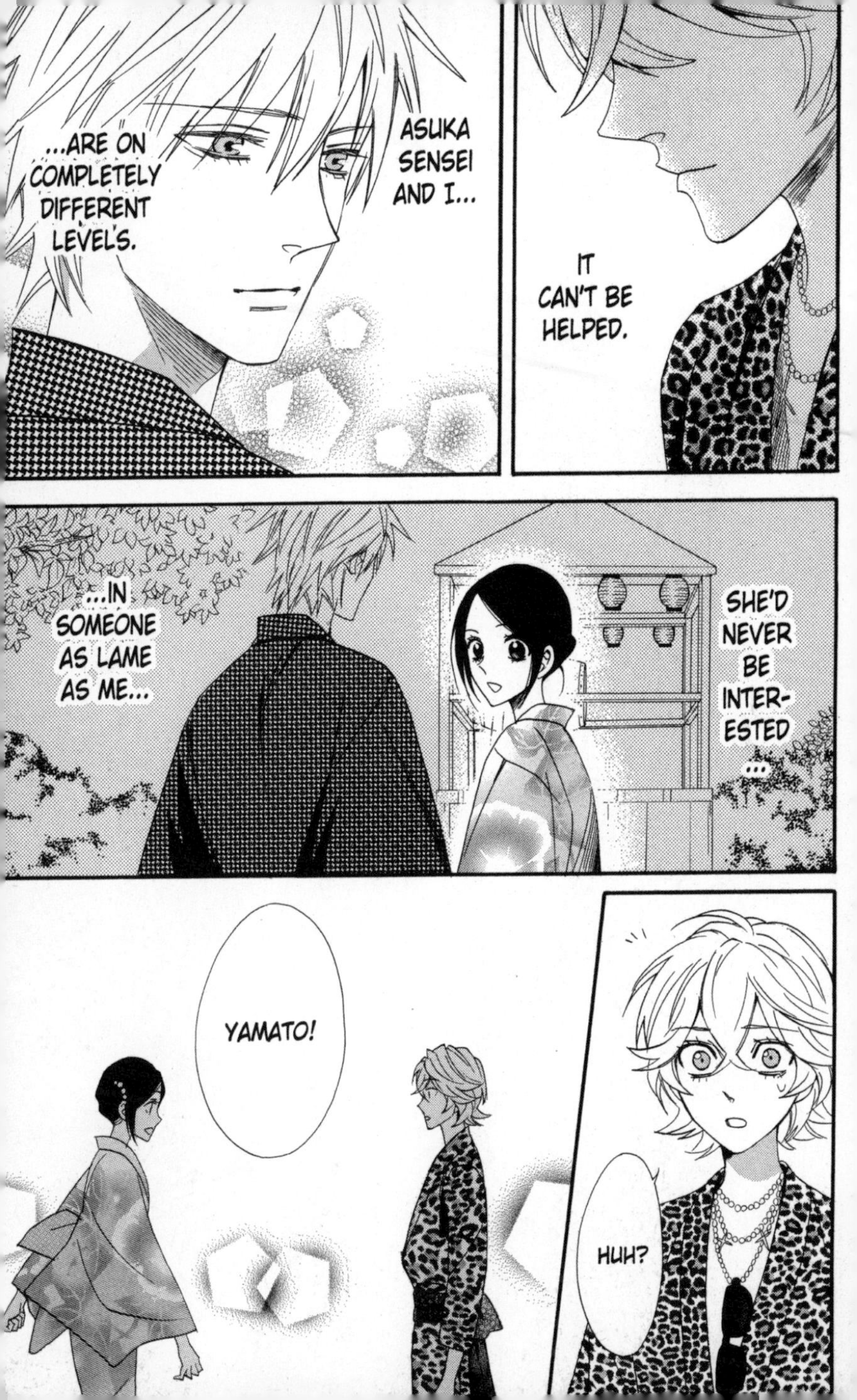
IT CAN'T BE HELPED.
ASUKA SENSEI AND I...
...ARE ON COMPLETELY DIFFERENT LEVEL'S.
SHE'D NEVER BE INTER-ESTED...
...IN SOMEONE AS LAME AS ME...
HUH?
YAMATO!

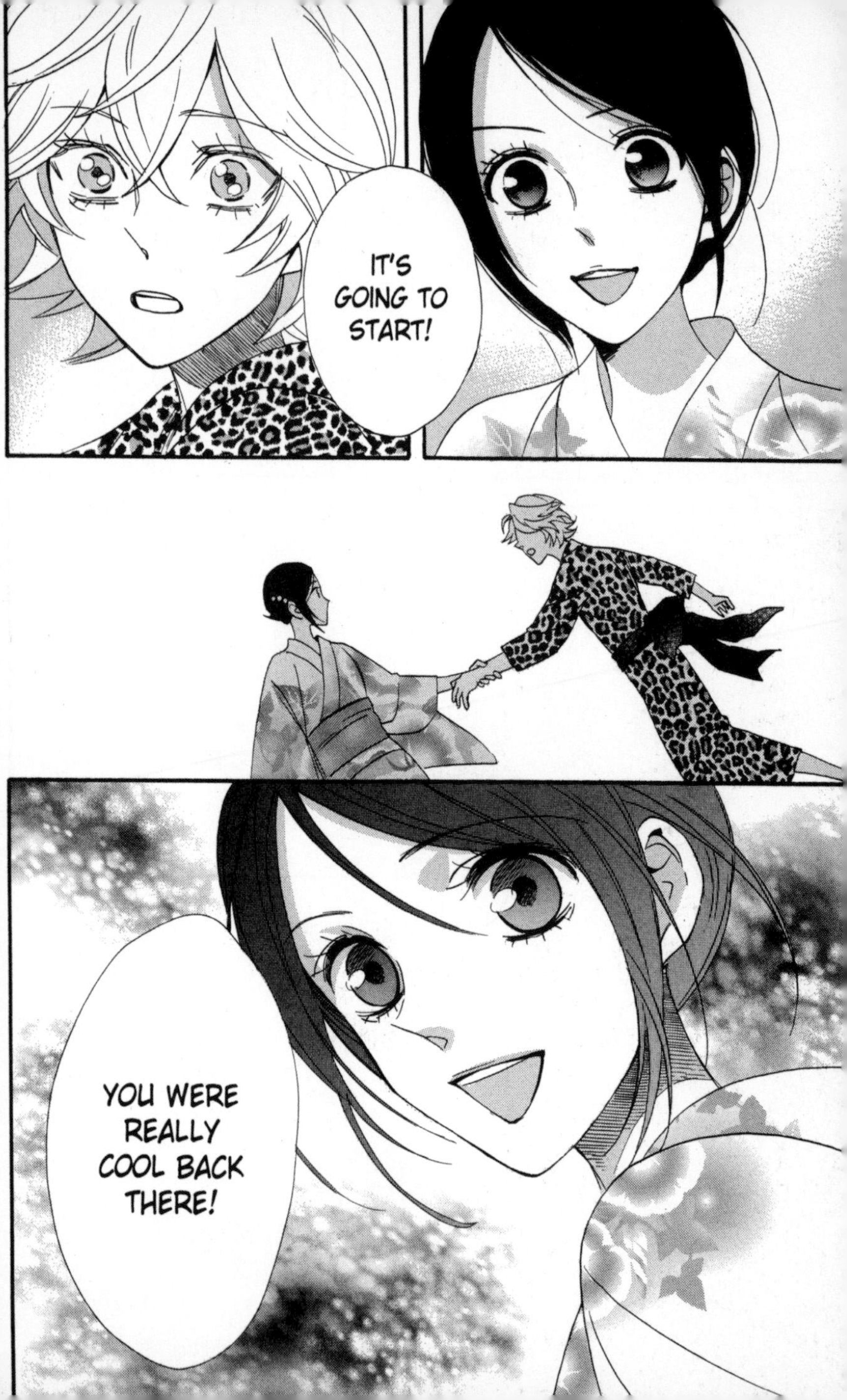
IT'S GOING TO START!
YOU WERE REALLY COOL BACK THERE!

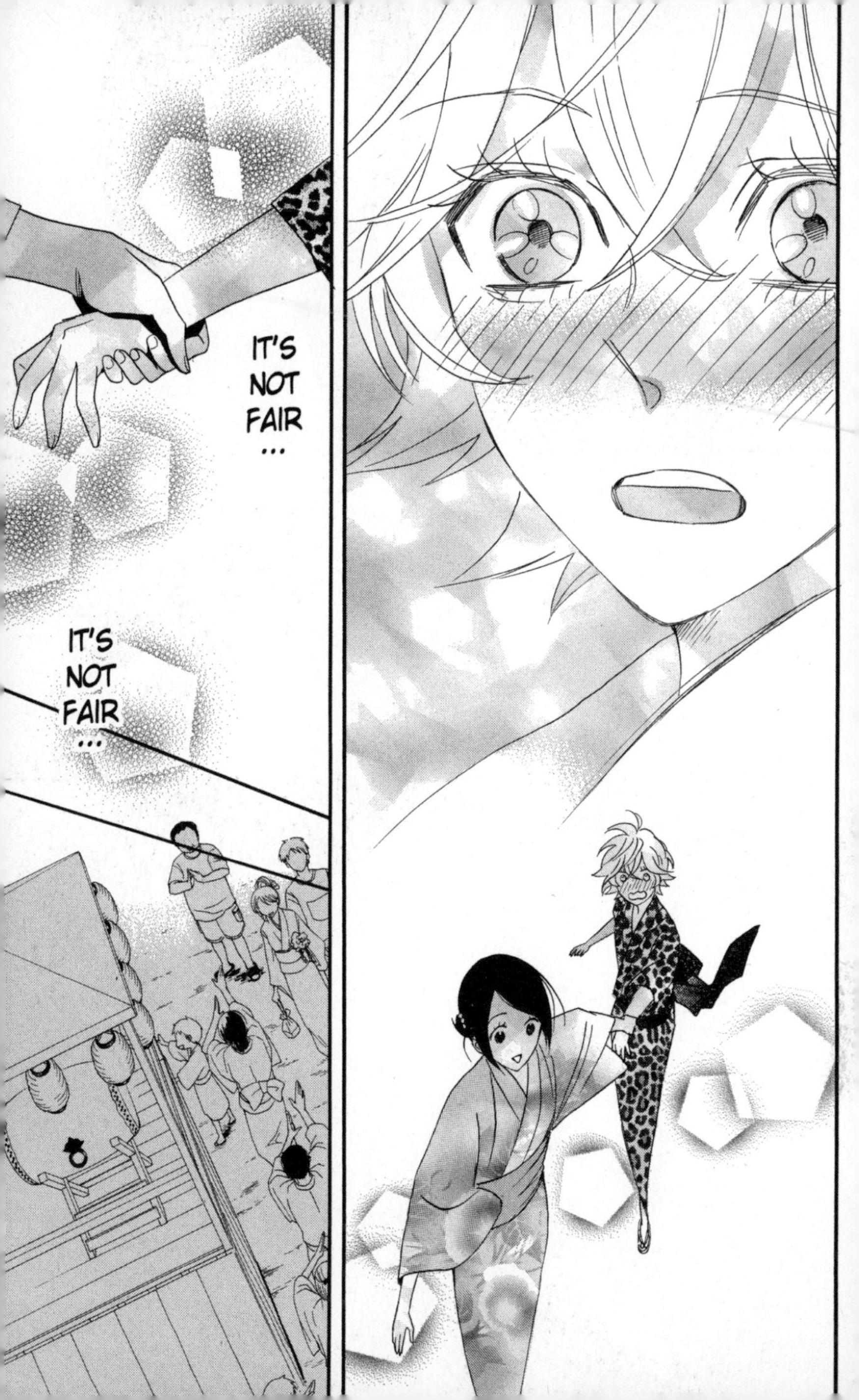
IT'S NOT FAIR ...
IT'S NOT FAIR ...

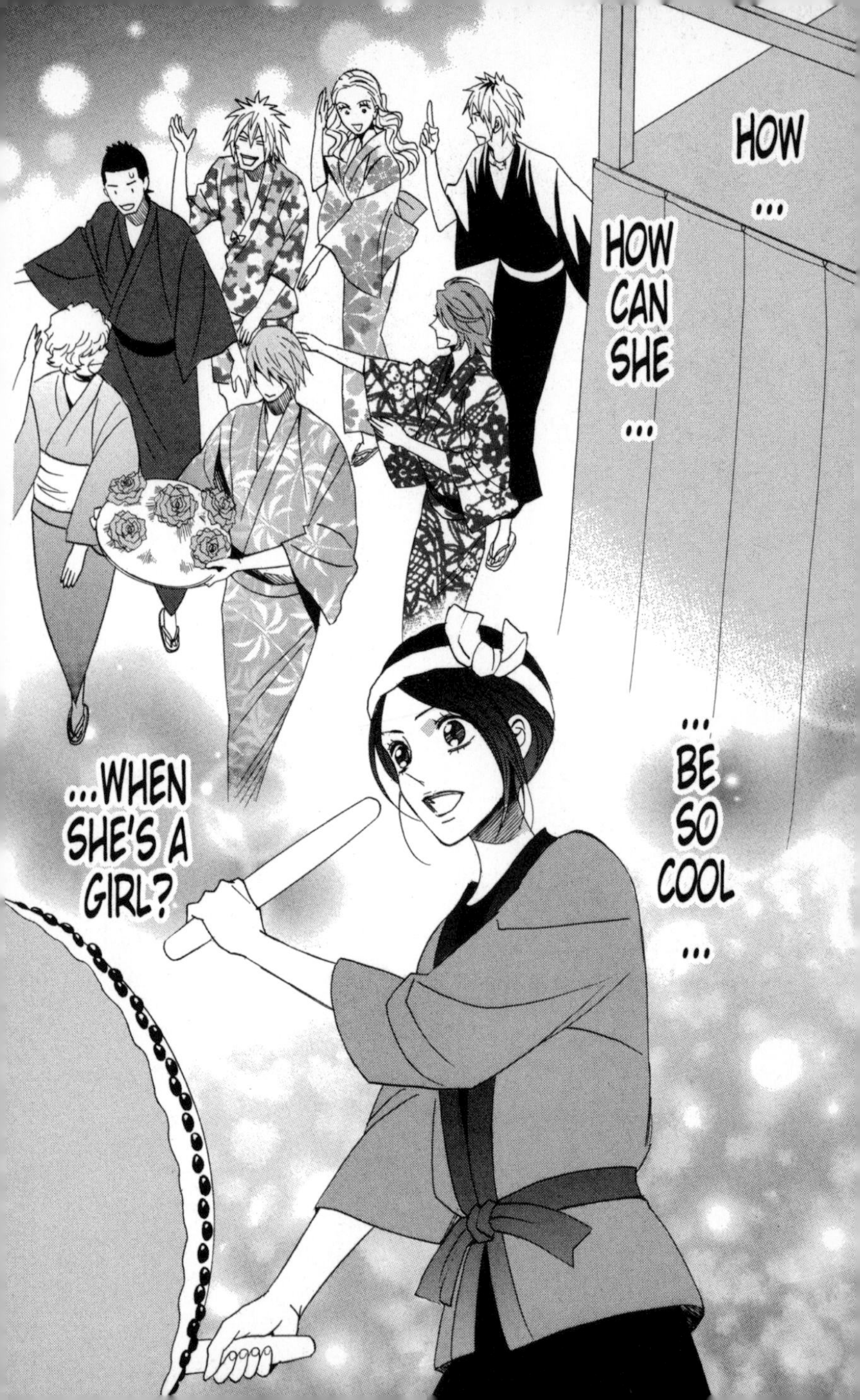
HOW ...
HOW CAN SHE ...
... BE SO COOL ...
...WHEN SHE'S A GIRL?

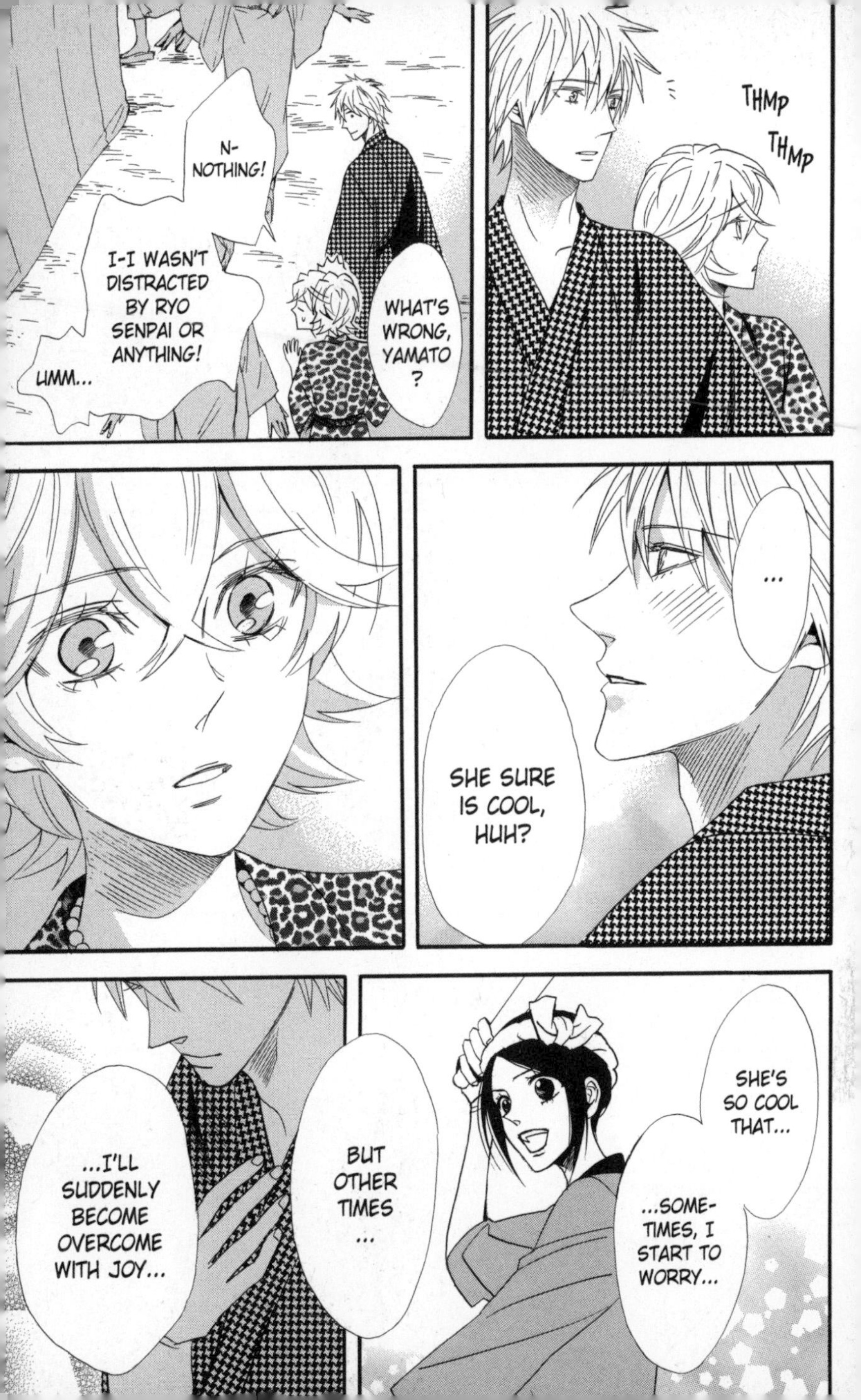
THMP THMP
WHAT'S WRONG, YAMATO?
N-NOTHING!
I-I WASN'T DISTRACTED BY RYO SENPAI OR ANYTHING!
UMM...
...
SHE SURE IS COOL, HUH?
SHE'S SO COOL THAT...
...SOME-TIMES, I START TO WORRY...
BUT OTHER TIMES...
...I'LL SUDDENLY BECOME OVERCOME WITH JOY...

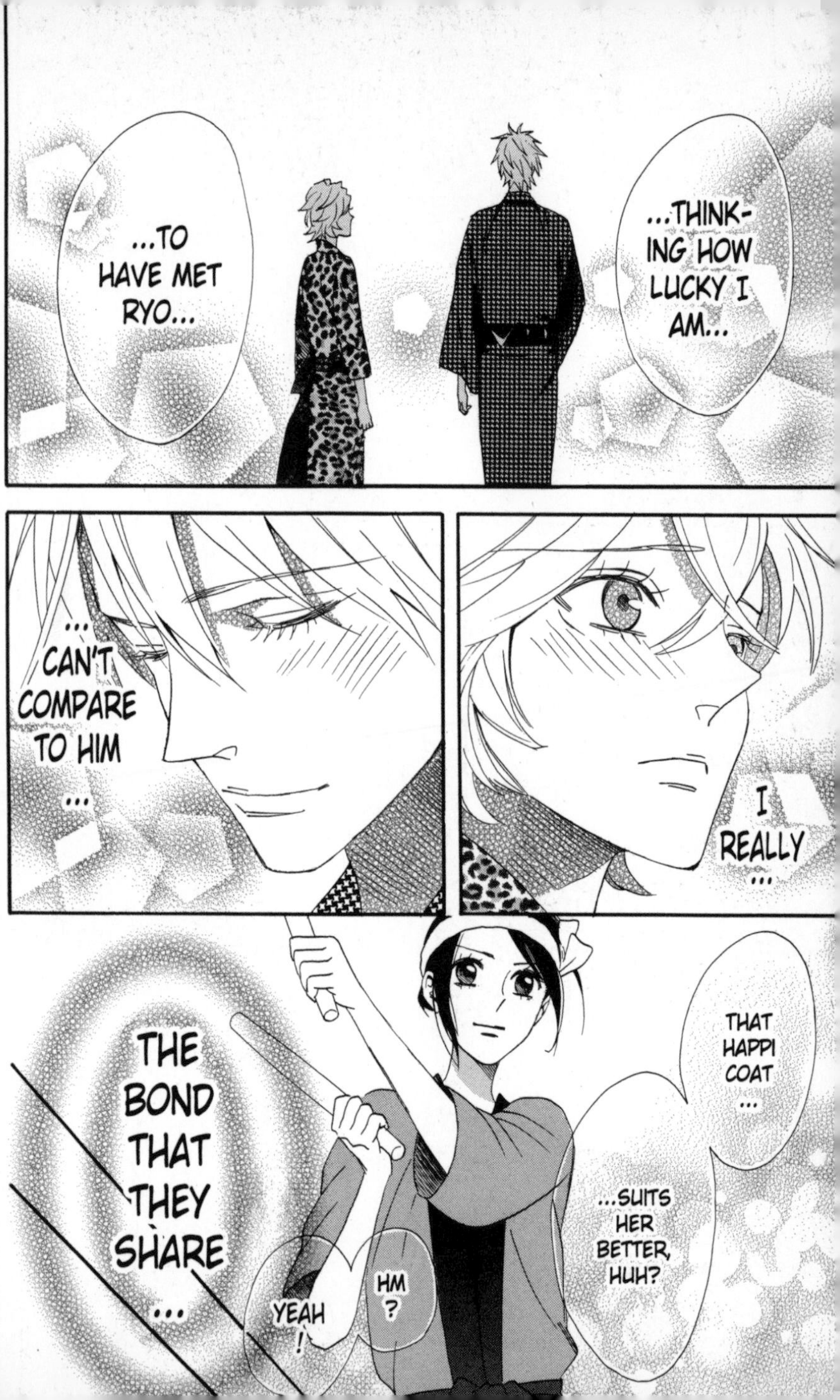
...THINKING HOW LUCKY I AM...
...TO HAVE MET RYO...
I REALLY ...
...CAN'T COMPARE TO HIM ...
THAT HAPPI COAT ...
...SUITS HER BETTER, HUH?
HM ?
YEAH !
THE BOND THAT THEY SHARE ...

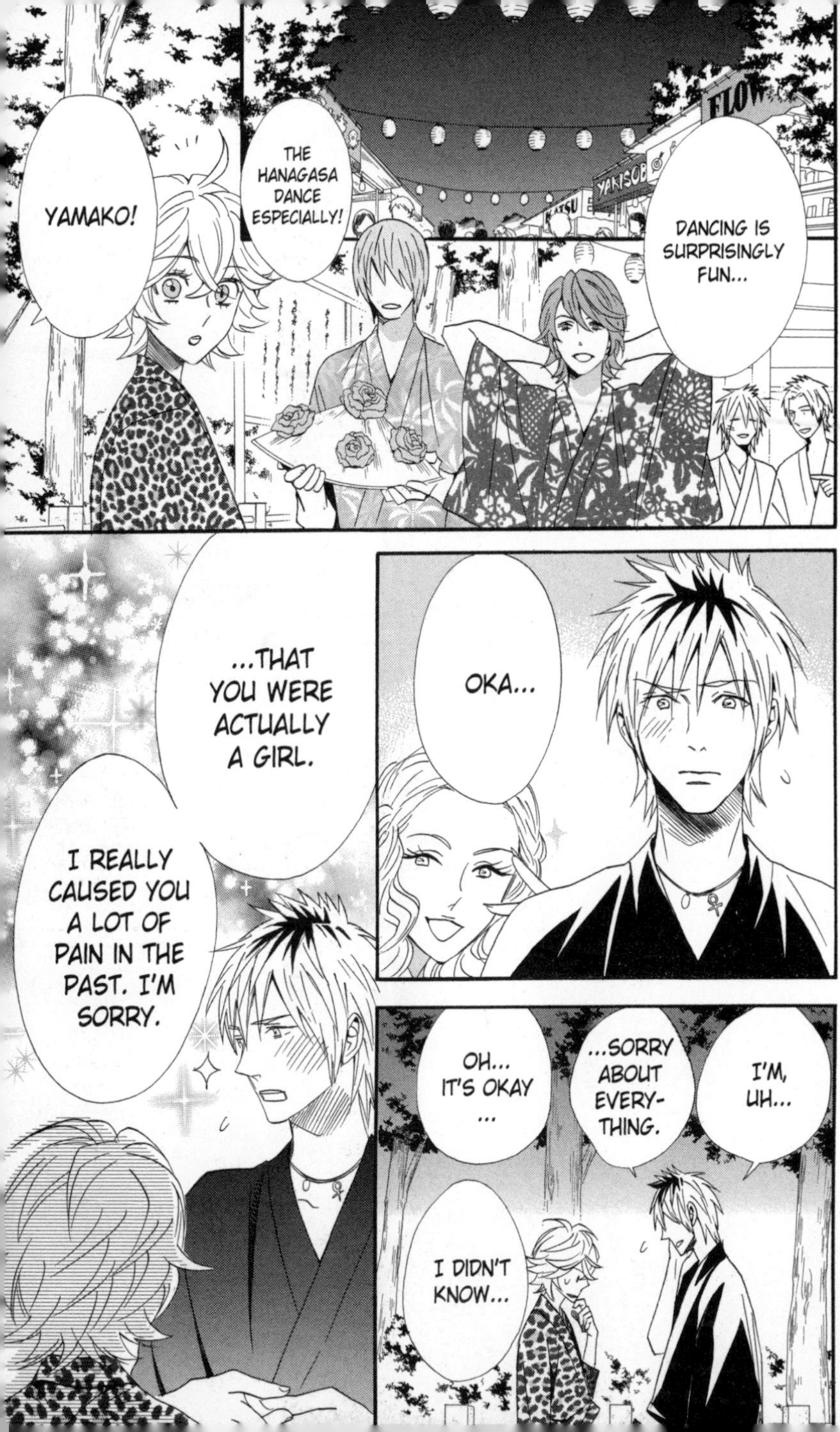
FLOW
YAKISOB
DANCING IS SURPRISINGLY FUN...
THE HANAGASA DANCE ESPECIALLY!
YAMAKO!
OKA...
I'M, UH...
...SORRY ABOUT EVERY-THING.
OH... IT'S OKAY ...
I DIDN'T KNOW...
...THAT YOU WERE ACTUALLY A GIRL.
I REALLY CAUSED YOU A LOT OF PAIN IN THE PAST. I'M SORRY.

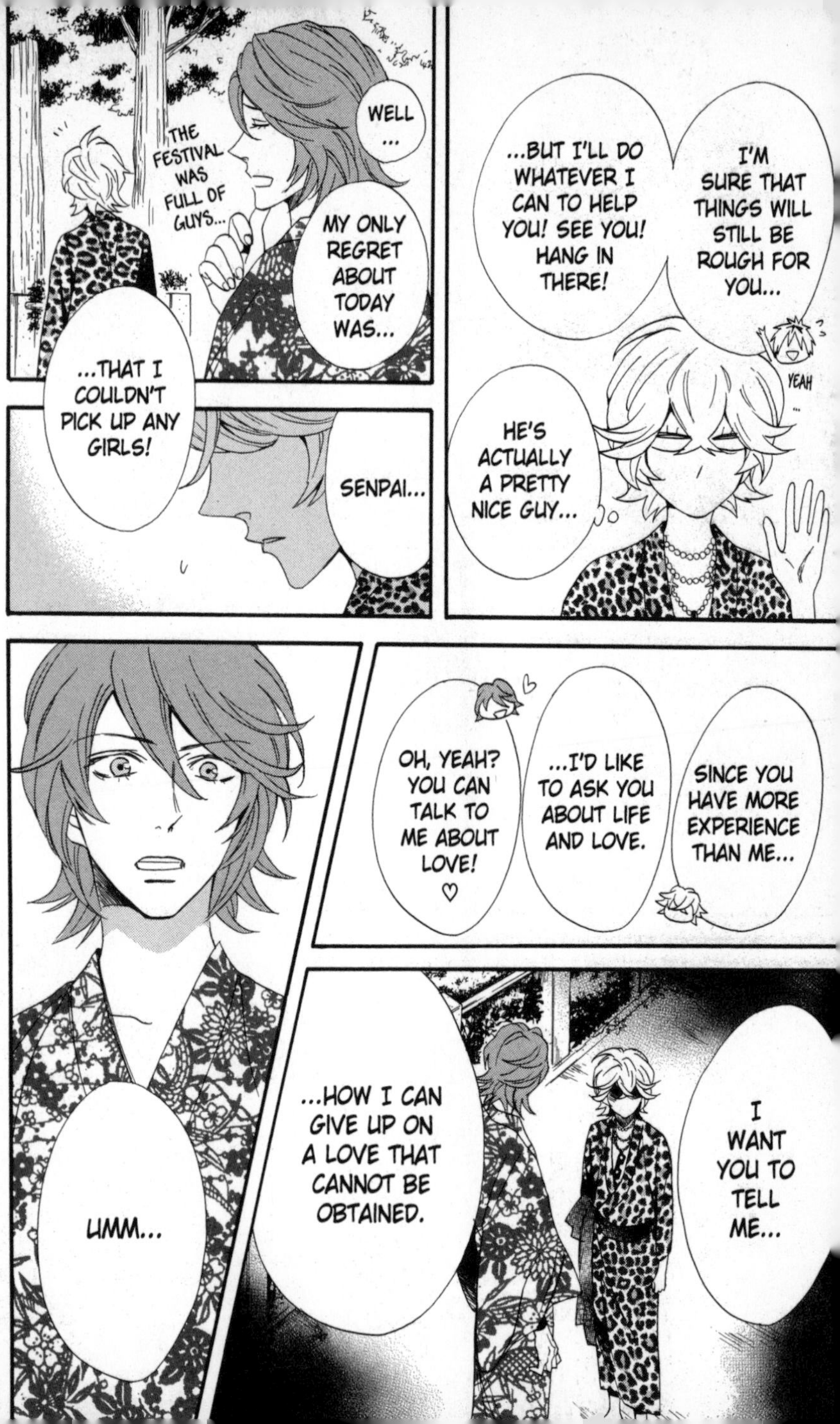
I'M SURE THAT THINGS WILL STILL BE ROUGH FOR YOU...
...BUT I'LL DO WHATEVER I CAN TO HELP YOU! SEE YOU! HANG IN THERE!
YEAH ...
HE'S ACTUALLY A PRETTY NICE GUY...
WELL ...
THE FESTIVAL WAS FULL OF GUYS...
MY ONLY REGRET ABOUT TODAY WAS...
...THAT I COULDN'T PICK UP ANY GIRLS!
SENPAI...
SINCE YOU HAVE MORE EXPERIENCE THAN ME...
...I'D LIKE TO ASK YOU ABOUT LIFE AND LOVE.
OH, YEAH? YOU CAN TALK TO ME ABOUT LOVE! ♡
I WANT YOU TO TELL ME...
...HOW I CAN GIVE UP ON A LOVE THAT CANNOT BE OBTAINED.
UMM...

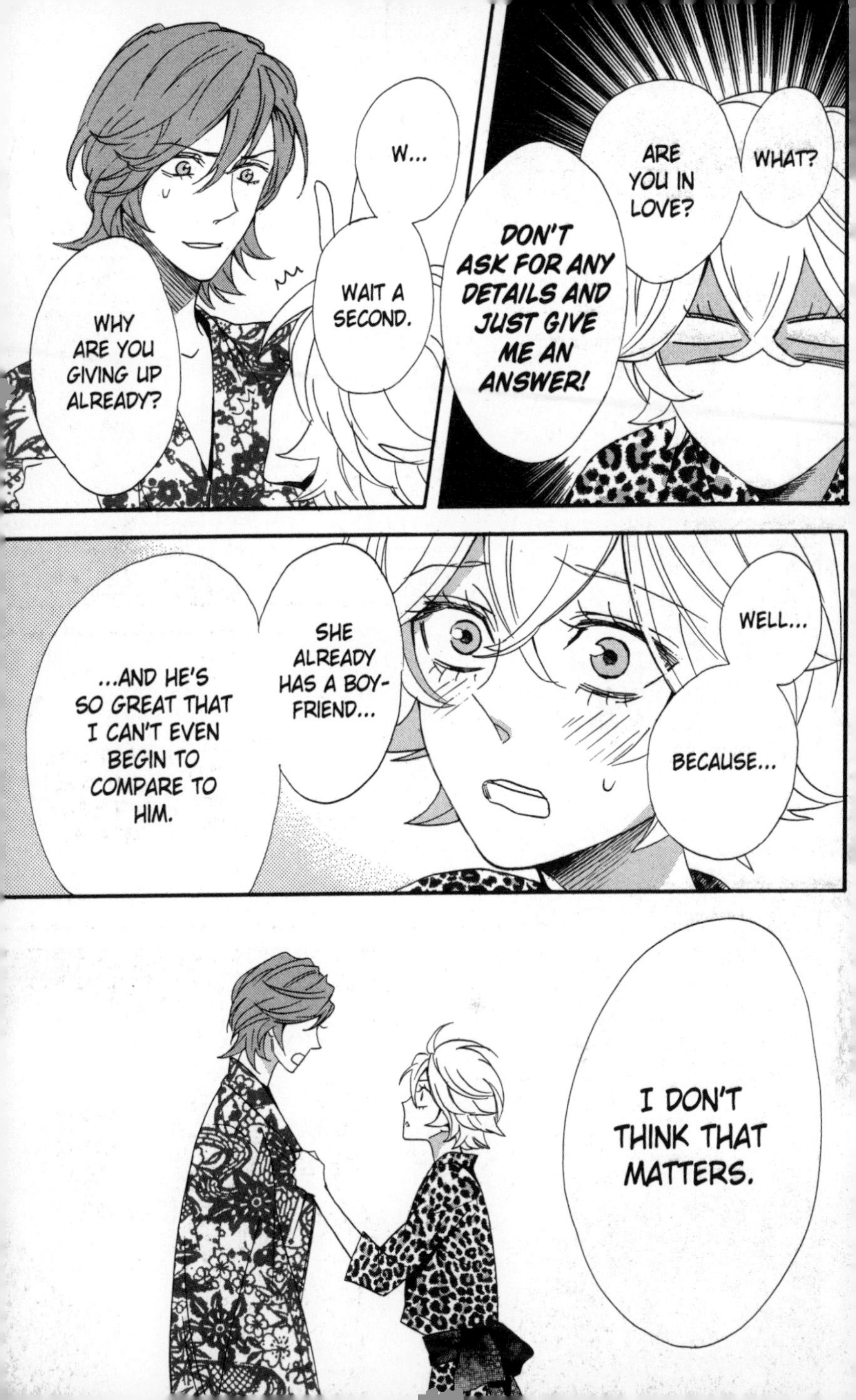
WHAT?
ARE YOU IN LOVE?
DON'T ASK FOR ANY DETAILS AND JUST GIVE ME AN ANSWER!
W...
WAIT A SECOND.
WHY ARE YOU GIVING UP ALREADY?
WELL...
BECAUSE...
SHE ALREADY HAS A BOY-FRIEND...
...AND HE'S SO GREAT THAT I CAN'T EVEN BEGIN TO COMPARE TO HIM.
I DON'T THINK THAT MATTERS.

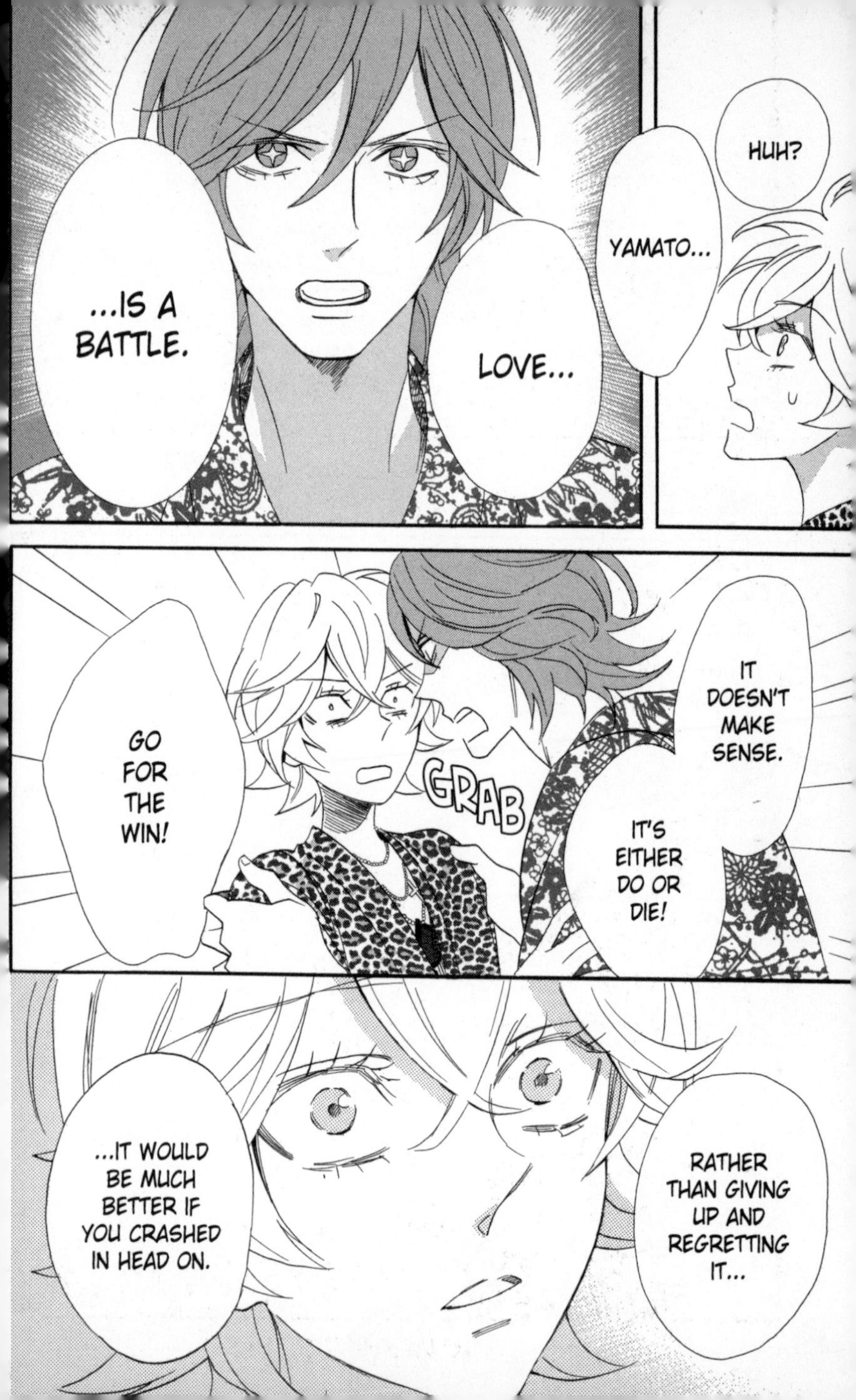
HUH?
YAMATO...
LOVE...
...IS A BATTLE.
IT DOESN'T MAKE SENSE.
IT'S EITHER DO OR DIE!
GRAB
GO FOR THE WIN!
RATHER THAN GIVING UP AND REGRETTING IT...
...IT WOULD BE MUCH BETTER IF YOU CRASHED IN HEAD ON.

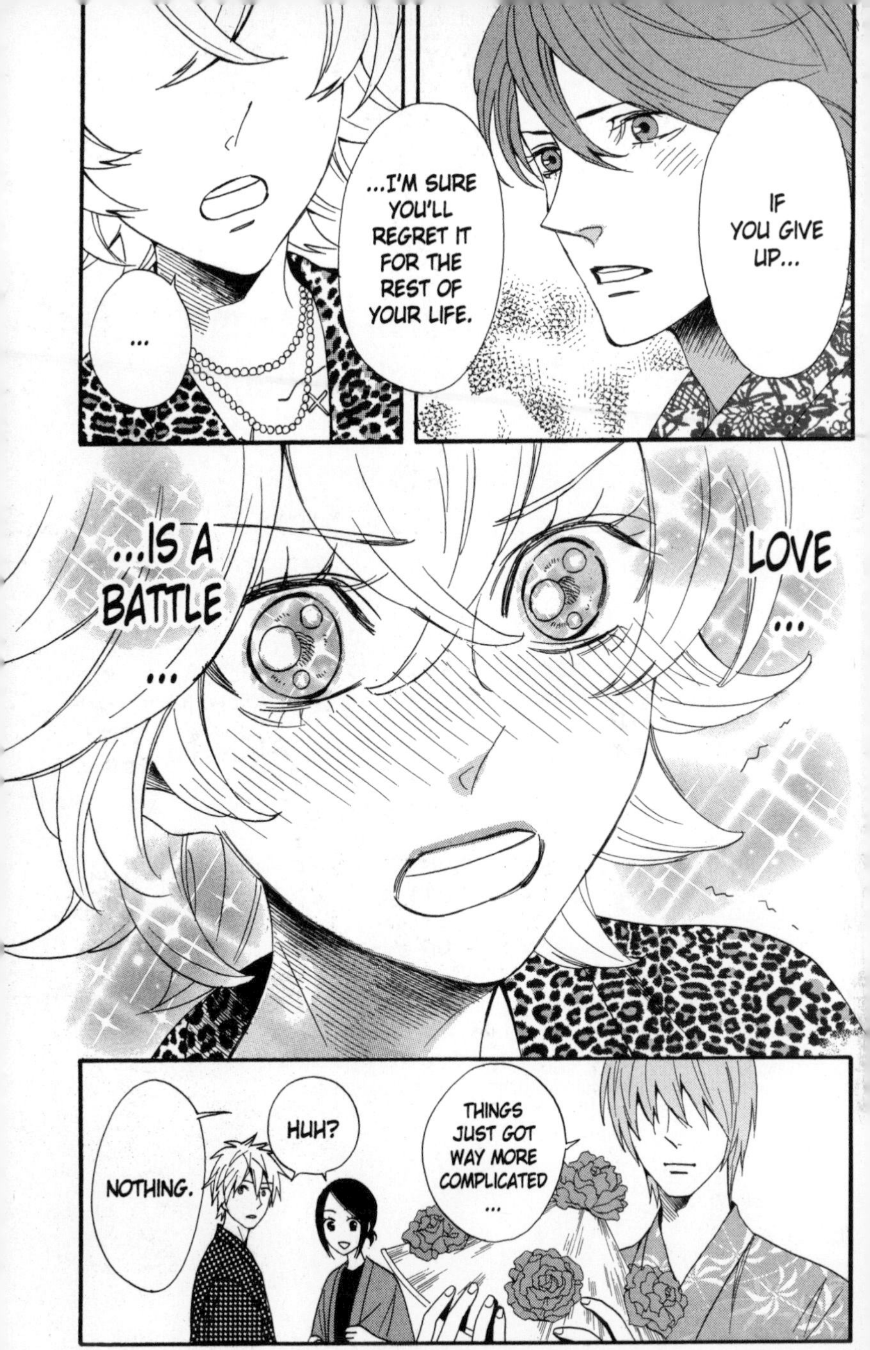
IF YOU GIVE UP...
...I'M SURE YOU'LL REGRET IT FOR THE REST OF YOUR LIFE.
...
LOVE...
...IS A BATTLE...
THINGS JUST GOT WAY MORE COMPLICATED...
HUH?
NOTHING.

OTOMEN ⑮ / THE END

# Confused by some of the terms, but too MANLY to ask for help?

Here are some **cultural notes** to assist you!

# HONORIFICS

**Chan** – an informal honorific used to address children and females. *Chan* can also be used toward animals, lovers, intimate friends and people whom one has known since childhood.

**Kun** – an informal honorific used primarily toward males; it can be used by people of more senior status addressing those junior to them or by anyone addressing male children.

**San** – the most common honorific title. It is used to address people outside one's immediate family and close circle of friends.

**Senpai** – used to address one's senior colleagues or mentor figures; it is used when students refer to or address more senior students in their school.

**Sensei** – honorific title used to address teachers as well as professionals such as doctors, lawyers and artists.

# NOTES

**Page 101, panel 1 | "Ko"**
"Ko" (子) is a popular ending for female names, so calling Yamato "Yamako" suggests that some of Yamato's grade school classmates thought he resembled a girl.

**Page 110, panel 1 | Happi Coat**
A *happi* coat is usually worn at Japanese festivals and has a crest on the back. The one shown here has the kanji character for "man."

**Page 111, panel 5 | Soiya**
In this panel, Ryo yells "Soiya"—a chant that men do during a Japanese festival.

**Page 128, panel 1 | Odawara Castle**
Odawara Castle in Kanagawa had a reputation of being impenetrable, so the fact that Ryo won the prize emphasizes her skill as a markswoman.

**Page 183, panel 1 | Hanagasa Dance**
The flower hat that Kitora is holding is used in the *hanagasa* dance, a special kind of festival dance from Yamagata Prefecture.

OSAMU TONOMINE

CITY COUNCIL CANDIDATE (Independent)

THE FINEST SOCIETY, THE FINEST LIVING

*THIS IS A FICTIONAL ELECTION.

TAKAKO TONOMINE

HAJIME TONOMINE'S OLDER SISTER

**Aya Kanno** was born in Tokyo, Japan.
She is the creator of *Soul Rescue* and *Blank Slate*
(originally published as *Akusaga* in Japan's
*BetsuHana* magazine). Her latest work, *Otomen*,
is currently being serialized in *BetsuHana*.

# OTOMEN

*Vol. 15*
Shojo Beat Edition

*Story and Art by* | **AYA KANNO**

*Translation & Adaptation* | **JN Productions**
*Touch-up Art & Lettering* | **Mark McMurray**
*Design* | **Fawn Lau**
*Editor* | **Amy Yu**

Otomen by Aya Kanno © Aya Kanno 2012
All rights reserved. First published in Japan in 2012 by HAKUSENSHA, Inc., Tokyo.
English language translation rights arranged with HAKUSENSHA, Inc., Tokyo.

The rights of the author(s) of the work(s) in this publication to be so identified
have been asserted in accordance with the Copyright, Designs and Patents Act 1988.
A CIP catalogue record for this book is available from the British Library.

The stories, characters and incidents mentioned in this publication are entirely fictional.

No portion of this book may be reproduced or transmitted in any form or by any means
without written permission from the copyright holders.

Printed in the U.S.A.

Published by VIZ Media, LLC
P.O. Box 77010
San Francisco, CA 94107

10 9 8 7 6 5 4 3 2 1
First printing, May 2013

# SURPRISE!

## YOU MAY BE READING THE WRONG WAY!

**It's true: In keeping with the original Japanese comic format, this book reads from right to left—so action, sound effects, and word balloons are completely reversed. This preserves the orientation of the original artwork—plus, it's fun! Check out the diagram shown here to get the hang of things, and then turn to the other side of the book to get started!**

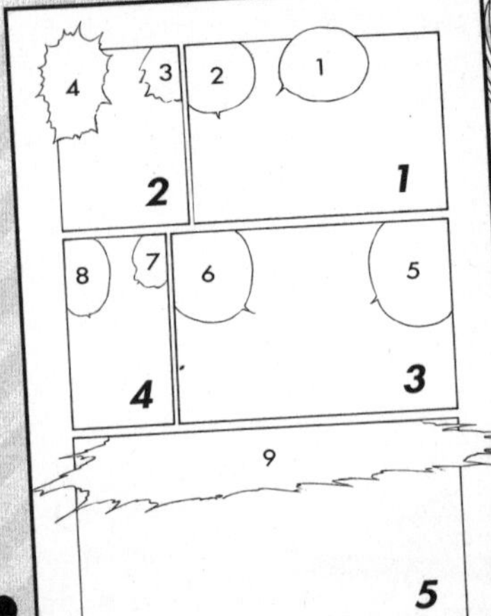
1
2
1
3
4
2
5
6
3
7
8
4
9
5
142

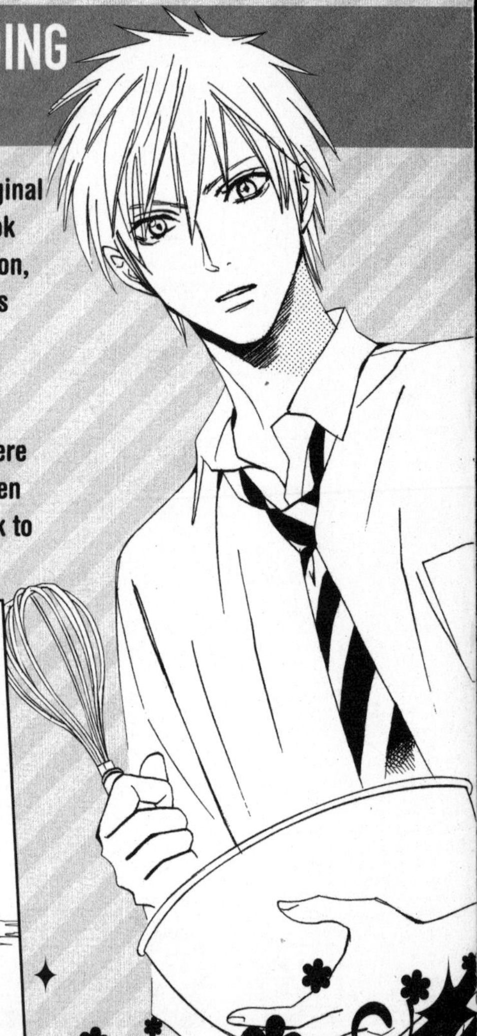

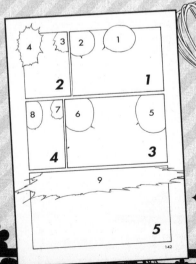